MEET THE PRESIDENTS

other books by Frances Cavanah

FRIENDS TO MAN

THEY LIVED IN THE WHITE HOUSE

TWO LOVES FOR JENNY LIND

WE CAME TO AMERICA

HOLIDAY ROUND UP
(*with Lucile Pannell*)

MEET THE PRESIDENTS

by

FRANCES
CAVANAH

in collaboration with
Elizabeth L. Crandall

Illustrated by Clifford Schule

MACRAE SMITH COMPANY: PHILADELPHIA

INTRODUCTION

This book offers the reader a chance to "meet the Presidents," both when they were young and when they grew older. The greatest among them have helped to change the course of history, and all have seen history in the making. Several of them grew up in one of the thirteen colonies, even before there was a United States, and later helped those colonies to become a nation. Others lived on the frontier and had an important part in transforming a wilderness into a prosperous land where millions of people now make their homes. In the experiences of the Presidents, from George Washington to Lyndon B. Johnson, one may find a vivid picture of America: America in peace and in war; America in colonial days; America as a struggling new country; America as a powerful nation.

There is a well-known saying that any American-born boy has a chance to become President. Some of the Presidents came from poor homes; others had well-to-do parents. Some went to college; others had to educate themselves. But most of them were real boys while they were growing up. They swam or went fishing or took part in athletic events—and sometimes played pranks. Each chapter begins with a story of a President in his youth. At the end of the same chapter, the reader meets him again at some high point in his career or in the history of his country. Not every President made his greatest contribution while he was in the White House. Sometimes it was before he went there to live, as was the case with James Madison, the "Father of the Constitution." With John Quincy Adams, it was toward the close of his life, while he was serving in Congress. Dramatic and amusing incidents in their lives have helped to reveal the personalities of our Presidents. A number of anecdotes have been included in this book so that the reader may have an opportunity to meet the Presidents as real people.

This new edition of *Meet the Presidents* includes an account of Lyndon Johnson's succession to the Presidency. The orderly manner of that succession eloquently affirmed what Thomas Jefferson once wrote in a letter to John Adams: ". . . And so we have gone on, and so we shall go on, puzzled and prospering, beyond example in the history of man."

The "At a Glance" section that follows each chapter lists many dates and significant events for which there was not space in the narrative.

INTRODUCTION

It is hoped that these summaries for easy reference will provide a concise history of the Presidents and the times in which they lived.

Space does not permit mention of the many books, magazine articles and newspapers consulted. I wish to thank Lena S. Bratter, who prepared the manuscript for the printer, for many helpful suggestions. Special acknowledgment is due my collaborator, Elizabeth L. Crandall, who was primarily responsible for the "At a Glance" sections and the chapters on Harry S. Truman and Dwight D. Eisenhower. I am grateful to her, as well, for her perceptive and critical appraisal of all the chapters.

FRANCES CAVANAH

WASHINGTON, D. C.

FEBRUARY, 1964

CONTENTS

CONTENTS

MEET THE PRESIDENTS

*". . . And so we have gone on, and so
we shall go on, puzzled and prospering,
beyond example in the history of man."*
—THOMAS JEFFERSON
IN A LETTER TO JOHN ADAMS

GEORGE WASHINGTON *Decides on a Career*

Sometimes George Washington felt that he had three homes. He really lived at Ferry Farm with his mother and her younger children, but he was always welcome in the houses of his two older half brothers. Austin Washington had a farm called Wakefield. Lawrence's broad acres overlooking the Potomac River were known as Mount Vernon, and to George Mount Vernon was the most beautiful plantation in Virginia.

Nor had there ever been a kinder brother than Lawrence, he decided one summer day in 1746 when he turned the horse's head in at the gate. Lawrence had been like a father to him, ever since their father died three years before.

The master of Mount Vernon and his young wife, Anne Fairfax, stood in the doorway. George at fourteen was so tall that Anne had to stand on tiptoe to kiss his cheek. Lawrence joked about his height.

"I believe you have added a few inches since I last saw you," said Lawrence heartily. "I am glad that you arrived today. Two naval officers, friends I knew in the war, have come for a visit."

He pointed toward the river, where a warship lay at anchor, its great mast rising bold and tall against the sky. It was on just such a ship that Lawrence had sailed when he went to war in the West Indies. This home he had built on the rise of the ground above the river had been named for Admiral Vernon, his old commander. At dinner George listened eagerly as the naval officers recalled tales of their adventures at sea.

Colonel Fairfax, Anne's father, later rode up from his estate, Belvoir, farther down the river, and the talk turned to the vast wilderness west of the Blue Ridge Mountains. Lawrence was convinced that in a few years thousands of people would be going west to live. Anne's father agreed.

"My cousin," he told the officers, "is Lord Fairfax, who has inherited thousands of acres out there beyond the Blue Ridge. He writes from England that he is coming over to look after his property. His plan is to have his land there surveyed and then mark it off into lots and estates to be sold to settlers."

George was silent, but he did not miss a word of what was being said. Adventures on land or adventures at sea—it seemed that Lawrence's friends were always talking of one or the other. The next day, when the naval officers left, the two brothers stood on the wharf watching as the ship sailed slowly down the river. George wondered what new experiences awaited the officers. What strange lands would they visit?

"I wish I could go to sea," he said.

"Perhaps you can. A life at sea would offer many advantages, and it would be a good career for you," Lawrence replied. "I have friends in the Royal Navy who may be able to get you a commission as an ensign. Or you might prefer to sail on a merchant vessel. In a few years you might become a mate, or even a captain. Would you like that?"

"Yes, Lawrence, I would. But I would like it even better if I could join the Royal Navy."

"Then I will write to my friends. You must not worry your mother, though," Lawrence warned. "Wait until I have some definite plan to suggest."

George's heart sank. He was afraid that Mrs. Washington would consider him too young to leave home. Could he ever make her understand how much he wanted to go to sea?

After his return to Ferry Farm, George thought of little else. He liked to imagine himself wearing a blue uniform with brass buttons and walking the deck of a big ship. He could almost feel the tang of the salt air against his cheeks. But he said nothing to anyone, not even to his sister, Betty, only a year younger than himself.

The little house where they lived was perched high on a bluff amid the pine trees overlooking the Rappahannock River. Every morning the two older children, with their three small brothers, walked down the steep slope to the ferry. They were rowed across the river to the town of Fredericksburg, where they attended the school kept by the Reverend Mr. Marye. One day while he was in town, George met Colonel Fairfax.

"I bring two letters from Mount Vernon," said the colonel. "One is for your mother. The other is for you."

On the ferry going home, George broke the seal of the letter addressed to him. Lawrence wrote that he had high hopes of obtaining a commission for George in the Royal Navy, but it would be necessary for Mrs. Washington to give her consent. The ferryboat had no sooner touched shore than the impatient boy raced up the hill.

As Mrs. Washington read the letter from her stepson, a flush mounted to her thin cheeks. "It would be well," she said, "if Lawrence remembered that *I* am the one to decide what is best for your future. This is nonsense. How can a boy of fourteen know anything about the sea?"

"I can learn," said George quickly. "Both Lawrence and Colonel Fairfax think it is a good plan."

"Colonel Fairfax, you say?" asked Mrs. Washington. The colonel was one of the leading men in the colony, and she respected his opinion. But she loved George dearly, in spite of her strict ways. She knew how much she would miss him if he left home.

"Enough!" she said. "You are my eldest child. I don't want you to go so far away."

"What will happen to me if I stay here?"

Mrs. Washington hesitated. She knew only too well how few advantages George would have in Virginia. His older half brothers had finished their education in England, but she would not have enough money to send her own sons away to school. Lawrence and Austin had inherited the larger part of their father's estate. For Mrs. Washington and her children there was only Ferry Farm, and there seemed little chance that George would ever own a big plantation. Perhaps the Royal Navy, or even a merchant vessel, would offer him a better future, but she clutched at one last excuse.

"Before I decide, I must write to your Uncle Joseph," she declared. "We shall see what he advises."

Mrs. Washington's brother, Joseph Ball, lived in London, and in those days it took several weeks for a letter to cross the ocean. George's fifteenth birthday came and went, and there had been no answer to his mother's letter. It was hard to wait, but he was not idle. One of the surveyors in the neighborhood agreed to teach him surveying.

Soon the boy began to put into practice what he had been learning. He would carry his instruments to the turnip patch or some other plot of ground. Under his direction, a colored slave would drive stakes into the ground and help him to measure the distances between them with a long metal chain. George would peer through his theodolite—a sort of telescope mounted on a tripod—and busily set down figures on a piece of paper. Afterward, he would write down the measurements and boundaries in a notebook. Then he would draw a careful map of the plots he had surveyed.

One day the following summer, when he returned to the house for dinner, his mother met him at the door. She handed him a letter. "It is from your Uncle Joseph," she said. "Read it for yourself."

George glanced at her tight-drawn lips before he opened the pages.

> *I understand that you are advised and have some thoughts of putting your son George to sea. I think he had better be put apprentice to a tinker, for the common sailor before the mast has by no means the common liberty of the subject, for they will . . . use him like a dog.*

George laid the letter down. His voice was low, but there was a note of desperation in it. "It will not be as Uncle Joseph thinks," he protested. "I will not be a common sailor. Lawrence will get me a commission."

He stopped in surprise. His mother—his stately mother—was weeping. It came to him in a flash then—her grief since his father's death, her hardships in caring for her five children and in managing the farm alone. A moment later she dried her eyes. She sat up straight. She was her old stern self again.

"I need you here," she said, "and I want to hear no more nonsense about going to sea."

George stumbled from the room and walked across the fields. Gone were his hopes for adventure on the wide oceans, he thought, as he picked up his surveyor's chain. There was a sort of comfort in the touch of the cool steel links between his fingers; in the feeling of the sun-baked earth beneath his feet. In every direction stretched the farm which someday would be his. He thought of how many more acres Lawrence owned at Mount Vernon. Then his face brightened. Soon he would be returning for another visit with his brother.

It was a long visit, and Lawrence let him survey some of the fields overlooking the Potomac. George also went foxhunting with the masters of the neighboring plantations; and Lord Fairfax, who had recently arrived from England, took an immediate liking to Anne's young brother-in-law. He often talked about the property he had inherited beyond the Blue Ridge.

"I hardly know myself how much land I own," he said one day. "Five million acres, I've been told, and it is high time that I find out exactly where my boundaries are. Squatters are moving in and settling there without so much as a by-your-leave."

"Are you going to have your land surveyed, sir?" George asked.

Lord Fairfax nodded. "I am sending an experienced surveyor and Anne's brother, George Fairfax, out into the wilderness. It is a savage country, with only Indians and wild beasts to keep them company, but they are brave fellows. I would like—" he peered at George out of nearsighted gray eyes—"I would like a third person to go with them."

"Yes, sir," said George.

"I have been watching you at your surveying instruments," the British nobleman went on. "I have seen your maps. You are careful; you don't make mistakes."

At this compliment, George bowed awkwardly.

"Yes, and I believe you have courage. Would you like to go with my surveyors? You could be of much help, and it would be good training for you."

He named a salary that sounded like a fortune to a boy just starting a career, and put out his hand.

George clasped it eagerly. "I shall be proud to serve you, sir," he said.

The surveying party set out for the wilderness on March 11, 1748, less than three weeks after George Washington's sixteenth birthday. It was a cold, rainy spring and the men often had to swim their horses across swollen streams. Sometimes they waded through water to set up their surveying instruments. Then as soon as they finished surveying the land in one place, they moved on to another. It was a hard, rugged life, and George enjoyed it. He had brought his journal with him, and he wrote in it at the end of nearly every day as he sat by the campfire. On one page he described his first meeting with a band of Indians:

They clear a large circle, and make a great fire in the middle, then seat themselves around it. The speaker makes a grand speech, telling them in what manner they are to dance. After he has finished, the best dancer jumps up and runs and jumps about the ring in a most comical manner. He is followed by the rest . . .

George smiled as he closed the journal in which he had been writing. Was it only a few weeks ago that he had wanted to join the Royal Navy? He had hoped to find adventure on shipboard. Instead he had found it in the wilderness. Later that night, lying on the ground wrapped in his blanket, he looked up at the dark sky and felt content.

He liked being a surveyor. He liked the calm beauty of the woods, and he was much impressed by the rich, fertile soil in this new country. Already he knew how he was going to spend the money that Lord Fairfax was paying him. He was going to buy land—and then more and more land as fast as he could earn the money.

The next five years were busy ones. George worked hard as a surveyor, and at nineteen he was appointed a major in the group of volunteer solders known as the militia. By the time he was twenty, his beloved brother Lawrence had died, and young Major Washington became the master of Mount Vernon. Meanwhile he had made several surveying trips into the western wilderness. These trips brought new adventures to record in his diary, and the experience he gained opened the way for another adventure when he was twenty-one.

It really began one day in October, 1753, during a conversation with Colonel Fairfax. George had been reading an article in the *Virginia Gazette*. The French in Canada, pushing southward into territory claimed by the British, had built two forts on the southern shore of Lake Erie. Unless they were checked and forced to turn back, they might try to claim all of the vast Ohio Valley. Robert Dinwiddie, the royal governor of Virginia, decided to send a letter to the commander of the nearest French fort, warning the French to leave British territory.

"The governor has not yet chosen a messenger to deliver his message," Colonel Fairfax told George. "It will be a difficult mission. A man is needed who has had experience in the wilderness, one who is strong and brave and can be trusted."

A messenger? The nearest French fort was five hundred miles away and the journey, especially with winter coming on, meant danger, but George's decision was made. He would volunteer to deliver the governor's letter. A few days later he mounted his horse and rode into Williamsburg, the capital of Virginia. Although he was outwardly calm, his heart was pounding when he dismounted before the Governor's Palace.

Robert Dinwiddie was a big man, so big that the slender chair behind his desk seemed hardly strong enough to bear his weight. He regarded George shrewdly as the young man made his request.

"Indeed, Major Washington, I do need a messenger," the governor replied, "and my friend, Colonel Fairfax, has spoken highly of you. The French have grown very bold. But they will soon learn they are mistaken if they think they can drive us out of territory that is rightfully ours. Englishmen can be bold, too."

As he spoke, his voice rose in indignation. George nodded respectfully.

"I shall give you a letter to the commander of the nearest French fort," the governor went on. "You are to deliver my message and demand a reply. While you are at the fort, learn all you can about what the French intend to do and how many soldiers they have. Then return with all haste to Williamsburg."

George chose three companions to go with him. Snow lay deep on the ground as their horses stumbled along the rough paths through the wilderness toward the French fort. On the return journey several weeks later, George had two narrow escapes. Once a treacherous Indian tried to kill him. Another time, in crossing an icy stream on a raft, the raft upset and he was nearly drowned. When he finally reached Williamsburg, he handed the governor a reply from the French commander.

As Robert Dinwiddie read it, his face grew red with anger. "Bah!" he exclaimed. "Fine words and nothing else. What the commander really means is that the French refuse to leave. What did you learn of their plans for the future, Major?"

"My news is not encouraging," George replied. "While I was at the fort, I heard the soldiers talking. It is as you suspected, sir. The French want to occupy the entire Ohio Valley. Unless they can be stopped, they will send a force southward in the spring. They have already turned many of the Indians against us, and I fear they will have some staunch allies among the red men."

As George described what he had seen and heard, Robert Dinwiddie listened carefully. "Major," said the governor, "will you please write out what you have been telling me? I want to read your report to the members of my Council."

Fortunately George had written in his diary nearly every day, and the diary helped in writing his report. It gave such a vivid picture of the territory beyond the mountains that the governor had it printed and copies sent to London. In Virginia, too, people were reading the report. They realized as never before that the rich Ohio Valley was in grave danger of becoming French territory unless England and the English colonies acted promptly.

And what about the young man who had taken the journey beyond the mountains? His friends looked on him with new respect.

Others who had not heard of him before were curious. "Who is this George Washington?" they asked.

The day was coming when everyone would know the answer to that question. George Washington's journey to the French fort was the beginning of forty-five years of service to his country. When the desire of both French and English to control the rich Ohio Valley brought on the French and Indian War, he fought bravely and became a colonel. After many months of hard fighting, the British and Americans felt certain of victory, and the young colonel resigned.

A week later George Washington married a pretty widow, Martha Custis. At twenty-six, he did what he had long wanted to do; he settled down at Mount Vernon to be a farmer. Martha had had two children by her first marriage, and George loved them as dearly as if they had been his own. The Washingtons were a hospitable couple, and the large, gracious house was usually filled with guests.

But after fifteen years, the happy, peaceful life at Mount Vernon came to an end. Ever since the French and Indian War, trouble had been building up between England and the thirteen American colonies. When the American Revolution began, George Washington was asked to take command of the Continental Army. He was General Washington now, and few generals ever faced greater difficulties. He himself served without pay, and there were times when he had no money to pay his soldiers. Sometimes it was hard even to feed them, but for six and a half years he managed to keep an army together. When the war was finally won, the thirteen colonies had become an independent nation—the United States of America.

Then at last General Washington could return to Mount Vernon, the place that he loved more than any spot on earth. He expected to spend the rest of his life there, but he soon found that his country still needed him. The new nation he had fought for was in grave danger because the central government had no real power. In 1787 he went to Philadelphia, where he presided over the Constitutional Convention. The delegates to the convention worked out a new plan for a stronger government. This plan, called the Constitution of the United States, provided that the head of the nation should be a President. A strong President, one whom everyone trusted, was needed to get the new government started, and there was only one man everyone wanted. That man was General Washington.

New York City was chosen as a temporary capital, and on April

30, 1789, George Washington stood on the balcony of Federal Hall. On the table beside him there was a Bible resting on a crimson cushion. The judge of the New York Supreme Court stood facing him and spoke the words of the oath of office. This was a promise, the same promise that every President since that time has made. George Washington placed his hand on the Bible and repeated the words.

"I do solemnly swear," he said, "that I will faithfully execute the office of President of the United States and will, to the best of my ability, preserve, protect and defend the Constitution of the United States."

Then he added, "So help me God," and leaned forward to kiss the Bible.

The judge turned toward the crowd waiting in the street below. "It is done," he said. "Long live George Washington, President of the United States."

The crowd that was watching the first inauguration in American history responded with a shout that seemed to reach the sky: "Long live George Washington!" And other voices answered: "God bless our President!"

THE FIRST PRESIDENT *at a Glance*

George Washington

Born: February 22, 1732   *Died: December 14, 1799*

As a boy. George Washington was born in Virginia on a plantation now known as Wakefield. He was the son of Augustine Washington, a planter, and Augustine's second wife, Mary Ball Washington. Later the family lived on another plantation, Hunting Creek, and then at Ferry Farm near the Rappahannock River. After his father's death when George was 11 (1743), the boy continued to live at Ferry Farm. He often visited his older half brothers: Lawrence, at Hunting Creek (which Lawrence had named Mount Vernon), and Austin, who had inherited Wakefield. George studied surveying as a youth and was a surveyor (1748–1752).

As a young man. After Lawrence died (1752), George inherited Mount Vernon. The next year, when he was 21, he carried a message from the colonial governor of Virginia to the commander of a French fort in the Ohio Valley, warning the French to leave. Their refusal helped bring on the French and Indian War, in which George fought (1754–1758).

As hero of the Revolution. Washington was a delegate (1774) to the First Continental Congress, which met in Philadelphia to consider the grievances of the American colonies against the British. In June, 1775, the Second Continental Congress selected Washington as commander-in-chief of the Continental Army. Washington took command of the army in Cambridge, Mass. (July, 1775), and drove the British from Boston (March, 1776). Following an unsuccessful campaign in New York, he won a great victory at Trenton, N.J. (December 26, 1776) after crossing the Delaware River on Christmas night to surprise the enemy. He held his ragged, hungry troops together at Valley Forge, Pa., during the winter of 1777–1778. With the help of a French army and fleet, he forced the British general, Cornwallis, to surrender at Yorktown, Va. (October, 1781). The British recognized U.S. independence in a treaty signed September, 1783. General Washington resigned as commander of the army (December, 1783) and returned to Mount Vernon, but left again to preside over the Constitutional Convention in Philadelphia (May–September, 1787).

As President (1789–1793; 1793–1797). After being elected President unanimously (February, 1789), Washington was inaugurated (April 30, 1789) in New York City, the first capital of the U.S. The first Presidential Cabinet, or group of advisers, included Alexander Hamilton, Secretary of the Treasury, and Thomas Jefferson, Secretary of State. Hamilton wanted to make the Federal, or central, government strong. Jefferson feared that a strong central government would interfere with the people's freedom and happiness. Disagreements between these Cabinet members led to the rise of the first U.S. political parties: the Federalist party, led by Hamilton, and the Democratic-Republican party, led by Jefferson. Washington, although he tried to stay out of political quarrels, supported Hamilton's efforts to organize a strong central government. Washington, often called "Father of His Country," refused to run for a third term, and returned to Mount Vernon (1797), where he died two years later. Soon thereafter, General Henry Lee described Washington as "first in war, first in peace, first in the hearts of his countrymen."

George Washington's family. Washington married a widow, Martha Custis (1732–1802). They had no children, but two of Martha's children, "Jackie" and "Patsy," and later two grandchildren, Nelly Custis and George Washington Parke Custis, were brought up in the Washingtons' home.

Other happenings. When Washington was President, the government moved from New York to Philadelphia, the nation's second temporary capital (1790–1800). Washington chose (1790) the exact site on the Potomac River for a permanent capital and helped to plan the city to be built there (Washington, D.C.). The first ten amendments (the Bill of Rights) were added to the Constitution (1791). Eli Whitney invented the cotton gin (1793). After General Anthony Wayne subdued (1794) the Indians in the Northwest Territory (the present states of Ohio, Michigan, Indiana, Illinois, Wisconsin, and part of Minnesota), great numbers of settlers flocked into the region.

The nation's population and growth. The population was almost four million in 1790, according to the first U.S. census. Three new states were added to the original 13: Vermont (1791), Kentucky (1792), and Tennessee (1796).

JOHN ADAMS *Changes His Mind*

It was a crisp winter night in the little town of Braintree, ten miles south of Boston in the colony of Massachusetts. Several boys were skating on the pond, and none was a better skater than John Adams. Out of the corner of his eye he could see several girls, bundled up to their ears in scarfs and shawls, who stood on the bank. They looked on admiringly as he lengthened his stride and made a swift, graceful circle of the pond.

"Watch John Adams," said one of the "females," as girls were then called. "He may be fat, forsooth, but he knows how to skate."

Her words carried distinctly across the frozen pond, and John needed no more encouragement. He twisted and turned and made a figure eight. There was another long-drawn-out "Oo-o-oh!" from the females who stood watching. John's round, plump cheeks were flushed with embarrassment, but he liked the feeling. Winter was even more fun than summer, he decided.

But when June arrived, he was convinced that summer was his favorite time of year. Roses framed the doorway of the brick and clapboard farmhouse where the Adams family lived. Lilacs blossomed in the yard, and the woods were cool and green. John Adams was busy, always busy. Once he whittled a canoe out of pinewood and launched it on the town brook. He often rode bareback around the pasture on one of his father's horses. He played with his younger brothers, Peter and Elihu. He and his Uncle Peter went fishing, and they were like two boys together.

"John is the talkingest nephew I have," Uncle Peter said.

It was true that John talked a great deal, but he could be quiet, too. He liked to wander off into the woods alone and take long hikes. Sometimes at the end of a hot, lazy afternoon, he climbed the hill back of the Adams farmhouse. In the distance, over the treetops, he could see Boston, and in Boston harbor were the clustered masts of many tall ships. Most of them were English ships, and John felt a stir of pride. England was the mother country, to which Massachusetts and the twelve other colonies belonged. Sometimes he stood there on the hill for more than an hour. It was always a thrill to watch as a ship spread its white sails and moved slowly out into the Atlantic Ocean.

Many years later, when John recalled the days of his boyhood, he said that they "went off like a fairy tale." Yet he was not always happy. He did not like to go to school. Many days, as he bent over his Latin grammar, pretending to study, he was counting the minutes until he could run outdoors and play.

There were two schools in Braintree. John wished that he could attend the school taught by Joseph Marsh; Mr. Marsh understood boys. The other school, where John went, was taught by Mr. Cleverly, and Mr. Cleverly was dull. Dull and cross. He sat on a high platform, his eyes seeming to look right through his students. His cane was beside him, ready for instant use on any boy who displeased him. One morning John heard the schoolmaster talking with the kind old clergyman of the village.

"If I were a monarch," said Mr. Cleverly in his harsh voice, "I would have in my dominion only *one* religion."

John had to bite back the words he wanted to say. What right would anyone, even a king, have to tell other people what they should believe? That was something every person had a right to decide for himself.

Occasionally, when John felt that he could not stand Mr. Cleverly's dull classes any longer, he played hooky. He might get a caning afterward, but usually it was worth it. One afternoon he came home from a long ramble through the woods to find Peter waiting back of the barn. Peter wanted to play Bat and Ball. John picked up the bat. He had just hit the ball a resounding whack when he heard his name called.

John at fourteen was a big boy, five feet, six inches tall, but at that moment he felt smaller than ten-year-old Peter. He also felt scared. His father was coming across the barn lot. Had Mr. Adams been talking with Mr. Cleverly?

"Peter, go into the house," said Mr. Adams. "John, put down that bat. Your schoolmaster has told me you were not in school again today. He says that you refuse to study. I think it is time that you and I have a long talk."

Another scolding! the boy thought ruefully. He would rather take a caning and have it over with. But his father just stood there, looking him up and down.

The silence became uncomfortable. John shifted from one bare foot to the other. The elder John Adams had what he called "an admiration for learning," but had left school at twelve to work on the family farm. It was the custom in many New England families for the younger boys to inherit the farm, and only the eldest son had a chance to go to college. Mr. Adams' older brother Joseph had attended the University at Cambridge, as Harvard was then called. Now Mr. Adams was looking forward to the day when *his* eldest son would enter Harvard. The trouble was that John did not seem to care if he ever went to school again.

Mr. Adams broke the silence at last. "John, why won't you study? You can learn well enough when you want to."

"I don't like my master," John mumbled.

"That is no excuse. Cleverly's Free Latin School is as good as any in the colony."

John did not answer. But the way he drew his lips together in a long, thin line showed that he did not agree.

"You will be fifteen next October," his father reminded him. "In one more year you will have to take your entrance examinations to enter the university. Do you think you will be ready?"

"No, sir," John admitted.

Mr. Adams sighed. "At least you are honest about it, and I suppose the fault is partly mine. I should have been more strict with you, and from now on I intend to be. There are to be no more fishing trips with Uncle Peter, no more Bat and Ball and *no more playing hooky.* You will have to study every evening, to make up for the time you have wasted."

John kept his eyes on the ground, as he traced a pattern in the dust with his toe. When Mr. Adams spoke again, his voice sounded even more stern.

"By the time you are sixteen," he said, "I shall expect you to be ready for the university. The examinations will be hard, but you can pass them if you try."

"I don't want to go to the university," John blurted out. "I don't ever want to go to school again. I hate school. I hate Latin. I hate Mr. Cleverly."

"If you don't want to go to school, what do you want to do?"

This was an embarrassing question. John could hardly answer that he wanted to go swimming, or hike through the woods, or wrestle with his friends.

"All of us must work in one way or another," Mr. Adams went on. "What work do you want to do, John?"

The boy did some fast thinking. "I would like to be a farmer like you."

"Very well, I shall give you a taste of farming. First, let me see—" Mr. Adams paused. "Yes, my meadow yonder needs a ditch. Since Latin grammar does not suit you, you may try ditching."

"I don't have to go to school tomorrow?"

"No. You may dig a ditch instead."

John could hardly believe his good fortune, and the next morning, with shovel over his shoulder, he started for the meadow. A soft breeze fanned his cheek; the birds were twittering in the trees. Why, this was going to be as much fun as spending the day in the woods. When he reached the spot where his father had told him to begin his ditch, he sank his spade into the ground. The rocky soil was surprisingly hard, and he had to bear down on the spade with all his weight. A shovelful of earth came up at last, but his shirt was wringing wet.

John stopped and wiped his face on his sleeve. Ditch digging was more difficult than he had expected. But he was stubborn; he was going to dig that ditch if it broke his back in two.

John never knew a day to be so hot. It became even hotter as the sun rose higher in the sky. His hair curled around his forehead in damp ringlets. His hands were blistered. By night he was so tired that he could hardly drag himself upstairs to bed.

The next morning he was back in the meadow. Again and again he glanced toward the cool house and wished that he were inside, studying his Latin. During the noonday meal, he kept his eyes on his plate but once when he looked up he noticed that Mr. Adams was watching him closely. The boy opened his mouth as though about to speak. Perhaps if he asked, very politely, his father would allow him to go back to his studies. Then he thought again of Mr. Cleverly's dull school. He rose wearily from the table and returned to the ditch that he was digging.

Somehow the afternoon dragged by. Every muscle in John's body seemed to ache. It was nearly evening when he went to find his father.

"The ditch is finished, sir."

"Good!" said Mr. Adams. "Now what task shall I find for you tomorrow? Would you like to——"

John looked up hopefully. "If you choose, sir," he said, "I would like to go back to my Latin grammar."

"I am glad, son. If you work as hard at your Latin as you have been working in the meadow, you should be ready for college in another year."

There was a wistful note in his voice, and John felt a pang of conscience. He knew how much it meant to his father to have him go to college.

"I will try, sir." John hesitated, then made himself go on. "I will do my best to please Mr. Cleverly."

"No," said Mr. Adams quickly. "Your mother and I have been talking it over. How would you like to go to Joseph Marsh's school?"

The boy let out a whoop. Why, he really liked Mr. Marsh.

A new world seemed to open to John Adams when he started in his new school. Joseph Marsh was a strict master but a kind one, and John worked harder than he had ever worked for Mr. Cleverly. There was not much time for hikes and fishing trips, but he no longer minded. Even Latin seemed interesting, for he was learning to translate the great epic poem by the poet Virgil. As he read about the voyages of Aeneas, he was surprised to find what remarkable adventures could be found between the pages of a book.

"Under my second master, who was kind," he said years later, "I began to love my books and neglect my sports. From that time on I have been *too* studious."

It was not like John Adams ever to do anything halfway. He studied so hard that, at sixteen, he passed his entrance examinations to enter Harvard. Four years later, one hot July day in 1755, his family arrived to see him graduate. Not only the students but the people of Cambridge and other New England towns looked forward to Commencement. Because there were so few holidays to celebrate in those days, everyone wanted to share in the fun. Tents had been set up in the college yard, and jugglers and acrobats were performing. Fiddlers were playing. Young people were dancing. Against this gay background, John Adams walked across the grass to welcome his parents, his brothers, and several uncles and aunts and cousins. His father in a new cocked hat and an embroidered waistcoat did not look like a farmer.

"I have been told," said Mr. Adams, "that you are graduating near the top of your class. You have done well, my son."

Mrs. Adams looked on, beaming with pride. Was this the same John who used to play hooky? How dignified he looked in his long black academic gown, his powdered hair neatly plaited in a pigtail at the back.

For such a lively boy, John Adams certainly did grow up into a very solemn man. After graduating from Harvard he taught school and studied law at the same time. Within a few years he had become a prominent lawyer and one of the leading patriots in Massachusetts. Before the American Revolution began, he protested vigorously every time he thought that the rights of the colonists were being threatened. He was a delegate to the Continental Congress which met in Philadelphia to try to find ways of settling the troubles with the mother country. After the American colonies went to war against England in 1775, it was John Adams who nominated George Washington to be the commander-in-chief of the new Continental Army. A year later he was a member of the committee appointed to work on a Declaration of Independence.

When Congress voted to adopt the Declaration, John Adams was elated. Back in Braintree, his wife Abigail, whom John had married twelve years earlier, was as staunch a patriot as her husband, and he wanted to share the good news with her.

The day "ought to be solemnized with pomp and parade," he wrote her, "with games, bells, and bonfires, from one end of this continent to the other, from this time forevermore."

John Adams continued to serve the new nation for many years. But as he grew older, he became bitter because he felt that he was not appreciated. He was accused of being blunt and haughty and proud, and one of his nicknames was "His Pomposity." Another nickname was "His Rotundity" because he was so plump. But "honest John Adams," as he is remembered today, was always devoted to his country. He may have been as stubborn and conceited as his many enemies said, but they had to admit that he was brilliant and conscientious.

When George Washington was elected the first President of the United States, John Adams became the first Vice President. Eight years later he was elected President. In 1800, toward the end of his term, he and other officers of the government arrived in Washington, D.C., the new capital city that was being built on the banks of the Potomac River. The stately mansion now called the White House was not yet finished, but John Adams moved in anyway.

Then he sat down to write a letter to Abigail, who was soon to join him. Many years later one sentence from that letter was to be carved over the fireplace in the State Dining Room:

I pray Heaven to bestow the best of blessings on this House and all that shall hereafter inhabit it. May none but honest and wise men ever rule under this roof.

THE SECOND PRESIDENT *at a Glance*

John Adams

Born: October 30, 1735   Died: July 4, 1826

Early life. John Adams, the son of a farmer, was born in Braintree (now Quincy), Mass. After graduating from Harvard (1755), he taught school in Worcester, Mass. and studied law at night. He began to practice law in 1758. He and his second cousin, Samuel Adams, actively opposed the Stamp Act, a law passed by the British Parliament (1765) to raise taxes from the American colonists. One of the staunchest of colonial patriots, John Adams was also a strong believer in justice. When British soldiers were accused of killing several civilians during the "Boston Massacre" (1770), he insisted that they should have a fair trial and acted as their legal counsel. Although he feared that public opinion would turn against him, he was respected for having the courage of his convictions. In 1774 he was a delegate to the First Continental Congress in Philadelphia.

In the struggle for independence. At the Second Continental Congress (1775) Adams nominated George Washington to be commander of the American troops. Adams was a member of the committee appointed (1776) to draft a Declaration of Independence. In 1778 Adams was in Paris as a member of a commission seeking French help in the Revolution. Two years later he went alone to Holland on a similar task. After the war, he was appointed to serve (1785–1788) as minister to Great Britain, the former enemy.

As President (1797–1801). After serving as Vice President during Washington's two terms (1789–1797), John Adams was elected President and was inaugurated in Philadelphia (1797). Adams' firm stand in a bitter dispute with France won popular approval. But many people turned against him when he supported the Alien and Sedition laws, passed by Congress (1798) in an attempt to silence criticism of the government. Other quarrels made him unpopular even with leaders of his own Federalist party. He was not elected for a second term. One of his last important acts as President was to appoint (1801) John Marshall as Chief Justice of the Supreme Court. Marshall was to become the first great interpreter of the Constitution.

The President's wife. Abigail Smith Adams (1744–1818), considered one of the most brilliant women of her time, was the first mistress of the mansion now called the White House. Mrs. Adams used the East Room of the unfinished mansion for drying the family wash.

Other happenings. When John Adams was President, the government moved from Philadelphia to Washington, D.C. (1800). The capital city had a population of a little more than 3,000. The Library of Congress was founded (1800).

The nation's population. According to the census of 1800, there were more than 5,300,000 people in the U.S.

TOM JEFFERSON *Climbs a Mountain*

I like living at Shadwell, Father," said Tom Jefferson. "I like it better than Tuckahoe."

Colonel Peter Jefferson seemed pleased. Shadwell was a plain frame house on the edge of the wilderness; Tuckahoe was a stately mansion belonging to the Randolph family in eastern Virginia. Mrs. Jefferson and William Randolph had been cousins, and after Mr. Randolph's death, Colonel Jefferson had taken his family to Tuckahoe, where he could look after the Randolph children. Their home was one of the finest in the colony, and the colonel was glad that Tom had not been spoiled by luxury.

"At heart you are a pioneer, just like me," said Colonel Jefferson.

It was a satisfaction to know that Tom shared his father's pride in Shadwell. Only a few years earlier, this farm—these fields of wheat and tobacco—had been a heavily wooded forest. Peter Jefferson, a regular giant of a man, had cut down the trees and cleared the land for planting with the help of a few slaves. Now Shadwell was prospering, but moving back had presented one problem. At Tuckahoe there had been a little schoolhouse on the plantation grounds. The Jefferson daughters, according to the ideas of that time, had had all the schooling they would need, but the colonel wanted Tom to prepare for college. The boy was nine years old, and it was time for him to begin to study Greek and Latin.

"I have been giving much thought to a teacher for you, a better teacher than you had at Tuckahoe," the colonel said. "I have been to see the Reverend William Douglas. He is a very learned man, and I bring you good news."

"Is Mr. Douglas coming here to teach me?" asked Tom eagerly.

"No, but he takes a few scholars into his home," Colonel Jefferson replied. "He has agreed that you may live with him."

The father paused in surprise. Tom looked disappointed; usually he liked to study. Peter Jefferson felt proud that his tall, redheaded son was so bright, even if some people might consider him too inquisitive. The colonel looked down with a teasing smile.

"I should think that a boy so full of questions would want to go to school," he said. "The right teacher, the right books, will help you to find many of the answers."

"I do want to go to school," said Tom slowly, "but I don't want to leave Shadwell. I want to be with you."

"And you shall be," Colonel Jefferson assured him. "Mr. Douglas lives close enough for you to come home every Friday afternoon. There will be longer vacations in the summer, and you and I can go hunting and fishing. But school is important, son. Although I never had a chance for much education, I want you to be a scholar."

During the next five years Tom spent a large part of his time in the home of Mr. Douglas. Here the boy studied French as well as Greek and Latin. He was good in mathematics. He read poems and stories and essays by great writers. When he went home he kept right on learning—but there he learned from the outdoors instead of from books. His father taught him to swim and ride and shoot.

"It is the strong in body who are both strong and free in mind," said Colonel Jefferson.

Tom was as good in sports as he was in his studies, and he loved the "upcountry," as this part of Virginia was called. It was a land of rugged hills. On the farther side of the Rivanna River, across from Shadwell, there was one hill so high that it was almost a mountain. It was Tom's favorite retreat, and he often swam his horse across the stream, then climbed on foot to the wooded summit. From there he could look out over an expanse of green valley to other hills half lost in a blue haze. In all the world, he believed, there could not be a scene more beautiful.

Often when Tom arrived home for a visit he found guests. Men in fine velvet coats stopped on their way to Williamsburg to attend meetings of the House of Burgesses—citizens elected from the different counties to make the laws for the colony. The colonel also had many Indian friends, and one evening he and Tom attended an Indian campfire ceremonial. The Cherokee chief, Ontassete, was about to leave for England to ask justice for his tribe from the English king. He arose, and holding out his arms to the moon that hung like a great golden ball in the sky, he began to pray. Although he spoke in the Cherokee language, Tom felt a cold chill up and down his spine. He did not need to understand the words to know that Ontassete was asking the Great Spirit to grant him a successful voyage and bring him safely home again to his own people.

Tom Jefferson never forgot that evening. Nor did he forget the evenings that his father's friend, Dr. William Walker, spent at Shadwell. He was the Jefferson family physician, but he was also an explorer. With a few hardy companions he had traveled west to a place the Indians called Kentucky. What lay beyond Kentucky no one seemed to know, and the men wondered what they would find if they could explore the western rivers. Tom wondered, too. What were the western lands like? He knew that he would never be satisfied until he learned more about them.

Then came the French and Indian War, which put an end to the evening discussions at Shadwell. Colonel Jefferson, who had always tried to be a friend to the Indians, felt sick at heart. Some of the red men from farther north, allies of the French in their war against the British, were spreading terror along the frontier. They raided villages and lonely cabins, killed the men, and carried the women and children off as prisoners. Whenever Colonel Jefferson learned of a raid on a neighboring farm, he led his militia against the savage foe. Often he arrived too late; the cabin was in ashes and the enemy had escaped.

By the time the war was over Peter Jefferson had died. His last wish had been for Tom to continue his education, and Dr. Walker, Tom's guardian, sent the boy to live and study with another teacher, the Reverend James Maury. Now when Tom came home for vacations Shadwell seemed very lonely. But he still liked to climb his little mountain. He shared it with Dabney Carr, a new friend he had met at school, and they spent many hours reading or just talking under the wide-spreading branches of an oak tree. In the tree's friendly shade all things seemed possible, as the boys told each other of their ambitions, their hopes and plans. Both Tom and Dabney were going to study to be lawyers.

One afternoon Tom confided to his friend that he also wanted to travel. He wanted to see some of the far places of the world. Then he would come home and build a house on this mountaintop. He would call it Monticello, the Italian word for "little mountain." It was going to be a beautiful house—the most beautiful in Virginia.

Tom fell silent as he looked out over the bright valley at his feet. It was a valley of pioneers, where every man was free and each had an equal right to carve out for himself the kind of life he wanted. That was the way that all Americans should live, thought Tom. Somehow, the freedom and the right to govern himself that the pioneer had found in the wilderness should belong to all men everywhere. Tom stretched out on the grass and looked up at the sky through a tangle of leaves. Already a dream was stirring in his heart.

Years were to pass—years of thought and study—before Thomas Jefferson worked out the ideas and found the words to help make the dream come true. He was not quite seventeen when he went to Williamsburg to attend William and Mary College. Here he discovered the answers to many of his questions, only to realize that he had new questions to ask. He studied the books of some of the great French and English thinkers who believed that each and every person had a right to freedom. After graduating at nineteen, he spent the next five years studying law under George Wythe, one of the most brilliant lawyers in the colonies. Part of the time, Tom read his law books at home, but he often went to Williamsburg to see his teacher. Frequently, when the House of Burgesses was in session, Tom would stand listening in the doorway.

He was still a law student when, one bright spring morning in 1765, he heard a rumor that the Burgesses would probably vote on an important matter that same day. As soon as breakfast was over, Tom hurried down the Duke of Gloucester Street. As he passed between two rows of white frame houses, he glanced back at the red brick buildings of William and Mary College at one end of the wide street. At the other end was the red brick Capitol. Most of the Burgesses were already seated in the Assembly Hall when Tom found a place in the crowded doorway. His friend Patrick Henry, a new member from the upcountry, glanced up and saw him.

Tom lifted his hand in greeting, trying not to smile. Patrick in his buckskin breeches, a coonskin cap resting on his knee, seemed out of place among the other members. Most of them were rich planters in fancy waistcoats with lace ruffles at their wrists. Not that it mattered how Patrick looked! thought Tom loyally. He had a golden tongue in his head, if ever a man did.

As the meeting droned on, Tom found it hard to keep his mind on what the speakers were saying. He, like many others that day, was thinking of the Stamp Act. This law, recently passed by the English Parliament, would require Americans to buy stamps to place on all legal documents and papers, even newspapers.

"The law is not legal." A tall gentleman who stood in the doorway spoke in a low voice.

Tom nodded in agreement. The colonists sent no representatives to Parliament, and Parliament had no right to tax them. Only their own colonial Assemblies, such as the House of Burgesses, should decide what taxes Americans should pay.

"Legal or not," a second man spoke up, "the law has been passed, and we shall have to obey it. At least that is what the Burgesses seem to think."

Not all of the Burgesses, however. Suddenly Patrick Henry stood up and began to read a list of resolutions condemning the Stamp Act. His voice was firm, as he demanded that the Burgesses send a copy of his resolution to the Parliament.

Tom was surprised; a newly-elected Burgess was not expected to make speeches. A murmur of disapproval—an angry murmur—ran through the room. Some of the Burgesses, although they lived in America, still thought of themselves as Englishmen. It was wrong, they muttered—what was more, it was dangerous—to criticize Parliament or King George the Third. They glared at the shabbily dressed young man who dared to make such a radical suggestion. Patrick Henry glared back. There was thunder in his voice when he spoke again.

"We must not yield to tyranny," he said.

Tom, listening from the doorway, felt deeply moved, but some of the Burgesses were shocked. They began talking among themselves, their voices raised in anger. But Patrick was determined to be heard.

"Caesar," he shouted, "had his Brutus. Charles the First his Cromwell, and George the Third——"

He was interrupted by cries of "Treason! Treason!"

Patrick Henry's face flamed a brighter red. He waited until the noise had died down. "George the Third," he said firmly, "may profit by their example. If this be treason, make the most of it!"

The arguments that followed were loud and bitter. But, like young Thomas Jefferson, a number of the Burgesses had fallen under the spell of Patrick Henry's golden flow of words. It was finally decided, with only one vote to spare, to send several of his resolutions to England.

"Patrick speaks as Homer wrote," thought Tom as he left the Capitol.

This time he had to smile. The fiery orator from the upcountry had probably never heard of Homer, most famous of Greek poets, nor had he read the great liberal writers whose books Tom had studied. Yet he spoke many of the same thoughts and in a way that thousands could understand.

Tom Jefferson was not surprised, in the weeks that followed, to learn that his friend's speech had been printed in newspapers throughout the colonies. The words "We must not yield to tyranny" were repeated by patriots from Massachusetts to Georgia. But on no one had they made a deeper impression than on Thomas Jefferson.

"I have sworn on the altar of God," he said years later, "eternal hostility against every form of tyranny over the mind of man."

After Thomas Jefferson completed his law training, he became a successful lawyer. He married and built the beautiful house of his dreams—his Monticello—on his mountaintop. He was still a young man, only thirty-three, in 1776, when he was elected a delegate from Virginia to the Second Continental Congress. Twenty-one months had passed since the delegates from the colonies had met in the First Continental Congress to try to find peaceful ways of settling the troubles with the mother country. Since then the American Revolution had begun; the fighting had been going on for more than a year.

And now the Second Continental Congress had an important question to decide. Should the colonists continue to fight merely for their rights as Englishmen living in America? Or should they start a new nation of their own? While the delegates argued the question, a committee was asked to prepare a statement giving the reasons why the colonies wanted to separate from England. The statement would be ready, then, in case the Congress voted for independence. Thomas Jefferson was on the committee and two other members were Benjamin Franklin and John Adams. Tom suggested that Mr. Adams should do the actual writing.

John Adams shook his head. He was not popular, and he was convinced that some of the delegates would object to anything he might write, simply because they did not like him. "Besides," he added, fixing his keen blue eyes on young Mr. Jefferson, "you write ten times better than I do."

For eighteen days Thomas Jefferson kept close to his room in the house where he was staying in Philadelphia. His quill pen scratched across a clean white sheet of paper, filling it with phrases that would go ringing down the years. He remembered some of the books he had read in college by authors who believed in freedom. He had before him a copy of the Declaration of Rights only recently adopted by a convention of patriots meeting in Virginia. That declaration had been written by his friend George Mason. Perhaps he thought of the stirring words of another friend, Patrick Henry.

Laying down his pen, Thomas Jefferson gazed down on a busy street. Horses clattered over the cobblestones carrying some of the delegates to an afternoon meeting. A fine gentleman in a velvet coat passed by. Workmen in leather aprons paused to chat with soldiers home for a few days' leave from General Washington's army. The document Tom was preparing was for them—for all of the people passing in the street. His thoughts went back to his pioneer boyhood, when he had first started to climb his little mountain: he also was writing for the people whose homes he could see from Monticello.

Yes, Thomas Jefferson decided, picking up his pen again, the Declaration of Independence must find words for what was in the hearts of many men. It must do more than announce the beginning of a new nation. It must make clear to the world that the United States of America was to be a new kind of nation.

As soon as the Declaration was finished, Tom showed it to John Adams and Benjamin Franklin. They made some suggestions and a few small changes and then it was read before the Continental Congress. When the delegation voted to adopt it, riders on swift horses set out to carry copies to other colonies. The date was July 4, 1776.

Four days later three thousand people gathered in the statehouse yard in Philadelphia to hear the Declaration of Independence read aloud. It began:

We hold these truths to be self-evident, that all men are created equal, that they are endowed by their creator with certain inalienable rights, that among these are life, liberty, and the pursuit of happiness.

The crowd listened intently, and when the reading was over the bells in all the churches set up a glad ringing. Cannons were shot off, and people shouted and sang. That evening bonfires were lighted, and the celebration went on far into the night.

As for Thomas Jefferson, he was busy with plans for making his stirring words come true. He was going to return to Virginia and work for the repeal of some of the old, unjust laws. His first task, he had decided, was to try to bring to the people of his own state a greater measure of "life, liberty, and the pursuit of happiness." In the years following 1776, the birthday of the United States was celebrated on the Fourth of July, the date on which the Continental Congress had voted to declare for independence.

The nation's twenty-seventh anniversary was a time for special rejoicing in Washington, D.C., the little capital city that had not even been in existence when the Declaration of Independence was adopted. By 1803 the town had several thousand inhabitants, and they were awakened at dawn the morning of the Fourth by a salute of thirteen guns. A few hours later throngs of people were hurrying along a wide, dusty road called Pennsylvania Avenue. They turned in at a big house, still unfinished, where the President lived. The President was Thomas Jefferson.

He was smiling as he stood shaking hands with the long line of callers who had come to congratulate him. Astonishing news had reached Washington the night before. The French government had agreed to sell an area of nearly a million square miles west of the Mississippi River. The President's ministers in Paris had actually bought all of Louisiana, a region several times the size of the state which later would be called by the same name.

The news was so unexpected that many people in Washington, and elsewhere throughout the nation, found it hard to realize that their country was now twice as big as it had been before. They knew in a vague way that Louisiana stretched westward from the Mississippi as far as the Rocky Mountains. But what were the exact boundaries and what was the country like? It was said that far to the west there was a high steep wall of mountains. Some people called them the Stony Mountains, others the Rockies, but no white man had ever crossed them. And what lay beyond those mountains? Sailors sailing their vessels along the coast of Spanish California and farther north knew about the Pacific Ocean. Captain Robert Gray of the United States Navy had discovered the mouth of a great river which emptied into the Pacific, but he had not followed the river to the source. How long was the river? How far was it from the Pacific Ocean to the Rocky Mountains?

President Jefferson had been asking these same questions. All his life he had been interested in western lands. Earlier in that same year of 1803 he had persuaded Congress to set aside $2,500 for an exploring expedition all the way overland to the Pacific Ocean. The President's trusted young secretary, Captain Meriwether Lewis, and Meriwether's friend, Lieutenant William Clark, were to be the leaders. The news about the Louisiana Purchase made Captain Lewis all the more eager to explore the unknown regions beyond the mountains, and he left Washington a few days later to join Lieutenant Clark in the frontier village of St. Louis.

There during the next few months the two young men were busy recruiting men and gathering supplies. By May, 1804, they were ready, and they sailed up the Missouri River, carrying with them a long list of instructions from the President. Soon the last frontier village had been left behind. . . . Weeks and months went by, and nothing was heard from Lewis and Clark or the forty-three men under their command.

Back in Washington, Thomas Jefferson was worried, and his suspense was shared by many others throughout the settled regions of the United States. It was feared that the explorers might have lost their way in the mountains or, perhaps, been killed by Indians.

One day toward the end of October, 1806, the President sat writing at his desk. It was two and a half years since the Lewis and Clark Expedition had left St. Louis. A long time for the men to be gone, unless . . .

He looked up at the sound of a knock on his study door. When a messenger entered and handed him a letter, Thomas Jefferson broke the seal impatiently, for he had recognized the handwriting of Captain Lewis. He glanced at the date at the top of the page. The letter had been sent from St. Louis a month before.

"Sir: It is with great pleasure," Captain Lewis wrote, "that I announce to you the safe arrival of myself and party at this place . . . In obedience to your orders, we have penetrated the Continent of North America to the Pacific Ocean."

How like the young captain! thought Thomas Jefferson. As always, Meriwether Lewis was unassuming and matter-of-fact, although he had just completed one of the most remarkable journeys in history. Going and coming, he and his men had covered eight thousand miles. Many of these miles, he reported, could be traveled in boats on the Missouri and Columbia Rivers and their tributaries. Whenever possible, the explorers had made friends with the Indians, some of whom had never seen a white man before. When Captain Lewis returned to Washington, he would bring the maps he and Lieutenant Clark had made, and also specimens of minerals and plants which they had gathered. He had much, much more to tell about the rich fertile country through which he had passed.

The President walked over to the window and looked out on the Potomac. But he was not really seeing the river or the Virginia shore; in his imagination he was climbing the tall Rockies and looking across two thousand miles toward the Pacific. Doubtless several nations would lay claim to this region, but the Lewis and Clark Expedition would strengthen the claims of the American government.

The President hoped that, like Louisiana, this Far Western country would belong someday to the United States. Then thousands of Americans would be going there to live.

When that day came—Thomas Jefferson took a deep breath—his ideas about liberty and self government, first expressed in the Declaration of Independence, could be tried on a grand scale. The sons of the pioneers who would settle in the empty spaces between the Mississippi River and the Pacific Ocean were "destined," as he said later, to fill "that vast and fertile country with arts, with science, with freedom and happiness."

The President thought often about his country's future. He knew that there would be times of trouble in the years ahead, just as there had been times of trouble in the past. But he had faith in the ability of the American people to solve their difficulties.

And Thomas Jefferson never lost that faith. In his old age, after he had returned to his beloved mountaintop to live, he corresponded regularly with his old friend, John Adams. The two ex-Presidents had been through a great deal together in the days when the country was struggling for its independence. They had been like two men in the same boat, "laboring always at the same oar," as Thomas Jefferson said in one letter.

"With some wave ever ahead threatening to overwhelm us," he went on, "we rode through the storm and made a happy port . . . And so we have gone on, and so we shall go on, puzzled and prospering beyond example, in the history of man."

THE THIRD PRESIDENT *at a Glance*

Thomas Jefferson

Born: April 13, 1743   *Died July 4, 1826*

Early life. Thomas Jefferson was born at Shadwell, near Charlottesville, Va. He was the son of Peter Jefferson, a planter, and Jane Randolph Jefferson. After graduating from William and Mary College at 19 (1762), he studied law and was admitted to the bar (1767). He was a member of the Virginia House of Burgesses (1769–1774). When a delegate to the Second Continental Congress in Philadelphia, he was on a committee appointed (June, 1776) to prepare a Declaration of Independence. The Declaration adopted July 4, 1776, was almost entirely Jefferson's work.

As a leading citizen of Virginia. In September, 1776, Jefferson returned to Virginia to try to put his democratic ideals into practice. Because of his efforts as a member of the state legislature (1776–1779), old laws were abolished that had prevented the great estates of the aristocracy from being broken up into smaller land holdings. A law was passed establishing religious freedom in Virginia. He tried, without success, to persuade the legislature to pass bills for the gradual abolition of slavery in the state and for the establishment of free schools. Jefferson was governor of Virginia (1779–1781) and was almost captured when the British invaded the state (1781).

As servant of the new nation. After the Revolution, when serving again in the Continental Congress (1783–1785), Jefferson prepared (1784) a plan for organizing and governing the Northwest Territory. His plan included a prohibition against slavery. Though Jefferson's plan was not used, it paved the way for the Ordinance of 1787 which later governed the territory and prohibited slavery in that region. In 1785, Jefferson succeeded Benjamin Franklin as minister to France, and was Washington's Secretary of State (1790–1793). He became leader of the Democratic-Republican party. He was Vice President (1797–1801) under John Adams. In 1801 Jefferson became the first President to be inaugurated in Washington, D.C.

As President (1801–1805; 1805–1809). Jefferson's desire to have the U.S. possess the port of New Orleans resulted in the purchase (1803) of the Louisiana region from France. His interest in the West led to the Lewis and Clark Expedition that reached the Pacific Ocean in 1805. By persuading Congress to pass an Embargo Act (1807) prohibiting trade with foreign countries, Jefferson tried to keep the U.S. from becoming involved in a war between Great Britain and France.

The President's family. Jefferson married a widow, Martha Wayles Skelton (1748–1782), who died before her husband became President. Their daughter Martha sometimes acted as her father's hostess.

Other happenings. When Jefferson was President, Alexander Hamilton was killed (1804) in a duel with Aaron Burr. Plans were made (1806) for building the Cumberland Road (now part of U.S. highway 40), the first national highway leading west. Zebulon Pike discovered (1806) in Colorado the mountain peak that bears his name. Fulton's steamboat, the *Clermont*, made a successful trip from New York to Albany (1807). Abraham Lincoln was born (1809).

The nation's growth. Ohio was admitted to the Union as a state, (1803), bringing the total number of states to 17.

The Sage of Monticello. At the end of his Presidency, Jefferson retired to Monticello, the home he had built on a hill near Charlottes-ville, Va. Great numbers of people wrote or visited him to ask advice. He founded the University of Virginia, which opened a year before his death. He and John Adams died on the same day (July 4, 1826), fifty years after the adoption of the Declaration of Independence. As Jefferson had requested, these words were inscribed on his tomb at Monticello:

Author of the Declaration of American Independence
of the Statute of Virginia for Religious Freedom
and father of the University of Virginia

The many-sided Jefferson. Besides being a statesman, diplomat and writer, Jefferson was the architect who designed Monticello and the buildings of the University of Virginia. He collected vocabularies of American Indian languages. He experimented with improved ways of farming, and he invented many useful things that can still be seen at Monticello.

JAMES MADISON *Finds a Way to Help*

"D on't you fret, Master Jemmy," said his old Negro mammy, trying to comfort him. "Colonel George Washington is going to drive those Indians back. He won't let those wicked redskins hurt you."

Like other four-year-old boys who lived near the western frontier of Virginia during the French and Indian War, James Madison had heard all about "redskins." His family never knew when their home might be attacked, and Jemmy never forgot those days of terror. Even after the Indians had been driven off, he would shiver with excitement when his mammy told him stories about them.

With the return of peace, Jemmy's father became more prosperous and built a fine house which he called Montpelier. It had a view of the Blue Ridge Mountains extending for miles in each direction. Here Jemmy grew up, playing with a succession of younger brothers and sisters. He was small for his age, rather shy, and never very well. Most boys in Virginia at that time liked to go to horse races or cock fights, but Jemmy preferred to wander alone through the woods. Sometimes he would lie for hours on the grass and gaze up at the sky, thinking deep, deep thoughts.

Better still, he liked to read and study. For a while he went to school in a neighboring county, and then he had a tutor at home. The boy had a restless, eager mind, and by the time he was seventeen he was ready to enter college.

One bright, sunshiny day in 1769, a big stagecoach came lumbering down an elm-shaded street in Princeton, New Jersey. It drew up at the door of Nassau Inn, and out stepped a young man in plush knee breeches and a richly embroidered lavender coat. A man in a gray wig tapering to a queue stepped forward to greet him.

"Is this Mr. James Madison, Jr., of Virginia?"

James removed his cocked hat and bowed.

"So I am called, worthy sir, at your service."

"I am Mr. Thompson, sophomore tutor. You will live in Nassau Hall. You will doff at once this foppish Virginia garb and provide yourself with the collegiate habit of cap and gown. These young men are your classmates."

He turned to two youths with black academic gowns thrown carelessly over their red cloth coats and sheepskin knee breeches. "Freneau and M'Knight, this is Mr. Madison, Jr., of Virginia. See that he is instructed in the college rules."

James's pale face flushed with pleasure. Back in Virginia he had often felt out of place with boys his own age, but there was something about these new companions that made him like them at once. By the time they were halfway to stately Nassau Hall with its tall belfry, they were talking like old friends. Much to James's relief the conversation was not about horse racing, but about books.

That afternoon he put on a black cap and gown and called on the president of the college. Tall and dignified in his white wig, Dr. Witherspoon looked down at the bashful youth out of kind eyes. "Study hard," he advised. "Make a future of which we can be proud. Look upon me as your father, for here I represent him. And now, my son, God keep you."

During the months that followed, James was busy from the moment the blowing of a big horn called the students to prayers at five o'clock in the morning. He did well in all of his classes, and he looked forward to the evenings spent with his new friends. Among them were Harry Lee and Aaron Burr, handsome and brilliant. James's roommate, Philip Freneau, liked to write poetry. As the young men sat before the blazing logs in the fireplace at Nassau Inn, they often talked far into the night.

Many of their discussions were about the Parliament in London and the taxes it wanted the colonists to pay. The students considered these taxes a threat to liberty—and liberty, Dr. Witherspoon said, was mankind's most precious possession. James and his friends heartily approved when the merchants in some of the colonial towns stopped buying anything from England. In New York the merchants met and signed an agreement not to import any more English goods, and a New York newspaper came out with the words printed in big letters: IT IS BETTER TO WEAR A HOMESPUN COAT THAN LOSE OUR LIBERTY.

The young patriots at Princeton agreed. They were always anxious to learn the latest news, and a crowd was usually on hand to meet the stagecoaches. The stagecoaches between New York and Philadelphia stopped at the inn, and some of the passengers brought newspapers with them. One day the news made the students very angry.

"For shame!" cried one young man, waving a newspaper high above his head. "Those New York merchants are cowards. I suppose they found that their patriotism was costing them money, and now——"

"What do you mean? What has happened?" the young man was asked.

"I mean," he replied, "that those New York merchants are buying goods from England again. What is worse, they have written to the Philadelphia merchants, asking them to do the same. The letter is printed right here in the paper. Read it for yourselves."

The newspaper was passed from hand to hand. James's pale blue eyes blazed with anger behind his spectacles. "Those New York merchants have broken their promise. They are cowards, every one of them," he said.

"They are traitors to the cause," a friend exclaimed. "Why don't we burn their old letter?"

Of course, James knew that in burning the newspaper they would be destroying only one copy of the letter. But it would be fun to have a bonfire, and it would show how they felt. Quickly the news spread, and the college yard was filled with students. From all directions they came running, their long, black academic gowns flapping awkwardly about their ankles. Wood was gathered, and the roaring flames leaped toward the sky. The bell in one of the college buildings began to toll, as though for a funeral. A shout went up from the students.

"Now burn the letter!" they cried. "Burn it! Burn it!"

Everyone became silent, watching as the newspaper was laid upon the flames. Slowly it blackened, and the wind carried it away in a thousand crisp pieces. Then a shout went up, "Hurrah! Down with all traitors!"

James felt a tingling up and down his spine, and he longed for new ways to show his patriotism.

A short time later, he helped to organize a debating club to discuss some of the burning questions of the day. It was called the American Whig Society, and James became so interested in the debates that he was no longer shy when it was his turn to speak. There was no other sound in the room when he talked about what good government could do to help the people.

James Madison continued to think and study about government after he returned home from college. For three years he was the tutor of his young brothers and sisters, but much of the time he was ill. When the colonies went to war against England, he longed to be a soldier but was not strong enough. One day early in 1776 he was reading a new pamphlet called *Common Sense*. The author, Thomas Paine, an Englishman who had recently come to America, believed that the Americans no longer owed any loyalty to George the Third. "Here is the vast continent of North America," wrote Thomas Paine. "It is suited to become the home of a race of free men. Let it no longer lie at the feet of an unworthy king."

James laid the book down feeling both thrilled and discouraged— thrilled because of the magic of the words, discouraged because he could not be a soldier. If only he could find some other way to help!

The chance came sooner than he had expected. In the spring of 1776 the citizens of his county elected him and one other young man as delegates to a Virginia Convention. When the two men rode their mud-splashed horses into Williamsburg one afternoon in early May, the little city was crowded. Everywhere there were soldiers, many of them still wearing the leather breeches and hunting shirts they had worn before they enlisted. Several officers in military coats and tri-cornered hats were entering Raleigh Tavern. There was a feeling of suspense and excitement in the air and James forgot all about not feeling well.

The next morning he put on a plain black suit and walked up the Duke of Gloucester Street to the Capitol. His hair, freshly powdered, was tied with a ribbon at the back. He wore a high, cone-shaped hat, which he hoped would make him look taller, but he did not feel at all tall when he entered the room where the convention was meeting. Most of the delegates towered above him. Patrick Henry and several of the others were more than six feet tall, and James seemed to shrink into his chair.

His friend and neighbor Thomas Jefferson was not present. Mr. Jefferson and several other leading Virginia patriots were in Philadelphia attending the Continental Congress. What instructions should the Virginia Convention send these men? Finally on May 15, 1776,

the convention passed a resolution. The Virginia delegates in Philadelphia were to propose to the other members of the Continental
Congress that they "declare the United Colonies free and independent States."

The people of Williamsburg wanted to celebrate the news. A big
picnic was held in a grove at the edge of town, and the soldiers were
invited; bonfires were lighted in the streets that night, and candles
burned in the windows of nearly every house.

James Madison had attended the meetings of the convention, listening quietly but seldom speaking. People noticed, however, that
when he did talk, he had something worthwhile to say. The day after
the celebration he was appointed to the committee that was to work
out a new plan of government, a new constitution, for the new state
of Virginia.

Never had James been so pleased, although he realized that he
was running a great risk in serving on the committee. If the Revolution failed, he and the other members would be tried as traitors.
Just how the war would end no one could tell, but the danger was
great. Enemy ships were anchored in the York River only a few miles
away; there were rumors that an army of 45,000 men was sailing
across the Atlantic to subdue the rebellious colonies. But the committee went on meeting every day until the new Virginia Constitution
was finished.

By that time Richard Henry Lee, one of the delegates to the Continental Congress, had returned to Williamsburg. He spoke of the
resolution he had read before the Congress on June 7:

"Resolved that these United Colonies are, and of right ought to be,
free and independent states."

The members of the Virginia Convention listened in tense silence.
Then someone asked, "Do you think the resolution will pass, Mr.
Lee?"

Richard Henry Lee hesitated. Some of the delegates to the Continental Congress had considered the resolution too radical. Others
had wanted to declare for independence at once. Mr. Lee had left
Philadelphia while the arguments were still going on, but he felt
hopeful.

"I have not the least doubt," he said, "that in a few days independence will be announced by the Congress."

News traveled slowly in 1776, and when the Virginia Convention
adjourned on the fifth of July the members had no way of knowing
that the Declaration of Independence had been adopted the day be-

fore. James Madison, riding his horse up the dusty road toward home, must have wondered what was happening in Philadelphia. Had history been made there? Suddenly he felt a warm glow of pride. He himself had had a part—a very small part, he thought—in making history in Williamsburg.

In later years James Madison was very modest about his work on the Constitutional committee. He said he had been too "young and inexperienced" to contribute very much to the Virginia Constitution. He little guessed at the time that the experience he had gained was to help him prepare for his part in writing another constitution— the Constitution of the United States.

In May, 1787, he attended a convention in Philadelphia. The meetings were held in the same red brick building where the Declaration of Independence had been signed nearly eleven years earlier, but this time the delegates came together to work out a stronger plan of government for the new nation. George Washington was the chairman, and the other delegates included such distinguished leaders as Benjamin Franklin and Alexander Hamilton, but no man there knew as much about government as "the great little Madison." He might be small and frail, but he had big ideas—sound, brilliant ideas. Many of his ideas were used in the new Constitution when, after four long, hot months, it was finally finished.

"We the people of the United States," read the Preamble, or opening words, "in order to form a more perfect Union, establish justice, insure domestic tranquillity, provide for the common defense, promote the general welfare, and secure the blessings of liberty to ourselves and our posterity, do ordain and establish this Constitution for the United States of America."

The Constitution was then sent to all the states for their approval, and by the following summer the success of the new plan of government was assured. In town after town, the people celebrated by holding parades. In Philadelphia the parade was a mile and a half long. On one of the floats there was a small ship called "Union" symbolizing the union of the states in one nation. Several thousand men marched in that parade, and as they tramped in the streets, their feet seemed to beat out the rhythm of three words: "We the people . . . we the people . . ." The marchers knew that they themselves were the people, and they took pride in those words, as Americans have ever since.

Some years after the Constitution was adopted, James Madison served his country as Secretary of State and then as President. But his greatest work had already been accomplished at the age of thirty-six, and it is as "the Father of the Constitution" that he is remembered most gratefully today.

THE FOURTH PRESIDENT *at a Glance*

James Madison

Born: March 16, 1751   *Died: June 28, 1836*

Early life. James Madison, the first of twelve children of James and Nellie Conway Madison, was born at his grandmother's home in Port Conway, Va. He grew up at Montpelier, his father's plantation in Virginia. He attended Princeton, then known as the College of New Jersey (1769–1772). His college friends included Philip Freneau, later known as the "poet of the American Revolution"; Aaron Burr, who became Vice President of the U.S. (1801–1805); and Henry (Light-Horse Harry) Lee, who won fame as a cavalry officer during the Revolution and who was to become the father of Robert E. Lee.

Early career. Madison was a delegate to the Virginia Convention (May, 1776) that declared Virginia independent of Great Britain. He also helped to write a constitution for the new state. Later he was one of Virginia's delegates to the Continental Congress (1780–1783).

As "father of the Constitution." In 1787 Madison was a delegate to the Constitutional Convention in Philadelphia and was a leader in drawing up plans for the U.S. Constitution. Together with Alexander Hamilton and John Jay, he then wrote a series of influential articles (later published as a book, *The Federalist*) arguing for the adoption of the Constitution. He was a representative in Congress (1789–1797) and Secretary of State under Jefferson (1801–1809). In 1809, Madison—who, like Jefferson, was a Democratic-Republican—became President.

As President (1809–1813; 1813–1817). Madison worked to keep the U.S. from becoming involved in ever-increasing difficulties between England and France. British interference with American ships finally compelled Madison to consent to a declaration of war against England (June, 1812). The War of 1812 lasted for over two and a half years. In August, 1812, the U.S. ship the *Constitution* ("Old Ironsides") defeated the British *Guerrière*. Oliver Perry won a great naval victory on Lake Erie (1813). On land, the Americans were less successful. The British captured Washington, D.C. (August, 1814) and burned the Capitol, the President's mansion, and other buildings. The President and the other government officials were forced to flee. Andrew Jackson won the Battle of New Orleans (January 8, 1815) before news of the peace treaty, signed in Ghent, Belgium (December 24, 1814), had reached America. The treaty resulted in little gain for either country, but the U.S. had become more firmly united because of the war.

The President's wife. Dolley Madison (1768–1849) was one of the most popular hostesses ever to live in the White House. When the British captured Washington in 1814, Dolley had Gilbert Stuart's portrait of George Washington cut from its frame and carried it to safety when she fled from the President's mansion.

Other happenings. When Madison was President, John Jacob Astor founded (1811) a trading post, Astoria, near the mouth of the Columbia River on the Pacific Ocean. General William Henry Harrison (later the ninth President) defeated the Indians at Tippecanoe, Ind. (1811). Francis Scott Key wrote the "Star-Spangled Banner" during a British bombardment of Fort McHenry, Md. (1814).

The nation's population and growth. The population was more than 7,200,000 (census of 1810). Two new states were admitted to the Union: Louisiana (1812) and Indiana (1816), bringing the total to 19.

JAMES MONROE *Crosses the Delaware*

It was fun to be a boy in Virginia in 1765. James Monroe lived on the strip of land between the Potomac and Rappahannock rivers, and sometimes the big ships from London moored at the landing near his home. People gathered from miles around to watch the unloading, while field hands, singing as they worked, carried box after box on shore. James knew that the boxes held coffee, tea, sugar, jewels, brocaded silks and all the other luxuries that had been ordered by members of the gentry families. London must be a wonderful place, indeed!

Then, when a ship had slowly sailed away, James would turn back to the fragrant Virginia woods. After all, what were silks and satins to a seven-year-old boy who had fish to catch and horses to ride across the sunny meadows? Often when James returned to the house after playing outdoors, he found that his uncle, Judge Joseph Jones, had arrived for a visit. Uncle Joseph lived in Williamsburg and seemed to know everyone in the colony's capital. Sometimes he talked about Tom Jefferson, then a tall, gangling law student, or about Colonel George Washington, who rode down from Mount Vernon every year to attend meetings of the House of Burgesses.

One spring day in 1765, Judge Jones brought news about a fiery new delegate from the backwoods named Patrick Henry. Young Mr. Henry had recently made a speech about a new tax law, the Stamp Act. It was a very eloquent speech and had caused quite a stir in the House of Burgesses. James looked up from his plate of fried ham and hominy, his eyes bright and questioning in his lean, tanned face. His uncle tried to explain.

"This law, James," said Judge Jones, "was passed by the British Parliament, and Mr. Henry insists that only our own local Assembly has any right to decide what taxes we shall pay. He says we must not yield to tyranny."

"Faith, Patrick Henry is right," said James's father, pounding on the table with his fist. "We send no representatives to Parliament, yet it tries to tell us what to do. Do the members of Parliament think that we are slaves?"

"Mr. Henry certainly convinced me," Judge Jones replied. "As patriots, we should protest, and keep on protesting, until the law is repealed. If Parliament is allowed to tax us now—if it is unfair in this matter—who knows what may happen in the years to come?"

Others felt as Judge Jones did. Not only in Virginia but in other colonies as well, many people simply refused to buy the stamps. Even boys as young as James were caught up in the excitement. There was a popular song they liked to sing:

> "With the Beasts of the Wood, we will ramble for Food,
>   And lodge in the wild deserts and caves,
>   And live poor as Job on the skirts of the Globe,
>   Before we'll submit to be Slaves,
>   Before we'll submit to be Slaves."

There was so much resistance to the Stamp Act that it was repealed the following year. But Parliament still insisted it had the right to tax the colonies. Other laws were passed which American patriots resented, and their anger mounted when the British government sent soldiers across the Atlantic to force them to obey. In nearly every town there were meetings and speeches, and James listened to many a heated discussion at his own dinner table. But in spite of all that was going on, he still had to study his lessons. Until he was twelve, he had a tutor at home. Then he tramped several miles each day back and forth to a school taught by a parson, the Reverend Archibald Campbell.

There he met a tall, fourteen-year-old pupil named John Marshall, and the two boys liked each other at once. John was boarding with the parson's family, but he often spoke of the log cabin where he lived, farther west on the edge of the wilderness. His black eyes snapped with merry good humor as he talked, and after he returned home James missed his new friend. He missed hearing stories about the frontier, although these stories were no more exciting than the news printed from week to week in the Williamsburg newspaper.

The troubles with Great Britain were growing more serious. In 1774, a short time after James entered William and Mary College, the Continental Congress met in Philadelphia, and the next year the American Revolution began. One morning, when James was a sophomore, startled cries were heard up and down the length of the Duke of Gloucester Street.

"The savages! The savages have come!"

The more timid residents drew their curtains, but a few men and boys ventured outdoors. Some strange-looking men were drilling on the Palace Green. They had buck tails fastened to their round black hats and scalping knives thrust through their belts. On the bosoms of their green homespun hunting shirts were the words, in large white letters, "Liberty or death." The students from William and Mary came rushing down the wide street.

"Why, those men are not savages. They're not Indians; they are soldiers," one student exclaimed. "Some of them are no older than we are."

James Monroe was staring at a dark-eyed youth at the head of the line. There was a grin on the young man's swarthy face, and he put out his hand.

"Why, John Marshall!" said James. "What are you doing here?"

"Lieutenant Marshall, if you please," John corrected his friend. "This is my company of minutemen—the first in Virginia. We march to join General Washington."

Both boys had grown taller and more rugged since they had been together at Parson Campbell's school. John at twenty seemed a full-grown man.

"Forward, march!" Lieutenant Marshall gave the command in a firm voice, and his volunteers turned their faces northward. James watched them as they disappeared up the street in a cloud of dust. He had been drilling with a company of students on the Palace Green, but he wanted to do more. He wished that he could join General Washington.

The next summer his wish came true. The Third Virginia Regiment, in which he had enlisted, was ordered North. In September, 1776, James Monroe, a shy, rawboned youth of eighteen, arrived in New York in time to take part in two battles. He had never been under fire before, but he proved himself brave and dependable. It must have been a proud day for him when General Washington commissioned him a lieutenant.

Even so, James had never felt so discouraged. Both battles had been disastrous defeats for the Americans, and the Declaration of Independence, signed only a few weeks earlier, seemed only so many empty words. It did not seem possible for George Washington to hold out much longer, and he retreated across New Jersey in a desperate effort to save what was left of his army. It was a raw, cold December day when he finally reached the Delaware River and sent out scouts to gather up all of the boats they could find for miles in each direction. Then his army escaped across the river into Pennsylvania.

The last of the American soldiers got across barely in time. The enemy arrived in hot pursuit, but there were no boats left for them to use. It did not matter, their commander, General Howe, decided. The river would soon freeze over; then it would be easy enough to cross on the ice. He ordered a detachment of Hessian troops—German soldiers who had been hired to fight the Americans—to stay on guard in the town of Trenton, on the New Jersey side of the river. He himself returned with his main force to spend Christmas in New York. He felt confident that the war would soon be over.

Nor was he the only one who thought so. Even many of George Washington's soldiers felt that they were fighting for a hopeless cause. They were hungry and cold in their ragged uniforms. Some were barefoot. Their general knew that they needed a victory to bolster up their courage, and he decided on a bold and daring move. He would attack the enemy in Trenton, when an attack was least expected—on Christmas night.

Lieutenant James Monroe and the general's cousin, Captain William Washington, with a small number of men under their command, were the first to cross the Delaware. Their small boat jammed against the cakes of floating ice that gleamed faintly white in the darkness. Snow was falling when the men landed, and it almost blinded them as they moved cautiously toward the intersection of two main roads. Their orders were to stand guard here until the main body of troops could cross the river and join them. In the meantime no one else was to be allowed to pass. James, straining his eyes in the dim light, could make out a lane and, in the distance, the outlines of a house.

At that moment some dogs set up a loud barking. The men stood rigid as statues, but the dogs could not be fooled. Lights flickered in the house. James saw a light moving toward him down a lane. A red-faced man, a lantern held high above his head, was peering into his face.

"What are you doing out on such a night?" the man thundered. "You're up to no good, I dare say. Get off my land."

James drew himself up to his full height. He looked much older than eighteen. "My advice to you," he said, "is to go back to your house and keep quiet. Otherwise, I shall have to arrest you."

"Arrest me?" said the man indignantly. "I tell you, I'll have no Redcoats or their Hessian hirelings——"

"We are not Redcoats," James interrupted. "We are with General Washington."

The man lowered his lantern. "You should not be out on a night like this," he said, his voice suddenly filled with concern. "Come and bring your men into the house and I'll give you something hot to eat."

"I am sorry, sir, but my orders are strict. We cannot leave."

"Then I shall bring some victuals to you out here. What is more, when you move on I am going with you. I am a doctor. If there is to be a battle, I may be able to help some poor fellow."

Several more hours passed before General Washington was able to move his troops and artillery across the river. Then the march on Trenton through a blinding sleet began in the early hours of December 26. The Hessians had been celebrating Christmas until late the night before. They were tired, and most of them were sleeping when the Americans dashed into the town at daybreak. The pickets left on guard were soon disarmed, but the other Hessians were aroused. There was fierce hand-to-hand fighting, and two Hessian gunners managed to reach their cannons. But before the big guns could be fired, young Captain Washington and Lieutenant Monroe rushed upon the gunners and captured them.

James felt a sharp pain. He wavered a moment, then fell to the ground, a bullet in his shoulder. Two of his soldiers carried him into a house close by where a surgeon was treating other wounded men. James was resting, after his own wound had been dressed, when he learned the good news.

The Hessians had surrendered. Nearly a thousand of them had been taken prisoner. James, although weak from loss of blood, felt a great surge of joy. It was a feeling shared by many patriots. The Americans had proved that they could still fight, even with all the odds against them.

After James recovered from his wound he took part in several more battles and then returned to Virginia, where he began to study law under Thomas Jefferson. Although he was never a brilliant student, he was hard-working and sincere. The same qualities of honesty and courage that won Mr. Jefferson's admiration were in time to make him very popular with the voters of Virginia. As the years went by, he was elected to several important public offices. In 1794 a new honor came to him when President Washington appointed him American minister to France.

Nine years later, after Thomas Jefferson had become President, James Monroe was sent to France again. The regular minister at that time was Robert R. Livingston, and James Monroe's assignment was to assist him in a very special matter. The new nation, only twenty years after it had won its independence, faced another crisis.

France had recently gained control of a vast region west of the Mississippi River, which the French called Louisiana. The American pioneer farmers, who used this river to take their goods to market, were worried. What if Napoleon, the dictator of France, refused to allow the Americans to use the port of New Orleans, near the mouth of the river? The pioneers' trade would be ruined! President Jefferson decided that the United States government must try to buy New Orleans from the French. The prosperity of the western farmers and the future success of the nation were at stake.

When James Monroe reached Paris in January, 1803, Robert Livingston had surprising news. Napoleon needed money and had offered to sell all of Louisiana. The purchase would include New Orleans, but he refused to sell New Orleans alone. The United States must buy the entire region or nothing at all.

What should be done? The ministers had been instructed to spend about two million dollars, not fifteen million, the price Napoleon was asking. Yet their nation was being offered a tremendous bargain—an area of nearly a million square miles for only a few cents an acre. They dared not take time to write to the President, for while they were waiting for an answer, Napoleon might change his mind.

The decision took courage, but neither the regular minister nor James Monroe lacked courage. They signed the treaties that Napoleon's ministers had prepared. "We have lived long," said Robert Livingston, "but this is the noblest work of our lives."

With a few strokes of the pen the two men had doubled the size of the United States, adding a rich, fertile region where one day millions of Americans would make their homes. The success of the mission also marked a turning point in the career of James Monroe. He was given other responsible assignments, and in time became so well known and so well liked that he was elected President. At his inauguration in March, 1817, the oath of office was given to him by an old schoolmate. John Marshall, tall and thin in his long black robe, was now the Chief Justice of the United States Supreme Court.

A brief smile passed between the two men. Both had served the new nation in war and in peace, and they had been rewarded with the two highest honors their nation had to give. They had not always agreed, but they had remained friends. Then, as an enthusiastic crowd of people looked on, James Monroe raised his right hand and repeated the words that made him President of the United States.

He proved to be a very popular President, and his years in the White House were known as "the Era of Good Feeling." During his second term he made the statement for which he is best remembered today. This statement—a warning to European powers that they must not interfere with the government of any nation on the American continents—was a part of his message to Congress in December, 1823. The policy he laid down in that message has been known ever since as the Monroe Doctrine.

THE FIFTH PRESIDENT *at a Glance*

James Monroe

Born: April 28, 1758   *Died: July 4, 1831*

Early life. James Monroe was born on his father's plantation in eastern Virginia. He entered William and Mary College at 16 but left to fight in the Revolution before he was graduated. At the age of 22 (1780) he began to study law with Thomas Jefferson.

Political career. Monroe was a member of the Virginia legislature (1782) and of the Continental Congress (1783–1786). Though a delegate (1788) to the Virginia state convention that ratified the U.S. Constitution, he opposed accepting the Constitution without a Bill of Rights. After serving as U.S. Senator (1790–1794), he was appointed by President Washington as minister to France and was in France (1794–1796) during some of the bitterest struggles of the French Revolution. He was governor of Virginia (1799–1802). He was then sent to France by President Jefferson to take part in negotiations that led to the Louisiana Purchase (1803). Other diplomatic missions took him to Spain and England (1804–1806). In 1811 he was again governor of Virginia. When Secretary of State (1811–1817) under President Madison, he also served for part of the time as Secretary of War. In 1817, Monroe, another Democratic-Republican, became President.

As President (1817–1821; 1821–1825). An agreement was reached with Great Britain (1817) for permanent disarmament of the Great Lakes. Florida was purchased from Spain (1819) for five million dollars. A bitter dispute between the North and the South as to whether to admit Missouri to the Union as a slave state was settled by the Missouri Compromise (1820): Missouri was admitted as a slave state; Maine, as a free state; slavery was prohibited in all regions (except Missouri) north of a line stretching along the southern border of Missouri from the Mississippi to the Rockies. Monroe was re-elected (1820) with only one electoral vote against him. (The opposing vote was cast by an elector who felt that Washington should be the only President to have the honor of being elected unanimously.) After several colonies in Latin America declared their independence from Spain, an alliance of European countries agreed to help Spain win them back. The President then issued a statement, now known as the Monroe Doctrine, warning against European interference in American affairs (1823).

The President's wife. Elizabeth Kortright Monroe (1768–1830) ordered fine new furnishings from France for the White House, as the President's mansion was called. It had been partly rebuilt and painted white since the British set fire to it in the War of 1812.

Other happenings. When Monroe was President, Congressman Henry Clay of Kentucky became known as the "Great Pacificator," or peacemaker, because of his help in arranging the Missouri Compromise (1820). The success of a trading expedition (1821) led by Captain William Becknell, "father of the Santa Fe Trail," stimulated trade with the Southwest. Liberia, a colony in Africa for freed American slaves, was founded in 1822. Its capital, Monrovia, was named for President Monroe.

The nation's population and growth. The population was about 9,600,000 (census of 1820). Five new states were admitted to the Union, bringing the total to 24: Mississippi (1817), Illinois (1818), Alabama (1819), Maine (1820), and Missouri (1821).

JOHN QUINCY ADAMS *Faces Danger*

John Quincy Adams put spurs to his horse and galloped down the road toward Braintree. He made regular trips into Boston for the mail, but never before had he returned home in such quick time. He was glad that he would find his father there. John Adams was often away attending the Continental Congress down in Philadelphia. But now he was home for a while, and Johnny had news to share—wonderful news! He did not pause until he drew rein before the slant-roofed farmhouse where he lived.

"Pappa! Pappa!" he cried.

John Adams rushed outside to take the letter bag from Johnny's trembling hands. Then he led the boy indoors to warm himself by the kitchen fireplace. "Tell me, Johnny. What has happened?"

"Oh, Pappa, you should see the people in Boston. They are shouting and singing in the streets. Bells are ringing. One man said——"

Johnny's father scarcely seemed to hear. He had opened the letter bag and was reading a letter. "God be praised!" he exclaimed, then turned to his wife, Abigail. "General Washington crossed the Delaware on Christmas night. He has taken Trenton from the Hessians."

"I have been trying to tell you, Pappa," Johnny said. "That is why the people in Boston are celebrating."

Johnny was excited, but he was used to excitement. The American Revolution had begun before he was eight. When British soldiers had occupied Boston Johnny had helped his mother care for many of the refugees who fled from the city. With her he had watched the battle of Bunker Hill from a hilltop near their home. Other battles had been fought close by, and the little house would rattle and shake when the big guns started firing. Those days were over now, for George Washington had finally driven the enemy soldiers away from Massachusetts. But the fighting had gone right on in the other colonies. The Americans had suffered one defeat after another.

"We can all take heart from your news, Mr. Johnny," said his father reassuringly. "General Washington's victory may well prove to be the turning point of the Revolution."

Encouraging though the news was, the United States was still a long way from winning its independence. Help was needed—help from abroad. A few weeks later John Adams received a letter from the president of the Continental Congress. He was asked to join two other American commissioners in Paris in trying to persuade the French government to send ships, supplies and soldiers to the aid of the struggling new nation.

The Adams children—Johnny, his older sister Nabby and two younger brothers—gathered close as their father told them the news. They listened eagerly, but Abigail's dark eyes were troubled. She knew that, the day her husband sailed, spies would probably carry the word to the commander of the British fleet. If one of the enemy ships gave chase and her husband was captured, he would be put in prison and tried for treason. He might even be hanged as a traitor, for George the Third considered him one of the leaders of the Revolution.

"I cannot bear to have you go so far alone, John," Abigail told him. "The children and I will go with you."

"No, Dearest Friend," John Adams replied, using the pet name that he often called his wife. "It would not be safe. But my country is in danger. I am needed and I must go."

"Then take Johnny along to keep you company," she said. "He is nearly ten and will profit from the journey."

She went on to talk about the good schools near Paris. The school in Braintree was closed because of the war. "Mr. Johnny," another pet name often used in the family, perhaps because Johnny was such a solemn boy, was brilliant. His mother realized the perils of a voyage in wartime, but to give Johnny the education he deserved would be worth the risk.

As Johnny listened, he felt that he could hardly wait to sail. But when the day finally came to leave, he hardly knew whether to be glad or sorry. Slowly he put on his new best velvet coat and knee-length breeches. He picked up his tricorn hat and closed his carpet-bag. After he had kissed the family good-bye, there was just time to give his mother another hurried hug. Then he mounted to the big horse behind his father for the ride to the harbor. When he reached the shore, he had his first glimpse of the *Boston,* the ship that was to carry his father and him to France. At the sight of those white sails glowing against the dull February skies, Johnny almost forgot that he was homesick. He was wondering what new adventures lay ahead.

The adventures began almost at once. The *Boston* was hardly out of sight of land when a squadron of British ships gave chase, and several times during the next two days capture seemed almost certain. Then, in a sudden gust of wind, the American vessel spread its white sails and skimmed over the waves, and a night without stars closed down and hid it from the view of the enemy ships.

Soon a new danger threatened: the wind that had carried the *Boston* to safety grew into a hurricane. After the storm had finally died down, one dull day followed another until one morning a sail appeared on the horizon. Another British ship!

Samuel Tucker, the captain, snapped out orders in quick succession, and the sailors rushed to their posts. Johnny and his father stood by the railing as heavy guns were dragged into place and ammunition was laid out beside them.

"I have been commanded by the Continental Congress," Captain Tucker told John Adams, "to carry you to France, and my first responsibility is your safety. With a good wind we may be able to escape. My force is smaller than the enemy's, and I feel it is my duty to avoid a fight, if possible."

"What if you can't avoid it?" John Adams asked.

Samuel Tucker glanced toward the ocean. The British ship was gaining. "Then we will give the enemy something to remember us by," the captain said.

He paused, fixing his stern blue glance on John Adams. "But you, sir, you and your son, are to go below. You are to remain there until all danger is over."

Down in their cabin, Johnny watched as his father opened their trunk and brought out a dispatch bag. Inside the bag were important papers, secret documents that must never be allowed to fall into the hands of the enemy. There were stones in the bag to give it weight. If John Adams saw that he was going to be captured, he would throw the bag into the ocean and the stones would cause it to sink quickly to the bottom. He glanced at Johnny, sitting on the bunk, and sat down beside him.

"I do not repent of my voyage, for I am in the way of duty," said

John Adams, "but I am sorry that I brought you, my son. I should never have exposed you to this danger."

"Do not be sorry, Pappa," said Johnny, but he sounded anxious. "Do you think we can escape? Or will Captain Tucker have to fight?"

There was no time for an answer. A great gun boomed overhead. Johnny ran to the porthole, where he could barely make out the outlines of the enemy ship through a haze of smoke. His father paced up and down the narrow cabin, his hands clasped behind him, his brows drawn together in a frown. *Boom—boom—boom!* Again and again the guns coughed forth their fearful message. John Adams grabbed a musket.

"Johnny, stay in the cabin," he said. "I am going up on the quarter-deck."

Again the enemy ship opened fire. Johnny, standing at the porthole, was blinded by a flash of light. The ship rocked violently, as one explosion followed another. John Adams had said nothing of his intentions, but Johnny guessed the truth. His father had joined in the fight and was now exposed to enemy gunfire. The boy wanted to rush up on deck, but he had been told to stay below. Even in this moment of terror he knew he must obey. Again the enemy ship spat fire, and again the *Boston* shuddered.

Suddenly the door of the cabin was flung open. The tall captain entered, pushing a very fat and perspiring John Adams in front of him.

"Again I ask," Captain Tucker sputtered angrily, as he forcibly sat Mr. Adams down on his bunk, "why were you on deck, sir? My orders are to carry you in safety to France and, by thunder, I will do it!"

If Johnny had not been so worried he might have laughed. His father, usually so dignified, looked like a small boy who had been scolded. He admitted, after the captain left, that a cannon ball from the enemy ship had struck the mizzen yard directly over his head.

At that moment a broadside woke the echoes. "Cease fire!" a voice called from overhead. The sailors cheered. The Americans had won.

When Johnny and his father went up on deck, a detachment of sailors from Captain Tucker's crew had boarded the captured vessel and were preparing to sail the British ship and her crew back to New York as prisoners. Her commander, Captain McIntosh, also a prisoner of war, was brought on board Samuel Tucker's ship. John Adams liked the British captain, enemy though he was, and the two men became friendly.

At last, six weeks after sailing from America, the *Boston* was approaching the green shores of France. Father and son were in their cabin, packing their carpetbags. "Well, Mr. Johnny," said John Adams, "we dock in a few more hours. We shall be in France, safe from British ships. And then——"

He was interrupted by a knock on the cabin door, and Captain McIntosh, the British prisoner, entered. He bowed in his usual courtly manner, but from the suppressed excitement in his voice Johnny knew that something must have happened.

"Mr. Adams," said the captain, "two British men-of-war are bearing down upon us. This ship will be captured by my countrymen, I warrant you, in less than half an hour. Let me take the liberty to say, sir, that I feel for you more than anyone else. I believe it is because of you that I have received such good treatment. Any good service I may render you with my country will be done with pleasure. You may depend on it."

Johnny's throat felt tight. The British captain was kind, but the boy knew that if the *Boston* was captured nothing could save his father; he would be carried off to England to stand trial for treason. But John Adams remained calm as he reached for his hat.

"Come up on deck with me, Mr. Johnny," he said. "We will not worry about the danger until we have seen it for ourselves."

The moon had gilded the deck in a white radiance, so that every spar, every mast and sail, stood silhouetted against the sky. Father and son walked over to the railing to get a closer look at the two British men-of-war. Were they coming closer? Would one of the captains hail the *Boston,* demanding to know the name of the ship and whither it was bound? But no, the men-of-war were gliding by. No sound came from them. They were moving out of sight. The American ship, if it had been seen, evidently had not aroused the suspicions of the enemy.

Johnny took a deep breath. Far to the west, across the moonlit waters, was the United States fighting desperately for freedom. Just ahead was France, the old nation which—it was hoped—would help the new nation to win its independence. Beautiful France, gallant America. The boy felt a hand on his shoulder. John Adams was smiling down at him.

That voyage across the Atlantic was the first of many for John Quincy Adams. He accompanied his father on several trips to Europe

—an experience that was to prove excellent training for the years ahead. As a man he was United States minister to several European countries. Later, as Secretary of State under President Monroe, he suggested and helped to write the Monroe Doctrine. His parents, living in retirement in Braintree, followed their eldest son's career with pride and joy. John Adams, the only President whose son also became President, was nearly ninety when "Mr. Johnny" went to live in the White House.

As President, John Quincy Adams was no more popular than his father had been, and for some of the same reasons. To all except his family and a few close friends, he seemed cold and blunt and very stubborn. But, also like his father, he was brilliant and courageous. After he was defeated for a second term as President, he was elected to Congress; and it was here, during the next seventeen years, that he did his finest work. The boy who had watched a handful of soldiers fight for freedom at Bunker Hill was now an old man, but there were new threats to freedom to be overcome.

Chief of these threats, thought many people in the North, was slavery. Petitions poured into Congress, asking that slavery be abolished. Many Congressmen wanted to ignore these petitions, and in 1836 several resolutions called "gag rules" were passed. John Quincy Adams considered such rules a threat to liberty. The right to send petitions to Congress, he insisted, had been guaranteed to the people in the United States Constitution.

Again and again the aging Congressman rose to speak. His voice was high and shrill. But he was so sincere and his arguments were so forceful that he became known as "Old Man Eloquent." Some people honored him for not being afraid to express his views, but he also made many enemies. He once said that he felt "forsaken of all mankind."

But John Quincy Adams dared to be unpopular. For eight years he tried to have the "gag rules" set aside, and he never lost courage. In the end his courage was rewarded, and the resolutions he considered so unjust were finally repealed. In championing the right of the people to petition Congress, John Quincy Adams also became one of the first champions in the struggle against slavery.

But he knew that he could not live much longer. "My career must close," he said, "leaving the cause at the threshold. To open the way for others is all that I can do. The cause is good and great."

THE SIXTH PRESIDENT *at a Glance*
John Quincy Adams

Born: July 11, 1767   *Died: February 23, 1848*

Early life. John Quincy Adams was born in Braintree (now Quincy), Mass. He was the eldest son of John Adams, the second President, and Abigail Adams. When he was 10, he went to Paris with his father, who was on a diplomatic mission for the Continental Congress. John Quincy attended school in Paris (1778) and, later, in Holland (1780) while on another trip to Europe with his father. At the age of 14 (1781) he was private secretary to the American minister to Russia. He returned to the U.S. (1785) to enter Harvard and was graduated in 1787. He studied law and was admitted to the bar (1791).

Political and diplomatic career. When Adams was 27 (1794), President Washington appointed him minister to Holland. Later he represented the U.S. government in Portugal (1796); in Berlin (1797–1801); in Russia (1809–1811); at Ghent, Belgium (1814), as one of the signers of the treaty ending the War of 1812; and in Great Britain (1815–1817). Between diplomatic assignments, he served in the U.S. Senate (1803–1808). As President Monroe's Secretary of State (1817–1825), he negotiated the purchase of Florida from Spain and had an important part in planning the Monroe Doctrine. In the election of 1824 Adams was one of four candidates for President. Since no candidate received a majority of the electoral votes, the House of Representatives had to decide the issue. The house chose Adams even though Andrew Jackson of Tennessee had received more popular and electoral votes.

As President (1825–1829). Many of Andrew Jackson's political admirers were angry because the House had chosen Adams as President. Adams, handicapped by their hostility and by his own tactlessness, was able to accomplish little. Both Adams and Jackson were Democratic-Republicans, but political quarrels led to a split in the party. The followers of Adams and his Secretary of State, Henry Clay, became known as National Republicans (later known as Whigs); the followers of Jackson were called Democrats.

In Congress. After leaving the Presidency, Adams returned to Washington as a Massachusetts Representative. For 17 years (1831–

1848) he served in Congress where he became known as "Old Man Eloquent."

The family of John Quincy Adams. In 1797 Adams married Louisa Johnson (1775–1852). Their son, Charles Francis Adams (1807–1886), was minister to Great Britain during the American Civil War. Their grandsons, Henry Adams (1838–1918) and Brooks Adams (1848–1927), were writers and historians. A great-grandson, Charles Francis Adams, was Secretary of the Navy (1929–1933) under President Hoover.

Other happenings. When John Quincy Adams was President, construction was completed on the Erie Canal (1825). Work was begun on the Baltimore and Ohio Railway (1828), and a great ceremony was held on July 4 when the first rails were laid. Charles Carroll, who was then nearly 91 years old and the last living signer of the Declaration of Independence, drove the first spade into the ground. "I consider this among the most important acts of my life," he said, "second only to that of signing the Declaration of Independence."

ANDY JACKSON *Meets the Enemy*

It was recess in the log schoolhouse. Andrew Jackson and one of the bigger boys rolled over and over in the dust. The next moment they were on their feet again, prancing back and forth in the road, eyeing each other cautiously. Andy, being very slender, was thrown once—twice—and then again. Each time, he bounced back on his feet with his brown fists flying.

"Look at Sandy Andy," cried one of his schoolmates who stood watching. "You can throw him, but he won't stay throwed."

Andy's cheeks were almost as red as his hair as he clutched his ragged, homespun trousers to his hips. He made his way gingerly over to a brier bush and plucked several sharp thorns, which he used to fasten his trousers to his shirt. Then, whistling blithely, he started off for home.

Andrew Jackson lived in what was then called the Waxhaw settlement, in the Carolinas. His father had died before he was born, and he and his mother and two older brothers made their home with an uncle, James Crawford, the Waxhaw storekeeper. Uncle James had been very kind. So had his brother, Squire Robert Crawford.

Andy's mother, a stout, comfortable-looking woman, met him at the door. "Son, I have news," she said. "Your Uncle Robert's militia is going south to the defense of Charleston. They will be passing along the post road any time now."

The boy's eyes widened. The American Revolution had been going on for more than a year, and the British Redcoats had overrun

66

parts of the Carolinas. Andy had often watched Robert Crawford drilling a company of men to fight the invaders.

"Ma," Andy announced, planting his bare feet firmly in the dust, "I want to go with the militia. I am plenty big enough to be a soldier."

Elizabeth Jackson smiled. Andy got his red hair from her; from her he also had inherited his dauntless spirit. "Why, you are just nine years old," she reminded him. "Let us hope the war is over before you are big enough to be a soldier. Now you'd better run along if you want to see the militia pass."

Trying to gulp down his disappointment, Andy turned away without another word. At recess the next morning he rounded up some of his schoolmates to play soldiers. They used sticks for guns, and from then on Andy drilled them every day. But pretending to be a soldier wasn't enough. He wanted to do some real fighting, he complained to his Uncle James.

"Your ma already told you; you are too young," said James Crawford. "But there is something else you *can* do. The Philadelphia paper came today."

Andy looked up expectantly. Newspapers were scarce in Waxhaw, and Uncle James always shared his Philadelphia paper with the neighbors. Andy could read better than most of the grown people in the neighborhood, and he often acted as "public reader."

"What do you think has happened up in Philadelphia?" James Crawford went on. "The Declaration of Independence has been signed!"

"The Declaration of Independence?" Andy did not know exactly what the words meant, but they had a pleasing sound.

"Yes, it's something Thomas Jefferson wrote," Uncle James explained. "It says that the colonies are free of England. It says that we are the United States of America now. All the neighbors are coming in to hear the news, and I want you to read it to them, Andy."

"Give me the paper, Uncle. I want to read that dec—declaration first. Then when all the folks come, I can read it right off without stopping to spell out any of the words."

That afternoon the neighbors came hurrying along the dusty country paths. They gathered, thirty or forty of them, before the store. Andy hitched up his trousers, smoothed down his hair, and followed his uncle out onto the porch. His hands shook a little as he held up the paper. He knew that he wasn't going to stumble over the long words, but the words said such big things!

" 'We hold these truths to be self-evident: That all men are created equal' "—Andy spoke every word distinctly—" 'that they are endowed by their Creator with certain inalienable rights; that among these are life, liberty, and the pursuit of happiness . . .' "

The neighbors listened, their faces grave and thoughtful. There was one phrase that Andy liked especially: "All men are created equal." It meant that plain folk had as many rights as rich ones. Anyway, Mr. Jefferson thought they ought to have, and Andy thought so, too.

The war came very close to Waxhaw during the next few years. Hugh, Mrs. Jackson's oldest son, joined the militia and died in battle. The old Waxhaw meeting house became a hospital. Here Andy and his brother Robert helped their mother care for the wounded soldiers lying on beds of straw. Once the whole family was forced to flee and take refuge with some distant relatives in North Carolina. When they returned in February, 1780, Andy learned that several of his friends had been killed.

"Ma," he said, "Robert and I can't stand it any longer. We've got to fight."

Elizabeth Jackson laid down her knitting. Hugh was dead, and now her younger sons wanted to go to war. Andy brushed a lock of sandy hair off his high forehead with an impatient hand as he stood there waiting for her answer, but she scarcely saw him through a haze of tears. He was only thirteen, and Robert was just three years older.

"Well, sons—" Elizabeth held out a hand to each of them. "With things as they are, I can't hold out against you any longer. If you feel you have to fight, then I reckon you have to."

The boys did not enlist in any organized corps. They had no uniforms, and they furnished their own guns. Whenever a party of soldiers passed through the neighborhood, Andy and Robert joined them, and they took part in several battles and skirmishes. One day the boys were helping to defend the Waxhaw meeting house when a company of British dragoons set fire to the church. The patriots were forced out into the open, and eleven of them were taken prisoner. Andy saw Robert dash away on horseback toward the swamp—and safety.

And then Andrew Jackson looked up to see a redcoated dragoon riding toward him. His heart seemed to stand still, but not his legs. They carried him over the ground in long, quick strides. He dashed in and out of crowds of fighting, sweating men. "If I can only reach the swamp," he thought. "If I can find Robert . . ."

Just ahead a horse reared, frightened by the noise of battle. Its rider must have been killed or wounded. Andy leaped on the horse's back, calming it by a soft touch on the neck. "Hurry, hurry," he whispered, spurred on by the sound of hoofbeats just behind him. The other rider caught up with him, and he recognized his cousin, Lieutenant Thomas Crawford, also trying to escape.

"The swamp!" he cried, and Andy nodded. Behind him came the Redcoats. Ahead lay a wide slough of water, and into this the boy plunged his unwilling horse. With a sigh of relief he finally drew up on dry land again.

"Tom—" he whispered.

Then he realized that he was alone. He turned to see Lieutenant Crawford sunk in the mire, surrounded by his enemies. His sword was raised trying to protect himself from their blows. Then the sword was knocked out of his hand and he was taken prisoner. At that moment the leader of the Redcoats saw Andy.

"There he is, the little chap," the leader yelled. "Get him next."

Andy, leaning low over his horse's head, made for the woods. The sound of shouting behind him grew fainter, and he decided that his pursuers must have turned back. After a search he found Robert hiding in a thicket. Together they waited for the night.

Even then the boys did not dare to leave their hiding place. The shadows of tall trees lay in frightening shapes upon the ground. A night owl hooted. Andy and Robert clutched each other. There was a gnawing pain in their stomachs, for neither had eaten for many hours. Not far away was Lieutenant Crawford's cabin. Tom's young wife would give them food.

"It's risky," said Robert, between chattering teeth, "but we've got to have something to eat. Besides, we ought to tell Tom's wife that he has been taken prisoner."

"We'll tether our horses here and hide our guns," said Andy. "As soon as it is light, we can slip up to the house."

When the gray light of dawn began to sift through the trees, Andy and Robert crept from the thicket and knocked softly on Lieutenant Crawford's door. His wife let them in, a baby in her arms and her other children clinging to her skirts. She paled when they told her that her husband had been taken prisoner. But there was no way that she could help him, and the boys needed food. She laid places for them at the kitchen table.

"Um!" Andy spread a piece of cornbread with thick slabs of yellow butter. He started to take a bite, when there was a pounding on the door.

"Who is it?" asked Mrs. Crawford.

No one answered, but the door was thrust open. The commander of the dragoons pushed into the room. "Ah, there you are," he snarled when he saw Andy.

Raising his sword, the ill-natured commander brushed all of the food from the table. He picked up a piece of crockery and hurled it against the cabin wall. The children ran, screaming, to their mother. Andy stood by helplessly, with no words for the rage that welled up in his heart.

"Now, you," said the commanding officer, "clean my boots."

Andrew Jackson, thirteen years old, drew himself up proudly. Whatever might happen to him, he was determined not to clean that officer's boots. "I am a prisoner of war," he said between clenched teeth, "and I claim the right to be treated as such."

The officer glared. Andy saw the terrible, shining blade of the officer's sword, and put up his hands. He was too late. He felt a burning streak of pain across his hand, another on his head. The room whirled around him in a dizzy circle, as the blood oozed from two deep gashes.

The two Jackson boys, Lieutenant Crawford and other prisoners were marched forty miles to the enemy prison in Camden, South Carolina. Here Andy was separated from his brother and cousin and robbed of his shoes and jacket. His wounds pained him, but no one came to dress them. There was no medicine, and he was given no food, except some moldy bread.

Smallpox broke out. One morning Andy awoke with his freckled face flushed a deep, unhealthy scarlet. The fever burned through his aching body, but he tried to keep his thoughts on his mother. He remembered how she looked, seated at her spinning wheel. Her face was calm, yet her eyes could flash with unexpected fire. Did she know that he was ill? Would he ever see her again?

"I hate these soldiers," he muttered, thrashing back and forth on the hard ground. "If I ever have a chance, I'll get even."

Not all of the soldiers were unkind. One day a redcoated guard brought him good news. "Listen, Andy," said the guard, "your mother is outside waiting for you."

"My mother?" Andy looked up at him out of dazed eyes.

"Yes, you and your brother are free. The British commander has consented to an exchange of prisoners. Five of you Waxhaw boys are going home today."

At the prison gate Andy was joined by his brother. Robert also had had smallpox, and Andy was shocked to see him looking so ill.

Their mother was coming toward them. How good it was to feel her arms around their shoulders.

"My sons!" Her voice broke. "My poor, dear sons, I have come to take you home."

Robert died as a result of his terrible experience. Andy was sick for a long time, but slowly his mother nursed him back to health. Some of the Waxhaw boys were not so fortunate. Several of them, including two of Andy's cousins, were ill with fever on board a British prison ship some distance away. Elizabeth Jackson and two of her neighbors obtained permission to take care of them. Elizabeth knew that the fever was contagious, but she did not hesitate. Before she left she had some last advice for her one remaining son.

"Remember, Andy," she said, drying her eyes on her apron, "never tell a lie, nor take what is not your own. Make friends by being honest. Keep them by being steadfast."

The sad news came a few weeks later. Mrs. Jackson had caught the fever and had died, leaving Andy an orphan at fourteen.

"I felt utterly alone," he said.

Andrew Jackson never forgot the bitter experiences of his youth, but he fought his way up with gusto. During the first few years after his mother's death, he was often reckless, but he finally settled down to study law. At twenty-one he made his way west to the little town of Nashville in the region soon to be admitted to the Union as the new state of Tennessee.

From the beginning, Andrew was one of Tennessee's leading citizens. During the War of 1812 with Great Britain, he also became well known as a soldier. The Creek Indians, egged on by the enemy, started to spread terror along the frontier, burning houses and killing settlers. Andrew Jackson led several thousand volunteer soldiers from Tennessee into the Indian country, where he defeated the Creeks so completely that they were no longer a danger. As a result he was commissioned a major general in the regular army.

Other American officers had been less successful. Since the war began, the Americans had lost battle after battle. The country was in despair toward the end of 1814 when British troops began landing near New Orleans. The picturesque city, acquired from France only twelve years earlier, was about to be taken over by Great Britain —or so it seemed to the people who lived there.

Then they learned that General Jackson was coming to their defense. His army of frontier soldiers was not as well trained as that of the enemy, but he inspired his men with his own confidence and courage. "Old Andy Jackson is as tough as a hickory tree," they said, and they called him "Old Hickory." Soon the French and Spanish residents of New Orleans were calling him Old Hickory, too. They joined with the American soldiers in digging trenches south of the city. Bales of cotton and hogsheads of sugar were piled high to form breastworks. So cleverly were the defenses planned that when the British attacked, the battle lasted less than half an hour.

The impossible had happened. Bold headlines in newspapers throughout the nation announced General Jackson's "almost incredible victory." People talked of his iron determination. They also talked about his boyhood—of how he had been left an orphan, almost without funds, yet had succeeded through his own efforts. This story had tremendous appeal for plain people everywhere. Of course not everyone liked him; a man so vigorous, so hotheaded, so sure of himself, was bound to make enemies. But General Jackson's friends outnumbered his enemies, and in 1828 he was elected President of the United States.

He was very different from the first six Presidents. They had been gentlemen from Virginia or Massachusetts. Andrew Jackson, although he had courtly manners and could be very gentle when he wished to be, had won his fame as a backwoods fighter, as a plain man from the West. His plan was to give positions in the Federal government to many of the plain people whose votes had elected him.

"Let the people rule!" was his motto.

And the people took him at his word. Thousands of them crowded into Washington for the inauguration. At a reception held at the White House men in ill-fitting homespun clothes and coonskin caps mingled with fashionable ladies and gentlemen from eastern cities. The fashionable gentlemen raised their eyebrows. Fashionable ladies whispered to one another behind their fans that they had never seen so many backwoods people at the White House before.

Not that the backwoods people cared. They felt, as one newspaper said, that General Jackson was "their own President." The tall, gaunt man with the thin, narrow face under bristling gray locks greeted all of his guests alike with simple dignity.

Andrew Jackson's two terms in the White House were one of the stormiest periods in American history. His enemies, who accused him of always wanting his own way, called him "King Andrew." But being called names never kept him from doing what he thought was right. The year after he became President, he had to make one of the hardest decisions of his life.

Many Southerners felt that a certain tariff, or tax law, which had been passed by Congress, would ruin them financially. The leaders of South Carolina believed that their state had a right to nullify the law, that is, to set it aside. At a banquet attended by President Jackson, the other guests were in suspense. He had been invited to give a toast, but what would he say? He was a Southerner, and he knew what hardship the tariff law meant for the South. Would he agree that a state had a right to nullify a law of which its people disapproved? What would he answer to the rumors that South Carolina might leave the Union unless the law was repealed? Everyone knew how much the Union meant to Old Hickory; he had fought for it even as a boy.

Andrew Jackson arose from his place at the table. His eyes, blue and searching under heavy brows, seemed to take in everyone in the room. He raised his glass, a signal for everyone to stand. A scraping of chairs was followed by silence. Everyone was waiting.

Then Andrew Jackson's voice came, firm and clear: "Our Union," he said. "It must be preserved."

No one was left in doubt of what the President meant. A law passed by Congress must be obeyed by everyone alike. No state had a right to leave the Union. Andrew Jackson was the first President to take a stand on this question which was to become more and more important as the years went by.

He also was the first President to give the plain people of the country a big share in running the government. The words "All men are created equal," which he had read for the first time as a nine-year-old boy, had never been forgotten.

THE SEVENTH PRESIDENT *at a Glance*

Andrew Jackson

Born: March 15, 1767   *Died: June 8, 1845*

Early life. Andrew Jackson was born in the frontier settlement of Waxhaw near the northern border of South Carolina. At the age of 13 he fought as an "irregular" in the American Revolution. At 17, he began to study law and was admitted to the bar three years later

(1787). In 1788 he went west to the area that later became the state of Tennessee and opened a law office in Nashville.

Early career. After Tennessee's admission to the Union (1796), Jackson represented the state in Congress as a Representative (1796–1797) and as a Senator (1797–1798). At 31, he became judge of the state supreme court (1798–1804). In 1804 he moved to the Hermitage, his plantation near Nashville.

As a military hero. When a major general in the Tennessee militia during the War of 1812, Jackson won a decisive victory over the Creek Indians (1814). As a major general in the regular army, he defeated the British at New Orleans (January 8, 1815). In 1817–1818 Jackson invaded Spanish Florida and subdued the Seminole Indians. After Florida was purchased from Spain (1819), Jackson was governor of the territory of Florida (1821).

As candidate for President. In 1824, while serving again as U.S. Senator, Jackson was a candidate for President. No candidate received a majority of the electoral votes, and the House of Representatives had to make the decision. The House chose John Quincy Adams, but four years later Jackson, a Democrat, was elected President by an overwhelming majority.

As President (1829–1833; 1833–1837). The phrase "to the victor belong the spoils" was first heard during Jackson's administration. Though Jackson gave Federal jobs to many of the people who had helped elect him, the "spoils system" of rewarding political supporters with offices was already in use in several states. In 1832 Jackson vetoed a bill to renew the charter of the United States Bank, where the government funds were on deposit. He believed that one bank, largely controlled by private bankers, should not have special privileges that enriched one group of men. Jackson's veto won great popular support, and in 1833 he had the government funds removed from the United States Bank and deposited in some of the state banks. When South Carolina refused to obey a Federal tariff law and threatened (1832) to secede, that is, to withdraw from the Union, Jackson announced that he would use force, if necessary, to see that Federal laws were obeyed. The issue was settled by compromise, and armed conflict was avoided.

The White House hostess. Jackson's wife, Rachel (1767–1828), died less than three months before her husband's inauguration. Her niece, Mrs. Emily Donelson, was the hostess at the White House.

Other happenings. When Jackson was President, the "Tom Thumb," the first steam locomotive built in the U.S., made a 26-mile trip (1830). Senator Daniel Webster, in a speech ending with the famous words, "Liberty and Union, now and forever, one and inseparable!" said that no state had the right to nullify a Federal law (1830). Cyrus McCormick patented the reaper (1834). Texas won its freedom from Mexico (1836) and became an independent republic. Narcissa Whitman and Eliza Spalding, traveling with their husbands from New York to the present state of Washington, were the first white women to cross the Great Plains and the Rockies (1836).

The nation's population and growth. The population was about 12,900,000 (1830 census). Two new states were admitted to the Union, making a total number of 26: Arkansas (1836) and Michigan (1837).

MATT VAN BUREN, *Boy Lawyer*

Ha, have you not heard what the Senator called the President?" asked one of the gentlemen at the table. "Here, lad, bring me another piece of apple pie."

Matt, who often waited on the table at his father's inn, brought the pie, but he did not miss a word of what the guests were saying. Some of the men were Federalists, of the party of President John Adams. Others, who called themselves Democratic-Republicans, were followers of Thomas Jefferson. Ten-year-old Martin Van Buren never tired of hearing them talk politics.

"Pray tell us, what was it that the Senator called the President?" asked a short-haired gentleman, whose somber breeches and waistcoat showed that he belonged to Thomas Jefferson's party. It was the custom in 1796 for men of the two political parties to dress quite differently.

Another man spoke up, and Matt could see from his velvet coat that he was a Federalist. "Is not 'His Excellency' a proper term of address for the President of the United States?" he asked sourly.

"Aye, for George Washington," the first man replied, "but President Adams is too fat, too round, to grace that title. At any rate, the Senator, the impudent fellow, has nicknamed Mr. Adams 'His Rotundity.' "

There was a shout of laughter. Even the Federalist lost his sour look. Matt, forgetting his duties as a waiter, began to giggle.

"So!" The gentleman who had told the joke turned on him, pretending to be displeased. "So Mr. Van Buren's son serves giggles with his pie?"

Matt's blue eyes twinkled in a round, jolly face. "His Ro-ro-ro-tundity! Ach, with that funny word you make me giggle, sir!"

The men roared. The boy was always ready with an answer, no matter how much they teased him. If he mixed an occasional Dutch word with his English, it was because he heard the Dutch language spoken in his own family. His ancestors on both his father's and his mother's side had come from Holland.

Something interesting was always happening in the low, clapboard tavern in Kinderhook-by-the-Hudson in New York state, where Matt lived. Famous men like Alexander Hamilton and Aaron Burr often pushed aside the swinging door to eat a hearty meal or to spend the night. Fat, good-natured Abraham Van Buren would make them welcome in his broken English, and Matt would run to take their carpetbags.

Matt decided that when he grew up he would be somebody important, like the guests who wore the fashionable cocked hats over their powdered wigs. He did not want to be like his father, never having quite enough money to go around, and Mrs. Van Buren understood how he felt. It made her proud to know that Matt wrote and talked better than any boy in school—at least that was what his teacher said. She scraped together enough money to send him to Kinderhook Academy for a while. Then one day when Matt was thirteen, he came into the kitchen and found her weeping.

"Ach, *mijn kind!*" she said. "My best I do, but now school you must stop and go to work."

"Do not mind, *mijne moeder,*" Matt replied, sounding more cheerful than he felt. He did not want his mother to know that he was disappointed.

"Your fadder has apprenticed you to the young lawyer, Francis Silvester," Mrs. Van Buren went on. "He home from Columbia College has come, to go into the law office of Mr. Gardinier."

"To be a law clerk, am I?"

Matt could not have been more pleased. Although he did not know Francis well, Mr. Aaron Gardinier often came to the inn. He was a likeable gentleman, as was Cornelius, Francis' older brother, owner of the village store. Mr. Cornelius was always one of the first to laugh at the quaint remarks of the innkeeper's son. But a few days later when Matt reported at the law office for work, he squirmed uneasily. At the door stood young Mr. Francis Silvester, every inch a dandy, from his triangular hat down to the silver buckles on his shoes.

"So," said the young man, "you are to be my clerk. Your duties are to dust, sweep the floors, keep the fire going on cold days, and clean the quill pens for both Mr. Gardinier and myself. Some of the easier law cases you will be allowed to copy. And oh, yes, my brother Cornelius desires you to sleep in his store the nights when his clerk is away."

Francis paused. Very slowly he looked his new law clerk up and down, and Matt was suddenly conscious of his homespun woolen breeches and coarse linen shirt.

"Well, Matt," said Francis, a thin smile curling his lips, "I see that we belong to different political parties."

Matt managed a grin, because he was used to being teased. Besides, he had made up his mind that he was going to like being a law clerk.

And he did like it. As the months went by he learned a great deal about law, but one of his most pleasant duties was guarding Cornelius Silvester's store at night. Matt slept on a cot behind some merchandise, and Cornelius often came in for a chat. He was an easy man to talk to, kind and generous, and very different from Francis. The elegant younger brother was always finding fault.

One day Matt came to work with a big tear in his jacket. Francis raised his eyebrows and flicked a spot of dust from the sleeve of his blue velvet coat. He sat down in his chair and crossed his silken legs.

"It vexes me," said Francis, "to see a lad careless in his dress. A gentleman always appears in fine raiment."

His precise voice went on and on. Matt said nothing, but the next morning he was missing from the office. The second day, when he did not appear, Francis began to worry.

"Zounds, has something happened to the lad?" he thought.

The third morning the door opened and Matt walked in. Francis blinked, and looked again to be sure it was really his grubby little law clerk. Matt was wearing a bright coat and handsome velvet breeches. His silver buckles shone at the end of his short legs, very shiny in their fine silk stockings. He took off his cocked hat and laid it on his table. No Federalist in Kinderhook looked more impressive.

"Good morning!" Matt spoke as calmly as though he came to work every day clad in silk and velvet.

Francis was so amused that he decided not to scold Matt for his absence. "My law clerk is no simpleton," he said to himself. "He must have gone to Albany to do some shopping, and I dare say he borrowed the money from Cornelius. Cornelius is that fond of the lad."

Matt's duties grew more interesting with each passing week. He began to go to court, which was often held in the village inn. One day, when Mr. Gardinier, the older member of the firm, was asked to defend a client in a town close by, he took Matt with him. The boy looked around curiously as he sat down at the counsel table. The room was crowded. Someday he hoped that he would be allowed to make a speech to a roomful of people. Less important cases were frequently intrusted to a clerk.

Matt opened the green bag in which the lawyer kept his papers and spread them out upon the table. Mr. Gardinier called his witnesses. The lawyer for the opposing side called witnesses. The case droned on. Finally the time came for the two lawyers to sum up their evidence and make their final appeals to the jury. Mr. Gardinier turned to his clerk.

"Say, Matt, you know all the facts in this case. Why don't you sum up? You might as well begin early."

There was a gasp of surprise from the spectators. The law clerk was fifteen, but because he was so short he looked even younger. No one was more surprised than Matt himself, and his heart seemed to take a dive down into his square-toed boots. But Mr. Gardinier was nudging him, and he had to stand up. He began to speak in a low voice. The words came haltingly.

"We can't see the little fellow," someone shouted.

Matt climbed on the table. Now that he towered above the spectators he felt more at ease. And soon he became so interested in what he wanted to tell the jury that he forgot to be frightened. He began talking in the hurried, racing manner that his friends knew so well, and Mr. Gardinier settled back in his chair.

"Well done," Mr. Gardinier whispered, when Matt had finished and came back to the counsel table. "I knew that you could do it."

Matt flashed him a smile of gratitude, then turned to watch as the jury filed out of the room. They were gone only a few minutes. When they came back, the foreman rose to read the verdict. The decision was in favor of Mr. Gardinier's client. Matt had won his first case!

"Hurrah for Matt Van Buren!" cried the spectators, and Mr. Gardinier pressed a shiny silver half dollar into his hand.

Because of that first success, Martin was allowed to try other cases from time to time. He was so popular that some of his Dutch neighbors called him "the Boy Lawyer" or "the Little Magician." Other neighbors shook their heads in disapproval. They were afraid that Matt might grow up to depend, not on brains and hard work, but on his wit and charm instead.

"Poor little Matty," they said. "Success has come too easily to him. Too much he thinks of his fine coat and silver buckles. Too much he counts on a slick tongue. Ach, the lad will do anything to take an advantage for himself."

About this last, the neighbors were wrong. One day, when Matt was sixteen, he heard the village cannon being fired. The Federalists had won the state election, and they were celebrating. That evening some of Mr. Silvester's friends gathered at his home. They were singing and shouting when Matt arrived at the house on an errand.

"Hurrah for the Federalists!" one of the men cried. "Down with the Democratic-Republicans."

Everyone was looking at Matt. Everyone seemed to be enjoying his embarrassment except Cornelius. He followed the boy outside and invited him to come back and join in the fun. But Matt felt too disappointed about the election. He hurried off to the store, where after several hours of tossing back and forth on his narrow cot, he finally fell asleep. About midnight he was awakened by a knocking at the door. Matt got up and raised the latch. Cornelius pushed his way into the room.

"Get back into bed, Matt," he said. "I want to talk with you, and please remember that I have your best interests at heart."

Cornelius pulled up a box and sat down. For more than an hour he urged Matt to become a Federalist. Matt listened, his eyes wide and troubled. An ambitious boy, he also was poor. He knew that most of the important people in Kinderhook were Federalists. He would have more influential friends to help him if he changed his politics.

"Mr. Cornelius," he said at last, "I am grateful for your kindness. But I believe in the policies of Mr. Jefferson, and I cannot be a Federalist."

Matt wondered if Cornelius would turn against him because of his decision, But, no, Cornelius was holding out his hand. "I'll never trouble you on this subject again, Matt," he said, "and whatever happens I will always be your friend."

Martin Van Buren never regretted his decision. Within a few years the Federalist party became very unpopular and went out of existence. In the meantime Matt had gone ahead with his law studies and had won success as a lawyer. From the start of his career he was interested in politics and soon became a leader in the Democratic party, as the old Democratic-Republican party was now called. After holding a number of other public offices, he was elected Vice President in 1832. Handsome, courteous, and charming, the "young magician" from Kinderhook had come a long way since he had stood on a table to argue his first law case.

"Mr. Van Buren," said his friend Washington Irving, the popular writer, "is one of the gentlest and most amiable men I have ever met."

Certainly President Andrew Jackson liked him. The older man regarded the younger one almost as a son, and Martin returned the President's affection. Before the end of the Jackson administration, Old Hickory let it be known that he wanted Martin Van Buren to be the next President. What Old Hickory wanted he usually got, and Martin was nominated. A few months later, he was elected— the first President who had lived his entire life under the American flag. The first seven Presidents had all been born before the United States declared its independence.

As it turned out, Van Buren's election was not the good fortune it appeared to be at first. Within a few weeks after his inauguration, hard times hit the country. Although the causes of the Panic of 1837, as the hard times were called, went back several years, many people considered him responsible. Thousands of voters who had lost their homes or could not pay their rent, and who often did not have enough to eat, had to have someone to blame for their troubles. And so they blamed the President.

After a long struggle, Martin Van Buren succeeded in getting Congress to pass a law that would improve the financial situation. But it came too late to help him when he ran for re-election in the fall of 1840. There were many uncomplimentary songs about him. Even behind the thick walls of the White House, he could hear the crowds on Pennsylvania Avenue shouting the refrain: "Van, Van, Is a used-up man!"

This song and many others were inspired by a new political party, the Whigs. Taking advantage of the misery of the people, they accused the President of being a haughty aristocrat who lived in luxury while thousands of other Americans went hungry. The Whig candidate, General William Henry Harrison, a valiant old Indian fighter from the Northwest Territory, was pictured as a homespun hero who lived in a log cabin on the frontier. It was seldom mentioned that the log cabin had been enlarged into a comfortable house of twenty-two rooms, neatly covered with clapboards. Or that General Harrison had been born into one of the oldest and most aristocratic families in Virginia.

In vain did Martin Van Buren's friends point out that he had been a poor boy, and that the White House was no more comfortable or luxurious than when some of the earlier Presidents had lived there. In spite of their efforts, he was defeated, but—in a time when there were neither telephones nor telegraph—the results were not known for some days. Martin Van Buren was coming out of church one Sunday in November soon after the election when a messenger met him at the door to tell him that the Whigs had won by an overwhelming majority.

Mr. Van Buren bowed. "Then General Harrison is your next President," he said.

Perhaps he was remembering a sentence he had written in his notebook as a law clerk just starting his career: "To yield to necessity is the real triumph of reason and strength of mind." He had followed that rule for many years, and he would follow it now. Whatever disappointment he may have felt, he allowed no one to see it, either during his final months in the White House or after his return to Kinderhook.

A large crowd was waiting on the steamboat wharf to welcome him when he arrived in his old home town the following spring. A brass band, marching before his carriage, led the way to the hotel. Here Martin Van Buren was called on for a speech, and he mentioned his hope that in time the American people would realize the wisdom of some of his acts as President. As for himself, he was not sad.

The ex-President smiled. In the crowd were some of his old neighbors who had known him as a boy. "I come to take up my final residence with you," he said, "not, I assure you, in the character of a repining, but in that of a satisfied and contented man."

THE EIGHTH PRESIDENT *at a Glance*

Martin Van Buren

Born: December 5, 1782   *Died: July 24, 1862*

Early life. Martin Van Buren was born in Kinderhook, N.Y. At 14, he became a clerk in a law office in Kinderhook. At 19, he went to New York City to complete his law training. He returned to Kinderhook two years later (1803) and began to practice law and to take an active interest in politics.

Political career. Van Buren gradually became very powerful in the

Democratic political organization of his state. After serving as a state senator and as attorney general of New York, he was elected to the U.S. Senate. As a Senator (1821–1828), he fought against the further extension of slavery and introduced bills against the practice of imprisoning debtors. Elected governor of New York (1828), he resigned soon after his inauguration to become Secretary of State (1829–1831) under Andrew Jackson. During Jackson's second term as President, Van Buren was Vice President (1833–1837). In 1836 he was elected President.

As President (1837–1841). An important cause of the financial "Panic of 1837" was the unwise loan policies of the state banks where the government money had been deposited after President Jackson refused to recharter the United States Bank. President Van Buren urged Congress to establish a government treasury, independent of banks of any kind, for keeping government funds. Many Congressmen opposed the idea, and three years went by before the Independent Treasury bill was passed (1840). The Independent Treasury system, with subtreasuries in several large cities, is, with certain changes, in use in the U.S. today.

The White House hostess. Hannah Hoes Van Buren (1783–1819) died 18 years before her husband became President. The President's daughter-in-law, Angelica Van Buren, a cousin of Dolley Madison, acted as White House hostess.

Other happenings. All during Van Buren's administration a war was being carried on with the Seminole Indians of Florida. It began in 1836 and did not end until 1842, when Van Buren was no longer President. An exploring expedition, commanded by naval officer Charles Wilkes, sighted the Antarctic Continent and sailed along its coast (1840).

The nation's population. The population was about 17,000,000 (census of 1840).

WILLIAM HENRY HARRISON *Goes West*

The Philadelphia innkeeper had news to share—distressing news. "The army that General Washington sent to subdue the Indians was all but massacred. General St. Clair's soldiers fell into an ambush, and most of them were slain. I tell you, evil times have come upon the settlers in the Northwest Territory."

William Henry Harrison, a handsome youth of eighteen, looked at the innkeeper out of flashing dark eyes. He had recently arrived in Philadelphia, which in 1792 was still the capital of the nation. William was studying medicine, but what he really wanted to do was to be a soldier. He wanted to go out west to help the settlers who were trying to make new homes for themselves in the Northwest Territory, that vast tract of land between the Ohio River and the Great Lakes.

"The savages have grown so bold," the innkeeper went on, "that they are murdering the white settlers on their doorsteps. They burn the cabins and carry off the women and children into captivity."

"The Indians have done that?" asked William.

"Worse than that, lad. They have murdered entire families. They have burned down whole villages. No white man is safe north of the Ohio, unless more soldiers go to their rescue."

"Have you not heard?" one of the guests at the inn interrupted. "President Washington has ordered that another regiment be sent west. Even now, it is being organized."

By the time William returned to his rooming house, his mind was made up. His father, Benjamin Harrison, had been one of the leading patriots in Virginia, a signer of the Declaration of Independence. Surely, if he were still living, he would not forbid his son to strike a blow for freedom in the Northwest Territory.

The next morning William went to see a family friend, Governor Henry Lee of Virginia, who was visiting in Philadelphia. "Lighthorse Harry," as he had been called during the Revolution, had been one of General Washington's trusted officers. Perhaps he could advise William about going into the army.

"So you want to be a soldier?" said Governor Lee. "But, William, you have such a kind nature. You would make a good doctor."

"I hope to be a good soldier, sir."

At first Henry Lee seemed doubtful. Perhaps he was thinking of Berkeley, the mansion overlooking the James River where William had been brought up. The boy knew nothing of hardship, and he did not look strong.

"Have you any idea what war in the wilderness is like?" the governor asked. "There would be long marches over rough country. Every tree and bush you pass might prove to be the hiding place for an Indian, waiting to pounce on you with tomahawk in hand. Many nights, even in the dead of winter, you might have to sleep on the ground, without shelter of any kind. Have you considered that?"

"I have," William insisted, "and I want to go."

Governor Lee arose and clapped him on the shoulder. "All right, lad. I like your spirit, and I shall speak to President Washington in your behalf. I shall tell him that you are a son worthy of your father. He knew and admired Benjamin Harrison. I feel sure if there is a vacancy, the President will give you a commission in the army."

"Thank you, sir."

"Not at all. I was your father's friend, and I am a friend of yours."

Within twenty-four hours William learned that there was indeed a place in the Tenth Regiment. By order of President Washington, the son of Benjamin Harrison was offered a commission, and he was sworn in as an ensign, as a second lieutenant in the army was then called. The new officer was ordered to report for duty to General Arthur St. Clair at Fort Washington on the north bank of the Ohio River. But he had another assignment first, and he lingered in Philadelphia long enough to recruit eighty soldiers to go with him.

In September Ensign Harrison and his recruits started west across the mountains. A month later they reached Fort Pitt, where the men built flatboats for their voyage down the Ohio. "Ohio" was the Indian word for "beautiful river," and it was well named, thought William one day, as he stood looking out over the wide expanse of water. The broad river flowed in majestic curves between wooded shores. Beyond those tall trees lay a wilderness—such a wilderness as Virginia had once been. His ancestors had been among the pioneers who developed Virginia into a great state. Now he, William Henry Harrison, was going to be a pioneer in this new wilderness called the Northwest Territory.

The eighteen-year-old ensign straightened his thin shoulders. His first duty, of course, would be that of a soldier. He was going to help General St. Clair to deliver the settlers from the terror of the Indians.

"Look!" shouted one of the recruits. "That must be Fort Washington."

It was a murky November afternoon when the flatboats drew up on the northern bank of the river. Through the mist William could see the outlines of a log stockade against a background of gray cliffs. Surrounding the fort was a cluster of log houses—the village of Cincinnati. Ensign Harrison lined up his men and marched them toward the stockade. As they passed through the wide gates, the recruits stared in shock and surprise; was this what war in the wilderness was like? Ragged soldiers, looking half starved, lounged before the log cabins inside the fort. Their eyes were like deep hollows in their thin, pinched faces, as they glanced up at the newcomers.

The new men learned what had happened. General St. Clair, in an expedition against the Indians, had been surprised by the enemy more than a hundred miles to the north. All of his supplies and the soldiers' baggage had been captured. Much worse, more than six hundred soldiers had been slaughtered on the battlefield. The ones who were able to escape had straggled back to Fort Washington in pitiful condition.

Never had William seen so much misery, but fortunately the Indians did not follow up their victory. The fort was not attacked, and the men took up the usual routine of army life. When William reported for drill on the parade ground, he met several cadets, young men about his own age; but they regarded him coolly, and seemed to be convinced that he would never be able to endure the hardships of army life.

The senior cadet, the son of one of the captains, was even more unfriendly than the others. One day he remarked—speaking loudly enough for William to hear—that the new officer had entered the army "through the window." William knew this was another way of saying that he had obtained his commission through special influence. Hurt and bewildered, he hurried to his cabin as soon as the day's duties were over.

From then on most of his free time was spent reading. He found several histories around the camp, and there was one volume on military tactics that he studied night after night.

One morning William was pleasantly surprised to meet an officer he had known as a boy. This gentleman, a recent arrival at the fort, had visited at Berkeley, and it was a relief for William to be able to confide in him.

"Has no one ever told you," asked the older man, "why the cadets resent you?"

William shook his head.

"It is because the senior cadet was in line for a promotion before you arrived, and his officers had promised to recommend him for the next vacancy."

"Is that the vacancy I was appointed to fill?" William asked.

"Yes, and the senior cadet had put in months of hard training. There is a general feeling around the camp that he deserved the appointment given to you. You are the only officer who has been admitted to the regiment without previous experience."

"But how was I to know?" asked William. "And now that I do know, what am I to do?"

"Resign your commission," his friend advised.

William was indignant. "Do you think I would give up so easily?"

"Why not? As a soldier, you will find little chance for advancement. Besides, the cadets may be right in thinking you are not husky enough for army life. I am returning East next month. Think it over and come with me."

"No," said William stubbornly, "my dander has been raised, and I intend to stay."

Perhaps, he admitted to himself, he had won his commission because the President had been his father's friend. But that was all the more reason why he must prove himself worthy.

A short time later William, with twenty men under his command, was sent with a train of packhorses to deliver supplies to another fort twenty miles away. Several other hard marches followed, through rain and snow, but Ensign Harrison never complained.

Then came a much harder test of his fortitude. A new general, who had taken command of Fort Washington, planned a longer expedition, hoping to recapture some of the supplies stolen at the time of General St. Clair's defeat. William spent his nineteenth birthday early in February marching in the face of a biting wind. The wet snow drifted into the tops of his leggings. Icy particles stung his cheeks, and that night he slept on the frozen ground.

Nearly every night during the next few weeks was spent sleeping on the ground. Two other forts were visited and a third outpost established, but because of the bitter weather all plans for attack had to be abandoned. The cold, however, did not prevent a surprise attack by Indians, but after a brief skirmish they were driven off.

Other enemies—rain and snow and sleet—simply had to be endured. For three weeks William stood guard every other night. There was no campfire to keep him warm, for fear that the light might attract the Indians. Because of the continued exposure, many of the men were taken ill. Some of them had pneumonia, but not William. He stood the rigors of those terrible weeks in the open better than most of his companions. They could not help but admire his skill as an officer and his pluck and good nature in the face of hardship. He was in high spirits when he returned to Fort Washington in early March.

"I recollect with great pleasure," he said years later, "that the prejudice against me when I first entered the regiment was soon removed. The cadets who were disappointed by my appointment soon received commissions and became my friends."

After that difficult expedition, William Henry Harrison was one of the most popular young men in his regiment. But the Indian troubles were growing worse. President Washington decided that a much larger army must be sent to protect the settlers, and General Anthony Wayne was placed in command. In the spring of 1792, he began to drill his army at Fort Pitt. The soldiers at Fort Washington considered it a great honor when one of their officers was chosen by the new general as an aide. That officer was William Henry Harrison.

No one felt more gratified than William. As the weeks passed, he found Anthony Wayne a stern drillmaster, but the general was quick to recognize the ability of his new aide. William was promoted to lieutenant and later to captain. In August, 1794, he marched northward with his general and helped to defeat the Indians in the Battle of Fallen Timbers, defeated them so decisively that the chiefs of several tribes promised never again to make war on the Americans. Also in exchange for presents amounting to about $20,000, they gave up thousands of acres of their land in what is now southern Ohio and southeastern Indiana. William, thinking that permanent peace had come, resigned from the army several years later.

In the meantime he had married and bought a farm at North Bend overlooking the Ohio. But he soon learned that his military service was only the beginning of his service to the Northwest Territory.

At twenty-seven William Henry Harrison was appointed governor of the western part of the territory. It was called Indiana Territory, and the old French town of Vincennes on the Wabash River was chosen as the capital.

One of the new governor's tasks was to make friends with the chiefs of the Indian tribes that lived close by. More and more settlers were going west to live. This meant that more and more land was needed that could be broken up into small farms for the settlers to buy. Governor Harrison obtained the land by making treaties with the chiefs of thirteen different tribes, and the Indians agreed to find new hunting grounds farther west. Some of the tribes sold their land; others allowed the United States to annex thousands of acres in exchange for gifts.

There was one Indian, the great leader Tecumseh, chief of the Shawnee tribe, who felt very bitter about these treaties. He claimed that the hunting grounds belonged to all red men alike, and that no tribe had a right to sell any land without the consent of all the other tribes. The time would soon come, he declared, when there would be no hunting grounds left, unless the American invaders were driven back east across the mountains. With the help of his brother, known as the Prophet, Tecumseh planned a great confederacy in which all of the tribes would unite against the white man.

After Governor Harrison heard of this plan, he invited Tecumseh to come to Vincennes, and a council was held in the walnut grove back of the governor's house. The great chief, tall and handsome, rose to his full height and began to speak.

"Until lately," said Tecumseh, "there were no white men in this country. Then it belonged to the red men, placed on it by the Great Spirit, to keep it, to travel over it, to eat its fruits, and to fill it with the same race. Once they were a happy race. Now they are made miserable by the white people who are never contented but always trespassing. They have driven us from the sea and forced us over the mountains, but we are determined to go no farther."

It was a moving, eloquent plea. The governor, seated in his armchair, listened attentively while it was being translated by an interpreter. In his reply he insisted that the Indians had been treated fairly, mentioning the money they had received for their lands. This last remark made Tecumseh very angry, and he began shouting in his own language. Thirty of his warriors, who had been seated behind him on the grass, jumped up, brandishing their tomahawks and war clubs. They looked to their chief, waiting for his orders. In the meantime the American guard had observed what was happening, and rushed up, their guns cocked.

Governor Harrison stopped them with a gesture; the guards were not to fire. Then he arose and drew the short sword that hung at his side. "You came under the protection of a council fire, and therefor you may leave in safety," he told the Shawnee leader. "But the council is over."

A short time later, the governor learned that Tecumseh had started south, hoping to stir up other tribes to join his confederacy. If he succeeded, thousands of settlers might be killed. The danger was great, and William Henry Harrison realized that he must strike first, before the Indians became too strong. Early in November, 1811, he marched a thousand soldiers toward the Shawnee village on the Tippecanoe River. Tecumseh had not yet returned, but his brother, the Prophet, was there.

"The Indians appeared much terrified at our sudden appearance before their town," one of Governor Harrison's soldiers told the story later. "A chief came out to the governor, begging him not to open hostilities; but to encamp with the troops for that night. The Indians, expressing their earnest desire for peace without bloodshed, solemnly promised to come into camp the next morning and hold a council."

To this proposal Governor Harrison agreed, and his men made camp outside the village. Several hours later they were awakened by bloodcurdling yells. The Indians, aroused to fury by the Prophet, were shooting down the Americans by the light of their own campfires. Although taken by surprise, the soldiers rallied, and in the bloody battle that followed the Shawnees were completely routed. By daybreak they were fleeing in all directions, and the camp ground was strewn with the bodies of dead and wounded men.

The battle of Tippecanoe was a great victory for the Americans, and put an end to Tecumseh's dream of driving the white men back east across the mountains. Later, during the War of 1812, William Henry Harrison fought gallantly and became a general. But it was in his battle against the Shawnees that he had won his greatest fame, and he was affectionately called "Old Tippecanoe." In 1840, when the Whigs nominated him for President, many rousing songs were written about his victory nearly thirty years earlier. From one end of the nation to the other, his admirers were singing:

JOHN TYLER'S *Rebellion*

The crowd of boys locked the schoolhouse door behind them, paying no attention to the yells coming from inside the building. They looked half scared, half jubilant. Their punishment would doubtless be severe. But they did not expect to be found out until morning, and for the moment they refused to worry.

All except John Tyler. He had begun to worry already. As he took his little brother William by the hand and walked across the road, he was wondering what his father would think. The Tylers lived in a big white house called Greenway Court, and Judge Tyler was one of the most distinguished men in Virginia. There was a close friendship between father and son, and they had been even closer since Mrs. Tyler died. John did not like to think how disappointed his father would be in him when he learned what had happened.

Judge Tyler was reading under the spreading willow tree on the lawn. "Good afternoon, boys," he said. "How was school today?"

That was a question neither boy wanted to answer. John, standing beside Judge Tyler's chair, looked down at the book he had been reading. It was a book about Virginia, and was open to a picture of the Virginia state seal. John leaned close to read the Latin motto *Sic Semper Tyrannis*. He spoke the words aloud, then translated them, "Thus ever to tyrants."

"Good!" his father said. "You are doing very well with your Latin, John. And you, William——"

The judge paused, puzzled by the expression on little William's face. William was quick to change the subject. "Tell us a story," he begged.

"Yes, Father," said John eagerly, "tell us about the time when you went to school with Mr. Jefferson."

Judge Tyler nodded. He was as proud as his sons were of his friendship with the President of the United States. They had been students together at William and Mary College.

"I can still see Tom as he looked then," said the judge. "Turned-up, freckled nose, and wide gray eyes that always looked curious about something. Tom could ask more questions than anybody in Williamsburg, and he was fun to be with. But he never let fun interfere with his school work. He studied hard. I know, because I used to study in the same room with him. He was a brilliant student, the kind of student I expect my sons to be——"

He was interrupted by a great bellow. James McMurdo, the schoolmaster, was pounding across the lawn. His face was red, his sandy hair uncombed, his jacket torn. He shook an accusing finger at John. The judge, astonished by his visitor's torrent of words, suggested that he sit down, catch his breath, then try to tell what had happened.

"What happened, indeed!" Mr. McMurdo replied. "Sir, your sons—I don't blame William too much. He is young and merely did the bidding of his older brother. But John was the ringleader——"

"The ringleader in what?"

Finally the story came out. "The young scalawags—my scholars, mind you—tripped me, then tied me up hand and foot. I might have had to stay that way in the schoolhouse all night, had not a passer-by heard my calls for help."

As Judge Tyler listened, expressions of surprise, disbelief, and consternation passed over his face in quick succession. Usually John was such a gentle boy—and at that moment he was a very frightened one. The judge noticed that he was trembling, but he stood by his father's chair, looking the schoolmaster straight in the eye.

The judge pursed his lips. "Tell me, Mr. McMurdo, what brought on this rebellion?"

"I was punishing one of my scholars, trying to whip some sense into him."

John could not keep silent any longer. "He was whipping all the sense out of him instead. That is what he is always doing. It's a wonder he doesn't whip the sense out of *all* his scholars."

"Quiet!" Mr. McMurdo thundered, exactly as though he were standing behind his desk at school. Then he turned back to Judge Tyler. "I am here to punish your son."

"First, shall we listen to what he has to say?"

"You mean you will take his word against mine?" asked the schoolmaster.

"I did not say that, but the accused has the right to testify in his own behalf. John"—the judge's voice was stern—"were you the ringleader in the rebellion at school today?"

He sounded exactly as he did when he was trying a case in court. John swallowed hard. "Yes, sir," he said.

"I am waiting for your explanation."

"Well, at recess somebody drew a funny picture of Mr. McMurdo wearing a dunce cap—the kind he makes us wear sometimes——"

Little William started to laugh, but thought better of it after a glance from his father.

"Go on, John," said the judge.

"Mr. McMurdo did not know who did it, and so he said he was going to thrash every boy in school. We didn't do anything until he started on the little fellows. He was whipping a boy not even as big as William—whipping him so hard we just could not stand it any longer."

"See, he admits it," said Mr. McMurdo. "I shall now cut the switches with pleasure."

"That, sir," said Judge Tyler stiffly, "is a pleasure that is to be denied you."

"You do not intend to let me punish your son, or to punish him yourself?" the schoolmaster asked aghast.

The judge frowned. Many a guilty man who had appeared before him in court was familiar with that frown. Mr. McMurdo seemed vaguely uneasy as he got to his feet.

The judge also rose, still holding his book. He opened it to the picture of the state seal and handed it to his visitor.

"This is the motto of Virginia, sir—the motto of every true Virginian," Judge Tyler went on. "Read it for yourself. You know your Latin."

When Mr. McMurdo glanced at the page, his face grew red. For once he could think of no reply.

"*Sic semper tyrannis!*" Judge Tyler thundered. "That is all I have to say to you, sir. And now I bid you good day."

After the schoolmaster's disgruntled departure, father and son had a long talk. John was grateful for his father's understanding; the judge realized why he had rebelled. All the same, Judge Tyler warned, he might not be so lenient if John got into any more scrapes.

"You are nearly twelve," the father said, "and I believe it would be better for you to attend the grammar school of William and Mary College in Williamsburg. But remember, I shall expect you to behave yourself. I shall expect a good record."

"Oh, I will, sir, and I give you my word of honor that I will be good in all of my studies." John was so relieved that he was willing to promise almost anything. Then he added, in a burst of confidence, "I want to be a lawyer like you and Mr. Jefferson. So I know I am going to have to work hard."

A smile crinkled the corners of Judge Tyler's mouth. "I shall hold you to your promise, John, and I suggest you start by improving your handwriting. I can scarcely read it, and writing well is absolutely necessary for a lawyer. Look at the handwriting of Mr. Jefferson—how much care he takes to write handsomely."

That was not the last John heard about his handwriting. A few months after he arrived in Williamsburg to attend grammar school, he received a letter from his father. "I can't help telling you," the judge wrote, "how much I am mortified to find no improvement in your handwriting; neither do you conduct your lines straight which makes your letters look so abominable. It is an easy thing to correct this, and unless you do how can you be fit for law business? Writing and ciphering well are absolutely necessary and cannot be dispensed with."

John must have taken this letter to heart, for in time he learned to write a good hand. After finishing grammar school he went to William and Mary College, where he graduated with honors. He then studied law, just as he had planned, and by the time he was nineteen he had become a lawyer. Even the exacting Judge Tyler was pleased.

John Tyler also followed his father's example by going into politics, and in 1840 he was nominated for Vice President. That was the year when William Henry Harrison was running for President, and the refrain "Tippecanoe and Tyler, too" was heard throughout the country. The two candidates were elected by a big majority.

After the inauguration the following March, John Tyler returned to Williamsburg, where he now lived. A happily married man, he was looking forward to spending some time at home with his wife and their large family. "My children are my principal treasures," he once said. He was a devoted father, as devoted as Judge Tyler had been to him, and he held his own sons and daughters up to the same high standards.

One morning in April he was playing a game of horseshoe with two of his sons when a foam-flecked horse came dashing down the street. The Vice President looked up in surprise when he recognized the rider. It was the chief clerk of the State Department. The man dismounted and came toward him holding out a letter. John Tyler read it hastily.

"Is there anything wrong, Father?" asked Tazewell, his eleven-year-old son.

"This letter," his father replied in a low voice, "is from the members of President Harrison's Cabinet. The President is dead."

The news was a great shock. John Tyler had been fond of President Harrison, but there was no time to think of grief. A boat was waiting at Yorktown ten miles away to carry him to Washington as speedily as possible. Before he left he called his family together.

"Now, my children," he said, "during the next few years you are to occupy the home of the President of the United States. Remember you will be much in the public eye. May you never, as the President's family, do aught which you will regret when you shall be nothing higher than plain John Tyler's family."

Later that evening, standing by the railing of the boat looking up at the dark sky, he was thinking of the awesome responsibility that had come to him so suddenly. For the first time in American history a President had died in office, and the Vice President must take his place. Several years—busy, troubled years—were to pass before he would be "plain John Tyler" again.

THE TENTH PRESIDENT *at a Glance*

John Tyler

Born: March 29, 1790   *Died: January 18, 1862*

Early life. John Tyler was born at Greenway, the Tyler home in eastern Virginia near Charles City. John's father, Judge John Tyler, was governor of Virginia from 1808 to 1811. At 17, John was graduated from William and Mary College. He was admitted to the bar two years later. At 21, he was a member of the state legislature and at 27, of the U.S. House of Representatives. He was governor of Virginia (1825–1827) and in 1827 became a U.S. Senator.

From Democrat to Whig. Andrew Jackson was President during most of the time that Tyler was a U.S. Senator (1827–1836). Tyler, originally a Democrat, disagreed with some of Jackson's policies. Hoping to win the votes of other dissatisfied Democrats, the Whigs nominated Tyler for Vice President (1840). Tyler and William Henry Harrison, the Whig candidate for President, won the election.

As President (1841–1845). Tyler became President when Harrison died (April 4, 1841) after a month in office. Tyler's administration was filled with conflict. The Democrats were hostile because he had been elected as a Whig. The Whigs were hostile because he supported the Democrats on many issues. When he vetoed (1841) a banking bill that the Whigs had sponsored, all but one Cabinet member resigned. The Whigs did not nominate Tyler for a second term. One of his last acts as President was to sign (March, 1845) a Congressional resolution permitting Texas to join the U.S.

The President's family. John Tyler had 14 children—7 by his first wife and 7 by his second. His first wife, Letitia Tyler (1790–1842), was an invalid when he became President, and the Tylers' daughter-in-law, Priscilla Cooper Tyler, acted as White House hostess. Letitia died during her husband's second year in office. In 1844 the President married Julia Gardiner (1820–1889). One of their sons, Lyon Gardiner Tyler (1853–1935), became president of William and Mary College.

As Ex-President. Shortly before the Civil War, John Tyler presided at a peace conference held in Washington (February, 1861) in an attempt to save the Union. After the conference failed, Tyler supported the South.

Other happenings. When Tyler was President, the Webster-Ashburton Treaty (1842) settled the question of the boundary between Maine and Canada. Samuel Morse sent the first message by telegraph (1844). Charles Goodyear obtained a patent for vulcanizing rubber (1844).

The nation's growth. Florida was admitted to the Union as the 27th state (1845).

Ambitious JAMES POLK

The campfire made a tiny spot of light in the dark forest. A boy, his face thin and pinched in the red glow, held an iron skillet above the embers. "Supper's ready, Pa," he said.

"All right, Jim." Samuel Polk took the wooden platter from his son and sat down on a fallen log. "Um—bacon and cornbread! Being in the woods certainly gives a man an appetite."

There was no reply. Mr. Polk watched, a worried frown between his brows, as James only picked at his food. He had been a frail boy of eleven when the family had left North Carolina to make a new home in Tennessee. He was often in great pain, and at fourteen he had mounted his horse to ride beside his father on another long journey into Kentucky. There they had consulted a pioneer doctor who said that James had gallstones and must have an operation. There were no anesthetics in those days, but James had clenched his teeth hard, and after the operation he had begun to feel better.

He was still pale and thin, however. His father had brought him along on this surveying trip into the woods, hoping that the outdoor life would help. But James seemed more listless than usual.

"Don't you feel well?" asked Samuel Polk.

"Of course, Pa. I'm all right."

"Then what is wrong? Don't you like——"

The father paused, afraid that he already knew the answer to the question he was about to ask. A few weeks earlier, a merchant in the village near the Polk farm had offered to take the boy into the store and teach him the business. At the time it had seemed a good idea; James might never be strong enough to be a farmer.

"Don't you like working in the store?" Samuel Polk persisted.

"No, I don't," James blurted out. "I want more schooling, Pa. I want to learn to be a lawyer."

Mr. Polk seemed to be considering. "I grant you this," he said. "You are smart and would probably make a good lawyer. But that is a career that would take too much close study. You could not stand it because of your health."

"I am getting stronger."

"Yes, but not strong enough. It will be much better for you to be a merchant."

James set his lips in a thin, stubborn line. He was trying to think of the right words to make his father understand how dull it was in the store. He hated standing behind a counter, weighing sacks of brown sugar, measuring off yards of calico for the frontier women, and bargaining with the farmers who brought produce in to sell. Each week that dragged by had seemed longer than the week before.

"Please, Pa," he pleaded, "I don't want to be a merchant. I'll never be a good one."

Still Mr. Polk hesitated. There were few schools in Tennessee in 1810, but a new academy had been started near Murfreesboro some fifty miles away. James would need further study before he could enter. "Are you sure that you feel well enough?"

"At least, let me try. Let me go to the academy."

"All right," his father answered. "We shall ask the Reverend Dr. Henderson to teach you. He will get you ready for the academy. You seem to know what you want, James. You know exactly what you want."

James definitely did know what he wanted. He wanted to learn all of the things that he had not had a chance to learn before. He did so well at the academy that in two years time he was able to enter the sophomore class of the University of North Carolina. Three years later he was back in Tennessee. Although he was still frail, poor health had not kept him from graduating with honors. A short time later he began to study law in the office of Felix Grundy, a well-known lawyer in Nashville.

Here James met his father's friend Andrew Jackson. General Jackson was not only a famous soldier but one of the best lawyers in

Tennessee, and he took a great interest in Sam Polk's serious-minded son. By the time James was twenty-nine, he, too, was a successful lawyer, and General Jackson encouraged him to go into politics. The young man was elected to the United States House of Representatives and later served as governor of his state. In 1844 he hoped to be nominated for Vice President, but a bigger honor was in store for him. When the Democratic party held its convention, there were several candidates for President, but not one of them could get enough votes to be nominated. The delegates finally decided—probably at Andrew Jackson's suggestion and certainly with his blessing—to nominate James Knox Polk.

The nomination came as a big surprise to the country. Although James Polk had served in Congress for fourteen years, he was so quiet and retiring that many people had never heard of him. He was compared to the "dark horse" that starts late in a race and then wins it. For this reason he was called "the dark horse candidate." An amusing story was told about one loyal Democrat who, when he heard the news, seemed pleased.

"Hurrah for—" the man shouted, then hesitated, a puzzled expression on his face. "What did you say his name was?"

Such stories did not bother James Polk. He knew exactly what he wanted if he became President. He wanted to see his country grow. Since the majority of Americans agreed with him, he was elected.

The West was in the people's blood. After settlers began filling up the old Northwest Territory there were many other Americans who wanted to go even farther. Thousands of them had already crossed the plains and mountains to make new homes on the western rim of the continent. Most of them had settled in Oregon, the vast region north of California, but how much of this rich, fertile country belonged to Great Britain and how much of it to the United States had never been decided. The year after James Knox Polk became President a treaty was signed which set the boundary between the western part of Canada and the western part of the United States where it is today. And then more and more people went to Oregon to live.

There were also a few settlers who crossed the mountains into California. This sunny land still belonged to Mexico, and President Polk's first idea was to buy it. But the Mexicans, although they were poor, were a proud people, and they refused to sell. They had already lost Texas to the United States, and in 1846 a dispute about the boundary between Mexico and Texas helped to bring on the Mexican War.

Although many of the President's own countrymen criticized him,

James Polk, thin-lipped and taciturn, said little about his real reasons for going to war. He wanted California, but so did the leaders in several countries in Europe. James Knox Polk knew that in a war Mexico would be too weak to hold out against a powerful European foe. Nor was Mexico strong enough to hold out against the United States. In less than two years the Mexican War was over, and the Mexican government agreed to give up the disputed region in Texas. It also gave up New Mexico and California, and for this vast area the American government later paid Mexico fifteen million dollars. James Knox Polk had succeeded in doing what he set out to do. Again, he had gotten what he wanted.

Pleased though the President was by the outcome of the war, even he had no real notion of the riches he had opened to the American people. During the summer and fall of 1848 news trickled through to the eastern states that gold had been found in California. Travelers returning from the West Coast brought back reports so exaggerated that they were hard to believe.

"We do not know what to think of this gold story," read one article in a Washington newspaper. "All Washington is in a ferment with the news of the immense bed of gold which it is said has been discovered in California. Nothing else is talked about."

One day the following December the Secretary of War called at the White House. He opened a small bag as President Polk and members of the Cabinet looked on. Out of the bag tumbled a number of shining gold nuggets, which had just been received from the commander of the United States Army in California, together with the officer's official report.

"We have now the highest official authority," a New York newspaper announced a short time later, "that from thirty to fifty thousand dollars' worth of gold is being collected daily; and this by using only the most common and primitive means, such as willow baskets and tin kettles. The people, it is said, actually pick gold lumps from the crevices in the rocks with a penknife. The mania for emigrating to California is spreading in every direction."

Never had the country witnessed such excitement! Men from every state in the Union sold their farms, gave up their jobs and closed their stores to raise enough money for the long sea voyage to California. Others joined the throngs trekking westward across plains and mountains to hunt for gold.

Meanwhile a new President had been elected—General Zachary Taylor, who had become famous after winning several brilliant victories during the Mexican War. James Knox Polk, worn out with hard work, had not wanted a second term, but there were times when only his devoted wife seemed to realize how much he had accomplished for his country. One of the campaign songs about "Old Zach" was very popular:

"Polk thought that when the war began
How grand *he'd* be in story!
He little dreamed how Zach would rise
And carry off the glory."

There was precious little glory for James Knox Polk for a long time to come. He died only three months after he returned to Nashville. During the crowded years that followed, years leading to the tragedy of civil war, the American people were too much concerned with other matters to think much about him.

Yet during his final weeks at his home in Nashville he must have read a great deal in the newspapers about the Gold Rush to California; about the new settlers pouring into Texas; about the many American families who were crossing the continent in covered wagons to settle in Oregon. Perhaps in those last days James Knox Polk found comfort in the knowledge that he, more than any other one man, was responsible for the new boundaries of the United States—a nation that reached from sea to sea.

THE ELEVENTH PRESIDENT *at a Glance*

James Knox Polk

Born: November 2, 1795   *Died: June 15, 1849*

Early life. James Polk, the oldest of 10 children, was born on a farm near Pineville, N.C. In 1806 the Polk family left North Carolina and settled in the wilderness of the Duck River Valley, south of Nashville, Tenn. After attending school in Murfreesboro, Tenn., and graduating (1818) from the University of North Carolina, James studied law in Nashville. At 25 (1820), he began to practice law in Columbia, Tenn. He was a member of the state legislature (1823–1825), a Representative in Congress (1825–1839), and Governor of Tennessee (1839–1841) before being elected President in 1844. Polk was a Democrat.

As President (1845–1849). Three months after Texas was formally admitted to the Union as a state (December, 1845), some American soldiers were killed by Mexican troops in a border area claimed by both Texas and Mexico. Polk asked Congress to declare war. He said: "Mexico has passed the boundary of the United States, has invaded our territory, and shed American blood on American soil." Although many Americans felt that war was not justified, Congress declared war (May, 1846). After General Zachary Taylor's successful campaign in northern Mexico (1846–1847) and General Winfield Scott's capture of Mexico City (1847), Mexico signed a treaty (February, 1848) giving up its claims to the disputed area. Mexico also agreed to sell California and New Mexico for fifteen million dollars. The region then known as New Mexico included the present states of New Mexico, Nevada, Utah, large sections of Arizona and portions of Colorado and Wyoming. The same year that the U.S. declared war on Mexico (1846) a dispute with Great Britain over ownership of the Oregon region was settled peacefully. Polk agreed to a division that gave the U.S. an area which later formed the states of Washington, Oregon, Idaho, and parts of Montana and Wyoming.

The President's wife. Sarah Polk (1803–1891) was a handsome, stately woman whose intelligent advice was welcomed by the President.

Other happenings. When Polk was President, Elias Howe's sewing machine was patented (1846). Ether was used as an anesthetic in a major operation (1846). Salt Lake City was settled by the Mormons (1847). Discovery of gold (January, 1848) at Sutter's Mill, Cal., led to the Gold Rush of 1849.

The nation's growth. Three new states were admitted to the Union, making a total of 30: Texas (1845), Iowa (1846) and Wisconsin (1848).

ZACH TAYLOR *Becomes a Soldier*

The children had heard their father tell the story many times, but they never tired of hearing it again. "It was Christmas Eve and bitter cold," said Colonel Taylor. "The Redcoats thought they had General Washington's army sewed up in a pocket, for there we were camped on the frozen banks of the Delaware River."

"But you didn't stay there?" asked Zachary.

"No, Zach, we didn't stay there," the colonel assured him. "Some of the Hessian soldiers that George the Third had hired to fight the colonies were encamped in the town of Trenton on the other side of the river, and the General decided to give them a surprise party. The soldiers had fetched all the boats they could find, and that night we rowed across the Delaware. To be sure, the river was clogged with blocks of ice, and our hands were so numb with cold that we could hardly hold the oars. But we men decided that if General Washington could stand it, we could. And then——"

"And then"—one of the other children took up the story—"you captured all those Hessians."

"That we did, and we took heart again," the colonel went on. "Some of us had thought the war as good as lost, but after that night we knew that General Washington was a great soldier. We had faith that he would lead us to victory, and heaven be praised, that was what he did!"

Mrs. Taylor looked up with her quiet smile. "Time for bed, children. William, fetch your father's rifle and see that it is loaded. Hancock, are all the windows locked? Zach, make sure that the bars are in place across the doors. We don't want any Indians walking in and surprising *us* the way General Washington's soldiers surprised those Hessians."

She spoke as calmly as though there were no danger. Yet she had lived with danger ever since she and her husband had crossed the mountains to start a new home in this beautiful wild land of Kentucky. That had been in 1785, when the eldest son, Hancock, was four years old, William three, and Zach still a baby. Their father had cleared the land for a large farm a few miles from the village of Louisville, and the farm was prospering. The log cabin in which they had lived for the first few years had been replaced by a comfortable two-story brick house. A younger brother and sister had been added to the family, and the Taylors would have been quite happy had it not been for the Indians.

Sometimes, when it was known that the red men were on the warpath, the family took refuge with other settlers at Soldiers' Retreat. In this big stone house with walls five feet thick, belonging to their friend, Colonel Anderson, the settlers found it much easier to defend themselves. Other times the Indians made a surprise attack on a lonely house or cabin. Often they came at night, and the Taylors never knew what might happen before morning.

On that particular evening, though, Zach was not thinking about Indians, as he snuggled down in a warm featherbed in his room on the second floor. He was remembering the story his father had told. Someday, the boy decided, he was going to be a soldier—perhaps even a general like George Washington. He was almost asleep when Colonel Taylor entered, carrying a candle in one hand and a sheaf of papers in the other. He opened the door of Zach's clothes closet, and twisted one of the clothes hooks. A panel above the closet swung outward, revealing a secret compartment. This was where money, important papers, Mrs. Taylor's silver and other family valuables were kept.

An understanding look passed between the colonel and his son. If Indians ever should enter the house, or if robbers came, they would never guess that anything lay hidden behind that smooth walnut panel. Zach was glad that the secret compartment was in his room. It made him feel very important and responsible.

The next morning, after a breakfast of corn pone and wild berries, Hancock, William and Zach set out for school. The log schoolhouse had been built by their father, who had invited some of their young neighbors to share it with them. As usual, each of the boys carried a gun.

"Come straight home after school and do not wander from the trail," their mother warned. "Be very careful."

Of course, thought Zach, they always had to be careful. Yet that afternoon, after they left the schoolhouse, the woods looked so peaceful that it was hard to realize the Indians could ever cause trouble again. The late afternoon sun, sifting through the leaves, made a pattern of light and shade upon the grass. As the Taylor boys walked along the trail with several of their schoolmates, William could not help boasting a little about his father. Kentucky, once a part of Virginia, had recently been admitted to the Union as a separate state, and Colonel Taylor had helped to write the state constitution.

"Someday my father thinks that Kentucky will be a great state like Virginia," William said.

"Not if the red men kill all of the white people first," one of the neighbor girls retorted.

"General Anthony Wayne won't ever let them do that," said Zach warmly. "He and Lieutenant Harrison are fighting the Indians up north of the Ohio River. After they drive the Indians farther west, then all of this country will be safe. My father says so."

"Listen!" the same girl interrupted, and her face grew pale. "Did you hear a noise?"

"Only the snapping of a twig," the girl's brother answered.

A soft whistle came from the underbrush. "Is that a red man signaling?" she asked again.

"It is just a bobwhite." Again the brother tried to reassure her. "Isn't it, Zach?"

"I—I don't know," Zach replied, "but I think we ought to hurry."

The children had reached a fork in the path. One way led to the neighbors' cabin; the other led to the Taylor home. "Good-bye," said Zach. "We'll see you at school tomorrow."

The three brothers waved to their friends, then trudged along the path toward their own door. They had gone only a few steps when a piercing shriek cut through the afternoon quiet.

"Indians!"

Zach recognized the voices of his friends. Indians—and the Taylor cabin was still many yards away! In the distance he could hear his mother's faint call, thin and shrill with fright. "Hurry, children, hurry!"

For a moment Zach's blood seemed to freeze. The Indians had divided into two bands, and one band was pursuing the young Taylors. Each of the boys turned and fired his rifle, but they did not dare to stop and reload. Arrows were falling all around them; the Indians were gaining. Zach was a thickset boy. His legs were short, but he seemed to cover the ground in great flying leaps. There was another shower of arrows, and he zigzagged back and forth across the path to avoid being hit.

Now the house was just ahead. His mother, her face white and drawn, was standing in the doorway. Zach was in the lead, and just behind him he could hear the pounding feet of Hancock and Wiliam. Then with a final burst of speed, all three of them were inside the house. There were tears in Mrs. Taylor's eyes, tears of relief, as she slipped the huge bar into place across the door.

The Indians, when they found the heavy door barred against them, turned back, but later Zach learned that his schoolmates had been the victims of the red men's scalping knives. His eyes smarted, and anger burned in his heart. If only he were old enough to join General Wayne and fight the Indians!

One day in the late summer of 1794, when Zach was ten years old, his father came home with news. "General Wayne has won a great victory at the Battle of Fallen Timbers," he said, "and sent the Indians fleeing into the forest. They must know by now that they cannot drive the white men back across the mountains."

"God be praised," said Mrs. Taylor.

"Hurrah!" shouted Zach, tossing his coonskin cap into the air.

The victory at Fallen Timbers, important though it was, did not end the troubles of the pioneers. The Indians continued to raid their homes, but as time went by the raids gradually ceased. The red men found new hunting grounds farther west, and more and more white people went to Kentucky to live. It was well on its way to becoming the great state dreamed of by Colonel Taylor and other pioneers.

In the meantime, Zach's boyhood wish had come true. A distant cousin, James Madison, the Secretary of State under President Jefferson, obtained a commission in the United States army for his young relative. For the next forty years Zachary Taylor was an officer in the service of his country. After fighting in the War of 1812 and in several wars against the Indians, he became a general.

In the rough old brown coat and battered hat that Zachary Taylor liked to wear, he never looked very much like a general. But he was kind and gallant and brave, and his soldiers loved him. "Old Zach," they called him and, sometimes "Old Rough and Ready," because he was always ready, no matter how great the peril.

The greatest test of General Taylor's courage came toward the end of his long army career. During the Mexican War, at the Battle of Buena Vista in Mexico, he faced an army that outnumbered his own forces more than four to one. Shortly before the battle began, Zachary Taylor received a message from the Mexican commander, Santa Anna, demanding that he surrender.

"General Taylor never surrenders," the American commander replied.

For ten hours the battle raged. It seemed impossible that 4,700 Americans could hold out against 20,000 Mexicans. Yet, as a result of General Taylor's wise strategy and the pluck and bravery of his men, the enemy was defeated. Back in the United States, "Old Zach" became a hero overnight. The next year, when the Whig party needed a popular candidate, he was nominated for President.

But was he fitted for this high office? He may have doubted it himself, for he knew nothing about government. The American voters, however, were impressed by his courage and common sense, and in 1848 he was elected President.

"General Taylor," said one admirer, "was able and honest and could be expected to do the right thing."

In the White House General Taylor was the same gentle, kindly man his soldiers had loved and admired. He became President at a very difficult time. The North and South had been quarreling about slavery, and by 1850 the quarrel had grown so serious there was grave danger it might lead to civil war. Some of the Southern leaders warned that their states might secede, that is, leave the Union, if certain laws were passed to which the South objected.

Zachary Taylor then showed the same firmness he had shown on the battlefield. Although he was a Southerner himself, he announced that he would put down any attempt at secession—by force, if necessary.

"There will be local questions to disturb our peace," he said in one speech, "but after all, we must fall back on Washington's farewell advice and preserve the Union at all hazards."

General Washington, his boyhood hero, was often in his thoughts during those troubled days in the early summer of 1850. On the Fourth of July the people of the national capital attended a big celebration at the monument then being erected to the memory of the first President. President Taylor, seated on the platform that had been erected in front of the monument, was listening to a speech by a United States Senator.

"Let me repeat George Washington's solemn words," the Senator was saying. " 'The unity of government which constitutes you one people, is a main pillar in the edifice of your real independence; of your safety; of your prosperity; of that very liberty which you so highly prize.' May these parting admonitions of the illustrious Washington sink deep into the hearts of his countrymen of the present generation. I entreat you, at this moment of awful peril to the republic, that you do your duty to the Constitution and the Union."

The President seemed deeply moved as he arose to congratulate the speaker. "The unity of government which constitutes you one people," George Washington had said. "And one people we must remain," thought Zachary Taylor.

He turned again to look at the Washington Monument. It was only a third the height it would be when it was finished. But perhaps in his imagination he could see the high white marble shaft which one day would rise high above the city.

THE TWELFTH PRESIDENT *at a Glance*

Zachary Taylor

Born: November 24, 1784   *Died: July 9, 1850*

Early life and army career. Zachary Taylor was born in Orange County, Va. When he was a baby, his family moved to the wilderness of Kentucky, where Zachary grew up. At 24 (1808), Zachary was commissioned first lieutenant in the U.S. Army. He fought in the War of 1812, the Black Hawk War (1832), and the Seminole War (1836–1837), gradually advancing to the rank of brigadier general.

As a Mexican War hero. In 1846, after driving Mexican troops from an area claimed by both Texas and Mexico, Taylor, now a major general, crossed the Rio Grande into northern Mexico and captured the town of Monterey. In 1847 he won a victory against great odds at Buena Vista, Mexico. This important victory made General Taylor a national hero, and, though he had previously taken no part in politics, the Whig party nominated him for President (1848).

As President (1849–1850). When Taylor became President, it had not yet been decided whether slavery should be allowed in the vast areas acquired (1848) from Mexico. Northerners disagreed with the many Southerners who wanted slavery permitted in the entire new region, which included California and a large part of the Southwest.

When California asked (1849) to be admitted to the Union as a free state, President Taylor, though a Southerner, wanted Congress to grant the request. Congress was still debating the matter when Taylor died, after 16 months in office.

The President's family. The President's wife, Margaret Taylor (1788–1852), did not enjoy entertaining, and the Taylors' youngest daughter, Mrs. Elizabeth Bliss, acted as White House hostess. Another daughter, Sarah, married Jefferson Davis in 1835 but died long before her father became President.

Other happenings. When Taylor was President, many thousands of gold-seekers took the overland trails or the sea routes to California (1849). A compromise plan suggested (January, 1850) by Henry Clay for settling the question of slavery in California and the other areas obtained from Mexico gave rise to a series of famous Senate debates. John C. Calhoun of South Carolina opposed the plan; Daniel Webster of Massachusetts supported it (March, 1850). Later, other important senators took part in the controversy, which continued into the next administration.

MILLARD FILLMORE *Learns a Trade*

Millard Fillmore sank his plow into the hard clay soil. The sun was very hot, and he paused to wipe the perspiration from his face. Glancing toward the cabin where the Fillmore family lived, in western New York state, he saw his father coming through the door. Mr. Fillmore was carrying a pail of water. He filled a dipper and held it out to his son.

"That tastes mighty good," said the boy.

"Come over and sit down in the shade," the father suggested. "I want to talk to you."

Millard smiled gratefully. As the eldest son, he had a great deal of responsibility. This was a new farm, and he had helped his father to clear the land of timber, to plow and plant and to do all of the other work that needed to be done to get a new farm started.

"I have been thinking it over," Mr. Fillmore was saying, "and I do not want you to go through the same hardships that I have known. I don't want you to be a farmer. Now that you are fourteen, you should start learning a trade."

"But, Pa, I'd rather go into a profession."

"I am sorry, son, but that would take money. You know that I cannot afford the training you would need."

Millard nodded. Why, his father could not even afford to let him attend school, except in winter. There was a log schoolhouse in the hamlet of Newhope a mile away, and here Millard had studied writing and arithmetic for a few months each year. The trouble was that with the coming of spring he had to stop to work on the farm again.

Then before he had a chance to return to school, he would forget much of what he had learned the year before.

"What trade did you have in mind, Pa?" he said aloud.

"Benjamin Hungerford who used to live in Newhope came to see me today," Mr. Fillmore replied. "Ben has moved to Sparta, where he is now a wool-carder and maker of cloth. He is back in Newhope to buy dye-goods and other materials that he needs in his business."

Millard squirmed uneasily. Benjamin Hungerford was a harsh man, with a lean, cruel face. The boy had never liked him.

"Ben has offered to take you into his shop for a three-months' trial," Mr. Fillmore went on. "If you are both suited, you may become his apprentice."

The man paused, noticing the look of despair on Millard's face. "Why, son, Mr. Hungerford has offered to teach you the business, and someday you can open your own shop. This is your chance to make something of yourself."

"All right, Pa," said Millard in a resigned voice. "I'll go whenever Mr. Hungerford is ready."

Mr. Hungerford was ready the next morning. His wagon was packed so full with the supplies he had purchased, and the load was so heavy, that Millard had to walk. It was a hundred miles to Sparta, and the fall winds blew sharp and chill as he trudged along in his worn jacket. After several weary days on the road, they reached the Hungerford home. There was salt pork for supper that night, and Millard only toyed with his food. He did not like salt pork, but there was also another reason for the strange feeling in his stomach. This was his first time away from home, and he was homesick.

The next morning when he entered the shop, the other apprentices were already at work. One seventeen-year-old boy picked up a big bunch of wool, greasy and full of dirt, just as it had come from the back of a sheep, and began to wash it with soap and water. Another apprentice fed the tangled fibers into a machine where roller after roller with comblike teeth straightened out the snarled mass. At the other end of the carding machine a third apprentice was removing the spools on which was wound the wool, now ready to be spun into thread.

Mr. Hungerford turned to Millard. "I want you to go outside and chop wood for the charcoal pit," he said.

Millard looked surprised. He did not see how chopping wood could help him learn to be a cloth dresser.

"Charcoal is very necessary in dressing cloth," Mr. Hungerford explained stiffly. "After you go into business for yourself there may come a time when you can't buy charcoal. Then you will be glad that I taught you how to make your own."

"Very well, sir."

Millard shouldered his ax and started for the wood lot. By night he ached in every muscle.

Several weeks went by, and Millard was still chopping. Mr. Hungerford was taking advantage of him, he decided, because he was the youngest apprentice. He had agreed to work for three months without pay with the understanding that he was to start learning a trade, and he was not being given a chance to learn. He still knew nothing about carding wool or dressing cloth. When he protested, Mr. Hungerford started to beat him, and Millard's temper suddenly blazed. The boy faced his master, ax in hand. Ben Hungerford was so taken aback that he turned and walked away.

"He is just an old tyrant," thought Millard fiercely, "but I guess many apprentices have a hard time. They are mistreated because they are young and poor."

Some good came out of the quarrel, however. From then on, Millard was allowed to work in the shop, but he counted the days until he could go home. The morning that his three months were up, he placed some bread and dried venison in his knapsack and started down the road alone. This time the one-hundred-mile walk seemed short, because he knew that at the end of the journey he would find his father and mother waiting.

The next year, Mr. Hungerford came to ask Millard to return to Sparta, but the boy firmly shook his head. His father found him another place in a cloth dresser's shop in Newhope, and Millard liked the new arrangement much better. He was to work as an apprentice from June until December of each year for the next five years. He would receive a small wage and learn the business. During the spring he was to help on the family farm and—what pleased him much more—he could go to school again during the short winter session.

When Millard was eighteen, he joined a small circulating library in the town. Except for a few books at school and the Bible at home, he had never had a chance to do much reading. Now as he pored over volume after volume, the big words puzzled him. Out of his small earnings he bought a dictionary, and propped it up against a desk in the shop. In his work of feeding the machine and removing the reels, he had to pass the desk every two minutes. It took only an instant to glance at a word and read its definition.

"Ambition," he said, "the desire for fame and honor."

"Ambition!" The word was often in his thoughts as he went about his tasks. Each book that he read whetted his ambition and made him want to read others. One day when he was visiting in another town close by, he passed the office of Judge Walter Wood. The judge was a well-to-do Quaker lawyer, with many farms and tenants in the surrounding country. But what especially interested Millard was the judge's big library. Judge Wood owned dozens of books, mostly about law. Millard wished that he had a chance to read them. He was still thinking about those books when he returned home for dinner.

His mother smiled at him across the table. "Millard," she said, "folks have been telling your pa that, given a chance, you could be something more important than a wool-carder."

"Yes, Ma." Millard looked surprised—and hopeful.

"Well, your pa decided to go see Judge Wood," Mrs. Fillmore went on. "The Judge says he will take you into his office on trial, until you have to go back to your apprenticeship next June. He is getting old and needs a young fellow to help him in looking after his farms. In your spare time, you can read the law books in his office."

Millard could hardly believe his good fortune. He was to have his chance at last.

Judge Wood liked his new assistant and suggested that the boy serve him the year round, and study law. For a small cash sum the wool-carder to whom Millard was apprenticed agreed to let him go, and he settled down in earnest to learn to be a lawyer. No one was more pleased at this change in fortune than Mr. Fillmore. One day, glancing at the boy with his brown head bent above a book, he turned to Mrs. Fillmore.

"Wife," he chuckled, "who knows but that our Millard will some day be President?"

Mr. Fillmore was not the only one who had faith in his son's future. A short time later, Millard met a young schoolteacher, Abigail Powers, who helped him with his studies. For a while he was able to teach school part of the time to pay for further law training. He and Abigail were married, and she also went on teaching several years, so that her handsome young husband could get ahead with his career. His advancement was rapid. He became a successful lawyer in Buffalo, went into politics, and finally was elected Vice President of the United States.

And then Zachary Taylor died very suddenly, only a few days after he had attended the Fourth of July ceremonies at the Washington Monument. He had been so popular that he was not an easy man to follow. Soon after Millard Fillmore had become President, he asked Edward, a White House servant who had been devoted to General Taylor, to go with him to inspect a carriage. A gentleman who was moving from the city had offered the carriage for sale.

"How do you like it, Edward?" the new President asked.

"It is a very handsome vehicle," was Edward's opinion.

"Yes, and it is just what I want," Millard Fillmore replied. "But do you think it would do for the President of the United States to ride in a second-hand carriage?"

"Why, your Excellency," Edward replied with a twinkle in his eyes, "aren't you a second-hand President?"

The new President was amused, and laughed heartily when, later, he told the story on himself.

His sense of humor was not much help, however, in solving some of the problems during the troubled weeks that followed his inauguration. Earlier that same year several laws, known as the Compromise of 1850, had been suggested in Congress. It was hoped that these laws would settle the quarrel between North and South, but the debates in Congress had grown more and more bitter as the weeks went by. President Taylor had been opposed to parts of the compromise, but President Fillmore signed them.

He even signed the Fugitive Slave Law which enraged many people in the Northern states. Sometimes slaves escaped from slave states into states and territories that were free, and many sympathetic white men and women wanted to help them. But the new law provided for severe penalties for anyone who tried to prevent the return of a runaway slave to his master. Perhaps in signing this law, the new President hoped to avoid a civil war between the two sections of the country. Whatever his reasons, his decision made him very unpopular, and he was not nominated for a second term.

Another act of President Fillmore's was more successful. After California was added to the Union and the nation reached from sea to sea, the American people began to think more about the lands on the far side of the Pacific. Millard Fillmore was anxious for the United States to trade with Japan, a beautiful island kingdom which for many years only a few foreigners had even been allowed to visit. Commodore Matthew C. Perry of the Navy was placed in command of a squadron of war ships, and toward the end of 1852 he set sail from the east coast of the United States on a voyage that was to carry him halfway around the world. With him he carried many handsome presents, among them a rosewood box. In this box there was a letter inscribed on parchment to the emperor of Japan from President Fillmore.

"Great and good friend," the letter read, "I have directed Commodore Perry to assure your imperial majesty that I entertain the kindest feelings toward your majesty's person and government, and that I have no other object in sending him to Japan but to propose to your imperial majesty that the United States and Japan should live in friendship and have commercial intercourse with each other.

"The United States of America reach from ocean to ocean, and our Territory of Oregon and State of California lie directly opposite to the dominions of your imperial majesty. I am desirous that our two countries should trade with each other for the benefit of both Japan and the United States."

By the time this letter reached Japan, Millard Fillmore was no longer President, but he lived to see treaties of friendship and trade established between the two countries. He probably did not realize— few people did at the time—how far-reaching these treaties were to be in their results. Once Japan had begun to trade with the people of the United States and other Western lands, it learned from them and became a modern nation almost overnight. For the American people, too, the treaties marked the beginning of a new interest in distant parts of the world.

THE THIRTEENTH PRESIDENT *at a Glance*

Millard Fillmore

Born: January 7, 1800   *Died: March 8, 1874*

Early life. Millard Fillmore was born in a log cabin on his father's farm in Cayuga County, N.Y. After a meager schooling and an apprenticeship as a wool-carder he began to study law (1819) while teaching school to support himself. In 1830 he moved to Buffalo, N.Y., where he built up a successful law practice.

Political career. Fillmore served in the N.Y. state legislature (1829–1831) and in the U.S. House of Representatives (1833–1835; 1837–1843). He was elected Vice President on the Whig ticket in 1848, and became President when Zachary Taylor died (July, 1850).

As President (1850–1853). Two months after Fillmore took office, Congress passed the long-debated measures known as the Compromise of 1850. The compromise provided for admitting California to the Union as a free state and for organizing the other areas acquired (1848) from Mexico into territories, without laws either for or against slavery. A strong fugitive slave law was also part of the compromise.

The President's wife. When Abigail Fillmore (1798–1853), a former schoolteacher, found that there were no books in the executive mansion, she started the first White House library.

Other happenings. When Fillmore was President, Harriet Beecher Stowe's antislavery book, *Uncle Tom's Cabin,* was published (1852). The death of the great Whig leaders, Henry Clay and Daniel Webster, in 1852 contributed to the breakup of the Whig party during the next two years.

The nation's population and growth. The population was over 23,000,000 (census of 1850). California was admitted to the Union (1850), bringing the total number of states to 31.

Mischievous FRANK PIERCE

Frank shook himself like a young puppy. But the water was still dripping from his clothes as he walked up the path to the log cottage near the river. A kind-faced woman opened the door in answer to his knock.

"Why, Franklin Pierce, what happened to you?"

"I fell in the river," he explained ruefully. "Whatever will my mother say?"

"I declare," the woman exclaimed. "Come right in and let me have your jacket. Take off those breeches, too; they are wringing wet. Fanny will get you a blanket, and you can wrap up in that while I dry and iron your clothes."

"Oh, thank you, ma'am." The boy grinned in relief and walked, dripping, into the kitchen.

Fanny, the woman's daughter, a girl about eight, went over to the clothes chest and threw back the lid. She knew Frank at school, but this was the first time he had ever visited in the little log house. He himself lived in a big square mansion surrounded by gardens, and was the son of General Benjamin Pierce. General Pierce had fought in the Revolution and was one of the most important men in New Hampshire, but that was not the reason Fanny liked Frank. She liked him for himself, as did most people in the little town of Hillsborough. He was good-natured and full of fun, and though he did a lot of roughhousing with the other boys, he was always doing nice things, too. Once he had stayed in at recess to help Fanny with her arithmetic.

"Here is the blanket," she said, blushing, then hurried from the room. When she returned, she found Frank wrapped in the warm folds while he huddled close to the fireplace. He watched as Fanny's mother placed a big flatiron over the embers to heat.

"You won't tell Mama, will you?" he asked anxiously. "She wanted me to keep my clothes nice. This is election day, you know, and we have company coming for dinner."

"I thought as much, with your pa such a big man," the woman replied. "Are you going to be a Democratic-Republican when you grow up?"

"Of course." Frank smiled up at her shyly, and repeated his question. "You're not going to tell Mama, are you?"

"Seems to me," the woman replied, setting up her ironing board, "that Mrs. Pierce must be plenty busy today. So we'll not worry her by sending her son home looking like a drownded rat. You just set your mind at rest. Fanny and I will have you looking spic-and-span in no time."

Now that he was no longer worried about discovery at home, Frank was soon laughing with Fanny. She held up his jacket and his breeches before the flame to dry, then handed the garments to her mother to be pressed. An hour later, he was walking down the path, his arms swinging free, his lips puckered in a whistle. When he reached the road, he turned to wave.

"Thank you," he called. "Thank you again."

"Ain't he an agreeable little fellow?" said Fanny's mother, watching from the doorway. "Handsome, too, but so happy-go-lucky I don't wonder he is always getting into mischief."

Frank remained a happy-go-lucky boy throughout most of his school days. At twelve he went away to school and at sixteen entered Bowdoin College up in Maine. Here he made many friends, including Nathaniel Hawthorne and Henry Wadsworth Longfellow, both of whom were to become famous writers. None of the students was any brighter or learned more easily than Franklin Pierce, but he seldom studied. The result was that the beginning of his junior year found him at the foot of his class, and he was so overcome with shame that he resolved never to attend another recitation. Perhaps, he declared hopefully, the faculty would then expel him, and he could go home.

Instead, his teachers decided to ignore his absence and his friends begged him to return to his classes. Franklin, moved by their concern for his welfare, finally agreed.

"But if I do," he told them, "you shall see a change."

And he did change. During his last two years he worked so hard that he graduated third in his class, and the experience seemed to mark a turning point in his life. After college Franklin studied law and became a successful lawyer. He was elected to Congress. When the Mexican War broke out in 1846 he enlisted as a private and within a few months was promoted to a brigadier general. Success came easily to him. His old friend Nathaniel Hawthorne spoke of the "fascination of manner," the source of which lay "deep in the kindliness of his nature."

"Few men," Hawthorne added, "possess anything like it."

Finally, in 1852, when Franklin Pierce was nominated President, most of his old neighbors were pleased and proud. One day he received a letter from his childhood schoolmate, Fanny.

"Neither have I forgot," she wrote, "when you was a boy with a little misfortune by falling into the River one Lexion Day you came to my mother & she dried your clothes & ironed them and you did not wish to let your mother know your misfortune, my mother said you was so agreeable in conversation that day she almost fell in love with you."

Fanny and her mother were not alone in their admiration for Franklin Pierce; but a few of his old friends seemed worried. During the election campaign a traveler stopped at a New Hampshire inn. "What about this man, Pierce?" the traveler asked. "Would he make a good President?"

The innkeeper hesitated. "Up here, he seems right smart," he finally replied. "But spread him over the whole country and I'm afraid he will be very thin in spots."

It was said that Franklin Pierce did not really want to be President; that he had accepted the nomination reluctantly. Perhaps he himself doubted his ability to hold that high office, but he was elected by a large majority. Then two months before his inauguration he and his wife, Jane, suffered a tragic loss. Their thirteen-year-old son, their last surviving child, was killed in a train wreck before their eyes. The new President was a deeply troubled man when he entered the White House, not only because of his personal loss and the grief of his wife, but because of the grave problems he knew he would be expected to solve.

That he would fail to solve them most of his fellow Americans became convinced, after he had been in office only a few months. They considered him weak and inefficient. Many of his most staunch admirers in the past turned against him when he signed the Kansas-Nebraska Act. This law, passed by Congress in 1854, would make it possible for slavery to spread to much of the free territory out West, and people who had thought the slavery question settled forever were bitter and angry. Instead of settling the quarrel between North and South, as some people had hoped, the new law only made the quarrel worse.

Indirectly, and unintentionally, President Pierce accomplished something else. For out in Illinois there was a lawyer named Lincoln. He was no longer interested in politics, or so he thought, but the Kansas-Nebraska Act aroused him to action. He began to make speeches warning people of the danger if slavery should be allowed in the territories that were still free. These speeches made Abraham Lincoln famous.

As for Franklin Pierce, he was undoubtedly convinced that the Kansas-Nebraska Act might keep the Union from breaking up. "I do not believe that I ever saw a day," he said toward the close of his life, "when I would not have made any possible personal sacrifice to maintain the Constitution of my country and the Union based upon it."

His tragedy was that charm is not enough to make a strong President. A bigger man was needed to lead the nation in a time of crisis.

THE FOURTEENTH PRESIDENT *at a Glance*

Franklin Pierce

Born: November 23, 1804   *Died: October 8, 1869*

Early life. Franklin Pierce was born in Hillsborough, N.H. His father, General Benjamin Pierce, fought in the American Revolution and later served as governor of New Hampshire. Franklin attended Bowdoin College in Maine, and after his graduation (1824) studied law.

Early career. At the age of 24 Pierce was elected to the New Hampshire legislature. Later he served in the U.S. Congress as a Representative (1833–1837) and as a Senator (1837–1842). During the Mexican War he enlisted as a private but soon became a brigadier general (1847). In 1852 Pierce was the Democratic nominee for President, and won the election by a large majority.

As President (1853–1857). In 1854 Congress passed the Kansas-Nebraska Act, which established Kansas and Nebraska as territories and allowed the settlers to decide the slavery question for themselves.

This meant that Kansas and Nebraska could later enter the Union as slave states if the majority of settlers so desired. People from nearby slave states immediately began to pour into Kansas, hoping to make it a slave state. Great numbers of Northerners, determined that Kansas should be a free state, soon followed. The territory became known as "bleeding Kansas" because of the conflicts between the two groups of settlers. Elsewhere in the U.S. people took sides about Kansas and heatedly discussed the whole question of slavery. Because the President had supported the Kansas-Nebraska Act, many blamed him for the increased tension, and Pierce was not renominated.

The President's wife. Jane Pierce (1806–1863), having lost her three sons by the time her husband became President, was a very sad White House hostess, but was much admired for her quiet charm.

Other happenings. When Pierce was President, the U.S. paid Mexico ten million dollars for land along the southern border of the present states of Arizona and New Mexico (Gadsden Purchase, 1853). The Republican party was started (1854) by men opposed to the extention of slavery into any of the U.S. territories. The already declining Whig party was completely disrupted by quarrels over the Kansas-Nebraska Act (1854), and by the time the Republicans held their first national convention (Philadelphia, 1856) many former Whigs had joined the new party.

JAMES BUCHANAN'S *Second Chance*

The boy saw his father open the letter and noticed that his face grew stern. "This is about you, James," said Mr. Buchanan. "Read it for yourself."

James was spending his summer vacation at his home near Mercersburg, Pennsylvania, but he expected to return in a few days to Dickinson College for his senior year. He gave a start when he glanced at the sheet of note paper in his hand. It was signed by Dr. Davidson, the head of the college.

"I can't understand it," said Mr. Buchanan. "You, a boy of seventeen, a young man, rather——"

James kept his eyes on the floor, but he could not shut out the sound of his father's voice. "Dr. Davidson has asked that you not return to school," Mr. Buchanan went on. "Your mother will be heartbroken when she learns that you have been expelled. You are bright enough. Look at me, James, and tell me why this happened. Why?"

James turned and rushed from the room. He could not bear to see the expression on his father's face, his kind, gentle father who had worked hard to give him a chance to go to college. One word kept pounding in his ears. "Why?" Mr. Buchanan had asked. James hardly knew himself. Perhaps he had been afraid that the other students would not like him if he seemed to work too hard. He had wanted to be popular, and instead of studying he had spent most of his time playing pranks.

And now he had brought disgrace on himself and his parents. He finally decided to talk with Dr. King, pastor of the church the Buchanans attended. He paused before the manse, his hand on the gate. It was not going to be easy to admit how he had wasted his time, but Dr. King was a trustee of Dickinson College. If anyone could help him, Dr. King could.

The elderly pastor heard his story in silence. "I believe you, James," he said finally. "I believe you are truly repentant. If I ask Dr. Davidson to take you back, will you pledge me your word of honor to keep out of mischief? Will you promise to do better work than you did last year?"

"Indeed, I will, sir," James replied. "If I can have a second chance, I'll make good use of it, I promise you."

As a result of Dr. King's letter to Dr. Davidson, James was allowed to return to college. He studied so hard that he had no time to get into mischief, no time for pranks. It was the custom of the college to award a "First Honor" and a "Second Honor" to the two most deserving members of the senior class, and James's heart was set on winning one of them. Toward the end of the year he was one of several candidates who appeared before the faculty to take a public examination. The professors asked questions—hard, searching questions—about the courses the students had been taking, and James answered each question correctly. When he left the room he felt confident that he was going to win the highest honor that his college had to give. How proud his parents would be!

And then the announcement was made. The faculty had decided to give the First Honor to one of James's friends. The Second Honor was awarded to another student. It was true that young Buchanan had answered every question correctly at the public examination. His grades and his conduct during his senior year had been excellent, but the faculty was thinking of his earlier record.

"It would have a bad tendency," they said, "to confer an honor of the college upon a student who had shown so little respect for the rules of the college and for the professors."

James was crushed when he heard the news. His friends, knowing how hard he had worked, were indignant, and several of them threatened to stay away from the Commencement altogether. This James refused to allow them to do, but he himself was determined to take no part in the exercises. Each student in the graduating class was supposed to write an oration. If James had won the First Honor, to which he felt he was entitled, he would have appeared first on the program. If he could not appear first, he declared proudly, he would not appear at all.

Then he received a note from one of his professors, urging him to change his mind. James, touched by the professor's kindness, took the unfinished oration from his desk and started to work on it again.

That evening he wrote to his parents. It was a hard letter to write, but he had to let them know what had happened. They had counted on his winning the First Honor, or at least the second one, and he knew how disappointed they would be. A few days later, when he received his father's answer, he was almost afraid to open it.

"I hope you will have fortitude enough to surmount these things," Mr. Buchanan wrote. "Your great consolation is in yourself. I approve of your conduct in being prepared with the oration; and if upon delivery, it be good sense well spoken, your audience will think well of it, whether it be spoken first, last, or otherwise."

He had won back his father's respect, thought James gratefully, then turned the page to read the last sentence: "We anticipate the pleasure of seeing you shortly, when I hope these little clouds will be dissipated."

Heartened and encouraged by this letter, James did well when the time came to give his Commencement oration. And as the years passed, his college had good reason to feel proud of him. He became interested in politics and government and served his country with distinction in Congress, as Secretary of State, and as a diplomat in Russia and Great Britain.

After more than forty years of public life, it was James Buchanan's misfortune—and a misfortune for the country—that he was elected President at a time when only a very great leader might have been able to avoid the tragedy of the coming Civil War.

In 1857, the year James Buchanan went to the White House, the quarrel between North and South was rapidly coming to a head, and in trying to please both sides he pleased neither. No state had a right to secede, he said. But almost in the same breath he insisted that the Federal government did not have the power to force a state to remain in the Union. Strangely enough, many of the people who blamed the President for lack of firmness were equally in doubt as to the wisest course to take.

As President, James Buchanan never had a second chance, nor did he want it. At the inauguration of Abraham Lincoln, he was a tragic figure—nearly seventy years old, wizened and bent, knowing that he was considered a failure.

"If you are as anxious to come into the White House as I am to leave it," he told his great successor, "this is certainly the happiest day of your life."

THE FIFTEENTH PRESIDENT *at a Glance*

James Buchanan

Born: April 23, 1791   *Died: June 1, 1868*

Early life. James Buchanan was born near Mercersburg, Pa. He was graduated from Dickinson College, Carlisle, Pa., at 18 (1809). He then studied law and was admitted to the bar in 1812. He was a volunteer in the War of 1812 but saw no active service.

Political and diplomatic career. At 23 (1814), Buchanan became a member of the Pennsylvania legislature. He was a Representative in Congress (1821–1831), U.S. minister to Russia (1832–1834), and U.S. Senator (1834–1845). As President Polk's Secretary of State (1845–1849) he helped work out with England the division of the Oregon country. He was U.S. minister to Great Britain (1853–1856). In 1856 Buchanan was the Democratic nominee for President, and in the election he defeated John Frémont of California, the first Republican presidential candidate.

As President (1857–1861). Buchanan's term in office was filled with mounting tension between the North and the South. The Supreme Court's "Dred Scott" decision (1857), stating that Congress did not have the right to prohibit slavery in any of the territories, infuriated most Northerners. In 1859 a rash attempt by the antislavery agitator John Brown to arm the slaves for an insurrection ended in failure. But the attempt angered and frightened the Southerners and added to the dangerous friction between the slave states and the free states. Then the worst crisis of all came when South Carolina carried out its threats to withdraw from the Union (December 20, 1860) and six other Southern states seceded in the next few weeks. Buchanan was unwilling to use force to prevent the secession of the Southern states and left the problem to his successor, Abraham Lincoln.

The White House hostess. Harriet Lane (1833–1903) was a popular hostess for her uncle, James Buchanan, who was a bachelor.

Other happenings. When Buchanan was President, the Lincoln-Douglas Debates (1858) made Abraham Lincoln a national figure. E. L. Drake's discovery of oil near Titusville, Pa. (1859) started the first oil boom. The Pony Express was established between Missouri and California (1860). A peace conference, meeting in Washington, D.C. (February, 1861), failed in its attempt to hold the Union together. Jefferson Davis was elected president of the newly formed Confederate States of America (February, 1861).

The nation's population and growth. The population was almost 31,500,000 (census of 1860). Three new states were admitted to the Union: Minnesota (1858), Oregon (1859), and Kansas (1861).

ABE LINCOLN'S *First Case*

Abe Lincoln and his friend Joe Gentry were on their way to the log schoolhouse. Nearly everybody in Pigeon Creek, a little pioneer settlement in Indiana, was going. This was the day of the trial. The justice of the peace was coming up from Rockport, the county seat, and he was bringing two lawyers with him.

"Ain't it exciting?" asked Joe.

He had to throw back his head to look up at Abe who, at seventeen, was taller than most men. Both boys wore buckskin breeches and coonskin caps. Joe was fourteen, but in contrast to Abe, looked much younger. "I reckon it is exciting," Abe admitted, "but it bothers me to have two friends set the law on each other—and all because of an old gray goose."

Strangely enough, it was a goose that had started the trouble. Jake Adams and Joshua Blake lived on adjoining farms, and each owned a flock of geese, which often mingled as they waddled over the meadows. One evening a goose belonging to Jake was missing, and he rushed over to Joshua's cabin to see if it was there.

"No," said Joshua, counting his own flock. "I have just the right number."

"Can't be," Jake insisted. "I see my goose right over there."

"That big gray one?" asked Josh. "Why, that's mine. What do you mean, trying to walk off with one of my geese?"

The argument had grown so bitter by the time Jake left that he was threatening to "have the law" on his old friend the next time a justice of the peace came up from Rockport to try cases at the schoolhouse. He would hire a lawyer to see that he got his goose back. Josh retorted that he would hire a lawyer, too. Unfortunately, the dispute had spread until most of the people in Pigeon Creek were taking sides. Everyone was talking about the "Gray Goose case" and wondering how it was going to end.

"Pa thinks Jake Adams is right," Joe went on, "but Ma says it's a cinch Mr. Blake would know his own goose. What do you think, Abe? Whose side are you taking?"

"Neither," said Abe shortly.

"But you've got to be on one side or the other. One of them has to own that goose."

"Maybe," Abe replied, "but going to law isn't going to help them find out which one. I reckon even the goose doesn't know."

When Joe and Abe reached the log schoolhouse, neither the justice of the peace nor the two lawyers had arrived. At one end of the long puncheon bench at the front of the room sat Jake Adams. At the other end, as far away as he could get, Josh Blake was sitting up very straight and staring straight ahead. Two other benches were filled with spectators. As Abe took his place among the men lined up against the wall at the back of the room, it seemed to him that nearly everyone was glaring at someone else. There was a restless shuffling of feet, and heads craned toward the door. Would the squire never come? What had happened to those lawyers?

For several minutes Abe stood, looking down at the floor. Suddenly he straightened his shoulders, and with an air of quiet resolution walked toward the front of the room. He paused beside the teacher's desk, the desk where the justice of the peace would sit. He turned and faced the people.

"Friends and neighbors," he said seriously, "what is the meaning of this-here gathering? Why are we here?"

There was a surprised murmur. Everyone was looking at Abe. He seemed embarrassed, but swallowed hard and repeated his question: "Why are we here? I'll tell you. We're here because," he dragged the words out slowly, "because—of—an—old—gray—goose."

The expression of mock despair, the funny drawl, were so unexpected that a titter rippled through the room. It died almost as soon as it started. Abe was speaking again, his gaze shifting gravely from Jake Adams to Josh Blake.

"Mr. Adams," said Abe, "has lost a goose. He claims that Mr. Blake has it. Now Mr. Blake says he hasn't any goose except his own; and both these men seem to think they're right. Not being able to settle the matter between themselves, they're going to law. And that, folks, is why we're here."

Was that a twinkle in Abe's eyes? Joe Gentry could not be sure.

"You, Mr. Adams," Abe continued, "say you have lost a gray goose. You're right sure that Mr. Blake has it, and you decided to bring the case to court. You hired a lawyer, is that right?"

All eyes were turned on Jake Adams. He nodded self-consciously.

"And you, Mr. Blake," Abe wheeled quickly, pointing a long finger at Josh Blake, "decided to hire a lawyer to defend your case."

Josh Blake nodded.

"Well, Mr. Adams and Mr. Blake, it looks as if you're going to get your trial." Abe looked accusingly from one to the other. "And after you've had it, what good is it going to do you? W-e-l-l, you, Mr. Adams, may get back your gray goose. And it's worth"—there was a long pause—"about two-bits."

Again the comical expression, the long-drawn-out words. This time several people laughed.

"If you win, Mr. Blake," Abe went on, "you'll get to keep your old—gray—goose. And it's worth——"

When Abe spoke the next words, most of the spectators were repeating them with him under their breaths. "And it's worth about —two—bits."

The sentence ended in a gale of laughter; Jake Adams and Josh Blake seemed to feel a little foolish. Only Abe continued to look serious.

"Now, you, Mr. Adams, and you, Mr. Blake," he went on earnestly, "if you win today you'll get back your goose, or get to keep your goose, as the case may be. But I'm telling you that whoever wins, you are both going to lose.

"Lose what, you ask? For one thing, you are neighbors, and you'll lose your friendship. And it won't stop there. Nearly everybody in this schoolhouse has been sitting here, glaring. You've started something that's got all Pigeon Creek riled up. It looks as how some folks in this neighborhood may never get back to being friends.

"And what is it all about?" Abe drew down his face again. "I'll tell you, folks. It's all on account of an—old—gray—goose."

The schoolhouse shook with laughter. Even Jake Adams and Josh Blake were on the verge of smiling.

"Why don't you stop this hair-pullin', fellows?" said Abe. "Settle the thing some way, and make up and be friends."

Jake Adams looked at Josh Blake out of the corner of his eye. Josh Blake fidgeted nervously.

"W-e-l-l, reckon I'm willing," said Jake at last.

Josh Blake jumped up, his hand extended. "Me, too. You skedaddle over to my place right now, Jake, and take that goose home with you."

"I wouldn't think of it, Josh," Jake protested, "you keep it."

There was a rustle at the back of the room. The squire and the two lawyers stood in the doorway.

"Reckon we don't need you after all, Squire," said Jake.

"No, we figure on settling out of court," Josh added. "Jake and I have made up."

"That's right," one of the spectators added, with a sly glance at the disappointed lawyers. "The gray goose case has done been laughed out of court."

Everyone left the schoolhouse in high good humor. Abe was always making speeches, and he always seemed to have a funny story to tell. But his speech today was the best yet.

"Why didn't you tell me you were going to speechify?" Joe asked.

"Didn't know it myself," Abe answered. "It struck me all of a sudden what a shame it was for those two fellows to waste their time and money going to court—and even more of a shame for them to waste their friendship."

As Abe took the trail that led through the woods to the log cabin where he lived, he was thinking of the two lawyers and the squire in their store clothes. Like them, he wanted to "be somebody," as the saying went, but he had only been to school "by littles." Sometimes when a schoolmaster came to Pigeon Creek Abe had attended for several weeks in a row, but his whole schooling had amounted to less than a year. Nor did he expect ever to have a chance to go to school again. It was the law that he must work for his father, or turn over any wages that he earned, until he was twenty-one. Tom Lincoln was poor, almost as poor as when he had arrived in Indiana ten years before to stake out a claim for a new farm.

Abraham Lincoln had been born in Kentucky. He was seven and his sister Sally was two years older when Tom brought his family to Indiana. Nancy, his mother, had been living then, and Abe remembered her with a great tenderness—the understanding smile and the sweet tones of her voice when she told him stories from the Bible. For a year after she died, he and Sally had been lonely and neglected.

Then their father had married again, and Sarah Lincoln, their stepmother, had lavished on them the same love that she gave her own three children. At times nine people lived together in the one-room cabin, with a loft above, but Sarah made everyone keep quiet when Abe wanted to study. She encouraged him to go ahead with his education, even when he could not go to school. He borrowed books from everyone who had a book to lend.

Today as Abe strode along the path, he pulled a book out of the front of his homespun shirt and began to read. The next morning he got up early and read before breakfast. He was working for one of the neighboring farmers, and he took his book to the fields. At noon when the other farm hands stopped for dinner, he perched on a rail fence with a piece of cornbread in one hand and his book in the other.

Some of the farmers thought him lazy because he read so much. Abe admitted that he did not like farm chores. There were many things he would rather do than plow fields, chop wood and grub roots out of the ground all day long, but he made a joke of it.

"My father taught me to work," he drawled, "but he never taught me to love it."

In spite of his jokes he was often restless and discouraged. He would walk along the forest trails, his head sunk forward on his chest, lost in gloom. Then one day he found a job more to his liking. He hired out to James Taylor, a farmer down on Anderson Creek. One of Abe's duties—the duty he liked best—was to operate a ferry across the creek. He also built a small rowboat of his own.

Anderson Creek emptied into the Ohio, and Abe liked being near the river. He liked to watch the flatboats floating downstream toward the Mississippi. He knew they were on their way to the city of New Orleans where the cargoes would be unloaded and sold. The handsome steamboats seemed even more remarkable as they plowed through the blue waters. They were too big to dock in the low water near the shore. There was an Ohio River ferry to carry passengers to the middle of the stream where the steamboats could be boarded.

This ferry boat was owned by two brothers, John and Benjamin Dill, who lived in Kentucky across the Ohio River from the Taylor farm. They had obtained a license from the State of Kentucky granting them the right to operate a ferry across the Ohio, but sometimes they forgot to attend to business. Again and again, Abe would notice a passenger waiting on the Indiana shore, ringing the ferry bell. After a while, if neither of the brothers appeared, he would take his own small boat and row the anxious passenger out to the steamboat. In this way he earned extra money, and one day two men each gave him a half dollar. Why, Jim Taylor only paid him six dollars a month, and Abe could hardly believe his good fortune. He had earned a whole dollar in less than a day!

But John Dill and his brother were furious, and John swore out a warrant for Abraham Lincoln's arrest. No one was more surprised than Abe himself. It had never occurred to him that he was doing anything wrong, and his hands were shaking a little as he tied up his rowboat on the Kentucky side of the river and climbed the steep bank that led to a dusty road. Just beyond an orchard where ripening fruit hung heavy on the trees, he came within sight of a large two-story house of hewn logs. A Negro servant waiting on the front porch showed him into the room where Samuel Pate, Esquire, justice of the peace in Hancock County, Kentucky, held his court.

The room was already crowded when Abe found a seat on one of the long benches facing the table by the window. He sat hunched forward, his hands clasped around his knees. There was a buzz of conversation, low-pitched as at a funeral.

It stopped abruptly when Squire Pate entered from another part of the house. Although he was a man in his early thirties, his pointed beard and cold gray eyes made him appear older. He carried a large book, Littell's *Laws of Kentucky*, which he placed on the table. He took an official-looking paper from his pocket, glanced at it briefly, and laid it beside the book. Then, dignified and unsmiling, he sat down behind the table and called the court to order.

"Today we hear the case of the Commonwealth of Kentucky versus Abraham Lincoln. The said Abraham Lincoln is charged with operating a ferry across the Ohio River without a license. Will the plaintiff please step forward?"

The taller of the two Dill brothers stood up.

"Name?" The squire almost smiled as he asked the routine question. The Dills were his neighbors. He had known them since they were boys.

"John Dill," was the answer.

"Business?"

"I'm a farmer. In our spare time, me and my brother run a ferry across the Ohio River."

"Do you have a license from the Commonwealth of Kentucky to operate said ferry?"

"Why, Sam, you know I have," said John Dill. "You made it out yourself."

Samuel Pate gave the plaintiff a withering glance. Even a boyhood companion must be made to understand that a justice of the peace should be addressed with respect. "So far as you know, Mr. Dill," he asked coolly, "does anyone else in this neighborhood have a legal right to operate a ferry across the Ohio?"

"No one but my brother Ben. He helps me."

"What is your complaint against the defendant"—the squire glanced again at the paper on the table—"Abraham Lincoln?"

"He's been running a ferry of his own, without a license. He's interfering with our business." John Dill's voice rose into a whine. "He's been taking fees we should be getting."

"When did the said Abraham Lincoln operate said ferry?" asked Samuel Pate.

"I don't know how many times he done it, but I seen him with my own eyes last Monday. He took two passengers from the Indiany side out to a steamboat in midriver."

"Was he rewarded for this service?"

"You mean was he paid?"

The squire nodded.

"Well, the two passengers put their hands in their pockets and handed him something. I figured they was paying him."

"Do you have a witness who can corroborate your testimony?" asked the squire.

"A what—who can what?" asked John Dill, bewildered.

There was a high cackle from an old man in the back of the room. Abe, usually the first to enjoy such a remark, did not even smile.

The squire rapped sharply for order and explained his question. "I mean, did anyone else see the said Abraham Lincoln transport said passengers to the steamboat?"

"Sure, my brother did," said the plaintiff in relief.

John Dill sat down, looking well pleased with himself, and Ben Dill took his place. After Ben finished his testimony, the squire opened the book of laws on the table. He stroked his chin as he read. He frowned ponderously.

"Will the defendant please step forward?"

Abe rose slowly. He was so tall that his head almost brushed against one of the beams in the low-ceilinged room.

"Name, please," said the squire.

"Abraham Lincoln."

"Where do you live?"

"Carter Township, Spencer County, Indiana."

"Be you guilty or not guilty?"

"Well—" Abe seemed to hesitate, then went on with more confidence. "Sometimes when a steamboat would come down the river, I'd see a man standing on the bank. He'd be ringing the ferry bell, impatient like, because he knew that the steamboat wouldn't wait. But I never took my boat out, except when the Dills were too busy or just plain weren't there to bring their ferry across the river."

"Then you admit you were guilty," said the squire.

Abe looked abashed. "I did what Mr. Dill said. On that Monday morning, there were two men on the bank with their trunks and carpetbags. On the other side of the river they could see the ferry, with no one to run it. The steamboat was coming and they seemed to be in a powerful hurry to catch it. They seemed to think I was doing them a favor."

"They paid you, didn't they?"

"Yes, your honor," Abe replied soberly, "but honest, I didn't know I was breaking any law."

"Ignorance of the law is no excuse," said Squire Pate sternly. "Anyhow, you knew the boundary of Kentucky reaches the low-water mark on the Indiana shore. You knew that when you were on the river you had to obey Kentucky laws."

"Yes, I knew that," Abe admitted.

"You knew you were running a ferry without a license?"

Abe scratched his head. "Never thought of my little rowboat as a ferry."

"For the benefit of the defendant," said the squire stiffly, "I shall read the law about ferries." He pulled the big book a little closer. *"If any person whatsoever shall, for reward, set any person over any river or creek, whereupon public ferries are appointed, he or she so offending shall forfeit and pay five pounds current money for every such offense."*

Abe's face grew longer and longer as Samuel Pate continued to read in a crisp, tight voice. If the defendant were found guilty, one half of the fine paid by him would go to the ferry-keeper nearest the place where the offense had been committed. The other half would be paid to the informer.

The Dill brothers exchanged smug, satisfied glances. They had been the ones to inform the squire about Abe's violation of the law and they hoped to collect the entire fine for themselves. The trouble was it was probably more money than Abe could pay.

Samuel Pate snapped the book shut.

"If a person found guilty of disobeying that law can't pay his fine" —the squire glanced at Abe's shabby, homemade clothes—"it is my sad duty to send him to jail. That seems like mighty harsh punishment, but the state has to protect the ferryman who forks out good money for a license. He's the only one who has any right to collect fees for setting passengers over the river."

Abe flushed, but his mouth was set in a stubborn line. "If I hadn't been around, your honor, there wouldn't have been any fees for anybody, and some folks would have missed their boats into the bargain. Take those fellows last Monday. They might still be cooling their heels over in Mr. Taylor's cornfield. I sort of figured I'd done right."

Samuel Pate looked uncomfortable. "I'm not here to decide if you did right. I'm not a preacher. I'm a justice of the peace, and my duty is to find out if you disobeyed a law of the sovereign State of Kentucky. Have you anything more to say before I pass sentence?"

There was a rustle in the courtroom, a low murmur of disapproval. The sympathies of most of the spectators seemed to be with the defendant.

Abe took another step forward. "May I ask a question?"

"Yes," said the squire briefly.

"That law book," Abe went on, pointing to the volume on the table, "says I can't set passengers over the river without a license, doesn't it?"

The squire nodded.

"Does the law say anything about not setting passengers part way over?"

"Of course not. What are you trying to do, young fellow? Tell me how to run my court?"

"No, your honor," Abe protested. "But you see, I never set any travelers *over* the river. I just took them out to the steamboats in midstream. If there isn't any law about taking passengers part way over, then I couldn't have broken it."

The stunned silence that followed was broken by another cackle from the old man in the back of the room. Someone else snickered. Samuel Pate's reaction was the strangest of all. Taking his bandanna handkerchief from his pocket, he vigorously mopped his face. When he took the handkerchief down, his face was so red he looked as if he might explode at any minute. The explosion threatened to take place in his throat. He strangled and he snorted. The justice of the peace was laughing.

"Case dismissed," he finally managed to say, and turned to the plaintiff. "Next time, John Dill, I'll thank you not to take up my time about a law that ain't been broken."

The disappointed Dill brothers stalked through the door. The spectators drifted away. Only Abe stayed in the courtroom, by order of the squire.

"Young man," he said, "with that sharp tongue in your head, you ought to be a lawyer."

There was a new and confident lift to the young man's shoulders as he walked back up the dusty road toward the river. He wondered if he could be a lawyer; there was so much a lawyer had to know. Well, he had learned something by attending his own trial, and the squire had invited him to come back the next law day. He also could go to Rockport, his own county seat, and listen to the lawyers argue. Perhaps he could borrow books about law. He had already read one law book, *Statutes of Indiana.* He had read it so often that he knew parts of it by heart.

Shadows were lengthening when Abe untied his boat and pushed out into the stream. The last rays of the sun lingered on the water, and a steamboat in the distance seemed bathed in golden light. He watched it wistfully as it disappeared around a bend in the river. It was on its way to that outside world that Abe Lincoln longed to see.

A chance to visit that outside world came when he was nineteen. He helped Allen Gentry, Joe's older brother, to build a flatboat. They loaded it with flour, corn, bacon and other products from Mr. Gentry's farm. Then they floated it down the Ohio and Mississippi rivers to New Orleans. Abe, standing on the wharf, saw ships from all over the world. He felt prickles up and down his spine as he realized that those ships were bound for cities along the eastern coast of the United States, and even in Europe—cities that he had read about in books.

Later, as he and Allen explored some of the narrow streets, they passed a slave market. An auctioneer stood beside the slave block, a sort of platform where Negro house servants and field hands took their places one by one. There was a hopeless expression in their dark eyes as the auctioneer asked for bids. The white men who stood below the block called out how much they were willing to pay. Abe turned away with a shudder. This was the first time he had ever seen human beings offered for sale.

"Let's go, Allen," he said. "I can't stand any more."

Abe kept thinking about that slave auction after he returned home. Not all slave owners were willing to sell their slaves to anyone who had the price to pay, and many white masters were kind. There was no law in the South against slavery, but Abe was convinced that it was wrong. No man had any right to own another, but what could be done about it? What could a boy from the backwoods do to help the slaves?

In the year 1828, he could not know that the time was coming when he would find a way.

At the age of twenty-one, Abraham Lincoln moved with his family to Illinois, and after helping his father clear land for a new farm, he settled in the village of New Salem. During the next six years he was a storekeeper, a postmaster, a soldier in the Black Hawk War and a surveyor. He was still very poor, but his new friends liked and trusted him. They called him "honest Abe," and when he was only twenty-five they elected him to the state legislature. In his spare time he studied law, and became a lawyer. Then he opened a law office in Springfield, the new state capital.

In his new home Abe was as well liked as he had once been in Pigeon Creek and New Salem. As time passed, he built up a good law practice, but in some ways he was still like the seventeen-year-old boy who had argued the "Gray Goose case" back in Indiana. He persuaded his clients, whenever possible, to settle their difficulties out of court, and he still told funny stories. Often he found that he could make people think by first making them laugh.

"I laughed," said one dignified judge—at least, he usually was dignified—"until I shook my ribs loose."

By the time Abraham Lincoln was forty-five he was one of the leading citizens of Illinois. But he might never have become well-known outside the state had it not been for the Kansas-Nebraska Act, a law passed by Congress in 1854. Until that time, slavery had not been allowed in the territory in the northwest part of the United States. It was expected that new states would be formed from this vast region. The new law would make it possible for the white people in each state to decide if they wanted to own slaves.

Ever since his visit to a slave market in New Orleans, Abraham Lincoln had been bitterly opposed to slavery. Now he began to make speeches against the Kansas-Nebraska Act, insisting that slavery must not be allowed to spread. In 1858 he was a candidate for the United States Senate, running against his old friend Stephen A. Douglas. The two candidates argued, in a series of debates, about the spread of slavery. These debates were held in seven different towns in Illinois, and people from all over the state came to hear them.

"Is slavery wrong?" asked Abraham Lincoln. What slavery really meant, he said, was this: "You work, and toil, and earn bread, and I'll eat it." It was not right for one race to make slaves of another race and "live by the fruits of their labor."

Although he was defeated for Senator, the Illinois lawyer had won the respect and admiration of thousands of men and women who had never heard of him before. People throughout the North began to think of him as the friend of freedom, and in 1860 he was elected President of the United States.

The next four years were the saddest in American history. Many Southerners refused to live under a President who was opposed to slavery. By Inauguration Day, March 4, 1861, several Southern states had withdrawn from the United States and started a new nation called the Confederate States of America. During the war that followed between the North and South—a war which President Lincoln called "the great trouble"—he had a chance to free the slaves. On New Year's Day, 1863, he signed the Emancipation Proclamation which declared that all slaves were free in those states then at war with the government of the United States.

The main purpose of the terrible struggle, however, was to keep all of the states together in one nation. The President insisted that no state had a right to try to break up the Union; that in a democracy everybody must be willing to obey the laws that most of the people wanted. In his famous speech four months after the battle of Gettysburg, he summed up in a few stirring words the purpose of the war: "that government of the people, by the people, for the people, shall not perish from the earth."

When Abraham Lincoln became President the second time, he said that the next great task would be to "bind up the nation's wounds." He wanted to help the people who had suffered, in both North and South.

Early in April, 1865, the Union armies won another great victory, and everyone knew that the brave Confederate soldiers could not hold out much longer. Outside the White House, in the streets of Washington, could be heard the sounds of celebration—the ringing of bells, the booming of cannon, and the shouts of the people. The President smiled. Often during the past four years he had felt as if he were living in a nightmare. But now the great trouble was nearly over.

"Thank God," he said, "that I have lived to see this."

[*The incident about the "Gray Goose" trial is based on a reminiscence of Joseph Gentry, who referred to the litigants merely as "Mr. A" and "Mr. B." The names, Jake Adams and Joshua Blake," were supplied by the author.]*

THE SIXTEENTH PRESIDENT *at a Glance*

Abraham Lincoln

Born: February 12, 1809   *Died: April 15, 1865*

As a boy. Abraham Lincoln, son of Nancy Hanks and Thomas Lincoln, a carpenter, was born in a log cabin near Hodgenville, Ky. In 1816, at the age of 7, he moved with his parents and sister Sarah, two years older than himself, to southern Indiana. His mother died two years later (1818). In December, 1819, Tom Lincoln married Sarah Bush Johnson, who arrived soon afterward in the Lincoln cabin with her own three children (Betsy, Mathilda, and Johnny). Abe attended several schools, two in Kentucky and three in Indiana, but altogether he had less than a year's schooling. At 17 (1826), he worked as a ferryman on Anderson Creek, and in 1828 he made a flatboat journey to New Orleans.

As a young man. Abe Lincoln moved with his family to Illinois (1830). In March, 1831, he began another flatboat voyage to New Orleans and then settled in New Salem, Ill., where he lived for six years (1831–1837). He enlisted (April, 1832) in the Black Hawk War to drive the Indians out of Illinois but did not take part in any battles. He served in the Illinois legislature (1834–1841). Meanwhile he had studied law, been admitted to the bar (1837), and moved to Springfield, the new state capital. There he bought (1844) a comfortable frame house where he and his wife and children lived until 1861.

As a leading citizen in Illinois. Lincoln served in the U.S. House of Representatives (1847–1849) and returned to Springfield to practice law again. Not until after the passage of the Kansas-Nebraska Act (1854) did he become interested in politics once more. In 1856 he joined the new Republican party, which had been organized to fight the spread of slavery. Two years later he was the Republican candidate for the U.S. Senate (1858) but was defeated by Stephen A. Douglas. As a result of the Lincoln-Douglas Debates, held in seven different Illinois towns (August–October, 1858), he became famous. He was nominated for President by the Republican convention meeting in Chicago (May 18, 1860), and was elected in November, 1860.

As President (1861–1865). By the time Lincoln was inaugurated (March 4, 1861) seven Southern states had left the Union and formed a new nation called the "Confederate States of America." Later four other states joined the Confederacy. Southern soldiers fired on Fort Sumter, a U.S. fort in the harbor at Charleston, S.C., on April 12, 1861. The North then went to war against the South to force the Confederate states back into the Union. On New Year's Day, 1863, President Lincoln signed the Emancipation Proclamation, which proclaimed all slaves free in any state then at war with the U.S. government. At the three-day battle at Gettysburg, Pa. (July 1–3, 1863) the Union forces won a great victory, and on November 19, 1863, Lincoln delivered his famous Gettysburg Address. He was re-elected and became President a second time (March 4, 1865). A few weeks later the main Confederate army surrendered (April 9, 1865). Peace was assured. But Abraham Lincoln was never able to carry out his plans for the South. He was shot by John Wilkes Booth while attending Ford's Theater the evening of April 14, 1865. When he died early the next morning, the Secretary of War, Edwin M. Stanton, said, "Now he belongs to the ages."

The President's family. Lincoln married Mary Todd of Kentucky in 1842. Their oldest son, Robert (1843–1926), later became Secretary of War (1881–1885) and U.S. minister to England (1889–1893). William, usually called Willie (1850–1862), died in the White House. Thomas, who was called Tad (1853–1871), was his father's greatest comfort during the trying days of the Civil War.

Other happenings. When Lincoln was President, the first telegraph line reaching from coast to coast was completed (1861). Congress passed the Homestead Act (1862), which offered 160 free acres out West to any settler who wanted to start a new farm. Congress also passed the Land-Grant College Act (1862) which offered government land to the states for the establishment of agricultural colleges.

New states. West Virginia was admitted to the Union in 1863; Nevada in 1864.

ANDY JOHNSON *Proves His Courage*

Through the open window Andrew Johnson could hear his friends at play. But inside the tailor shop ten or twelve hours of labor stretched ahead of him before he would be free to join them.

"Careful, Andy," said his master, James Selby. "You must make your stitches smaller."

Andy bent his black head closer over the coat that he was stitching. His back ached as he sat on the hard bench, pushing his needle in and out, but he wanted to be a good tailor. When he and his older brother, Bill, had become apprentices in Mr. Selby's shop in Raleigh, North Carolina, they had promised to serve him until they became of age. They lived in Mr. Selby's home while he was teaching them his trade, and he also furnished them with clothes and food. These last were very important, for their father was dead and their mother was very poor.

"Good morning, boys. Here is Dr. Hill to read to you."

Andy looked up from his work, his black eyes glowing with sudden interest. In the doorway stood Mr. Litchford, the foreman of the shop; behind him, holding a book under his arm, was Dr. Hill. Dr. Hill often read to the apprentices as they worked, and to Andy it seemed nothing short of magic that the doctor could look at those little black marks on a white page and make them form the stirring words of a speech. Andy himself could not read, for there was no school in Raleigh.

"Are you ready for Dr. Hill to begin?" asked Mr. Litchford. He spoke to all the boys, but he looked straight at Andy.

"Yes, sir, please do," said Andy eagerly.

"Very well," said Dr. Hill. "I have here Enfield's *American Speaker*. But today, instead of reading a speech by some great statesman, I shall read you an essay on how to make a speech. Who knows —perhaps someday one of you will be an orator!"

"An orator?" Andy's heart stirred. The neat stitches grew under his flying fingers, but his head was cocked so as not to miss a word. The most important thing in making a speech, the essay said, was to learn to speak slowly and clearly. It ended with the couplet:

> *Learn to speak slow, all other graces*
> *Will follow in their proper places.*

Andy repeated the words to himself. He looked up to see Dr. Hill standing beside him.

"Please, sir," Andy asked, "may I see the letters on the page?"

"Of course. Here is the couplet I just read. Look at the first word." Dr. Hill's finger pointed out each letter. "L-e-a-r-n spells 'learn.' "

"L-e-a-r-n, learn!" A light seemed to break over the boy's face. "Oh, sir, would you show me some of the other letters? And would you let me borrow the book? Perhaps *I* can learn to read."

The weeks that followed were magic weeks to Andy Johnson. He could not write, he could not cipher; but now the great world of books was opening to him. Dr. Hill dropped into the tailor shop every few days, and Mr. Litchford snatched a moment now and then from a busy day to stop beside Andy's bench to help him with a word. As Andy pored over the book, he never ceased to marvel at the miracle of those little black marks. Gradually they straightened themselves out into words and then the words became sentences. The sentences brought to him new ideas, ideas so interesting that when he was reading, he almost forgot the hard, humdrum life in the tailor shop.

Soon Andy was able to read the essay on elocution for himself. He took its advice seriously, and he decided that he would become an orator. He practiced again and again, making himself speak slowly and clearly. When the time came to return the borrowed book, he could hardly bear to part with it.

"You have done very well," said Dr. Hill, "and I think you deserve a reward. You may keep the book."

The boy could hardly believe his good fortune. "Oh, thank you, sir," he said.

In spite of his studious habits, Andrew Johnson was probably the most harum-scarum apprentice in the shop. On holidays he went fishing in the creek, and sometimes he fell in. Then he would return to his master's house dripping wet. In the evenings, after the day's work was over, he climbed the tallest trees, and he was always tearing his clothes. One night he had a big rent in his trousers and tried to slip into the house unnoticed. But Mrs. Selby, the master's wife, saw him.

"I declare, Andy," she said, "once you start playing, you seem to forget everything else. You look more like a ragamuffin than an apprentice to a tailor. But I'll fix you, young man."

Mrs. Selby did "fix" him. She made him a coarse homespun shirt, long enough so that he needed no other clothes and so heavy that no amount of tree climbing could tear it. The new garment made him look something like a barrel, and the other apprentices roared with laughter.

Andy pretended that he didn't mind. He just went on climbing trees.

One Saturday night, feeling restless after a hard week's work, Andy was walking down the street with his brother Bill and two apprentices from another shop. As they passed the house of an old lady named Mrs. Wells, one of the other apprentices picked up a rock.

"Bet I can hit her chimney with this," he boasted.

"Dare you to try," said Bill.

Bang! The rock crashed into the side of the house.

"I can do better than that," said Bill, and another stone crashed against the house.

Soon all four boys were throwing stones, just for the fun of it. Then without warning, the door was flung open. In the lighted doorway stood Mrs. Wells, shaking her fist.

"Run!" whispered Bill. "It's dark. Maybe she can't see who we are." And the boys raced down the street.

Sunday morning Bill beckoned Andy to one side. He was as fair as Andy was dark, and now his blue eyes were frightened. His freckled face was pale. "She saw us, Andy. She knows who we were."

"Who?"

"Mrs. Wells. She says she is going to persecute us tomorrow."

Andy realized Bill meant "prosecute," and that meant Mrs. Wells could probably send both boys to jail. "We've got to run away," said Andy.

"What if Mr. Selby catches us and brings us back?"

Andy hesitated. If they ran away before their apprenticeship was over, they would be disobeying the law. If they were caught, their master would have the legal right to punish them. But they were sure to be punished if they stayed.

"We'll just have to take a chance that we won't be caught," Andy decided. "Tomorrow is Sunday. It will be Monday before anyone misses us in the shop."

Early the next morning the two brothers put on their blue cloth coats and their best homespun breeches. The rest of their belongings they tied up in handkerchiefs. Then they slipped quietly out of town. They said little as they trudged along the dusty road leading away from Raleigh. They walked all day, and when darkness came they found a secluded place behind some trees to spend the night.

"I wonder what Mr. Selby will do when he finds out?" thought Andy just before he dropped off to sleep.

What Mr. Selby did when he came into the shop on Monday morning was to grow very red in the face. "What? Two apprentices run away? It's that stubborn Andy Johnson's fault, I'll warrant. Just wait till I can get my hands on him. I'll put a notice in the paper. I'll offer a ten-dollar reward for 'em. I'll offer a ten-dollar reward for Andy alone. That will fetch 'em back."

With his coattails flying along behind him, James Selby rushed down the street to the office of the *Raleigh Gazette*. He took a quill pen from its holder and started to write a description of the two runaways. The pen made a scratching noise across the page as he wrote.

TEN DOLLAR REWARD

Ran away from the Subscriber on the night of the 15th instant, 2 apprentice boys, legally bound, named William and Andrew Johnson. The former is of a dark complexion. . . . The latter is very fleshy, freckled face, light hair and fair complexion. . . . I will pay the above Reward to any person who will deliver said apprentices to me in Raleigh, or I will give the above Reward for Andrew Johnson alone.

All persons are cautioned against harboring or employing said apprentices on pain of being prosecuted.

JAMES J. SELBY, *Tailor*

Raleigh, N.C. June 24, 1824

The other apprentices must have smiled when they read that advertisement. Mr. Selby, in his excitement, had described Bill for Andy and Andy for Bill.

In spite of the mixed description, things looked bad for the boys. It seemed likely that someone would recognize them and try to send them back to Raleigh in order to claim the reward. But the days lengthened into weeks and the weeks into months, and there was no word of either boy.

Meanwhile, Andy and Bill had walked seventy-five miles to the town of Carthage. There they opened up a tailor shop in a little shack. Business was good, so good that they were afraid that their old master might hear of their success. The following winter they moved farther on to the town of Laurens, South Carolina, where they took up their trade again. Nearly two years went by, but Andy was not satisfied. He realized now that he had done very wrong to run away, and there was only one way to clear his conscience. He must return to Raleigh and finish his apprenticeship.

At the thought of facing Mr. Selby, a cold sweat broke out on the boy's forehead. What would Mr. Selby say? What would he do? To go back would take more courage than running away.

Bill decided to go with him, and the two brothers worked their way back to Raleigh. When they arrived, they learned that Mr. Selby had closed his shop and had moved twenty miles out into the country. Well, at least they had tried to make amends, Bill argued, but Andy did not agree. He set out alone to walk to Mr. Selby's new home. With every step he dreaded the meeting more and more.

"So you are back!" Mr. Selby opened the door and bent a dark look upon his one-time apprentice. "Humph!" he said. "So you came back."

"Yes, sir." Andy's steady dark eyes did not flinch. "I came to say that I am sorry I ran away. I am ready to work out my time."

"You'll never work for me again." His old master's voice rose in indignation. "You broke the law, and no other tailor will hire you either."

"But, sir——"

"Get out!" Mr. Selby shouted and closed the door.

Andy turned away with a heavy heart. He grew even more discouraged, as the days passed, and he could not find another job. Although he had tried to do the right thing by coming back, Mr. Selby was right. No one wanted to hire a runaway apprentice. His mother had married again, but his stepfather was as poor as his own father had been. Andy could not be a burden on them. They hardly had enough for themselves.

"What shall I do, Ma?" he asked one day, slumping into a chair. "Folks say there is plenty of free land in Tennessee for anyone who wants to come and take it. If——"

"Let's go, Andy," said his mother, "all of us. Your step-pa can get us a two-wheeled cart and we'll pile all our belongings into that."

"Yes," said Andy eagerly, "out in Tennessee, maybe we'll all have a better chance."

When Andrew Johnson returned to Raleigh forty years later he came as the President of the United States. In his neat black broad-cloth suit and high collar, he looked very dignified and quite different from the harum-scarum apprentice who had once been the despair of Mrs. Selby. Much had happened since Andy had left for Tennessee. In the town of Greeneville, where he had settled, he had opened his own tailor shop. He married a lovely girl, Eliza Mc-Cardle, and only Andy knew how much she had done for him. She taught him to write, and with her help he had been able to educate himself. Before he was twenty-one, he had started on a political career that finally led to his election as Vice President.

And then after Abraham Lincoln's tragic death, Andrew Johnson had become President. The following year, he returned for a visit to the town where he had been an apprentice. His old friends now felt very proud of the man who had had such a hard time when he had lived among them. The people of Raleigh listened attentively when he stood up to speak.

"I have no other ambition in life," he said, "but to mend and repair the breaches in the torn and tattered Constitution of my country."

Down in the audience one old lady who had known Andrew Johnson as a boy turned to a neighbor. "Bless Andy's dear heart," she whispered. "Do you think he is coming back to open up a tailor shop?"

If Andrew Johnson learned of this remark, it is hoped that it brought a smile to his face. He had little reason to smile during his years in the White House, for even Abraham Lincoln had not faced greater difficulties. The new President would never forget the last Cabinet meeting, held only a few hours before his great predecessor died, toward the close of the Civil War.

"I hope there will be no persecution, no bloody work, after the war is over," Abraham Lincoln had said. "Enough lives have been sacrificed. We must extinguish our resentments if we expect harmony and Union."

This was the policy that Andrew intended to follow; he wanted to make it easy for the Southern states that had tried to secede to take their rightful places once more in the nation. But certain selfish leaders in Congress were more interested in revenge and in keeping the North more powerful than the South. The South, they said, should be treated as conquered territory, and the Confederate leaders should be severely punished. They soon learned, however, that the new man in the White House, though he lacked Lincoln's tact, had just as much courage. Andrew Johnson was very stubborn and determined. He opposed the Congressional leaders in every way he could, and tried to keep the harsh bills from becoming laws.

By February, 1868, the quarrel between the President and his enemies in Congress had become so bitter that the House of Representatives voted to impeach him—that is, to accuse him of certain "high crimes and misdemeanors." A trial, presided over by the Chief Justice of the Supreme Court, was held in the Senate. If two-thirds of the Senators decided he was guilty, he would then be forced to give up his office.

As the trial dragged on, day after day, the American people began taking sides. Many of them agreed with the President's enemies. Others said that the charges against him were false, "trumped up." They were convinced that some of the Senators were not interested in conducting a fair trial, but only in trying to force the President out of office so that they themselves might be more powerful.

During those difficult weeks there was little change in life at the White House. The President made no mention of the trial when he greeted his callers. He spent long hours at his desk, and for relaxation he took his grandchildren on picnics in Rock Creek Park. Sometimes his secretary noticed him reading Joseph Addison's long dramatic poem, "Cato." This hero of ancient Rome had died rather than submit to injustice, and the President must have found comfort in the lines

> *'Tis not in mortals to command success,*
> *But we'll do more . . . we'll deserve it.*

Perhaps sometimes in the evening he read the poem aloud to his wife. In the days of their poverty she had been the one to read to him, as she sat beside him in his tailor shop and he stitched on a suit for one of his customers. Eliza was now an invalid and spent most of her time in her upstairs room at the White House, but she was still helping and encouraging him. Her complete faith in her husband's innocence and wisdom made the suspense easier to bear as the day approached when the Senate would decide his case.

On May 16, when a vote was taken on the most important charge that had been made against the President, the Senate galleries were crowded. As the clerk called the roll of Senators, the Chief Justice asked each one in turn:

"Is . . . Andrew Johnson, President of the United States, guilty or not guilty . . . ?"

"Guilty!" "Guilty!" "Guilty!" a number of Senators answered.

"Not guilty!" others replied.

And so it went, the spectators in the galleries growing more anxious as the clock on the Senate wall ticked off the minutes. As soon as the last Senator had voted, Colonel Crook, a member of the White House staff, hurriedly left the Capitol and drove down Pennsylvania Avenue. Andrew Johnson and a few close friends were waiting in his study at the White House to learn the verdict.

"Mr. President," Colonel Crook announced, "you have been acquitted."

The President's eyes were moist—but only for a moment. He thanked Colonel Crook, who then hurried upstairs and knocked on Mrs. Johnson's door. "I knew it, I knew it," she said happily. "I knew that he would be acquitted, but thank you for coming to tell me."

That night the members of a brass band gathered before the White House to serenade the President, and in the days that followed he received many friendly letters. To visitors who called to congratulate him, he seemed as calm as he had during the trial. Probably only Eliza knew how relieved he was that it was over.

Andrew Johnson's term as President came to an end the following March, but a few years later he was elected Senator from Tennessee. Public opinion was turning more and more in his favor, and he came back to Washington in triumph. Many people once in doubt now believed he had been right, and his enemies wrong, during the impeachment trial. In a speech he made before the Senate, he did not hesitate to denounce the men he felt were responsible for the spirit of hate that was still abroad in the land and which he feared could still wreck the Union. He begged the Senators to lay aside their personal feelings and to give themselves up to "this grand work of saving the Constitution—saving the country." The safety of one, he said, meant the safety of the other.

"Let peace and prosperity be restored to the land," he went on. "May God bless this people; may God save the Constitution."

THE SEVENTEENTH PRESIDENT *at a Glance*

Andrew Johnson

Born: December 29, 1808   *Died: July 31, 1875*

Early life. Andrew Johnson was born in Raleigh, N.C. His family was very poor, and Andy was apprenticed to a tailor when he was 13. At 17 (1826), he opened his own tailor shop in Greeneville, Tenn.

Political career. In 1828 Andrew Johnson was elected alderman in Greeneville. Two years later he became mayor. He served in the Tennessee legislature (1835–1837, 1839–1843); in the U.S. House of Representatives (1843–1853); as governor of Tennessee (1853–1857); and in the U.S. Senate (1857–1862). When the Southern states seceded (1860–1861), Johnson was the only Southern Senator who supported the Union and the only one who did not resign from Congress. In 1862 he was appointed military governor of the part of Tennessee already occupied by Union troops. When the Republicans renominated Lincoln for President (1864), they chose Johnson, a Democrat, as candidate for Vice President, in hope of winning Democratic support. Lincoln and Johnson were elected. When Lincoln died six weeks after his second inauguration (April 15, 1865), Johnson became President.

As President (1865–1869). President Johnson and Congress disagreed bitterly over plans for "reconstructing" the Southern states, that is, for restoring them to their rightful places in the Union after the Civil War. Congress disliked Johnson's policy of friendly help for the defeated states and in 1867 passed its own reconstruction program, which included military control of the South. Johnson's many enemies in Congress were angered by his constant opposition to their plans. They wanted to remove him from office, and when he further defied them by dismissing a member of his Cabinet without the consent of Congress, the House of Representatives impeached him (1868). A trial, presided over by the Chief Justice of the U.S. Supreme Court, was held in the Senate, but the attempt failed to have the President removed from office.

The White House hostess. Eliza Johnson (1810–1876) was an invalid when her husband was President. The Johnsons' elder daughter, Mrs. Martha Patterson, usually acted as White House hostess.

Other happenings. When Johnson was President, slavery was abolished in the U.S. by the 13th Amendment to the Constitution (1865). A permanent telegraph cable was completed between America and Europe (1866). Alaska was purchased from Russia for $7,200,000 (1867).

The nation's growth. Nebraska was admitted to the Union (1867).

Johnson as ex-President. Six years after leaving the White House, Johnson returned to Washington (1875) as a Senator from Tennessee.

LYS GRANT *Never Turns Back*

I am sorry, Lys, but Mr. Ralston wants too much money for the colt."

"But, Papa," Ulysses Grant persisted, "maybe Mr. Ralston will take less if I ask him."

"Maybe so," Jesse Grant admitted. He took off his gold-rimmed glasses, wiped them, and put them on again. Then he smiled; he knew how much his son liked horses. "Suppose you ride out to Ralston's farm," he suggested, "and offer twenty dollars for the colt."

"What if Mr. Ralston won't take twenty dollars?"

"Then you'll have to give twenty-two fifty. If he won't take that, say twenty-five. But not one cent more, mind you."

So anxious was Ulysses to own another horse that he lost no time in riding out to Mr. Ralston's farm. "I've come for the colt," he said. "Papa says that I may offer you twenty dollars for it. But if you won't take that, I am to offer twenty-two fifty. And if you won't take that, I'm to give you twenty-five."

Mr. Ralston threw back his head and laughed. "All right, Lys, you may have the colt—for twenty-five."

Soon the story was making the rounds of Georgetown, the village where the Grants lived in southern Ohio. "Hey, there!" someone would shout. "What'd you pay for your horse?"

It was the kind of joke to embarrass a shy, eight-year-old boy, but Ulysses tried not to let it bother him. He knew a good horse when he saw one, and he was convinced that the colt was worth much more than the price he had paid. Besides, he was used to being

153

laughed at. Sometimes the neighbors laughed because of what they considered his peculiar habit of never turning back.

"One of my superstitions," he said later, "had always been, when I started to go anywhere or to do anything, not to turn back or stop until the thing intended was accomplished."

And so it happened that if Ulysses forgot his cap, he would not return for it. Instead he would circle the house. When he reached the front door again, he *then* would go inside and get his cap.

His schoolmates also laughed because he was bashful and slow. They made the mistake of thinking he was dull, and called him "Useless."

But Ulysses was not dull. Although small for his age, he probably turned out more work than any boy in the neighborhood. Jesse Grant, a well-to-do tanner and farmer, expected his eldest son to help. From the time Ulysses was eight, he hauled all of the wood needed in the house and in his father's tannery shop. The wood was loaded on a wagon pulled by a horse. Horses were then used for many farm tasks later handled by machinery, and Ulysses handled horses well. His father's friends often brought their colts to him to be broken. No matter how lively the colt, the boy could usually gentle it in a few hours, and no one in the village could ride any better than Ulysses. People gasped when they saw him standing on a horse's back, balanced on one foot, as the animal galloped down the street.

When Ulysses was ten years old, a circus came to town. Excitedly he watched the antics of a trick pony. The ringmaster cracked his whip to get attention.

"Here is a five-dollar bill for the boy who can ride this pony. Anyone want to try it?"

"Sure, that's easy. I can ride it," boasted one of the bigger boys.

The pony had neither bridle nor saddle. But it seemed patient enough—until the boy mounted. Then it kicked its heels into the air, and the rider found himself lying in the ring, his mouth full of sawdust. The crowd jeered good-naturedly.

"Anyone else want to win this five-dollar bill?" asked the ringmaster. "Who will ride the pony?"

One boy after another came up. One after another was thrown. Ulysses stepped forward.

"I'd like to try," he said.

He soon realized why the other riders had been thrown. Not only had the pony's mane been cut off, but its back was greased. But Ulysses had made up his mind that he was going to hang on.

"Get up," shouted the ringmaster, and the pony started around the ring. It ran like lightning, but Ulysses kept his seat. The pony kicked and reared. Ulysses put his arms around its neck and held on tight. A crack of the ringmaster's whip, and the pony was off again, going faster and still faster.

"Good for you, Useless!" someone cried.

The ringmaster looked worried. He had felt sure he had a pony that no boy could ride. But now it looked as though he might have to part with that five-dollar bill he had offered as a prize. Hastily he brought out a monkey and commanded it to jump on the pony's back. The crowd again laughed, but Ulysses paid no attention.

"Up on his shoulder!" urged the ringmaster, and the monkey obeyed. Ulysses did not seem to notice.

Then, at another sharp command from the ringmaster, the monkey climbed on the boy's head. The pony started to kick, but Ulysses kept his mount.

"Hurrah for Lys!" his friends shouted, forgetting that they had ever called him "Useless."

The ringmaster wiped the perspiration from his face. "Whoa!" he called to the pony, and turned to the successful rider. "Here is the prize money. You really earned it."

Ulysses blushed and backed away from the cheering crowd. "That pony was slick as an apple," was all he said.

Because Ulysses seemed to be able to do almost anything with horses, his father trusted him to make long trips alone. Sometimes he hitched the team to the family carriage and drove passengers to the steamboat landing on the Ohio River, and sometimes even farther than that. At fifteen he drove a passenger to Flat Rock, Kentucky, seventy miles away. While he was in Flat Rock, he saw a saddle horse he wanted, and persuaded the owner to trade it for one of the carriage horses. The new mare was not accustomed to harness, but that did not worry Ulysses.

"The horse is not vicious," he said. "I guess I can manage her."

That same day he met a neighbor, Mr. Payne, and offered to drive him back to Georgetown. They started the next morning, the new mare hitched to the carriage beside Mr. Grant's old horse. All went well for a few miles. Then a fierce dog ran out into the road and began to bark. Both horses were frightened, and the mare began to kick.

"Whoa, there! Whoa!" shouted Ulysses, and with a quick turn of the wrist barely saved the team from running into a tree. With another tight pull on the reins, the horses came to a quivering stop.

"Quiet, there!" Ulysses spoke soothingly, but Mr. Payne seemed worried. "This is where I get out," he said.

"I think the team will be all right after they rest awhile," Ulysses told him. "Besides, my uncle lives in Maysville. He'll lend me another horse for the rest of the trip."

"But Maysville," Mr. Payne sputtered, "that's more than halfway to Georgetown."

"We'll get there," said Ulysses matter-of-factly, and started to drive on.

But the mare gave another terrified snort. She began to run, the old horse tearing along beside her. They were on a side road, but at this point the road led into the turnpike. Mr. Payne drew in his breath sharply. Even Ulysses grew pale beneath his freckles. Twenty feet away, on the other side of the turnpike, was a deep ditch.

"Whoa!" he shouted again with a sharp tug on the reins. "Steady—whoa!"

At the very edge of the ditch, Ulysses pulled the runaway team to a stop. The mare was trembling so that she could hardly stand. Ulysses jumped out of the carriage and gently stroked her nose.

But even the horses were not so scared as Mr. Payne. "Good-bye," he said, clamping his hat down firmly on his head. "The freight wagon will be along soon. I'm taking it! I'll meet you at your uncle's house in Maysville—if you ever get there."

With a last backward glance at the struggling team, Mr. Payne was gone, but Ulysses kept calm. "Giddap," he said, picking up the reins.

Again the mare began to kick. The boy let her rest, then tried once more. She snorted and pawed the ground with a wild look in her eyes. Ulysses rumpled up his chestnut-colored hair and wondered what to do. Suddenly he had an idea. He took a bandanna handkerchief from his pocket.

"A blind horse never runs away," he thought.

Once blindfolded, the mare was no longer afraid, and Ulysses found her easier to manage. The next day he reached Maysville, where Mr. Payne had already arrived. He looked surprised to see the boy, and perhaps a bit ashamed. After borrowing a fresh horse, they drove on together. The boy realized that he had used poor judgment in trying to drive a horse not accustomed to harness—but at least he had not turned back.

About this time, Ulysses had a long talk with his father about a future career. Jesse was looking forward to having his oldest son work in the family tannery, not realizing how much Ulysses detested the work.

"I don't like the tannery and never will," said the boy firmly. "If you want me to, though, I'll work at it until I am twenty-one."

"Why, son," Jesse Grant replied, "I would not want you to do any work you do not like."

Jesse finally decided to write his Congressman, asking that Ulysses be given an appointment to the United States Military Academy. The appointment came through when Ulysses was seventeen, and he left for West Point to begin his training as a cadet. Although the new cadet's full name was Hiram Ulysses Grant, the Congressman made a mistake. He sent in the name as "Ulysses Simpson Grant," since "Simpson" had been Mrs. Grant's name before she married. After Ulysses arrived at the academy he tried to have the mistake corrected, but became so involved in army "red tape" that finally he gave up. After all he was a cadet, which was what was important.

As it turned out, being a cadet was something of a disappointment. At home, he had been given almost complete freedom, but now his days were made up of rules, rules, rules.

"If I had known how strict the life would be, I never would have come," he confided to a friend. "But as I have started, I am bound to go through with it."

He did go through with it, and his four years at the academy were not all unpleasant. There were spirited horses to ride, and by his senior year he had made some fine friends. Grant might be shy, they said, but he certainly had a way with horses.

"It was as good as any circus to see Grant ride," one of the cadets said later. "There was a dark bay horse so fractious that it was about to be condemned. Grant selected it for his horse. He bridled, mounted, and rode it every day at parade, and how he did ride! His gentleness with a horse was proverbial, but he handled the refractory creature as a giant would a child. The whole class would stand around admiring his wonderful command of the beast and its graceful evolutions."

It was a long time before Ulysses S. Grant had such an admiring audience again. When he graduated from West Point in 1843, he was commissioned a second lieutenant and stayed in the army for several years. He fought in the Mexican War and served at various army posts, but finally, after many months of garrison duty in far-off California, he decided to resign. He was now a married man, and he was homesick for his family.

The next eight years were probably the most discouraging period of his life. Although he tried several jobs, he did not succeed at any of them. In 1861 he was clerking in a leather store in Galena, Illinois, for fifty dollars a month, and on this meager salary he was trying to support a wife and four children. At the age of thirty-nine he considered himself a failure—as did most people that he knew.

But failure or not, when the Civil War began, he wanted to fight for the Union. He began by drilling a company of volunteers in Galena, then went with the men to Springfield, the capital of Illinois. There, as a member of the governor's staff, he helped to organize the state militia. On May 25, he sent the following letter to the War Department in Washington:

> *Having served for fifteen years in the regular army, including four years at West Point, and feeling it the duty of every one who has been educated at Government expense to offer their services for the support of that Government, I have the honor, very respectfully, to tender my services, until the close of the war, in such capacity as may be offered. I would say, in view of my present age and length of service, I feel myself competent to command a regiment, if the President, in his judgement, should see fit to entrust one to me.*

This letter was never answered. U. S. Grant, it seemed, had failed again. But no: the governor appointed him a colonel of the Twenty-first Illinois Volunteers, and Ulysses soon had a chance to prove both his ability and his bravery. By summer he had risen to the rank of a brigadier-general, and within a few months he had won several brilliant victories in the western part of the Confederacy. After a fierce battle between Federal and Confederate forces at Fort Donelson in Tennessee, the Confederate commander sent a message through the lines: On what terms would General Grant accept the surrender of the fort?

The answer came back promptly: "No terms, other than unconditional surrender."

From then on U. S. Grant was known as "Unconditional Surrender" Grant. He won victories by fighting, fighting, fighting—by never giving up—by never turning back.

Meanwhile in the East the war had not been going well for the Union. In March, 1864, President Lincoln called General Grant to Washington to take command of all the Federal forces. Crowds cheered him as he rode in a carriage down Pennsylvania Avenue to see the President. As he sat in his carriage, a short, heavy-set man puffing away at a cigar, he seemed somewhat embarrassed to find himself a hero.

"He had a slightly seedy look," said one newspaper reporter. But he also had "a clear blue eye and a look of resolution, as if he could not be trifled with."

The reporter was right. General Grant might not look like a hero, but he was resolved to bring the war to an end as speedily as possible. Regardless of the cost, he gave the enemy no rest. "I propose to fight it out on this line," he said during one battle, "if it takes all summer."

By April, 1865, the gallant Confederate commander, Robert E. Lee, realized that the cause of the South was hopeless. Brave though the Confederate soldiers were, they could not hold out much longer against the bigger armies of the North. To avoid needless suffering, General Lee wrote to General Grant, asking for terms of surrender. The two men met in the town of Appomattox Court House in Virginia.

"What General Lee's feelings were I do not know," General Grant wrote later in his *Memoirs*, "but my own feelings, which had been joyful when I received his letter, were sad and depressed. I felt like anything rather than rejoicing at the downfall of a foe who had fought so long and so bravely and had suffered so much."

When the Union general learned that Lee's soldiers had been living mostly on parched corn for the past three days, he arranged to send rations to them at once. Also he made the terms of surrender as generous as possible. All property belonging to the Confederate government was to be turned over to the Union forces. But the Confederate soldiers were to be paroled on their honor—that is, they would be allowed to return to their homes after promising not to take up arms again against the United States government.

General Lee's grave, handsome face showed his gratitude. "These terms will have a happy effect on my army," he said, "but there is one thing I would like to mention. My men in the cavalry and artillery brought their own horses with them. Will they be allowed to keep their animals?"

General Grant nodded. He understood how much a horse can mean to a man. Besides, he knew that most of the soldiers in the Confederate ranks were small farmers. Their farms had been stripped bare by two armies, and many Southern families would go hungry the next winter unless crops could be put in at once.

"Yes, your soldiers will need their animals for the spring plowing," said General Grant. "Any man who claims to own a horse or a mule will be allowed to keep it."

"That will be very gratifying to my men," General Lee replied, "and will do much toward conciliating our people."

General Grant had done more than any one man—except Abraham Lincoln—to win the war and to preserve the Union, and in 1868 a grateful people elected him President. Later, after he had left the White House, he wrote his *Memoirs*.

"It is probably just as well that we had the war when we did," he said in this book. Before it took place, he went on, the monarchies of Europe "generally believed that our republic was a rope of sand that would part the moment the slightest strain was put upon it."

Well, the American people had proved that this was not true, General Grant reflected with satisfaction. They had proved—in spite of the terrible war and the difficult problems still to be solved—that their republic, their form of government, was no "rope of sand."

THE EIGHTEENTH PRESIDENT *at a Glance*

Ulysses Simpson Grant

Born: April 27, 1822   *Died: July 23, 1885*

Early life. Ulysses S. Grant was born on his father's farm at Point Pleasant in southwestern Ohio. While Ulysses was still an infant, the family moved to Georgetown, Ohio. In 1839 he entered the U.S. Military Academy at West Point, N.Y. Graduating in 1843, he was commissioned second lieutenant. During the Mexican War he rose in rank to captain (1847). At 32 (1854), he resigned from the army and settled in Missouri. In 1860 he moved to Galena, Ill., where he clerked in a leather store.

In the Civil War. Grant was commissioned colonel of an Illinois volunteer regiment in the spring of 1861. Later that year he was made brigadier general. He captured Fort Henry and Fort Donelson, Confederate strongholds in northwestern Tennessee (1862). His seizure of Vicksburg on the Mississippi (July 4, 1863) gave the Union the control of the river and split the Confederacy in two. After being placed in command of all the Union forces (March, 1864), he fought several great battles in Virginia against General Robert E. Lee. Lee surrendered to Grant at Appomattox Court House (April 9, 1865).

After the war. Commissioned a full-rank general in 1866, Grant was the first U.S. army officer ever to receive so high a rank. In 1868 Grant was elected President on the Republican ticket.

As President (1869–1873; 1873–1877). By 1871 all the Southern states had been restored to their places in the Union. But in some of these states, government was controlled by Northerners who went south after the war to seek their fortunes. These men were known as "carpetbaggers" because, it was said, they arrived in the South owning nothing except what was in their cloth satchels, or carpetbags. The "carpetbag" state governments usually were corrupt and extravagant and were able to stay in power only because they were protected by Federal troops stationed in the Southern capitals. Great corruption also existed in the national government in Washington. Although the President himself was completely honest, some of the friends he appointed to high office cheated the government out of large sums of money. *Grant's wife,*

The President's family. Julia Dent Grant, (1826–1902) was a well-liked hostess. The Grants had three sons, and their daughter Nellie was very popular. She was married (1874) at the White House to an Englishman, Captain Sartoris.

Other happenings. Ceremonies at Promontory, Utah (May, 1869) marked the completion of the first transcontinental railroad. The 15th Amendment to the Constitution gave equal voting rights to citizens, regardless of race or color (1870). Much of Chicago was destroyed by fire (1871). A severe financial panic (1873–1876) caused much suffering. Alexander Graham Bell patented the telephone (1876). The Centennial Exposition in Philadelphia (1876) celebrated the nation's 100th birthday. General George Custer and his soldiers were killed at Little Big Horn, Mont., by Sioux Indians (1876).

The nation's population and growth. The population was about 38,500,000 (1870 census). Colorado was admitted as the 38th state (1876).

As ex-President. Grant lost all his money through a business failure (1884). The next year, though in great pain from a fatal illness, he wrote his *Personal Memoirs* to provide for his family's future.

"*His Honesty*" RUTHERFORD B. HAYES

"O Sire, I pray thee grant me my wish!"

Fanny Hayes fell on her knees before Rutherford, her younger brother, who seemed to be having a hard time remembering his lines. "Nay, fair Ellen," he said at last, "do not be afraid."

The two children were acting out their favorite poem, "The Lady of the Lake," which Fanny had made into a play. She was taking the part of the beautiful Ellen Douglas. Ruddy pretended that he was King James V, wandering through the Scottish highlands disguised as James Fitz-James, the knight. He gave Ellen a ring and told her, if she should ever be in trouble, to take it to the king of Scotland.

Now came the final scene of the play, in which Ellen went to the castle. To her surprise she learned that James Fitz-James was none other than the king himself. Rutherford's voice rang out loud and clear as he took the ring that Fanny gave him:

> ". . . Thou still dost hold
> That little talisman of gold,
> Pledge of my faith, Fitz-James' ring——
> What seeks fair Ellen of the king?"

In a trembling voice Ellen asked that her lover be freed from the castle dungeon.

"Malcolm, come forth!" the king demanded.

There was no one to take the part of Malcolm, but Fanny seemed satisfied to embrace the empty air. She sighed blissfully.

"Oh, Ruddy, wasn't it grand?" she said.

Ruddy nodded, his cheeks even redder than usual. For the past hour he had forgotten that he was living in the year 1832 in a comfortable two-story red brick house in the little town of Delaware, Ohio. In the big yard where he had been "play acting" with his sister, the honeysuckle was in bloom. But the children's imagination carried them far away, so that they saw instead the rugged crags of Scotland.

"Let's play it all over again," said Rutherford.

"Wouldn't you rather read?" Fanny suggested. "I'll go in the house and get the Shakespeare book."

Although Ruddy was ten, he still liked to hear Fanny read aloud. When she returned, he stretched out on the grass, content to listen to the music of the words as she read Marc Antony's famous speech in *Julius Caesar*. Someday, Rutherford thought dreamily, he was going to make speeches. He was going to grow up to be a famous man.

First, of course, he wanted to go to college, and he knew that his Uncle Sardis would help him. Ruddy's father was dead, but Sardis Birchard, his mother's brother, seemed more like a father than an uncle. He took a great interest in his nephew's education, and when the boy was fifteen, sent him to a preparatory school in New England. A year later, Rutherford returned to Ohio and entered Kenyon College. A likeable, good-natured youth, who liked to fish and tell funny stories, he soon became very popular. He was also a good student, and he entered with zest into discussions of the political questions of the day.

Like many older people at that time, the young men at Kenyon argued about slavery. At the Fourth of July program in the college chapel in 1839, a Northern student made a speech that offended some of the Southern boys, and Thomas Kane from Kentucky heckled the speaker. Within a few minutes nearly everyone in the chapel was taking sides. Rutherford was afraid that the meeting would end in a riot.

Then two of his classmates stood up. Shouting to make themselves heard above the noise, they suggested that everyone form in line for a short march to the tune of "Yankee Doodle."

"This was immediately agreed to," Rutherford wrote in his diary that night. "The spirit-stirring notes of the favorite air recalled at once to the minds of the combatants the fact that we were all Americans. The dispute was amicably settled and we were better friends than ever. I trust all other sectional disputes may always be as fortunately ended as this."

This hope was not to be realized, for twenty-two years later the Civil War began. By then Rutherford Birchard Hayes had opened a law office in Cincinnati, Ohio, but in May, 1861, he gave up his law practice to join the Union army. He fought bravely and became a major general. While he was still in the army, his friends back in Ohio elected him to Congress, but he refused to take his seat until the war was over.

Later he was elected governor of his state and was living in Columbus, the capital, in June, 1876, when the Republican party nominated him for President. In a letter accepting the nomination, he declared that he would run for one term only. "I really think," he said, "that the President could do more good in one term if untrammelled by the belief that he was fixing things for his election to a second term."

Governor Hayes hoped, if elected, to bring about some much-needed reforms. The Democratic candidate, Samuel J. Tilden, was also for reform, and on election day in November he received a quarter of a million more votes than did Hayes. But the President of the United States is not chosen by a direct vote of the people. Instead, the voters in each state vote for electors who then choose the President. By evening of election day, it appeared that Tilden would win enough electoral votes to make him the President. Rutherford and his wife Lucy went to bed, thinking he had lost.

By the next evening they were not so sure. There were rumors that the votes in several Southern states had not been counted correctly. As the days passed, some of the followers of both candidates accused one another of fraud. THE MAMMOTH NATIONAL DOUBT, read the headline in one newspaper. WHICH? read the headline in another. For several weeks, the whole nation was in suspense. In other countries, too, people were wondering what was going to happen.

"Such a state of affairs," read an article in the London *Times,* "could not occur anywhere else in the world. The entire area of the country agitated by the uncertain issue of the political struggle, yet not one shot fired. . . ."

Governor Hayes quoted from this article in a speech before a large group of his admirers. It made him feel proud that—although

in the part of Ohio known as the Western Reserve had been started by James' father, but he died before James was two years old. Since then the "Widow Garfield" had had a hard time making both ends meet. James earned extra money doing chores for the neighbors, but in between jobs he attended the log schoolhouse close by. He borrowed every book that he could find, but his books only made him more anxious to go out and see the world. Sometimes it seemed that he could not bear the humdrum life of a farm boy any longer.

After the two girls married and moved away, and Thomas left to work on a farm in Michigan, James felt even more restless than before. In the spring of 1848, when he was sixteen, he found a job chopping wood for a farmer who lived on the shores of Lake Erie some miles away. He liked being near the lake, for the blue waters reminded him of the books he had read about the sea. Sometimes, as he watched a vessel disappear over the horizon, he would imagine that he was one of the sailors on board. He could see himself pacing the deck and giving orders to other sailors, or keeping watch at night.

The picture stayed with him when he returned home, but after a talk with his mother he promised to give up the idea of becoming a sailor. He went back to the drudgery of doing odd jobs for the neighbors. He chopped wood at fifty cents a day; he cut grass at fifty cents an acre; he helped at house-raisings; he plowed and hoed corn. But each job seemed more uninteresting than the last.

One night, after a hard day in the hayfield, he strode up to the house. "Mother, I can't stand it any longer. Don't make me keep my promise," he begged. "Please let me be a sailor."

Mrs. Garfield looked at her son sadly. "All right, James," she said at last. "You may try one trip on Lake Erie."

With a light heart James gathered a few clothes together in a bundle, placed them on a stick over his shoulder, and kissed his mother good-bye. He had a plan. He would go to Cleveland, board one of the vessels in port, ask for the captain, and say that he wanted to learn the business of sailing. The captain, looking hale and hearty like a captain in a story, would answer, "Aye, lad," and clap him on the shoulder as a sign of welcome.

With thoughts like these racing through his brain, the long walk to Cleveland seemed short. There was only one vessel tied up on the shore, but one was enough. James smoothed down his fair hair, walked up the gangplank, and spoke to one of the deck hands.

"I'd like to see the captain, please."

The deck hand gave him a strange look. "The cap'n's below. He'll be up soon."

At that moment a sudden roar caused James to turn around. A brutal-looking man was staggering toward him.

"What do you want hyar? I'm the captain of this vessel," he snarled.

James was amazed. Nothing like this had ever happened in the stories he had read. From the looks of this fellow, he would just as soon make a boy walk the plank as not. But James was not going to let anyone see that he was afraid. He looked the angry seaman in the eye.

"Could you use another deck hand, sir?" he asked.

The captain lifted a heavy fist and began to swear. "Get off my vessel, you country greenhorn. Get off, before I——"

The sailors broke into laughter, and James hurried down the gangplank much faster than he had gone up.

For several hours he walked the streets of the city, his face burning with shame. Finally he remembered that his cousin, Amos Letcher, was in command of the *Evening Star,* a boat making regular trips on the canal between Cleveland and Pittsburgh. He would hurry down to the canal and see if the boat was in.

"Why Jim!" exclaimed Captain Letcher. "What are you doing in Cleveland?"

"I am looking for work," Jim replied. "I came here to ship on the lake, but one captain called me a country greenhorn and ordered me off the boat."

"You'd better try your hand on smaller waters first," Amos Letcher suggested. "How would you like to be a canaler? I have nothing better than a driver's berth to offer you, but if you would like to work for me I can pay you twelve dollars a month."

James nodded. "Thank you, Cousin Amos," he said. It was not the job he had been hoping for, but he needed the money.

The *Evening Star* carried freight, and the deck hands were filling up the front half with copper ore. But Captain Letcher led the way toward the stern half of the boat, where a cabin took up most of the space. Inside, James saw a row of iron frame bunks hinged against the wall, with canvas stretched over each one to form a bed. He laid down his belongings, still tied up neatly in a handkerchief, on the bunk his cousin pointed out.

Early next morning he began his work as driver. He walked behind a pair of mules and guided them along the path that ran beside the canal. To the mules' harness was attached one end of a long tow line. The other end was fastened to the boat.

"Gedap, Kit! Gedap, Nance!" James shouted, and the team heaved forward. The long rope attached to the boat grew taut as the *Evening Star* began to glide along the canal.

Why, the work was easy, thought James—and it was fun. Although a man stood at the rudder of the boat and steered it, it was really the mules that made it move. They obeyed every touch of James' hands upon the reins. When he urged the mules forward, they went faster. Tightening the reins made the mules slacken their pace. And when he pulled, they stopped altogether. In one way, thought the new driver, it was he, James Garfield, who was making the boat move through the waters of the canal.

But after several hours, busy thinking about his own importance, the boy failed to notice that the mules were slowing down, or that the boat was drifting ahead of the team. Then—splash! Driver and mules were floundering in the canal! The water was cold. James could not swim, but he threw his arms around Kit's neck and climbed on the mule's back. Somehow he managed to hang on while he reached out and grasped Nance's reins. Then he guided both animals toward shore, and they scrambled up on dry land again.

"Careful there, landlubber!" a deck hand shouted.

James decided that being a driver was not as easy as it looked. During that first trip he fell into the canal several times. Still, he did his work so well that when the boat returned to Cleveland he was promoted to the job of bowsman. He felt very proud, clad in his new heavy oilskin coat and pants, as he stood at the bow and acted as lookout. It was his task to see that the boat did not come too near the bank or other boats. Sometimes he used a long pole to guide the *Evening Star* through a long channel.

"Bang!" One day the pole slipped from James' hand. It hit Dave, a deck hand, and set him sprawling.

"I'm sorry!" cried James. "I didn't mean to hit you."

Dave staggered to his feet, his eyes blazing. "Didn't mean to, eh?"

He made a lunge toward the boy, but James did not move. He did not want to fight, but if he had to it might as well be now. When Dave was almost upon him, James jumped aside. He dealt his opponent a blow behind the ear and the older, heavier man fell to the deck. In a moment the boy was on his back.

"Pound him! Pound him!" shouted Amos Letcher. "A man who will get mad at an accident ought to be thrashed."

Jim paused, his fist raised in mid-air. Somehow he couldn't strike. "Get up, Dave," he said. "It's all right."

Sheepishly, Dave picked himself up. "I'm sorry I lost my temper."

From then on the deck hands looked on their sixteen-year-old bowsman with new respect.

James liked being a canaler. He liked the times when the boat horns stirred the early morning echoes and the long procession of boats began creeping along the narrow channel. He liked the times when the *Evening Star* tied up at a dock and curious crowds gathered to watch the cargo being unloaded. Most of the nights were spent tied up at some dock; but if Captain Letcher was in a hurry to deliver a cargo, he might continue his journey through the darkness. James never minded as he stood at the bow looking out over the water that gave back the bright reflection of the stars. He did not even mind the nights when the canal was shrouded in silver mist, and the stillness was broken only by the swishing of water against the hull.

One rainy midnight Captain Letcher went down into the cabin and shook James awake. "Twelve o'clock," the captain said. "Time for you to keep watch."

James sleepily stumbled out of his berth and took his place on the narrow ledge below the bow deck. The tow line was lost in darkness, but on the towpath a little ahead to the right James could make out a moving light—the lantern of the driver sitting astride one of the mules. Half-asleep, James leaned a little too far over the edge and his foot slipped. He cried out and grasped a rope to keep himself from falling overboard.

The rope held for a moment, then began to unwind. Down, down, he felt himself slipping. His feet touched the cold water. He felt it on his legs and then his knees. He shivered as it reached his waist. He began to murmur the prayer that his mother had taught him as a child. The rope continued to unwind, lowering him by inches into the canal.

"Help! Help!" cried the boy, but no one heard.

"I'm drowning!" thought Jim, as he felt the water close above his shoulders.

But no, by some miracle the rope had stopped unwinding. It held, and the boy was able to lift his chin above the stagnant water and get a breath of air. This gave him strength, and, pulling himself up hand over hand, he drew himself to safety on the deck. Wet and shivering, he bent over the rope. What was it that had caused it to stop unwinding at the very moment he was about to drown?

His throat suddenly felt very tight as he saw that the rope had been drawn into a crack just where it came over the edge of the boat, and there it had knotted itself. Weakly James sat down in his wet clothes, his back to the rudder post. He thought of his mother; not once had he written her since he left home. How she must have worried! When she learned of his narrow escape, would she say that he had been saved for some career more important than canaling?

A short time later James was taken ill, and he left the boat for home. He was very sick for five months, but his mother finally nursed him back to health. Never once did she reprove him for the worry he had caused her, but her eyes were sad when he began to talk of returning to the canal.

"James," she said quietly, "you are still weak. If you go back to the canal right away, you may get sick again. Why don't you go to school again this year? With a little more schooling, you may be able to teach in the wintertime. If you teach winters and go on the canal in the summers, you will have employment all the year round. You always did well at your books. Maybe you'd like to go to the seminary."

James leaned back in his chair. The seminary was only a few miles away in the next town, and indeed he would like to go there. But he knew that he did not have enough money saved to pay his entrance fees. His mother smiled mysteriously and walked over to the bureau. She opened a drawer, and when she came back her hands were filled with coins and a few bills.

"You can earn your way at the seminary after you get started," she went on, "but in the beginning you'll need some more money to pay your fees. Thomas and I have saved a little—seventeen dollars—and it's all for you."

She pressed the money into his hands, but James could find no words to express his gratitude. He tried to smile. He knew that his mother was making him a gift of all she had.

James never went back to his old job. His mother's gift had opened the way to a future very different from what his life might have been as a canaler. After working his way through the seminary, he attended Hiram College, and then went East to Williams College. Following his graduation, he returned to Hiram as a teacher, became its president within a year, studied law on the side, and at the age of twenty-nine was elected to the Ohio State Senate. In 1861 he interrupted his political career to join the Union army, and rose rapidly to the rank of brigadier general. While serving in the army he was elected to the United States House of Representatives, where he remained for the next seventeen years.

Naturally James' mother was very proud of her famous son. But never had she felt so proud as on the morning of March 4, 1881. There had been a storm the night before, but neither snow nor hail could dampen the enthusiasm of the thousands of people who had crowded into Washington to witness another inauguration. When the white-haired old lady now known as "Grandma Garfield" took her place on the high platform in front of the Capitol, she looked down upon a vast throng. In the row just in front of her sat James' wife and his five children. But she had eyes only for the distinguished-looking, bearded man who was taking the oath of office as President of the United States.

As James Garfield repeated the solemn words, his mother listened quietly. Was she remembering the day when she had persuaded him to give up his life on the canal and encouraged him to go back to school? Was James remembering, too?

"After taking the oath of office," reported one newspaper reporter who described the inauguration, "the President reverently kissed the Bible. Then turning about, he kissed first his mother, then his wife. We believe there is no precedent for this recognition of the family, but the gesture was most pleasing to the spectators who rent the air with cheers."

As for Grandma Garfield, in the words of another spectator, her "happiness seemed to be overflowing."

She knew that James Garfield had remembered.

THE TWENTIETH PRESIDENT *at a Glance*

James Abram Garfield

Born: November 19, 1831   *Died: September 19, 1881*

Early life. James Garfield was born in a log cabin at Orange, Ohio. As a youth, he worked as a farmer and as a canal bargeman. He attended Hiram College and then Williams College, from which he was graduated in 1856. Returning to Ohio, he became a teacher at Hiram College and later its president. While at Hiram (1857–1861), he studied law and also served as state senator for two years (1859–1861). Early in the Civil War he joined the Union army and was commissioned a lieutenant colonel (1861). He saw active service in several battles, won several promotions, and in September, 1863, was commissioned major general for gallantry in battle.

Political career. On President Lincoln's advice, Garfield resigned from the army (December, 1863) to serve in the House of Representatives, to which he had been elected the previous year. He was in Congress for 17 years. In 1880 the Republicans nominated Garfield as President.

As President (March–September, 1881). Four months after becoming President, Garfield was shot (July 2, 1881) by an office seeker who was angry because he had not been given a government job. The wounded President died the following September.

The President's family. Lucretia Garfield (1832–1918) and James Garfield had been schoolmates at Hiram College and were married (1858) after he became the school's president. One of their sons, Harry A. Garfield, became president of Williams College (1908–1934). Another son, James R. Garfield, was Secretary of the Interior (1907–1909) in Theodore Roosevelt's Cabinet.

CHESTER ARTHUR, *Boss*

Chester Arthur's friends gathered around him, waiting to hear more about his plan. It had been raining hard, leaving a small rivulet flowing down the side of the muddy road. Chester's idea was to build a dam across the little stream, thus making a reservoir that would really hold water.

"Sure, Chester," said one of the boys. "Tell us how to do it."

"All right. You carry over some of those big stones. And you"— he turned to another boy—"bring some sticks—lots of them. We'll stand them up in the ground, and then we'll fill in the spaces between the sticks with sod and mud."

Chester, standing with hands in his pockets, gave his orders crisply. The boys obeyed without question. They brought what he asked for. They got down on their hands and knees and forced the mud into place against a background of stones and sticks. Chester nodded in approval.

"Now it will hold water all right. That's a good dam we made."

"We?" asked one of the boys indignantly, as he glanced down at his dirty hands and the mud on his trousers. "Well, Chester, I see that you didn't get any dirt on your hands."

It was true. When Chester took his hands from his pockets they were white and clean. But his friends did not really mind. They probably would never have built the dam at all, if that Arthur boy had not suggested it and then told them how.

Chester was the son of the Union Village Baptist minister, who had recently come from Vermont to this little town just over the New

York state line. Already Chester had made many friends. Although he studied harder than the other boys, he was always ready to go fishing or swimming or to take part in sports and games.

By the time Chester was fourteen, he was becoming interested in politics, and his friends followed his lead in this, as they did in other things. In 1844, Henry Clay was the Whig candidate for President. He was one of the most popular men in the United States and, because of the ash trees growing near his home in Kentucky, his admirers had made the ash tree his symbol. Chester, who like his father was an ardent Whig, thought Henry Clay one of the greatest men who ever lived.

"Let's plant an ash tree in his honor," Chester suggested one day. "That's what Whigs everywhere are doing now."

The other boys answered with a whoop of delight. In the woods close by they dug up a small ash tree to transplant. They worked quickly and quietly. There was a keen rivalry between them and the boys whose fathers were Democrats, and the young Whigs did not want their rivals to find out about their plan until the ash tree was planted firmly in the ground. Just as they were pressing the soft earth around the roots, the sound of singing was heard in the distance. Chester leaned on his shovel to listen. The Democratic boys were singing a song about their candidate, James Knox Polk:

"When a boy James K. Polk left his state and his home
And the friends of his youth, o'er the Union to roam . . .
And the people all said, when this boy is a man
In freedom's great cause he'll one day lead the van,
And be a true-hearted statesman."

Chester's young Whigs worked furiously, the blood rising to their faces. The Whig party also had its songs, and there was one in particular that seemed very suitable just then. Defiantly they sang:

"Ye aristocratic Democrats:
One word and I have done;
I'll leave you in the people's hands,
By Henry Clay led on."

The young Democrats were coming closer. Jeering and shouting, they made a rush toward the ash tree. The Whigs looked at Chester. He was their leader, and they waited for his command.

His handsome face was flushed. "Drive them back, fellows!" he cried. "They shan't touch our ash tree."

With dark head lowered, he led the attack upon the enemy. There were shouts on both sides: "Down with Polk!" "Vote for Clay!" "Polk's the man to vote for."

"At 'em, boys, at 'em! We'll drive them off!" Chester shouted his orders in a quick, tense voice.

The Whigs charged, their arms flying as they dealt blows to right and left. With howls of anger and disappointment the young Democrats turned and fled.

That was Chester Arthur's first political victory, but his triumph did not last very long. On election day that November Henry Clay was defeated. But there would be other political battles in the years ahead, and Chester intended to win them.

After graduating from Union College with honors at the age of eighteen, Chester Arthur taught school, and studied law in his spare time. He then went to work for a law firm in New York City, won several important cases, joined the newly-organized Republican party, and became an enthusiastic member of the local Republican organization. When General Grant was inaugurated as President, Chester Arthur was appointed Collector of the Port of New York. The employees who served under him, about a thousand of them, had been given their positions as a reward for service to their party, and with so many jobs to give out, Chester Arthur had a great deal of power. He was one of the "bosses" of the Republican organization in New York state—"the gentleman boss," he was called, because he was so handsome and charming and had so many friends. He sincerely believed, as did many political leaders of his time, in the old saying "To the victor belong the spoils."

And then Rutherford Hayes was inaugurated as President. He was just as firmly convinced that men and women should be chosen for government positions because they were capable and not because of political influence. There was no question that Chester Arthur himself was honest and efficient, but he refused to stop making political appointments. For this reason Arthur and two of his associates were the first to be removed from office—an action that caused quite a stir throughout the nation.

In the Republican party, one faction approved of what the President had done. Another faction was very angry with him. An effort was made to appease the latter in the convention of 1880 by nominating Chester Arthur for Vice President. Earlier during that same convention, James Garfield had already been nominated for the

Presidency. No one could know that a few months after his inauguration he would be shot by a half-crazed assassin.

When Vice President Arthur learned of the shooting, he was in despair. He did not want to become President through the death of another man, and he felt a great sense of relief when James Garfield's physicians held out hope that he would recover. But the physicians were wrong. Although President Garfield put up a brave fight, he died a few weeks later, and Chester Arthur was inaugurated that same night.

"No more lonely and pathetic figure was ever seen assuming the powers of government," said Arthur's friend, the distinguished statesman, Elihu Root. "He was bowed down by the weight of fearful responsibility and crushed to earth by the feeling that he took up the burden surrounded by dislike, suspicion, and distrust. . . ."

The knowledge that many Americans did not trust him cut deep. But the people who at first feared that Chester Arthur might be influenced by party bosses were in for a big surprise. He proved to be an able and conscientious leader. He no longer believed that "To the victor belong the spoils." He was as insistent as ex-President Hayes had been that employees in government positions should be chosen because of merit. In 1883 he supported and signed the Civil Service Reform Act, which marked the beginning of a more fair and efficient system of giving out government jobs. The change in Arthur's attitude angered some of the prominent politicians who had once been his friends, and he failed to win the nomination to run for President in his own right.

What Chester Arthur did win was to him much more important. "My sole ambition," he once said, "is to enjoy the confidence of my countrymen." In this he had his wish.

"He made himself President of the nation and not of a party, still less of a faction within the party," said another friend. "As President he gained the confidence of the whole people."

THE TWENTY-FIRST PRESIDENT *at a Glance*

Chester Alan Arthur

Born: October 5, 1830   *Died: November 18, 1886*

Early life. Chester A. Arthur was born at Fairfield in northern Vermont. After graduating from Union College, Schenectady, N.Y.

(1848), he studied law while teaching school in Pownall, Vt. In 1853 he became a lawyer in New York City. During the Civil War he was quartermaster general of New York State (1861–1862).

Political career. After the war, Arthur became very active in Republican party politics. In 1871 President Grant appointed him Collector of the Port of New York. Seven years later (1878) President Hayes removed Arthur from this office because Arthur opposed the President's policy of civil service reform. In 1880 when the Republicans nominated James Garfield for President, they nominated Arthur for Vice President. They were elected and took office March, 1881. When Garfield died (September, 1881), Arthur became President.

As President (1881–1885). As head of the nation, Arthur, though formerly a "machine" politician, refused to play party politics. He also came to realize the dangers of the "spoils system" in making government appointments. In 1883 he signed into law a bill passed by Congress establishing a Civil Service Commission whose duty it was to see that certain government positions were filled by competitive examinations. Arthur's support of the Civil Service Act and other reform measures angered the "machine" politicians, and he was not nominated to run for another term.

The White House hostess. Ellen Herndon Arthur (1837–1880) died shortly before her husband became Vice President. When Arthur was President, his sister, Mrs. Mary McElroy, acted as his hostess.

Other happenings. When Arthur was President, the Standard Oil Co. joined with a number of other companies (1882) to become the first of the great "trusts," or large business combinations, that gained control of various fields of American industry. Congress passed a bill limiting Chinese immigration (1882). The opening of the Brooklyn Bridge (1883) connected Brooklyn, N.Y., with Manhattan Island.

Independent GROVER CLEVELAND

It was Saturday morning. Through the window ten-year-old Stephen Grover Cleveland could see a long hill gleaming under a layer of ice. He could hear the shouts of his friends as they shot down that smooth incline on their sleds. He thought wistfully of his own sled waiting for him outside the kitchen door.

But Grover had been told to get baby Rose Elizabeth to sleep before he went out to play, and duties were taken seriously in the Cleveland household. Back and forth, back and forth, he rocked the baby's cradle. He tried singing to her, but she only looked up at him with an unblinking stare. She was watching him so intently he decided that just seeing him might be keeping her awake.

"I know what I'll do," he muttered under his breath.

With that he crawled under the cradle, but he continued to rock it as he lay on the floor. The baby was so quiet, he decided that she must have gone to sleep at last. Now he could slip out the back door, get his sled, and join the fellows on the hill. Cautiously he raised his head and looked over the side of the cradle.

"Coo! Coo!" said Rose Elizabeth.

This was too much. There were tears of exasperation in Grover's eyes as he crawled under the cradle and started rocking it again. Soon the boys on the hill would be going home for dinner, and there would be no sledding for Grover Cleveland that morning.

He felt a gentle touch on his shoulder. His big sister was bending over him. "It's all right," she said, "I'll rock Rose Elizabeth to sleep. You go out and play."

Before his sister had a chance to change her mind, Grover grabbed his cap and coat, and the back door slammed behind him. He started up the hill, pulling his sled. When he reached the top, he looked down at the smooth path between the mounds of snow.

"Watch me!" he shouted to his friends as he lay down on his sled. Someone behind gave him a push. Grover seemed to be flying through the air as the sled bore him swiftly downward.

"Whee!" he said. "That was worth waiting for!"

Grover was one of nine children and, though they were poor, there was always something interesting going on in such a large family.

In the summer Grover went fishing with his brothers. Sometimes he went alone, with only his dog for company. His father, the Reverend Richard Cleveland, was the Presbyterian minister in the little town of Fayetteville, New York, and in his study were many books that Grover liked to read. He knew *Pilgrim's Progress* almost by heart. In the kitchen he and the other children sometimes helped their mother make candy, or they gathered around the fireplace and popped corn.

But when Saturday night came, the young Clevelands knew that the week's play was over. Toys were put away, and the big sisters set up the tubs on one side of the kitchen to give the younger children their weekly baths. On Sunday they all went to church, to Sunday school, and then to church again.

When Grover was fourteen, the family moved to Clinton, New York. Here William, an older brother, went to Hamilton College. Grover attended the Clinton Liberal Institute and looked forward to the time when he, too, would go to college.

One evening, after prayers, Mr. Cleveland laid his hand on Grover's arm as the boy was about to leave the room. "Stay," he said. "I want to talk with you alone."

There was a long pause. Mr. Cleveland seemed to be having a hard time finding the right words. "Son," he said finally, "I simply can't make both ends meet. Would you mind stopping school for a while? There is a job waiting for you in Deacon McVicar's store in Fayetteville. He will pay you fifty dollars the first year, besides giving you board and room. The second year you could earn a hundred dollars. If you are willing to work for the Deacon——"

Grover tried not to show his disappointment. His father had not been well, and the boy knew extra money was sorely needed. "Of course, I'll take the job," he said quietly.

Into Mr. Cleveland's eyes came the old happy look his children knew so well. "When conditions are better, you can go on with your studies," he said hopefully. "You can go to college later."

"Of course," Grover said again.

Back in Fayetteville, Grover's heart sank when he saw the room over the store where he and his fellow clerk, a youth named F. G. Tibbitts, were to live. There was no carpet on the floor, no paper on the walls. The only furniture was a plain pine bed with a straw-filled mattress. But after his first day in the store Grover was so tired he did not care where he slept. He sank down gratefully on the hard bed beside his roommate. In the middle of the night he woke up.

"What's that noise?" he asked.

Again came a strange rustling sound, as though tiny feet were scampering across the floor. The noise stopped—began again—grew louder.

"There it is! Hear it?"

"Oh, *that!*" said Tibbitts. "That is just the rats."

"Rats?"

"Sure! The rats get into the store, and sometimes they come up into our room."

"Ugh!" Grover shivered at the thought.

Soon he began to shiver for another reason. He was cold; he had never been so cold in all his life. There was no stove in the room, and the fire in the stove downstairs was kept up only during the day. As the winter wore on, the temperature often sank to below zero. But no matter how cold it was, the deacon's clerks had to get up at five-thirty.

"B-b-b-beat you g-g-getting dressed!" Grover would shout through chattering teeth. "B-b-beat you d-d-downstairs!"

"B-b-b-bet you d-d-don't!" Tibbitts would reply.

Down in the store, the boys soon had a fire roaring in the stove. They heated water in a tin wash basin, washed their faces, and ate breakfast. By the time Deacon McVicar appeared at the front door at seven o'clock, the store was swept and dusted and the goods laid out on the counters.

When summer came, the work was not quite so hard. Besides, Grover had his dog. It followed at his heels when he made deliveries for the store. He had taught it several tricks: to stand on its hind legs and walk, and to lie on its back and play dead. Now he was training it to climb a ladder. The boy would lean the ladder against the wooden balcony outside his bedroom window. Down below the dog would wait patiently while its young master raced upstairs, stepped out on the balcony, leaned over the railing, and gave the words of command:

"Ready, now. Up the ladder!"

Rung by rung the dog would begin the slow climb.

"Come on, old fellow, you can do it. There now—only four more rungs. Now only three—now two—ah, here you are!"

One day, as the boy reached out to help his pet over the railing, something happened. On the last rung of the ladder, the dog missed its footing and fell.

Grover was downstairs in an instant, kneeling beside the dog. It tried to rise, then lay back with a whine. With tears raining down his cheeks, Grover took it in his arms. The dog stretched out a pink tongue to lick its master's cheek.

A man from the village came up. "Too bad," he said. "We'd better shoot the poor creature right away."

"Shoot my dog?" asked Grover indignantly. "You shan't."

"I know how you feel," the villager replied, "but its legs are broken. We can't let it live."

Grover rose carefully, still holding his pet. "I can fix his broken legs," he said stubbornly. "I know I can."

The boy carried the poor, frightened animal to his room. There with gentle hands he bound the legs in splints. In a few weeks, to the villager's surprise and to Grover's deep satisfaction, his pet was well and trotting stiffly but happily at its master's heels.

After nearly two years in the store, Grover returned home, expecting to continue his preparations for college. He hoped to study law, but he found that his father's health was much worse. Richard Cleveland died soon afterward, leaving his widow almost penniless. It was up to the three older boys to care for her and the younger children. College was now out of the question, for Grover had to go to work again.

But such jobs as he could find he did not like, and at eighteen he made plans to go West. In the year 1855, Ohio seemed like "the West" to a boy living in New York state, and a family friend lent him twenty-five dollars for the journey. Grover took the train for Cleveland, but stopped off in Buffalo to see his uncle Lewis Allen, who lived on a farm on the outskirts of the city.

Grover had visited the family several years earlier, and Mr. Allen was delighted to see his sandy-haired nephew again. "Why, Grover, what are you doing here?"

"I'm on my way to Cleveland to find work."

"Cleveland?" Mr. Allen seemed surprised. "What made you decide to go there?"

To this question, Grover had no easy answer. His only reason for choosing Cleveland was that the name appealed to him because it was the same as his own.

"There is no need for you to go to a strange city, where you would have neither money nor friends," Mr. Allen went on. "You can live with us for a few months, and work on my farm. You say you are interested in law. I'll be looking around, and maybe I can find a place for you with a law firm."

Grover could only stammer his gratitude. He had been disappointed in not going to college, but there were other ways to get an education. Perhaps he could be a lawyer after all.

Five months later Lewis Allen, true to his promise, found a place for his nephew with a law firm in Buffalo. Grover was to be a clerk, and in the time that could be spared from his duties he could study the law books in his office.

The first day he reported for work, Mr. Rogers, the head of the firm, did not seem very enthusiastic at the thought of breaking in a new clerk. He pointed to a table and the new clerk sat down. Mr. Rogers walked over to a bookcase, and came back carrying a copy of Blackstone's *Commentaries*. As he threw it down on the table the long-undisturbed dust ascended in a cloud. "That's where they all begin," he said gruffly.

Eagerly Grover opened the book—probably the most famous law book in the world—and became so interested in it that it no longer seemed to matter whether Mr. Rogers was grumpy or not. Several hours went by, but Grover was so absorbed in what he was reading that he looked up with a start at the sound of a key clicking in the lock.

Why, it was noon. He was alone. Mr. Rogers, the other members of the firm, and the other law clerks had left for dinner. Grover had been so quiet that they had forgotten he was there. As usual, they had locked the door upon leaving the office, not realizing that they were locking in the new clerk.

Grover could not help laughing. "Someday," he promised himself, "I shall be better remembered."

Grover Cleveland kept that promise, but he never dreamed how well-remembered he really would be in the days to come. After winning success as a lawyer and in several minor political offices, he was elected mayor of his adopted city. He had grown into a big man, with a ruddy complexion and a firm mouth that could not be hidden by his drooping blond mustache. He was blunt, but he was honest. When he made a promise, he kept it. People trusted him, and a year later, when he was forty-four, he was elected governor of New York state.

His election as governor took place during a period when "bosses" in both political parties made it a practice to tell government officials what to do. A political boss was usually influenced by wealthy business leaders, and used his influence to see that officials they approved of were elected and kept in office.

Although Governor Cleveland knew that without the help of the bosses he might never be elected again, he steadfastly maintained his independence. His only interest was in providing an honest and efficient government for the people who had elected him. The reforms he put through, both as mayor and as governor, made him famous. By 1884, an election year, he was being talked of as a possible Democratic candidate for President.

In that same year the Republicans held their nominating convention in June, a month before the Democrats were to meet. When the convention was over, a group of prominent Republicans, who had become very angry about boss rule in their own party, announced that they could not conscientiously support the Republican ticket in the coming election. Instead, they declared, they would work for the election of the Democratic nominee, provided that the Democrats selected a worthy candidate.

At this turn of events, some of the other Republicans—the "regulars"—were furious. The "rebels" who had "bolted" the party were called "Mugwumps," an old Indian word meaning "big chiefs." So they considered themselves smarter than the rest of their party, did they? the regulars scoffed. There was a popular song which, it was hoped, would laugh the Mugwumps out of existence.

"Oh, we are the salt of the earth,
    And the pick of the people, too;
We're all of us men of worth,
    And vastly better than you."

Although people did laugh at the song, the Mugwump movement became very popular. There had not been a Democratic President since before the Civil War, but now the Democrats realized they might have a chance if they selected the right candidate. At their convention in July they nominated Grover Cleveland, not because the political bosses in his own party liked him, but because they thought they might possibly win the election with the "reform governor" of New York as their candidate.

As his campaign motto Grover Cleveland chose the slogan "Public office is a public trust." It was a bitter campaign, filled with abuse and cruel accusations by the followers of each candidate against the nominee of the other party. Grover Cleveland kept calm. The plain-spoken governor of New York, who three years earlier had hardly been known outside of Buffalo, was running against James G. Blaine, one of the most colorful, brilliant and polished politicians in the country. The election was close, but—with the help of the Mug-wumps—Grover Cleveland won. He himself could hardly believe it had happened.

"Sometimes," he said, shortly after he went to the White House to live, "I wake at night and rub my eyes and wonder if it is not all a dream."

This victory, President Cleveland realized, was only the beginning of a harder struggle. In his first message to Congress, he served notice that neither "threats" nor "allurements" could keep him from doing what he was convinced would lead "to better government for the people." As the months passed he became known as "the veto President," because he vetoed so many bills passed by Congress. Especially did he show his independence in opposing the high tariff rates which were then being charged.

At that time there was a surplus in the Treasury—much more money than was needed to run the government—and about two-thirds of it was from the tariff, the tax collections on goods and articles imported from abroad. The tariff made it necessary for the American merchants who sold the imported articles to charge a higher price for them. The owners of American factories also were able to price their goods high without fear of competition.

The result was that a few of the manufacturers were making large fortunes. At the same time there were thousands of men and women who found it hard to pay the higher prices being asked for the goods they needed. The remedy, both for high prices and the surplus in the Treasury, President Cleveland concluded, was a lower tariff. In the fall of 1887 he decided to take up the tariff in his annual message to Congress but some of his advisers suggested that he wait.

"Election is next year," they reminded him. "You are sure to be re-elected, but not if you send that message to Congress now. Wait until after the election before you raise the tariff question."

"That would not be fair to the country," Grover Cleveland replied.

"But, Mr. President," one of his advisers argued, "such a message will offend some of the big manufacturers. They have much influence and could defeat you."

The President leaned back in his big chair, which creaked beneath his weight. "It is more important to the country," he said stubbornly, "that this message should be delivered than that I should be elected President. I do not wish to be re-elected unless the people understand where I stand on the tariff question. What is the use of being elected, unless you stand for something?"

In spite of the protests of his friends and advisers, the entire message which the President sent to Congress that December dealt with the tariff. The huge surplus in the Treasury was mentioned, and a demand was made for a reduction in certain tariff rates. The President's recommendations were praised by some and criticized by others, and the tariff question was hotly argued during the next election campaign. Grover Cleveland lost.

"My friends all advised me," he admitted to a young man who came to call on him shortly afterward, "that if I sent in that message to Congress, it would probably defeat me. Perhaps I was mistaken from the party standpoint, but"—and he brought his fist down on his desk with a mighty bang—"it was right. I have at least that satisfaction."

"Yes, Mr. President, it was right," the caller assured him, "and I want to say to you, not only that it was right, but that the young men of the country are with you. Four years from now we mean to put you back in the White House."

Grover Cleveland shook his head; he thought that his political career was over. At the end of his term in 1889, he and his lovely young wife moved to New York City, where he practiced law for several years.

Meanwhile there were rumblings of discontent throughout the nation. Down in Washington, the surplus in the Treasury was rapidly disappearing because of lavish spending by Congress. Another tariff bill was passed, imposing new and higher taxes on imports, and many people feared there might be another financial panic. Some of the opponents of ex-President Grover Cleveland were opponents no longer. Perhaps, they said, he had been right about the tariff. There was a growing demand that he run for President again.

> "Grover! Grover!
> Four more years of Grover!
> In he comes,
> Out they go,
> Then we'll be in clover."

At the Democratic convention in 1892, when he was nominated for the third time, bands played in the convention hall, and banners waved as enthusiastic delegates chanted the new song.

In the campaign that followed, the Mugwumps again worked for the election of Grover Cleveland. As stubbornly independent as ever, he refused to make any promises to any politicians or groups of people. He was going to "have the Presidency clean," he said, "or not at all." On the evening of election day, a few close friends were invited to his home to wait for the returns, but it was past midnight before the final result was known.

Grover Cleveland had won an overwhelming victory. The candidate who had been defeated four years earlier was the only man in American history to become President a second time after a lapse of years. His friends were jubilant. Outside the house, a crowd had gathered, their voices raised in song:

> "Grover! Grover!
> Four more years of Grover . . .
> Now we'll be in clover."

A shadow passed over the face of the President-elect. Grateful though he was for the faith the American people had shown in him, he knew they would not "be in clover" during the next four years. The United States was threatened with another financial panic, and his second administration would probably be more difficult than his first term had been. He was being called on to serve his country in a time of crisis, and he would try to do what was right, but he did not feel like celebrating.

Turning to a friend, he said, "It is a solemn thing to be President."

THE TWENTY-SECOND AND THE TWENTY-FOURTH PRESIDENT *at a Glance*

Stephen Grover Cleveland

Born: March 18, 1837   *Died: June 24, 1908*

Early life. Grover Cleveland, the son of a Presbyterian minister, was born in Caldwell, N.J. His family moved to Fayetteville, N.Y., when he was 4, and 10 years later to Clinton, N.Y. After working in a store and teaching in an institution for the blind, he became a clerk in a Buffalo, N.Y., law office (1855). At 22 (1859) he was admitted to the bar and began to practice law in Buffalo.

Political career. Cleveland was assistant district attorney (1863–1865) and county sheriff (1870–1873). Later he served as mayor of Buffalo (1881–1882) and as governor of New York (1883–1885). He was elected President on the Democratic ticket in 1884.

As President (First term: 1885–1889). A large surplus in the Treasury encouraged Congress to pass many Civil War pension bills, in hope of pleasing the voters back home. Whenever Cleveland's own investigations proved the pensions were not deserved, the President risked popular disapproval and vetoed the Congressional bills. Since the country's high tariff had resulted in an increased cost of living as well as in too large a Treasury surplus, Cleveland urged Congress (1887) to reduce the import tax on many articles. A tariff reduction bill, introduced in Congress, failed to pass, and tariff became the main issue when Cleveland ran for re-election (1888). Although he received more popular votes, his opponent, Benjamin Harrison, who received more electoral votes, became the next President. Four years later (1892) Cleveland ran again and defeated Harrison.

As President (Second term: 1893–1897). Soon after Cleveland took office for the second time (March, 1893), a severe financial and business depression spread across the nation. One cause of the depression was a fear that there was too much silver in the government Treasury and not enough gold. Many people did not trust silver money, which kept decreasing in value as more and more silver was mined in the West. Cleveland agreed with those who felt that the nation's money policy was unsound, and he persuaded Congress to stop government purchases of silver and to take measures to increase the Treasury's supply of gold. In 1894 the President sent Federal troops to Chicago to stop the disorders in a great strike by workers of the Pullman Co. and the railroads. In 1895 a boundary dispute between Venezuela and a British colony in South America led Cleveland to make it very clear that he intended to uphold the Monroe Doctrine, which warned against European attempts at further expansion on the American continents. For a while, there was a possibility of war between the U.S. and Britain, but the British finally agreed to arbitrate the boundary question.

The First Lady. The President, a bachelor when he took office, was married at the White House in 1886. His wife, Frances Folsom Cleveland (1864–1947), the daughter of Cleveland's former law partner, was probably the most popular First Lady since Dolley Madison. Esther, the Clevelands' second child, was the first child of a President to be born in the White House (1893).

Other happenings. During Cleveland's first term as President the surrender of the Indian chief Geronimo to U.S. troops marked the end of Apache raids in the Southwest (1886). A bomb thrown by an anarchist during a labor rally in Haymarket Square, Chicago, killed seven policemen and wounded many others (1886). The Statue of Liberty was dedicated (1886). The Interstate Commerce Act of 1887 placed railroad rates under government control.

During Cleveland's second term some American-built automobiles began to appear on the roads: the Duryea, the Ford, and the Haynes. The World's Columbian Exposition was held in Chicago (1893). Two steam-driven model airplanes, built by Samuel P. Langley, were the first self-propelled, heavier-than-air machines to fly successfully (1896).

The nation's growth. When Cleveland became President the first time, there were 38 states in the Union. No new states were added during his first term, but 6 new states were admitted to the Union while Benjamin Harrison was President. During Cleveland's second term in office Utah was admitted as the 45th state (1896).

BEN HARRISON and His Grandfather's Hat

The general lifted his high silk hat and bowed as he passed by in the parade. Every time anyone shouted, "Hurrah for Tippecanoe," or, "Hurrah for the hero of Maumee," William Henry Harrison lifted his hat and bowed again. Ben, the general's chubby, seven-year-old grandson, squared his shoulders proudly. All of those people in the parade, and all of the people who stood watching by the side of the road, wanted his grandfather to be the next President. They called him "Tippecanoe" and sometimes "Old Tip" because he had defeated the Indians in the battle of Tippecanoe. Before that he had taken part in another famous battle on the Maumee River, and the words "Tippecanoe" and "Maumee" were on everybody's tongue.

And now a band was passing. It struck up the tune of a song that was very popular in the summer of 1840:

> "When my old hat was new,
>   The friends of liberty
> Well knew the merits of old Tip
>   While fighting at Maumee.
> Come now, huzza for Harrison
>   Just as we used to do . . .
> When my old hat was new."

Ben glanced up at his grandfather, dignified and distinguished-looking in a tall silk hat. When the boy turned back to watch the parade again, a log cabin mounted on a float was rolling by. A 'coon skin was nailed to the wall, and real smoke was coming from the chimney. Behind the float marched several men carrying a large banner with the slogan TIPPECANOE, THE LOG CABIN CANDIDATE.

A bewildered expression passed over the grandson's face. Why, Grandpa Harrison didn't live in a cabin. His home in North Bend, Ohio, where Benjamin often came to visit, was a handsome two-story house with many rooms. There were several questions Ben wanted to ask. But as soon as the parade was over, General Harrison was surrounded by friends talking about the coming election. Finally Ben walked back to the house alone, his tow head bent in thought.

His grandmother stood in the doorway, smiling a welcome, and Ben ran up and threw his arms around her. She led the way into the dining room, tucked a napkin under his chin and gave him his dinner. As she sat down opposite him she noticed the worried frown between his eyes.

"What's the matter, Ben?" she said.

"What do folks mean," he asked gravely, "calling this house a log cabin?"

"Oh, that is just part of their campaign talk," Mrs. Harrison explained. "There are two political parties, as you know—the Whigs and the Democrats. When the Whigs nominated your grandfather to be President, one of the Democratic newspapers made fun of him because he lived in a log cabin."

"But he doesn't," said Ben indignantly.

"Not now, but this house was a log cabin when your grandfather and I were first married. After a while he had the logs covered with boards, and two wings were added. The house was painted to look just as it does today."

Benjamin selected a large red apple from a bowl in the center of the table, and sank his teeth into it. "Isn't it all right to live in a log cabin?" he asked.

Mrs. Harrison could not help smiling as she glanced around the comfortable room. "That is what the Whigs think," she replied. "Many voters seem to like the idea of having a plain, sturdy, honest man as President, and if he once lived in a log cabin, so much the better."

The boy walked over to the fireplace and gazed up at the portrait above the mantel. A dark-haired, kindly man with a long, lean face and fearless black eyes seemed to gaze back at him. Ben knew that his grandfather was a member of one of the most famous families in America—the son of an earlier Benjamin Harrison, who had been a signer of the Declaration of Independence. As a young man, William Henry had come west to fight the Indians, and because of what he and others like him had done, the Northwest Territory was now a safe place for white people to live in.

"I hope that Grandpa wins," Benjamin exclaimed.

General Harrison did win. One day in November, soon after the election, the President-elect took Benjamin with him to the little city of Cincinnati close by. As they walked through the streets, the general was stopped again and again by admirers who wished to shake his hand. Ben was getting tired—and very hungry. During one long conversation, he shifted impatiently from foot to foot, but his eyes brightened when he saw a fruit stand. Walking over, he helped himself to an apple. It was delicious, and he took another. He filled his pockets, in case he should get hungry later on. The woman who stood in back of the stand was staring at him, but the boy did not notice.

"Come, Ben, we must be going now," said his grandfather.

Ben had started on his third apple, and his mouth was too full to speak as he took his grandfather's hand. They were walking away when a shrill shriek rent the air.

"That boy did not pay me," the apple woman cried. "He took several of my apples, and not one cent did he pay me."

General Harrison turned in surprise. Benjamin's cheeks grew red. The way the woman looked at him made him feel like a thief. At home anyone who cared to come into the orchard could have as many apples as he could eat, and during the recent presidential campaign they had been given out freely.

"How much were the apples?" the general asked quietly.

The woman stopped spluttering and told him. He placed a coin in her hand; then walked on with his grandson.

"I didn't know apples ever cost money, Grandpa!"

"It's all right; never mind," the general answered in a kind voice. And Benjamin breathed a sigh of relief as he bit into another apple.

Although Ben visited his grandparents often, his real home was at The Point, a farm five miles farther west where the Great Miami and Ohio rivers flowed together. His father, John Scott Harrison, had built a log schoolhouse overlooking the Ohio, and here the Harrison children went to school. In the evening their mother would light the candles and they would gather around the big center table in the dining room to study their lessons.

By February, 1841, the young Harrisons were almost too excited to study. The inauguration would take place early in March, and their grandfather boarded the stagecoach for Washington. Their grandmother, who had been ill, planned to join him later.

April came. The broad Ohio, flowing on its tranquil way at the foot of the farm, shone like a long bright mirror in the sunshine. The trees put out their first tender buds, making a pattern of pale green lace against the sky. Up in the big house in North Bend Mrs. Harrison was preparing for her journey to the nation's capital when she received a melancholy message. Her husband had died exactly one month after he became President.

The next time Benjamin saw his grandmother, she was pale and sad. A lump came into his throat when he lifted his eyes to the portrait above the fireplace.

Many times during the years that followed, Benjamin looked at that portrait. They were busy years. He had chores to do on the farm. He caught fish in the river, and hunted for squirrels in the woods. At fourteen he left home to attend a preparatory school in Cincinnati. He was an excellent student, and two years later he was ready to enter Miami University at Oxford, Ohio.

When he came to tell his grandmother good-bye, she walked with him to the gate. She watched wistfully as he mounted his horse and rode away. A fine boy, she thought, warm and affectionate with those who knew him best. With most people, however, he was so shy that he probably would never be as popular as the general had been. All the same, the grandson had inherited the grandfather's keen sense of duty. Benjamin Harrison would serve his country well; of that his grandmother was convinced.

After Ben finished college, he studied law, married his college sweetheart and opened a law office in Indianapolis, the capital of Indiana. He was a good lawyer and worked hard. Clients sought him —partly, it was suspected, because he was a Harrison. In the meantime Ben had joined the new Republican party, and one day a group of enthusiastic Republicans rushed upstairs and into his office.

A political meeting, they said, was being held in the street outside. They wanted Ben to make a speech, and they only laughed when he protested. Paying no attention to his struggles, they picked him up forcibly and carried him downstairs. This was easy, because Ben was not very big. A minute later he found himself standing on an upturned box facing a large crowd. And then one of his "captors" introduced him.

"We shall now hear," the audience was told, "from the grandson of General William Henry Harrison, once governor of Indiana Territory, the famous hero of Tippecanoe, and the ninth President of the United States."

Proud though Ben was of his ancestors, this introduction made him angry. He drew himself up until he looked much taller than his actual five-foot, six-inch height.

"I want it understood," he said defiantly, "that I am the grandson of nobody. I believe that every man should stand on his own merits."

And then he made a short talk. Reserved though Benjamin Harrison was in private conversation, he was an excellent public speaker. This talent, as well as his illustrious name, brought him ever increasing success in his law practice. Eight years later, when the Civil War began, he interrupted a promising career to enlist.

"I love to feel," he wrote in a letter to Carrie, his wife, "that I am in some humble way serving a country which has brought so many honors to my kindred and such untold blessings to those I love."

Benjamin Harrison's part in the war was by no means humble. He proved himself a fearless soldier and officer, advancing rapidly from the rank of captain to that of brigadier-general. After the war he returned to his law practice in Indianapolis, and in 1880 was nominated for the United States Senate. One day during a political campaign, when Benjamin Harrison was about to leave Indianapolis to make a speech in another town, a neighbor took him to the railroad station.

"Now, Ben, I know you'll capture them with your speech," the neighbor said, "but for heaven's sake be a human being down there. Mix around a little with the boys after the meeting."

This advice was well meant. But when Benjamin Harrison tried to "mix with the boys," he only succeeded in feeling miserable and ill at ease. "I tried it but I failed," he admitted later to his friend. "I'll never try it again. I must be myself."

In being himself, Benjamin Harrison did not always impress people in the same way. To his family and a few close friends he was kind and gentle. To the page boys in the Senate he was always considerate and polite. When he raised his hand—the sign the Senators used whenever they needed a boy to run an errand—there was a rush among the pages to see who could serve him first. With his fellow Senators, however, he seldom unbent. But when he rose to make a speech, he was listened to with respect.

Benjamin Harrison's eloquence undoubtedly helped him to win the Republican nomination for the Presidency in 1888. There were still people living who remembered the song "When My Old Hat Was New" that had been sung when William Henry Harrison had been a candidate for the same office forty-eight years earlier. And now another campaign song about a hat was sweeping the country:

"Yes, Grandfather's hat fits Ben—fits Ben.
　　He wears it with dignified grace,
　　　Oh, yes!
　So rally again and we'll put Uncle Ben
　　Right back in his grandfather's place."

The words "Grandfather's hat" became a sort of campaign slogan, and the election sent Benjamin Harrison to the White House. A few weeks after he became President, he was invited to New York to take part in the centennial celebration of George Washington's inauguration. That first inaugural of the first President had been held in New York, the nation's first capital, on April 30, 1789. When the twenty-third President rose to speak, a hush fell over the vast audience. To them he represented a great tradition: not only had his grandfather served as President but the great grandfather for whom he had been named had signed the Declaration of Independence.

One hundred years after George Washington took the oath of office on the porch of old Federal Hall, one newspaper later described the event, *Benjamin Harrison, a great grandson of one of the illustrious men who had helped him to fashion this great free government, stood on the same spot, on the same stone, and rested his hand on the same Bible . . .*

When the President finished his brief speech, the applause was almost deafening. What changes had taken place since George Washington's inauguration a century before! thought some of the people in the audience. Neither they nor Benjamin Harrison could possibly know how much greater would be the changes in the century that lay ahead.

THE TWENTY-THIRD PRESIDENT *at a Glance*

Benjamin Harrison

Born: August 20, 1833　　　　　　　　*Died: March 13, 1901*

Early life. Benjamin Harrison was born in North Bend, Ohio, seven years before his grandfather, William Henry Harrison, was elected ninth President of the U.S. Benjamin grew up on his father's farm near North Bend. After graduating from Miami University, Oxford, Ohio (1852), he studied law. At 21 (1854) he moved to Indianapolis, Ind., where he became a well-known lawyer. During the Civil War he served in the Union army (1862–1865) and rose to the rank of brigadier general.

Political career. Harrison served in the U.S. Senate (1881–1887). In 1888 he was the Republican Presidential candidate, and in the election defeated President Grover Cleveland, who was seeking a second term.

As President (1889–1893). In 1890 President Harrison signed the McKinley Act, a law increasing the already high tariff rates. He also signed (1890) the Sherman Antitrust Act, which declared that "combinations in restraint of trade" were illegal. This antitrust law was supposed to prevent large business combinations, or trusts, from controlling the price of important products and services, but for a number of years the law was seldom enforced, and the trusts became more and more powerful. The first Pan-American Conference, with representatives from the Latin American countries and the U.S., was held in Washington (1889–1890). A quarrel with Germany over political and trading rights in the islands of Samoa resulted in both the U.S. and Germany's sending warships to the islands. After a hurricane destroyed the ships, the dispute was settled peacefully.

The President's wife. Caroline Scott Harrison (1832–1892) was the first president-general of the Daughters of the American Revolution. In 1896, the ex-President married his first wife's niece, Mary Lord Scott Dimmick (1858–1948).

Other happenings. When Harrison was President, Congress opened part of the Indian Territory (now Oklahoma) to settlers; many thousands took part in a famous "run" for choice land (April 22, 1889). More than 2,000 people were drowned when water from a broken dam flooded Johnstown, Pa. (1889). A battle between 300 Pinkerton guards and the striking employees of a steel plant in Homestead, Pa., resulted in many casualties (1892).

The nation's population and growth. The population was about 63,000,000 (census of 1890). Six new states were admitted to the Union, bringing the total to 44 (North Dakota, South Dakota, Montana, and Washington in 1889; Idaho and Wyoming in 1890).

Patient WILL McKINLEY

Three boys sat on the bridge that spanned Mosquito Creek, near the village of Niles, Ohio. Their bare legs dangled over the edge while they baited their fishing hooks. Their fishing lines cast thin, wavering shadows on the water as the hooks sank beneath the surface.

"I'm going to catch a lot of fish," said Joe Fisher.

"Sh!" said the boy named Allison.

The fat boy who sat between them said nothing. His round, rosy cheeks glowed from a recent scrubbing, and every black hair lay smoothly in place. An hour passed without a nibble. Joe stood up and yawned. Eight-year-old William McKinley did not stir.

"The fish just aren't biting today," Joe complained. "Why don't we go swimming?"

"All right," said Allison, throwing down his line. "Come on, Will."

Will shook his head. He had come to the creek for fish, and he didn't intend to stop until he had a good catch. After his friends had gone farther downstream, he could hear their squeals as they plunged into the cold water. He paid no attention, and by the time they came back, his patience had been rewarded. When he went home, there was a long string of fish dangling from the pole across his shoulder.

"Will is good at anything he goes at," said Joe, a touch of envy in his voice.

This was true. At home Will was one of eight children, and though his father owned a foundry, money was scarce. To help out, Mrs. McKinley kept a store at one end of the house, and Will waited on customers after school. At school he seemed to think that recess was more fun if he had studied his lessons first, but he was so good at sports that no one ever thought of calling him a sissy. Everyone liked Will McKinley.

It was the same way after the family moved to Poland, Ohio. This town was larger than Niles and the schools were better, and when Will was ten he entered Poland Seminary. Here he and some of his new friends decided to start a club and have debates. They named it the Edward Everett Debating Society in honor of a famous orator, and Will was elected president. Permission was obtained to use one of the rooms in the seminary for a clubroom, and the girls took up a collection to buy a new carpet. It was a very handsome carpet, with gold wreaths scattered over a green background.

"Isn't it just beautiful?" said one of the girls.

"It is good-looking, all right," Will agreed.

"Yes, and the first day it rains," the same girl retorted, "you boys will walk across our nice new carpet in your muddy boots and just ruin it."

"What can we do about it?" asked Will. "You know what the streets are like when it rains."

No one answered for a moment. Everyone knew that the streets in Poland were like a muddy swamp in bad weather. And then one of the girls had an idea.

"I know what we can do," she said. "We girls can knit slippers for all of us to wear on rainy days. No muddy boots are going to touch *our* carpet."

The next Saturday Will woke up to hear a steady *pat-pat* of rain on the roof, but he hardly noticed. This was to be a big day for him —the day when he, as president of the Edward Everett Debating Society, was to preside at the first meeting in the new clubroom. On the way to the seminary he had to walk ankle-deep in mud, but he was not worrying about the weather. He was too busy thinking what he was going to say at the meeting.

When he reached the clubroom, he found the other boys waiting outside the door. Just inside the room stood the girls. One of them seemed close to tears.

"You can't come in here with those muddy boots," she wailed. "Look at your feet."

Will glanced at the boots his friends were wearing. They were caked with mud. He looked down at his own boots. They were muddy, too.

"It isn't our fault the streets are muddy," one boy protested.

"That doesn't mean you have to ruin our new carpet."

"Well, what about those slippers you promised to knit?"

"We didn't have time; we had too much to do getting the club-room ready. But we'll finish the slippers before the next meeting."

"That doesn't help us now. This time we'll just have to wear our boots."

The boys started to push into the room, but the girls still barred the way. "We took off our shoes," one of the girls pointed out. "You can do the same."

In the argument that followed, the girls won. Will, like the rest of the boys, stooped over to pull off his boots. Going barefoot when he went fishing was all right. But he certainly was not going to look very dignified, speaking to the debating society in his stocking feet. And then he had to laugh. Everyone was laughing, as he padded into the room and took his place behind the president's desk.

From the big picture on the wall, the solemn eyes of Edward Everett seemed to be watching every move. And suddenly the members felt very solemn, too. William seemed to have forgotten that he stood before them without the dignity of shoes.

"Ladies and gentlemen," he said in the earnest, quiet voice that later was to win many people over to his way of thinking, "the meeting will please come to order."

Some of the members of the debating society remembered that meeting a quarter of a century later when their former president was elected to Congress. In the years that followed his election, they heard him speak at other meetings with hundreds in the audience. Afterward, when some of William McKinley's old school friends went up to the platform to greet him, they were smiling as though they shared some secret joke. Perhaps they were thinking of the day when a group of girls had made a future politician take off his shoes.

By the time William McKinley was elected to Congress he had known both great happiness and great sorrow. He served in the Civil War, coming out of the war a major, and from then on he was usually called Major McKinley. After studying law, he opened a law office in Canton, Ohio, where he soon became very popular. His many friends rejoiced over his happiness when he married Ida Saxton, one of the town's prettiest and most vivacious girls.

The young couple's happiness seemed complete after the birth of their two daughters, but then both children died and Mrs. McKinley became an invalid. Her husband's devotion won the admiration of everyone who knew him. His patience in caring for her never wavered, either while living in Canton or later, after he was elected to Congress.

In Washington McKinley was as well liked as he had been in his own home town. "No one could help feeling at ease in his presence," said one who knew him well. "It was his one idea in life to make those around him feel he was their friend."

As Congressman, Major McKinley was known chiefly as the author of the McKinley Tariff Bill. By making the high tariff rates still higher, he hoped to protect American industries from foreign competition and at the same time raise the wages of American working men. Many voters, however, disapproved of the law, because they claimed it chiefly benefited the rich manufacturers. The major was defeated for re-election to Congress in 1890, but it turned out that his defeat was his good fortune. Two years later he was elected governor of Ohio, and his success as governor led to his nomination for the Presidency.

During the Presidential campaign of 1896, William McKinley made most of his speeches from his own front porch in Canton. There was a festive air about the town. Houses were decorated with flags. Banners, waving in the breeze, displayed the campaign slogan: "Elect McKinley, the advance agent of prosperity." Parades marched through the streets, and nearly every train brought a new crowd to hear the Republican candidate.

Although William was often called "the friend of big business," he appealed to all kinds of people. His patience, his good nature and his reassuring speeches made his listeners feel confident that he was the man to lead the nation. His speeches were printed in newspapers from coast to coast, and William McKinley was elected on a wave of popular enthusiasm.

On the night before he was inaugurated, he had dinner at the White House with Grover Cleveland, the retiring President. Although the two men had disagreed about the tariff, they liked and admired each other personally. Both were worried about the threat of war. The Spanish colony of Cuba had revolted against Spain, and American newspapers were filled with stories about the cruelty of the Spanish rulers. Many Cubans were hoping for help from the United States. Many Americans sincerely felt it was the duty of their government to send a military force to drive the Spanish soldiers out of Cuba. Because the American people felt so strongly about the situation, Grover Cleveland had given up hope that war could be avoided. The next day, during the ride back to the White House after the inauguration exercises, he turned to his successor.

"I am deeply sorry, Mr. President," said Grover Cleveland, "to pass on to you a war with Spain. It will come within two years. Nothing can stop it."

William McKinley was more optimistic. He hoped that Spain might be persuaded by peaceful means to deal less harshly with Cuba, if only the Americans would be patient. This hope was not to be realized. In February, 1898, the United States battleship *Maine*, while on a visit to Cuba, was blown up, and two hundred and sixty sailors and officers were killed. Who was responsible for the explosion is still a mystery, but at the time it was suspected that Spanish commanders had ordered the vessel destroyed.

REMEMBER THE MAINE! read the headlines in the newspapers, and excited and indignant people from every state in the Union soon took up the cry. "Remember the Maine!" they shouted, and demanded that the government send troops to help the Cubans in their fight for freedom.

"I am not anxious about the result of war," the President told a friend. "There can be but one result, and it will not be long delayed. What I have in mind is what will come after war—the problems we do not see now but that are sure to come in some other way. And they will not be easy problems. Other nations have had that experience, and we shall not escape it."

Although the new President had hoped to avoid using military force, he soon had to give in to the popular clamor. On April 11, 1898, he asked Congress for a declaration of war against Spain.

The Spanish-American War was fought not only in Cuba but also thousands of miles away in the Pacific. Even before the first American troops reached Cuba, a squadron of United States naval vessels under the command of Commodore George Dewey steamed into Manila Bay in the Philippines. These islands also belonged to Spain. A Spanish fleet was anchored in the bay, but surrendered after a few hours of sharp fighting on May 1. American ships and land forces were equally successful in Cuba, and by the middle of August Spain was asking for terms of peace.

The American people were jubilant. The war had been won in a shorter time than many had thought possible, and Spain had agreed to grant Cuba independence. Other Spanish possessions—the beautiful green island of Puerto Rico, east of Cuba, and the smaller island of Guam in the Pacific—were ceded to the United States. But what should be done about the Philippines? This was one of the hardest decisions President McKinley had to make.

Many Americans thought it would be wrong for their nation to own distant colonies; they did not approve of a policy that they called "imperialism." Others argued that it would be cruel to turn the Philippine Islands back to Spain. Several times in the past the Filipinos had revolted, hoping to gain their independence. The revolts had always failed. But were the islands ready for independence? At that time only a few Filipinos had ever had the education needed for people to govern themselves.

"When I realized that the Philippines had been dropped into our laps, I confess I did not know what to do with them," the President told a group of callers at the White House in November, 1898. "I sought counsel from all sides—Democrats as well as Republicans—but got little help. I thought first we would take only Manila; then other islands, perhaps, also. I walked the floor of the White House night after night; and I prayed for guidance . . ."

One night the right answer seemed to come to him: the nation should take over the islands and educate the natives. In December, when the final peace treaty was signed, the American government agreed to pay Spain twenty million dollars, and the Philippines became an American possession.

"It is not the purpose of the United States to annex the islands permanently," read a Senate resolution passed a short time later, "but to prepare the people for self-government."

The Spanish-American War, coming at the end of the nineteenth century, marked a turning point in American history. The nation had become a world power almost overnight, and the Americans had become more interested in distant lands. There was much enthusiasm for the Pan-American Exposition held in the city of Buffalo during 1901—an exposition celebrating one hundred years of progress in the countries of North and South America. Several thousand people gathered to hear William McKinley when he arrived at the exposition to speak on President's Day, September 5.

How much closer distant countries now seemed! he thought. Swifter means of communication had drawn the peoples of the world closer together. New inventions had made it possible to produce more goods than ever before. And now, he told his audience, new markets must be found. William McKinley realized that some of his old ideas about the tariff might not work in the new century. If the people in

TEDDY ROOSEVELT *Does the Unexpected*

Theodore Roosevelt wanted to be a naturalist. Even in New York, the city where he grew up a hundred years ago, he never missed a chance to find out everything he could about the great world of nature. He collected rocks and stones, specimens of plants and abandoned birds' nests. By the time he was eight years old, his collection had grown so large that it threatened to overflow his bedroom.

"Mother says I may keep my collection in an old empty bookcase on the third floor," he told his cousins Johnnie and Jimmie Roosevelt. "Why don't we start a museum? We could call it the Roosevelt Museum of Natural History."

"The Roosevelt Museum," said Johnnie, rolling the words over his tongue, for he liked the sound of them. "Teedie," as his family called him, nearly always had something interesting, something unexpected, to suggest.

"All three of us could be directors of the museum," Jimmie suggested. "We can find lots of things to add to it."

That afternoon the boys went exploring. Teedie's family—his parents, his big sister Anna, and Elliott and Corinne, his younger brother and sister—lived in a tall brownstone front house on a busy street. But New York was much smaller then than now, and the young directors did not have far to walk until they came to some big open spaces. Each boy carried a large bag, and the bags were soon filled with an assortment of rocks and stones. They had started home when Teedie saw several toads.

"Quick!" he said. "Don't let them get away. We never have had any toads in our collection."

"How can we carry them?" asked Jimmie. "My bag is full, and so are my pockets."

"That's easy," Teedie replied. "We can put them under our hats."

Each boy put a toad on top of his head and clapped his hat down tightly. As they turned into their own street, they met a very dignified lady, Mrs. Hamilton Fish, a friend of their mothers.

"Good afternoon, boys," she said.

Jimmie and Johnnie looked at Theodore, wondering what to do. They understood all too well what their parents would expect of them; what Mrs. Fish was waiting for. Politely, though reluctantly, the three boys tipped their hats. Down jumped the toads and hopped away.

"They were our best specimens, too," said Teedie as they walked on.

His troubles were not over. One day he found some mice and put them in his mother's icebox for safekeeping. When he returned for them, they were gone. His mother had thrown them out. She tried to explain that no good housekeeper likes to have mice in her icebox, but Teedie would not listen.

"What hurts me," he sputtered, "is the loss to science."

His mother was careful not to laugh. Both she and his father, Theodore Roosevelt, Sr., were glad that he was so interested in his collection. This interest made it easier for him when he was ill, and Teedie was ill much of the time. He suffered from asthma. He wheezed and coughed. Sometimes, in order to get his breath, he had to sit up in bed all night.

But there was nothing the matter with his enthusiasm. He was curious and eager to know about everything, especially about animals and plants. His father gave him books on natural history to read, but he looked troubled when Teedie talked about being a naturalist.

"You have the mind, son," he said one day, "but not the body. Without the body the mind cannot go as far as it should. You're going to have to build up your strength."

"I'll try, Father," Teedie promised. "I'll try hard."

Mr. Roosevelt turned an upstairs porch into a gymnasium, with a trapeze and parallel bars and a rack for Indian clubs, and Theodore did exercises there nearly every day. Summers were spent in the country where he went on long walks. All of the children looked forward to the summertime, for then they could run barefoot, climb trees, and have all kinds of pets—not only dogs and cats but also rabbits and guinea pigs and even a raccoon. When Jimmie and Johnnie came to visit, the three boys wandered off into the woods to hunt for specimens.

Sometimes Teedie went alone. One morning, a few weeks before his twelfth birthday, he found a squirrel's nest in a chestnut tree. What had happened to the mother he did not know, but there were three tiny gray babies with their eyes not yet open. Teedie took them home, but they were still too young to lap milk from a saucer.

How was he to feed them and keep them alive? He solved the problem by buying a small syringe and then squeezing a few drops of milk into each little throat. After a few tries, the squirrels got the idea, seized the syringe in tiny paws, and sucked the milk for themselves.

Soon afterward, when Teedie had a bad attack of asthma, his parents decided that he might benefit from a change in air. He went off to spend a few days in the Berkshire Hills but forgot to mention, before he left, that he was starting a collection of field mice. The first his family knew about it was when Anna, his older sister, answered a knock at the door. Several boys were waiting outside, cap in hand, and in each cap there was a field mouse.

"Your brother advertised for these in the paper," Anna was told. "The ad said he would pay ten cents a mouse."

One of the smaller children held out a cap in which there were several wriggling little rodents. "Yes," the child added, "and thirty-five cents for each family of mice."

Anna hesitated, then reached for her purse. "All right, I'll pay for the mice," she said. And then she laughed. She had been surprised, but not too surprised. One never could tell what that brother of hers was going to do next.

When Teedie returned, he seemed to feel better, but the improvement did not last. Two years went by. Even when he was in the country, where he spent most of his time outdoors, attacks of asthma continued to sap his strength. There were many days when he sat in a big chair, propped up by pillows, feeling too miserable even to talk. But he never felt too ill to read. Among his favorite books were stories of real heroes like Daniel Boone and Davy Crockett who were brave and strong. Teedie decided that he was going to do brave deeds, too—after he got well.

One morning he picked up a book of poems by Robert Browning, and read "The Flight of the Duchess." This long poem was about a young duke who wanted to be brave like his ancestors but never did anything to make his wish come true. Theodore was feeling very uncomfortable as he laid the book down.

Why, he wasn't any better than that young duke, he thought. He had done a great deal of daydreaming, but had he been trying hard enough to make himself strong and husky? He made a resolution that from then on he was going to work even harder at his exercises.

He thought of this poem again a few weeks later, when two strange boys started to make fun of his long, thin legs. "Pipestems! Pipestems!" they chanted. "Your legs look just like pipestems."

Theodore was furious. When he could not stand the teasing any longer, he challenged the young bullies to a fight. They seemed to think this a huge joke, and good-naturedly took him on, one at a time. Theodore struck out with his fists, but each boy handled him as easily as if he had been a kitten. He was not hurt, but this made him more ashamed than if they had given him a black eye.

"The next time I get into a fight," he told his father afterward, "I am going to be able to defend myself."

"How?" asked Mr. Roosevelt.

Theodore thought it over. "I might take boxing lessons," he said. "Perhaps they would make me stronger."

As soon as the family returned to the city, Mr. Roosevelt arranged for an ex-champion in boxing to teach his son. But Teedie seemed no better, and the boxing lessons were interrupted when the family went abroad. They went first to Egypt, where, it was hoped, the mild dry air would help in Theodore's search for health.

Theodore himself had been looking forward to the trip for a different reason. He had recently been fitted with eyeglasses, and he had been studying taxidermy, the art of preserving birds and animals as they are preserved in big museums. Now that he could see better, he was a much better shot, and he set out to make a systematic collection of birds of different species. When he came home thirteen months later, he brought with him several hundred specimens which he himself had shot and prepared. It was a remarkable collection for a boy of fifteen, a collection to be proud of.

Soon after his return, Theodore started boxing lessons again, and this time he was able to keep on with them week after week. During his year abroad he had grown tall, but he was still pale and much too thin. He had made up his mind that boxing was going to help, and he spent hours every week trying to get into condition for his first match. He chinned himself on the parallel bars. He jumped rope to strengthen the muscles in his legs, and he banged away at the punching bag.

One day the boxing instructor announced that he and two other boys about the same weight were to try for the lightweight championship of the class. Theodore wanted a chance to test himself, but was he ready? If only he could win, he thought, it would prove that he was getting stronger.

He must win, he told himself fiercely—and he did.

Clutching his prize, Theodore hurried home to show his family. The prize was a pewter cup, and he carried it to his room and put it on his bookcase. He stood and looked at it for a long time. Theodore Roosevelt, bird collector, was very proud of his collection. But at that moment Theodore Roosevelt, lightweight champion, was even prouder of his pewter cup.

By the time Theodore entered Harvard University, his health had improved so much that he was able to take part in college sports. He was also an excellent student, but his courses in natural history were a disappointment. Instead of wandering through woods and fields searching for specimens, his teachers seemed to spend most of their time peering through microscopes. A very dull way to study nature, Theodore decided. He had once thought he wanted to teach natural history, but if he became a professor there would be so much else that he would not have time to do.

He also considered becoming a writer, and he started his first book while still in college. He was a very restless young man, however, and he was afraid that writing alone would never satisfy him. A few days before he graduated, he came to a decision.

"I want to help the cause of better government," he told a friend.

Two years later, at the age of twenty-three, he was elected to the New York State legislature. Although he was the youngest member, he was becoming well known throughout the state when tragedy struck. The death of his mother was followed twenty-four hours later by the death of his lovely young wife whom he had married after he finished college. Theodore, refusing to give in to sorrow, finished his term in the legislature.

Perhaps it was his grief that helped to bring on another serious attack of asthma, and his thoughts kept turning toward the West. Two years earlier, while taking a vacation in the Dakota Territory, he had fallen under the spell of that stark, beautiful country. He had bought a cattle ranch, called Chimney Butte, and hired two experienced ranchmen to look after the cattle. Now, in the summer of

1884, he decided to go back. He was through with politics, he said. He was going to live in Dakota.

Soon after his arrival at Chimney Butte, Theodore began to suspect that his ranch manager, Will Merrifield, considered him just another tenderfoot. One morning Theodore suggested that they go hunting, and they rode into the little town of Medora to ask Mr. Fisher, the storekeeper, to go with them.

"Say, Fisher," said Will slyly, "let's take the Sully Trail. I don't believe Mr. Roosevelt has ever seen it."

This trail skirted the edges of tall cliffs and was slippery because of recent rains. Riding it took nerve. Will Merrifield chuckled to himself, wondering how long "the dude from the city" could hold out. He was in the lead when he heard hoof beats behind him. He glanced back, expecting to see Fisher.

But it was Theodore. Fisher, far in the rear, had dismounted and was cautiously leading his horse over a wet, slippery stretch of ground. His companions waited until he had mounted and caught up with them.

Finally the three men reached the top of a grassy slope and reined in their horses. It made them all slightly dizzy to look down—down— at the dry creek bed far below. But Merrifield grinned and pretended to see a deer.

"Look, Mr. Roosevelt, there it goes," he called. "Let's get it."

Theodore saw the grin and guessed the truth. There was no deer. But if Merrifield wanted his little joke, he should have it. As he started down the steep hillside, Theodore followed, slipping and sliding. At any instant he expected to be tossed into the air, but he held on grimly. Once the horse stumbled, but he drew the reins taut and kept his seat. When he reached the bottom of the hill, he turned and looked around.

Fisher was walking and leading his horse. Will Merrifield's horse, having thrown his rider, was calmly cropping grass a hundred yards above. Will himself was rolling down the hill. When he finally picked himself up, he was not hurt, but his face was very red. It was Theodore's turn to grin, but he tried to act disappointed.

"Why, Merrifield," he said, "look how you frightened that deer away. It must be all the way to Montana by now."

All three men burst out laughing, and from then on Will Merrifield had more respect for his boss. It was a respect that increased as the weeks and months went by. Theodore was writing a book about his experiences, and he did a great deal of reading besides. The rest of the time he lived the same rough life as did the cowboys who had been hired to work on the ranches. He liked and admired these blunt, hard-working Western men, so different from anyone he had ever known before.

And they liked him. No matter how hard and grueling the work, he could always be counted on to do his share. During a roundup he slept on the ground. In stormy weather he sometimes spent fourteen or sixteen hours in the saddle, riding among the herds to see that all was well with the cattle; yet he never complained. He seemed to glory in hardship.

And why shouldn't he? he thought. He was no longer the frail young man who had arrived in Dakota two years before. The rough outdoor life had worked the miracle for which Theodore had been hoping since he was a boy. He had grown robust and strong. He was thirty pounds heavier. His shoulders had broadened. Even his neck looked thicker, and his face was tanned from long days in the sun.

"I really enjoy this life," he wrote to his sister. "The loneliness and freedom, and the half adventurous nature of existence appeals to me very powerfully. . . ."

Part of the appeal of this strange new country was its variety. Some days when Theodore went hunting he rode across plains where green grasses stretched away as far as he could see toward the horizon. The next morning might find him guiding his horse along the edge of a winding canyon, and he looked up at steep mountains called buttes making a jagged outline against a bright blue sky. Sometimes he was worried by what he saw. He came upon forests—or what had once been forests—where the trees had been ruthlessly cut down. He galloped across plains that were parched and dry for lack of rain. If only water from some of the rivers—waters now going to waste—could be brought to those dry areas, what a land it would be!

How he was going to miss this wild, free country when he went home! After much thought, he had come to the conclusion that, much as he liked the West, his place was in the East. In 1886 he returned to New York and was a candidate for mayor of the city. Although he lost, he took his defeat good-naturedly. "Anyway, I had a bully time," he said.

During the next twelve years, events moved rapidly for Theodore Roosevelt. He married a childhood friend, Edith Carow, and they went to live in a big, rambling house called Sagamore Hill, on Long Island. From his study on the third floor, Theodore could look down on the waters of Oyster Bay and Long Island Sound, and here he began to write what was to be the first of a series of four books called *The Winning of the West*. But he wanted to make history as well as write about it, and he was soon back in politics. He held several important positions in government, and whenever Theodore Roosevelt took a new position things usually began to happen. He was interesting and colorful, and he was very much in earnest.

"He has the knack," said one newspaper reporter, "of doing things, and doing them noisily, clamorously. While he is in the neighborhood, the public can no more look the other way than a small boy can turn his head away from a circus parade followed by a steam calliope."

Most reporters found that he made good "copy," and newspaper readers from coast to coast learned about the vigorous young man from Sagamore Hill. They read about him more and more after the Spanish-American War began. This war, which the Americans fought to help Cuba win independence from Spain, lasted less than four months, but that was long enough to make Theodore Roosevelt famous. His cavalry regiment, the Rough Riders, fought valiantly in Cuba, and their colonel soon proved his bravery in battle. "Teddy," as the newspapers had begun to call him, was constantly in the headlines, and when he came home, he found himself a hero. A few weeks later he was elected governor of New York State. Someday, his friends said—perhaps in 1904—he would make an excellent candidate for President.

When the Republican Convention met at Philadelphia in June, 1900, President William McKinley was nominated for re-election. The daring young colonel had been mentioned more and more frequently as a candidate for Vice President during the past weeks, and the convention hall rang with the cry, "We want Teddy! We want Teddy!"

Theodore Roosevelt won the nomination and then the election. Not everyone liked him, however. Although he was popular with the people, some of the leading politicians considered him too independent—too inclined to go his own way. "But you can't stop that man," said one of them, "any more than you can stop Niagara Falls."

Theodore Roosevelt had been Vice President only a few months when William McKinley's tragic death made him President. At forty-two he was the youngest man who had ever held that office, but he faced his new responsibilities with courage. Shortly after his arrival in Washington, he had two callers. One was his friend, Gifford Pinchot, head of the Forestry Bureau. The other was Congressman

Francis Newlands. Both men were passionately interested in the subject of conservation, as was Theodore Roosevelt himself.

"Mr. President," said Gifford Pinchot, "what are we going to do
about our forests? Our trees are being cut down at a reckless rate,
yet many people seem to think that they will last forever. Unless the
waste is stopped and new seedlings are planted, what is our country
going to do for timber?"

"I, too, have been growing more and more concerned about the
destruction of our forests," Theodore Roosevelt replied.

"What I am chiefly concerned about," said Congressman Newlands,
"are the desert lands out west. You have lived in the West, Mr. President. You know that much of the soil is too dry for farming. Yet with
irrigation, as many people could live in the western part of the
United States as now live in all the rest of the country."

"What do you suggest, Mr. Newlands?"

"That large dams be built to create artificial lakes, where water
can be stored from our western rivers," the Congressman replied.
"But the cost of irrigation on such a large scale would be very great.
The Federal Government would have to finance it."

Theodore Roosevelt regarded the two men thoughtfully. Important though the reclamation of arid lands and the saving of the
forests were to the welfare of the country, they were only part of the
problem of conservation. He knew that many natural resources were
being wasted. In the early days the government's first concern had
been to see that the big empty spaces in the country were settled.
Settlers had been able to buy land for very little money, and sometimes they made no payment at all. Big companies or corporations
also had bought up land, or it had been given them by careless
government officials. Gradually these corporations, representing a
few rich men—"land grabbers," Theodore Roosevelt called them—
had gotten a stranglehold on many natural resources which the
President felt should by right belong to all Americans.

"Gentlemen," he said, turning back to his guests. "If you will prepare some notes for me, I shall take up the matter of conservation in
my first message to Congress."

The first result of that message was the Newlands Reclamation
Bill, which Congress passed the following June. This law provided
for building several huge reservoirs or dams in the western part of
the country, the cost to be met by the sale of public lands. The first
battle in the struggle for conservation had been won, but it was a
struggle that was to go on and on. Whenever the President recommended new measures to conserve natural resources, there were

certain big businessmen who objected. They brought pressure to bear on some of the members of Congress not to pass the laws he wanted.

Most Americans had no understanding of what was happening to many of their natural riches, and Theodore Roosevelt set out to inform them. He wrote magazine articles. He made numerous speeches. Unless the government assumed control of public property, he warned, there might be nothing left for future generations.

"No man is a true lover of his country," he said, "whose confidence in its progress and greatness is limited to the period of his own life. We cannot afford to forget that our country is only at the beginning of its growth."

Theodore Roosevelt's efforts in behalf of conservation were a part of his campaign against selfish rich men. Whenever he felt that any of the people of the country were not given "a square deal" he fought for their rights, and he fought vigorously. "I have always been fond of the old West African proverb," he said. " 'Speak softly and carry a big stick.' "

Cartoonists frequently drew pictures of the popular "Teddy" wielding a "big stick." His prominent teeth, his firm jaw, his eyes glinting behind his thick-lensed spectacles, made his face an interesting one to draw. Most of the cartoons, and there were thousands of them, pictured him in action. But there was one that showed a different side of his nature. The President was hunting in Mississippi when one day his guide brought a bear cub into camp. Theodore Roosevelt refused to shoot it. "Let it go," he said sternly.

A news dispatch describing the incident gave a Washington newspaper cartoonist an idea, and the next day his cartoon showed the President refusing to shoot a frightened little black bear. An alert toy manufacturer made toy "teddy bears" to sell, and the new toy immediately caught on. Thousands of children began to play with teddy bears, just as their grandchildren still play with teddy bears today.

Whatever Theodore Roosevelt did made news, for he was always doing the unexpected. He invited diplomats and government officials to take "point to point" walks in the wild, beautiful woods in the capital known as Rock Creek Park. After deciding on a goal, they walked straight toward it. The one rule was that they must never turn aside. If there was a high cliff in the way, they climbed over it. If they came to a creek, they swam across. The public never seemed to tire of reading about the President's strenuous activities both at play and at work, and when he ran for a second term he was elected. The first time he became President, he had not liked the feeling that he was benefiting through the misfortune of another; and he was pleased and gratified by his victory at the polls.

"Tomorrow," he said to a friend the night before his inauguration, "I shall be coming into office in my own right. Now watch me."

There was much to watch during Theodore Roosevelt's second term. In November, 1906, he visited the Isthmus of Panama where thousands of laborers were at work on the Panama Canal. For many years men had dreamed of cutting a water route between the Atlantic and Pacific, but it had been President Roosevelt who pushed through arrangements for American government engineers to undertake that mighty engineering task. When the fifty-mile canal across the Isthmus of Panama was finished, it would furnish a short cut between the two oceans. Ships would be able to pass through the canal in a few hours instead of making a long voyage of several thousand miles around South America.

Meanwhile, Theodore Roosevelt had continued his efforts to conserve the riches and beauties of the country for the benefit of the entire population. Among other measures, he had set aside millions of acres of timberland as national forest reserves. An old law passed by Congress in 1891 gave the President the authority to do this. And then suddenly in 1907, this authority was threatened. Congress added a rider, or amendment, to the appropriations bill that provided money to operate the Department of Agriculture. This rider stated that Congress, and not the President, would have the right to set aside forest reserves in the future. When Theodore Roosevelt learned about this, he sent for Gifford Pinchot.

"I dare say," the President told him grimly, "that the Senators who suggested that rider have some influential friends among the land grabbers. I can think of certain rich businessmen who might like to get their hands on some good, cheap timberland out west."

"You will have to sign the appropriations bill, won't you?" said Mr. Pinchot in dismay.

"Of course, and my opponents in the Senate know it. The Department of Agriculture must have the money to operate, this coming year. But, by George"—the President slapped his hand down on his desk—"I won't have to sign it for several days. The bill is still in the Senate."

"But how will a few days help?"

With an impatient gesture, the President seemed to brush this objection aside. "A few days are all we need," he said. "Listen, Gifford, I have an idea. Your men have been making a survey, haven't they, of that western forest land?"

Mr. Pinchot nodded.

"Well, that's just bully. Will you please have maps made for me at once, showing the forest areas in six states?"

He counted the areas off on his fingers: "Colorado, Idaho, Montana, Oregon, Washington and Wyoming. I want to know every single acre that has a tree on it, or even a bush."

He laughed uproariously, and Gifford Pinchot was smiling when he left the White House.

The next few nights the lights burned late in the offices of the Forestry Bureau as Mr. Pinchot and his men worked day and night to prepare the maps that were needed. As soon as they were finished they were laid before the President. Beside them were neatly typed executive orders, which he promptly signed, transferring sixteen million acres of public lands to the forest reserves. Whatever might happen in the future, those sixteen million acres could never be sold.

The next day the appropriations bill arrived from the Senate. Theodore Roosevelt drew it toward him with a low chuckle. "Now I can sign the bill that will prevent my ever doing again what I have just done," he said. "When my opponents learn about it, they will doubtless turn handsprings in their wrath."

The President's action was so unexpected that his opponents may have felt like turning a few angry handsprings. He rather enjoyed the joke he had played on them. It was the kind of joke that would benefit the American people.

"It is my belief," he said, "unless such action is forbidden by the Constitution or the laws, that it is not only the President's right but his duty to do anything that the needs of the nation demand."

Four years went by. Theodore Roosevelt was no longer President when, in March, 1911, he visited Arizona to dedicate the big reservoir named for him. The Roosevelt Dam, started during his administration, was one of the largest irrigation structures in the world. From the rocky floor to the top of the high parapet walls, it measured more than two hundred and sixty feet—thirty times the height of the average room. That magnificent stone reservoir held enough water to irrigate nearly a quarter of a million acres. In a region that had been too dry to raise crops, there would now be rich and fertile farms—enough farms to support about fifteen thousand families.

When the ex-President looked out over the large audience waiting to hear him speak, he saw several boys and girls seated near the front. They made him think of another child—himself forty years before. How disappointed he had been when his mother threw away the mice he had put in her icebox for safekeeping! At the age of eight, he had blamed her bitterly for what he had called the "loss to science." The words were now only an amusing memory. Yet he knew that many people believed he would have made a brilliant naturalist.

Had he been wise to choose a career in politics instead of science? Yes, he decided. Although he had gone into politics, he had never lost interest in nature, and through his books he had shared that interest with thousands of readers. As President he had been able to serve his fellow Americans in many ways. Most important, perhaps, he had been able to preserve for them many of the natural riches of their own country.

His decision had not been a "loss to science" after all.

THE TWENTY-SIXTH PRESIDENT *at a Glance*

Theodore Roosevelt

Born: October 27, 1858   *Died: January 6, 1919*

Early life. Theodore Roosevelt was born in New York City, where his father was a well-to-do merchant. After graduating from Harvard (1880), Theodore studied law (1880–1881). He served in the New York State legislature (1882–1884). From 1884 to 1886 he lived on a ranch he owned in North Dakota (then still a part of Dakota Territory).

Political and military career. When he was 28 (1886), Roosevelt returned to New York City and was an unsuccessful candidate for mayor. He served as a U.S. Civil Service Commissioner in Washington (1889–1895), as president of the New York City Police Board (1895–1897), and as Assistant Secretary of the Navy (1897–1898). During the Spanish-American War (1898) he helped organize a volunteer cavalry regiment, known as the "Rough Riders." As lieutenant colonel and later colonel of the regiment, he fought in Cuba and led the Rough Riders in a famous charge known as the Battle of San Juan Hill. He was governor of New York (1899–1900). In March, 1901, he was inaugurated as Vice President. He succeeded to the Presidency upon the death of President William McKinley (September 14, 1901).

As President (1901–1905; 1905–1909). Throughout his Presidency, Roosevelt strove to protect the interests of the public. During a coal strike in 1902, he threatened to have the government seize the mines if the mine owners would not arbitrate. The owners then agreed to arbitration, the strikers won an increase in wages, and the country was saved from a heatless winter. He had the Attorney General start legal action against more than forty large business combinations, or trusts, which, he believed, were destroying free competition. At his insistence, Congress passed (1906) a Meat Inspection Act and a Pure Food and Drug Act to protect consumers. Because of his efforts, many important steps were taken to conserve the country's natural resources. Roosevelt also worked to build up the nation's defensive strength and its importance in world affairs. In 1903 a treaty with the Republic of Panama gave the U.S. the right to construct a canal through the Isthmus of Panama. Roosevelt helped arrange a peace settlement (1905) in a war between Japan and Russia, and was awarded the Nobel Prize for Peace in 1906.

The President's family. Roosevelt's first wife, Alice Lee Roosevelt (1861–1884), died after the birth of a daughter, Alice. Roosevelt and his second wife, Edith Carow Roosevelt (1861–1948), had four boys and one girl. These five children, together with their half-sister Alice, made life in the White House happy and exciting. Alice married Nicholas Longworth, a Congressman (1906). Theodore Roosevelt was a fifth cousin of Franklin D. Roosevelt, the 32nd President, and the uncle of Franklin's wife, Eleanor Roosevelt.

Other happenings. When Theodore Roosevelt was President, Orville and Wilbur Wright made the world's first successful flights in a motor-powered airplane (Kitty Hawk, N.C., December 17, 1903). In San Francisco an earthquake (April 18, 1906) was followed by a great fire.

The nation's growth. Oklahoma was admitted to the Union as the 46th state (1907).

As Ex-President. Roosevelt went to Africa on a big game hunting expedition (1909–1910). In 1912 at the Republican convention he tried to win the Presidential nomination. When President Taft, his successor at the White House, was nominated instead, Roosevelt became the candidate of a new Progressive party, organized by Republicans who felt Taft was too conservative. The party split resulted in defeat for both Taft and Roosevelt and in the election of the Democratic candidate, Woodrow Wilson. In 1914 Roosevelt headed an exploring expedition in Brazil. In 1917, when World War I broke out, he offered to raise and lead a division of troops. By then he was nearly sixty and in failing health, and the offer was not accepted.

As author. Throughout his busy career Roosevelt found time to write books, including *The Winning of the West* (4 volumes), *African Game Trails, Through the Brazilian Wilderness,* and his *Autobiography.*

Big BILL TAFT

W hy, it's snowing again!" said Bill Taft when he left the schoolhouse.

"Yes, and that Butchertown crowd will be laying for us, if you
ask me," one of the other boys replied. "It's just the day for a snowball fight."

Bill laughed—a deep, rumbling chuckle that shook his round, fat
body as he stooped to pick up a handful of snow. Behind a clump of
bushes a few feet away, he had a glimpse of a red muffler. A soft
rustling sound betrayed the presence of the "enemy," but he pretended not to notice. "Don't look now," he went on in a low voice,
"but we'd better get some snowballs ready."

William Howard Taft lived on Mount Auburn, one of the seven
hills overlooking downtown Cincinnati and the winding Ohio River.
On the hill to the east of Mount Auburn lay Butchertown, to the west
lay Taylorville; and the boys of the different districts carried on a
good-natured warfare. The feuds grew very exciting in the winter
when there was snow to furnish ammunition. As Bill bent over—
wham!—a snowball sped through the air from behind the bushes and
caught him squarely in the back. The Butchertown crowd was already
on the job.

Neither Bill nor his friends paid any attention, as they continued
to scoop up snow and roll it into shape. "Hurry with the snowballs,"
Bill urged. "Make 'em faster. Make 'em bigger."

Not until the Mount Auburn boys had a reserve supply of ammunition ready did Bill give another command. "Go after the enemy," he shouted. "Drive them off. Let's see them run."

Bill, in spite of his size, was quick on his feet. He and his friends advanced in a rush, and the Butchertown forces were too busy defending themselves to roll any fresh snowballs of their own. Finally they turned and fled amid the jeers of their rivals.

"No wonder those Mount Auburn fellows always win," grumbled a member of the defeated crowd. "They have big Bill Taft on their side."

The fight over, Bill started home, but one of his chums protested. "Don't go in yet," he said. "We're going to build a snow fort over in my yard."

Bill paused inside the gate before the big two-story brick house where he lived. "I have to get my lessons," he said.

"You can get your lessons after a while."

"No, I have to get them now."

He grinned as he spoke, then disappeared inside the front door. His friends turned away. They couldn't understand Bill. There was no boy in school who could be so much fun, or one who was any better in athletics. When he played, he played hard; but when the time came to get his lessons, he studied hard. Big Bill really seemed to like to study.

Most of the time this was true. Bill wanted to be a lawyer when he grew up, and then a judge, like Alphonso Taft, his father. If he was to realize this ambition, Judge Taft often reminded him, he must do good work in school.

At times, however, William wavered in his ambition. There were evenings when he put off doing his homework so he could play marbles with his brothers. One afternoon, after he had taken an examination at school, he came home dragging his feet. He hoped that his father wouldn't ask him how he had done; more than anything he wanted Judge Taft to feel proud of him. Of course, Judge Taft did ask, and Bill had to admit that he had come out fifth in his class.

There was silence in the room. Finally Mrs. Taft spoke up, trying to make excuses for their son.

"No, my dear," her husband told her, "mediocrity will not do for William."

Bill knew that his father was right. It was not enough to do just ordinary work. If he wanted to grow up to be a respected judge like Alphonso Taft, he must do his best work always.

This determination stayed with him as he grew older. At seventeen he entered Yale University and four years later was graduated with honors. After attending the law school in Cincinnati, where he tied for first place in his class, he practiced law. By the time he was thirty, he realized his ambition to become a judge. By the time he was forty-four, he was a judge in the Federal Circuit Court in his native state and made such a brilliant record that he became nationally known.

One day in January, 1900, Bill received a telegram. It was from President McKinley, asking him to come to the White House at once.

William Taft was both puzzled and elated. What could the summons mean? he wondered when he boarded a train for Washington. Perhaps one of the justices on the Supreme Court had resigned; perhaps the President wanted to appoint William Howard Taft to fill the vacant place. To sit on the bench of the Supreme Court, to share in the important decisions that the court made about the laws of the land, was the most important work a lawyer could ever hope to do.

Two days later, he was shown into the President's study. Elihu Root, the Secretary of War, was also present.

William McKinley came to the point at once. "Judge Taft," he said, "we would like you to go to the Philippines. We are sending a commission of several members to set up civil governments as soon as possible. You are a skilled lawyer, and your help is needed."

In his surprise Judge Taft hardly knew what to reply. He did know, of course, that the Philippines had been a possession of the United States since the Spanish-American War. The islands, under the control of the Secretary of War, were being ruled for the time being by army forces. Some of the same rebels who had once revolted against Spain were now in revolt against American authorities, and fighting was still going on on some of the islands.

"But, Mr. President," Judge Taft protested, "I was opposed to our annexing the Philippines. You should ask a man who is more in sympathy with the government's policy."

"I didn't want the islands either," William McKinley replied. "But the point is, we have them. It is our duty, as soon as the revolt is put down, to give the Filipino people a form of government suited to their needs. We must prepare them for the day when they will have learned to govern themselves. It was never our purpose, as you know, to annex the islands permanently."

"If I should accept—" Judge Taft did not go on.

"You would be doing your country a great service," Secretary Root reminded him.

Judge Taft still hesitated. "It would probably mean the end of my judicial career," he said.

Secretary Root looked at him sharply. "This is a task worthy of any man. You may go on holding the job you have in a humdrum way. But here is something that will test you; something in the way of effort and struggle. The question is, will you take the harder or the easier task?"

It was a hard decision to make, and Judge Taft asked for a week to think it over. "I confess I love my present position," he wrote one of his brothers. "Ought I to allow this to deter me? The opportunity to help along in a critical stage in the country's history is very great."

"You can do more good in that position in a year than you could in a dozen on the bench," his brother replied.

This advice was followed. The following June Judge Taft was on board a vessel, the *Hancock,* steaming into the harbor at Manila, which was then the capital of the Philippines. He was seven thousand miles from home. Behind those lush green trees that lined the shore, beyond those tall mountains, lived several million brown-skinned people very different from any he had ever known. When he walked down the gangplank he seemed just as strange to the people of Manila. This handsome giant of a man was six feet, two inches tall. He weighed more than three hundred pounds, and many of the small, muscular Filipinos regarded him with a mixture of curiosity and awe.

Soon after his arrival, Judge Taft interviewed a number of men in Manila. He also made frequent trips into the interior, making friends with the inhabitants of the villages. On one trip into the country of the Igorots, a Malay mountain tribe, he had a surprising experience. Several brown-skinned children approached him and bowed low.

"Good morning, Mrs. Kelly," they said.

Judge Taft turned to his guide. Why should the children call him Mrs. Kelly? The answer was simple. Several years earlier a man named Kelly had visited the region to investigate a gold mine. His wife had started a school for the children, and had taught them to greet her with the words "Good morning, Mrs. Kelly." Judge Taft was the first white person they had seen since she left, and they assumed that anyone with a fair skin was named Mrs. Kelly.

The big man with the red cheeks roared with laughter. His whole body seemed to shake. And then the children laughed, too, not because they understood the joke, but because they liked him.

Most of the Filipinos were very poor. Many reforms were needed, but Judge Taft was convinced that the majority of the people had no sympathy with the rebels. These desperate men were still carrying on a fierce guerrilla warfare on some of the islands, but they were finally captured by American army forces. By March, 1901, the last of the rebels had taken the oath of allegiance to the United States. Military rule was no longer needed, and William Howard Taft was appointed the first civil governor of the Philippines.

The day of his inauguration—July 4, 1901—the plaza in front of the cathedral in Manila was gay with American flags. A band played American music. The tall, mountainous man who stood on the covered pavilion delivering his inaugural speech was wildly cheered. Many of those in the crowd massed before the pavilion were tribesmen from the distant hills. They had not understood a word he said, but he was jovial and good-natured. When he smiled his warm smile, they seemed to know that he had come to help them.

After William Howard Taft became governor, he appointed to government positions a number of Filipinos who had proved themselves capable. New roads were built, harbors improved, and many new schools started.

"We hold the Philippines," said the new governor, "for the benefit of the Filipinos, and we are not entitled to pass a single act or to approve a single measure that has not that as its chief purpose."

Although Governor Taft was working from ten to twelve hours a day, there were many problems for which he could find no solution. The Filipinos were divided into factions, and disagreed violently with one another. Robbers roamed through the hills, preying on their countrymen. Crops failed, and there was a famine. Sanitary conditions were improved, yet many Filipinos continued to die of disease. Governor Taft became ill from overwork, not only once but several times.

On one occasion, when he was beginning to recover, he went to a resort high in the mountains for a much-needed rest. He had to travel on horseback up a steep road under a broiling sun—a hard journey for a man who weighed more than three hundred pounds. The news had reached Washington that he was ill, and Secretary Root sent him a cable inquiring about his health.

STOOD TRIP WELL, Mr. Taft replied. RODE HORSEBACK TWENTY-FIVE MILES.

Back from Washington came another cable: HOW IS THE HORSE?

Governor Taft, who was used to jokes about his great size, found this one too good to keep. It was published in a local newspaper and soon was being told all over Manila.

The following October he received a more serious cable. This one came from his friend Theodore Roosevelt, who was now President. There was soon to be a vacancy on the bench of the Supreme Court, and the President wanted to appoint William Howard Taft as an associate justice. There was no position he would rather have, and he knew that the chance might never come again. But his work on the islands was not finished, and he could not desert the Filipino people. He felt he must refuse, but three months later the offer was made again.

This time the President insisted that Mr. Taft return to Washington to fill the vacancy on the Supreme Court. Word that the governor was to leave soon spread through Manila, and a crowd gathered before the governor's palace. A long line of Filipinos, marching single file, passed through the palace gates. Many of the men carried signs with the Spanish words, "*Queremos* Taft." A few of the signs had the same words in English, "We want Taft."

A shout went up: "Taft! Taft! *Queremos* Taft."

The governor and his wife stepped out on the balcony to acknowledge the cheers. There they were joined by several Filipino leaders, each anxious to make a speech. "The Filipino people," said one man, who only two years earlier had been in revolt against the United States, "trust the home government will not tear from their arms their beloved governor."

The governor was touched when he learned that a number of prominent men in Manila had sent urgent telegrams to the White House. The cables informed the President that Señor Taft had performed a "miracle" in uniting all the different factions on the islands. He was the only man who could count on their cooperation. He had won the confidence of everyone. Two days later Governor Taft received a cable signed "Roosevelt."

"All right, stay where you are," the cable read. "I shall appoint someone else to the court."

This news was received with rejoicing by the Filipinos, but their governor was not to stay with them much longer. A few months later, back in Washington, Elihu Root announced that he must resign as Secretary of War, and Theodore Roosevelt offered the place to William Howard Taft.

"If only there were three of you!" he wrote. "Then I would put one of you on the Supreme Court, one of you in Root's place as Secretary of War, and one of you permanently governor of the Philippines. No one can quite take your place as governor, but no one of whom I can now think can take Root's place as secretary."

Again William Howard Taft had a hard decision to make. He had sacrificed his ambition to be a Supreme Court justice to help the Filipino people. Yet he consented to be Secretary of War, because in this position—although it appealed to him far less—he would still be in charge of the islands. In Washington he might have an even greater opportunity than in Manila to help his "little brown brothers."

"I have a deep affection for the Filipino people," he said, "and I mean to do everything that in me lies for their benefit."

As Secretary of War, Big Bill Taft—as he was often called in the newspapers—traveled not only to the Philippines but to Cuba, to the Canal Zone, and to Japan. He became a sort of "trouble shooter" for Theodore Roosevelt, who decided, as his administration drew to a close, that he wanted William Howard Taft to be his successor in the White House.

It was not the position Secretary Taft really wanted, nor was it the position for which he felt he was best suited. But the outgoing President and the Taft family urged him to be a candidate, and he yielded. Without much effort on his part, he was nominated by the Republican convention in the summer of 1908. That fall he was elected President.

During the next four years he had a number of accomplishments to his credit, but these were often overlooked at the time because of the noisy quarrels that began to divide his party. Those members who called themselves progressive did not like him, because they considered him too conservative. Theodore Roosevelt, when he returned from a hunting trip in Africa, was disappointed because some of his own cherished ideas had not been carried out. At the Republican convention in 1912, Mr. Roosevelt tried to take the nomination away from his old friend. When Taft won the nomination, Roosevelt became the nominee of a third party, the Progressives, made up mostly of dissatisfied Republicans.

In the election that followed, both Taft and Roosevelt lost, and the victory went to the Democratic nominee, Woodrow Wilson. Some of Mr. Taft's friends were bitter; they felt confident that he would have won if the Republican vote had not been divided. He himself bore no grudge.

"I try to keep my mind tranquil," he said, "and in that way I stand the knocks better."

After leaving the White House, ex-President Taft became a professor of law at Yale University. As the years went by, his opinion was sought on many public questions. He was a firm believer in settling disputes between nations by peaceful means, and after World War I he made speeches urging that the United States join the League of Nations. He often thought about the two chances he had passed up to be an associate justice. He still longed to be on the Supreme Court.

And then one day in June, 1921, he received a telegram from President Warren G. Harding. The President was offering to appoint him, not as an associate justice but as Chief Justice of the United States. This time he could accept. After he took the oath of office in October, he and the eight associate justices called at the White House.

As Mr. Taft passed between the tall white pillars, he realized that he was the only American who had ever been both President and Chief Justice. The Presidency—the position usually considered the highest honor an American could ever have—had brought William Howard Taft little happiness. For him the most satisfying office in the world was to be Chief Justice of the United States.

An old, old dream was coming true.

THE TWENTY-SEVENTH PRESIDENT *at a Glance*

William Howard Taft

Born: September 15, 1857   *Died: March 8, 1930*

Early life and career. William Howard Taft was born in Cincinnati, Ohio. After graduating from Yale (1878) and from the Cincinnati Law School (1880), he practiced law. At the age of 30 (1887) he became a judge of the Ohio Superior Court. He served as U.S. solicitor-general (1890–1892) and as U.S. circuit judge in Ohio (1892–1900). He went to the Philippines (1900) as head of a U.S. commission and later became the first civil governor of the islands (1901–1904). He served as Secretary of War (1904–1908) under President Theodore Roosevelt. With Roosevelt's backing, he won the Republican Presidential nomination in 1908.

As President (1909–1913). Though more cautions and conservative than Roosevelt, Taft often defied "big business" in the public interest. He was even more active than his predecessor in taking legal action against large business combinations that were strangling free competition. Because of his strong support, Congress ignored the protests of private bankers and established a government postal savings system (1910) and, against the wishes of the express companies, created a parcel-post system (1913). During Taft's term the Republicans were split by quarrels between conservative and progressive groups. The progressives were angered by Taft's policy on the tariff and conservation and other matters. When he was renominated at the Republican Convention in 1912, they organized a Progressive party with Theodore Roosevelt as their candidate. Both Taft and Roosevelt lost the election to the Democrat, Woodrow Wilson.

The President's family. The President and his wife, Helen Herron Taft (1861–1943) had three children who later had distinguished careers of their own: Robert (1889–1953) won prominence as a U.S. Senator; Helen (Mrs. Frederick J. Manning, born 1891), as dean and professor of history at Bryn Mawr College; and Charles (born 1897), as a lawyer and civic leader. As a result of Mrs. Taft's interest in planting Japanese cherry trees in the capital's Potomac Park, the mayor of Tokyo presented the city with 3,000 of the young trees (1912). Those blossoming cherry trees still draw thousands of sightseers every spring.

The nation's population and growth. The population was about 92,000,000 (1910 census). In 1912 two states, New Mexico and Arizona, were admitted to the Union, making a total of 48.

Other happenings. When Taft was President, Admiral Robert E. Peary discovered the North Pole (1909). The Boy Scouts of America was established (1910). The 16th Amendment to the Constitution, giving Congress the right to collect income taxes, was adopted (1913).

As Ex-President. Taft was a professor of law at Yale (1913–1921). After World War I, he favored U.S. membership in the League of Nations. As Chief Justice of the U.S. (1921–1930) he was much happier than he had been as President.

WOODROW WILSON *and His Great Dream*

Tommy Wilson had a new ball and bat. The bat was of polished hickory wood, and he swung it back and forth as he walked down one of the shady streets in Augusta, Georgia. He paused before a vacant lot, where some boys were practicing baseball. It had never occurred to them to invite Tommy to play, perhaps because he looked so pale and scrawny. Tommy himself had been too shy to suggest it.

But on this day he leaned his bat against the trunk of a tree, and began tossing his ball into the air. It was a real baseball, not at all like the homemade ball of yarn which Joe Lamar, his next-door neighbor, was about to pitch. Another player, Pleasant Stovall, was at bat. The bat was so old Pleasant was afraid it might crack if he hit the ball too hard.

"Hey, there, Tommy," Joe called. "Where did you get them?"

"You mean my ball and bat?" asked Tommy casually. "My father gave them to me."

Practice was forgotten as the boys gathered around Tommy to admire his present. "Say, don't you want to join our team?" one of them asked.

"All right," Tommy agreed, trying not to sound too eager. "You may use my ball and bat."

Tommy was not too good as a baseball player. But he was good at organizing, and within a few days he was making most of the rules for the team. They decided he could be their president.

"Let's call ourselves the Lightfoots," he suggested, and the other members agreed that it was a good name.

Sometimes the boys played against other neighborhood teams, but Tommy was much more interested in the correct way to conduct a meeting. One afternoon he led the way to the red-brick stable back of his home. The boys climbed the ladder leading into the loft and sank down on the mounds of hay, wondering what was going to happen next. All eyes were on Tommy, as he stood up before them, holding in his hand a book called *Robert's Rules of Order*.

"The meeting will please come to order," he said in a firm voice.

No one spoke. Tommy laid the book down, and picked up a piece of paper covered with his own handwriting. "I have made a constitution for the club."

"A constitution? What's that?" someone asked.

The question was soon answered. Tommy's constitution stated, first of all, the name and object of the Lightfoot Club, then gave a list of rules. "Will someone move that the constitution be adopted?" Tommy asked.

The boys were puzzled, but their president began turning the pages of *Robert's Rules of Order*. "This book tells us what to do," he explained. "Now, first of all, if you like this constitution, one of you must say, 'I move that the constitution, as drawn up by Tommy Wilson, be accepted.' Then somebody else must say, 'I second the motion.'"

"All right," said Joe Lamar. "I move that this constitution, as drawn up by Tommy Wilson, be accepted."

"I second the motion," Pleasant Stovall added.

Tommy pounded on the table. "All in favor say 'Aye.'"

"Aye!" all the boys shouted.

"The motion is carried," said President Tommy, beaming at the success of his plan.

During the weeks that followed, the Lightfoots played some ball but they more often held debates. Whatever the boys may have felt about having their baseball team turned into a debating society, Tommy's father seemed amused and pleased. Doctor Wilson, a Presbyterian minister, taught Tommy at home. The boy had always been too frail to go to school, but he liked having lessons with his father. Although he had to study hard, lessons—the way Dr. Wilson taught them—seemed more like a game.

One game both of them liked to play was with words. Whenever Tommy came across an unfamiliar word in his reading, his father told him to look it up in the dictionary. And then he was to use it again and again until he could use it easily. The purpose of words,

Dr. Wilson often said, was to express the exact meaning of what one wished to say.

Tommy also liked to write. One day he spent several hours on an essay. It was good, he decided—good enough to show his father.

Dr. Wilson blew a great cloud of smoke from his clay pipe as he picked up the essay. He read it slowly, while Tommy waited, leaning against the desk. Finally, Dr. Wilson took his pipe from his mouth. He pointed to the paper.

"Exactly what did you intend to say in this?"

"Why, I—I—" Tommy stuttered and floundered. He grew silent. He thought for a few moments. Then, simply, and directly, he told his father just what he had meant to say in his essay.

"Then why not say it?" Dr. Wilson asked quietly, tearing the paper into tiny pieces and dropping them into the wastebasket.

Tommy looked down at the floor. And after that he was careful to try to use exactly the right words to express his thoughts.

Sometimes, on a Sunday morning, when Dr. Wilson was preaching in the red-brick church across the street, he would hesitate. Tommy, seated in the family pew, would try to guess what his father was going to say next. He did not succeed very often, but sometimes he did. When, an instant later, Dr. Wilson used the same word Tommy had thought of, the boy would lean back in his seat with a satisfied sigh.

One Sunday morning Dr. Wilson arose in his high pulpit and made a strange announcement. "I have just received an urgent message," he said. "A great battle is raging in Virginia today."

Tommy's eyes, behind his spectacles, looked big and round. Although Augusta had never been attacked, he knew all about the war that was being fought between the North and South. Nearly every day he passed the factory where ammunition was made for the soldiers at the front. He had seen them march away to war in their new gray uniforms. He had seen wounded men come back, straggling along on crutches, or riding in wagons because they were too ill to walk.

"Our Southern soldiers are in grave need of ammunition," Dr. Wilson went on in his deep rich voice. "This congregation has been asked to meet at the ammunition factory and roll cartridges. We must all do our duty."

After singing the doxology, the congregation filed out of the church. Their faces were grave. For their pastor to suggest that they work on the Sabbath meant that the situation must be desperate.

It was to become more desperate as the months went by. During the summer of 1864, the town was thrown into a panic when it was learned that General Sherman and his Union army were marching across Georgia toward the sea. Bridges were blown up and crops destroyed. Houses were set on fire. This time it seemed that Augusta could not escape invasion, and yet it did.

But it did not escape sorrow. Messages were received more and more frequently of Augusta men who had been wounded or killed. The following April the news came that the Confederate commander, Robert E. Lee, had surrendered. Brave, gallant General Lee! Realizing that the South could not possibly hold out much longer, he had surrendered to spare his men unnecessary bloodshed.

Among the Southern soldiers who returned to Augusta after the war, was an officer, Joseph T. Derry. He started a school, and by the time Tommy was thirteen his health had improved enough so he could attend. One bright May morning in 1870, Mr. Derry called all of the pupils together.

"Young gentlemen," he said, "I have great news. General Robert E. Lee is coming to visit Augusta."

For a moment there was not a sound in the room. And then there was a shout. The pupils seemed to forget they were in school, but Mr. Derry understood. The general was the hero of every boy in the South, and Tommy could hardly wait to rush home and tell his family.

The whole town turned out to welcome General Lee, and Mr. Derry's pupils were among those who stood in line to have a chance to shake hands with the distinguished visitor. Gradually the line moved forward, until there were only four boys ahead of Tommy. Then there were only three boys, and then only two. And now at last it was Tommy Wilson himself who was standing before the general and looking up into the kind gentle face.

It was the face of a hero, Tommy thought, with a quick intake of breath—a hero who had been willing to sacrifice everything for the cause in which he believed.

There was time only for a brief handclasp, a warm smile, before Tommy's place was taken by the boy next in line. But Thomas Woodrow Wilson was to remember that moment all of his life.

The year after this meeting with General Lee, Tommy moved with his parents, his two older sisters, Marion and Anne, and little Joe, his four-year-old brother, to Columbia. Of all the cities in the South, Columbia, the capital of South Carolina, had probably been the most unfortunate. General Sherman's forces, when they invaded the South, had marched into the town and set fire to the entire business district. Now only the charred ruins of the old Capitol were left standing. Many homes also had been destroyed. Tommy felt sick at heart as he walked past the gaunt framework of what once had been beautiful mansions.

Was war always so cruel? he wondered. The sights that he saw every day were turning him into a very solemn boy.

Much too solemn, his mother felt. Too solemn, and still too shy. One evening Marion and Anne were attending a party given by their friends, Mr. and Mrs. MacMaster. Mrs. Wilson decided, now that Tommy was fifteen, he was old enough to escort his sisters home.

"Tommy," she said, "I have told the girls that you will call for them. You'd better leave at once."

"Yes, ma'am," he replied, but his feet felt like lead as he walked down the street.

The closer Tommy came to the MacMaster house, the more shy he felt. He stepped up on the veranda. He stood there for a few minutes in the shadow of one of the pillars, trying to get up enough nerve to lift the knocker on the front door. Inside he could hear voices, among them the voice of his sister Anne. When she moved closer to the window, he could see her shadow, and this gave Tommy courage. He walked across the veranda and rattled the blind.

"Anne," he whispered, but there was no response.

Tommy swallowed hard and tried again. "Anne! Anne!" he called. "Mother wants you and Marion to come home."

Anne hastily summoned her sister, and the two girls joined their brother on the porch. "I was never so embarrassed in my life," said Anne. "Why couldn't you just knock on the front door and ask for us?"

Mrs. Wilson also was embarrassed. Wouldn't Tommy ever get over his shyness? She hoped that going to a new school would help.

The classes in the Columbia school were conducted in a barn, because Dr. Charles Barnwell, the founder, had no place else to hold them. He had been left destitute by the war, but he was a very learned gentleman and the ideal teacher, Dr. Wilson decided, to help Tommy prepare for college.

Tommy did not seem to care very much for mathematics and some of the other subjects in the regular course of study, but history and politics interested him, and he tried to find out everything he could about government. What made some governments good and others bad? How had men learned to govern themselves? There were books and magazines in his father's library in which he tried to find the answers. Often, during the next few years, the lamp in his room burned far into the night as he turned page after page. Above his desk hung a picture of William Gladstone, the great English prime minister who had brought about many important reforms in the British Isles.

One day while Tommy was studying, his cousin Jessie Bones came to see him. He had often played Indian with her when they were younger, but at sixteen Tommy was so serious that Jessie was a little bit in awe of him. He did not even want to be called Tommy any more, but had decided to use his middle name.

"Hello, Tommy—I mean Woodrow," Jessie said. "Who is that dignified-looking man over your desk?"

For a moment the boy did not answer. His thoughts seemed to be far away, but his eyes lighted as he glanced at the portrait.

"That is a picture of William Gladstone, the greatest statesman who ever lived," Woodrow Wilson answered, "and I intend to be a statesman, too."

Some of the happiest years of Woodrow Wilson's life were spent in the town of Princeton, New Jersey. He went there first as a student and graduated from Princeton University in 1879. Eleven years later he came back as a professor. In the meantime he had studied and practiced law, had taught in two colleges, and was the author of several books. He had married, and when he returned to Princeton, he brought his lovely wife, Ellen, and three small daughters.

"His home life," said one man who was a frequent guest in the Wilson home, "was as charming and delightful as that of anyone I have ever known."

With strangers Woodrow Wilson might still seem shy and reserved, but the friends who came to know him well were constantly being surprised by his sense of humor. To his three growing daughters, he was a curious mixture of dignity and fun, but mostly fun. One of their earliest memories was of their father dancing a jig, with a high silk hat perched on the side of his head. He seemed to have an endless supply of amusing stories, and he liked limericks. Although the girls considered their father handsome—an opinion which he did not share—he could always make them laugh when he recited,

> "For beauty I am not a star,
> There are others more handsome by far,
>   But my face—I don't mind it;
>   You see, I'm behind it;
> It's the fellow in front that I jar."

As professor and later as president of Princeton University, Woodrow Wilson continued to write books on government and history. He became nationally known both as an author and an educator, but he had not forgotten his boyhood ambition to be a statesman.

"I am tired of a merely talking profession," he confided to a friend. "I want to do something."

The chance soon came. In 1910 he was elected governor of New Jersey, and in this office his record of wise reforms soon became the talk of the nation. How about Woodrow Wilson for the Presidency? some of the members of his political party began to ask. In June, 1912, he was nominated by the Democratic Party, in November he was elected, and the following March he became the twenty-eighth President of the United States. During the next nineteen months, Congress passed—at his suggestion—a number of forward-looking laws to help the average man.

In many ways 1914 had been a year of triumph. But it was a year of anxiety and worry as well. During the summer a terrible war, World War I, had started in Europe. The Central Powers, made up of Germany, Austria-Hungary, and Turkey, were fighting England, France, Russia and several other countries, known as the Allies. Most of Europe was suffering the hardships of war. President Wilson was determined, as were most of his countrymen, that the United States should remain neutral—that it should not take sides.

The President also had suffered a deep personal sorrow when his wife Ellen died. The next year he married Edith Bolling Galt, who proved to be as loyal and devoted as his first wife had been. The second Mrs. Wilson's understanding and courage were to prove a great help to her husband during the difficult months that lay ahead.

For as time passed, it was increasingly hard for the nation to remain neutral. There was a growing conviction among the American people that Germany was in the wrong. There was fear also of the autocratic German government. The Kaiser, or emperor, and his military leaders were ambitious. They were suspected of wanting to control Europe. What if they should win? Would the United States be the next victim of German aggression?

Feeling ran high when merchant ships on which Americans were traveling were ruthlessly sunk by German submarines. Even hospital ships were sunk. The submarines, firing their torpedoes from under the surface of the water, could not be seen before they attacked. Several hundred American men, women and children were sent to their deaths.

As a result of Woodrow Wilson's firm protests, the German government finally agreed that, in the future, submarine commanders would notify the crew before sinking a passenger vessel. Then crew and passengers would have time to take to the lifeboats and save themselves. Another crisis was passed, or so many people thought at the time.

After his re-election in 1916, the President offered to act as peace-maker for the countries at war. He suggested that they settle their differences without any more bloodshed, even though no nation was victorious. But the idea of "peace without victory" did not appeal to either side. The Allies wanted nothing less than Germany's complete surrender. The German military command responded by going back on its promise and announcing a new policy of submarine warfare. From that time forward, all vessels found near the British Isles were to be sunk without warning.

The Germans soon made good their threat. More American ships were sent to the bottom. More American lives were lost. The United States could remain neutral no longer. President Wilson, who loved peace, knew that he must lead his country into war.

On April 2 both houses of Congress were called into special session. No one present was ever to forget that evening when Woodrow Wilson asked for a declaration of war against Germany. Every seat was taken in the hall of the House of Representatives, and the galleries were crowded with visitors. The justices of the Supreme Court and members of the Cabinet occupied chairs placed in a half circle in front of the rostrum. There was a hushed silence when Woodrow Wilson began to speak.

He made it clear that he did not blame the German people. They had never been consulted by their autocratic leaders about going to war. But his face was grim when he spoke of the German government's use of submarines, which he called "a warfare against mankind." The United States did not want any new territory, he pointed out, and the Americans had "no selfish ends to serve." They would be fighting for "the ultimate peace of the world."

"The world must be made safe for democracy," he said.

A few days later Congress declared war on Germany, at a time when the Allies were in grave danger of defeat. Their situation was desperate, but that was soon changed. The American government lent large sums of money to the Allied governments. More American ships were built and rushed into action. Many tons of food were sent overseas. American factories speeded up the production of munitions.

Especially important, as the months went by, was the arrival of

American troops in France, where most of the fighting took place. A half million of them took part in one battle alone. During the long-drawn-out campaign in the Argonne Forest, more than a million Americans helped to drive the Germans back toward the Meuse River. Twice that number went overseas. More than a hundred thousand of them gave their lives in the struggle which the President called "a war to end wars."

For that was Woodrow Wilson's great dream. To him the war was a crusade. The troops fought with guns; he fought with ideas—expressed in stirring speeches that put heart into the Allied soldiers and their families behind the lines. In another address to Congress on January 8, 1918, he summed up the Allied aims in Fourteen Points. One point he stressed was "a general association of nations." Only through a league of nations, he was convinced, could future wars be prevented.

Again and again Woodrow Wilson spoke of peace—"peace with justice"—for all peoples alike. His speeches were sent by wireless to distant lands. They were printed in leaflets and dropped behind the German lines. Many Germans weary of the rule of their autocratic military masters began to feel that President Wilson spoke for them, as well as for the other downtrodden populations of Europe.

By the fall of 1918 it was the German people who were desperate. With fresh American troops pouring into Europe every month, Germany was threatened with invasion. There were uprisings among the people, and the Kaiser was forced to flee. Some of the German leaders had been writing President Wilson, asking him to arrange for a treaty on the basis of his Fourteen Points. The leaders of the Allied countries had already agreed to consider a peace on the same terms. Finally on November 11, 1918, representatives of a new German government met with Allied commanders in France. There they signed the temporary terms of surrender known as the Armistice.

The news spread quickly, and there was rejoicing throughout the Allied nations. THE WAR IS OVER and GERMANY GIVES UP, American newspapers announced in bold headlines. In Washington, as in every other town and city, on that first Armistice Day, the streets were jammed with people. Men and women were shouting and singing. Strangers clasped hands. Church bells were ringing. Bands played "The Star Spangled Banner." That afternoon the President rode through cheering throngs to the Capitol to address Congress. Here he was cheered again when he made the formal announcement that the war was over.

But the President's speech contained a warning. "To conquer with arms," he reminded the Congressmen, "is to make only a temporary conquest."

Yes, the real conquest—the realization of his great dream to bring permanent peace to the world—was still to come. Woodrow Wilson had faith that it would come. During the evening, as the jubilant crowds surged down Pennsylvania Avenue, he stood watching at the White House gates. In recalling that night several years later, Woodrow Wilson's secretary said, "I shall never forget how happy he looked."

Early in December, the President sailed for France as head of the American Peace Commission, to help write the Peace Treaty. At that time he was probably the most influential man in the world. In his speeches he had given expression to the hopes and dreams of hundreds of thousands of men and women.

The Polish people, among others, had been deeply stirred when he talked of the rights of small nations. Poland had had a very sad history. Its territory had been annexed by more powerful countries, Russia, Austria-Hungary, and Prussia (which had become a part of Germany). Polish patriots wanted their country to be independent. They wanted to have their own government. They—like the patriots of a number of other nations—now looked to the American President to help them.

Were they expecting too much of him? he thought uneasily. "It is to America the whole world turns," he said to a friend on shipboard. "Yet these ancient wrongs are not to be remedied in a day. What I seem to see—I hope I am wrong—is a tragedy of disappointment."

Woodrow Wilson was the first American President who had crossed the Atlantic while in office, and it seemed that everyone in Paris wanted to honor him. The Champs Élysées, one of the most beautiful boulevards in the world, was lined on either side with crowds. "*Vive Wilson! Vive l'Amérique!*" they cried, as the carriage in which he rode beside the President of France passed down the street.

People on the sidewalks tried to press closer. People leaned out of windows and tossed flowers into the carriage. Men and boys, perched on the branches of the stately horse chestnut trees, kept up a continuous shouting. Woodrow Wilson turned from side to side to acknowledge the cheers. When he looked straight ahead, he saw a sign stretched across the street: HONOR TO WILSON THE JUST.

Yes, he must try to be just, he thought. He must try to be just, even to the enemy.

While waiting for the Peace Conference to begin, Woodrow Wilson was visited several times by groups of peasants from neighboring countries. One day a group of Polish farmers in white wool suits gaily decorated with red embroidery arrived at the house where he was staying. Two of them, who had lived in America years before, stepped forward and doffed their shaggy fur hats. One of them began to speak haltingly in English, a language he had almost forgotten.

"We go on feet two days," he said, "then two weeks on train, so we can see you. We think you help us if you understand."

"How can I help you?" Mr. Wilson asked.

The men tried to explain. The President, in his Fourteen Points speech, had said that Poland should once more be an independent nation. There was a rumor that another independent nation, Czechoslovakia, was to be created by the Peace Conference. The Polish farmers had heard that the region in which they lived was to be made a part of Czechoslovakia.

"We do not want to be swallowed up by a people of different blood and religion," the Polish farmer went on earnestly. "I have read your speeches, Mr. Wilson. I told my friends I was sure you would not let us be a part of this other country."

The President was deeply touched by the men's faith in him. But his ideas about justice—which had brought hope to the Polish peasants and to many other people in Europe—were not popular with everyone. Some of the Allied leaders who had gathered in Paris to make a Peace Treaty did not seem to care what happened to any country except their own. They were less interested in justice than in revenge. The Peace Conference met in the palace at Versailles, a few miles from Paris, and as the days passed, a number of suggestions were made, of which Woodrow Wilson did not approve. But he had to give in. "Only with give and take," he told his wife, "can we come to an agreement."

Again and again the President compromised in order to get his way about a League of Nations. This great dream of an international organization had been growing in his mind and heart for many months, and he insisted that the League be made a part of the Treaty. The League provided for a court where nations, both great and small, could send their representatives to present their grievances. After the bitterness caused by the recent struggle had been forgotten, Woodrow Wilson believed that the mistakes of the Treaty could be corrected in this court. Most important, the League could settle disputes between nations that might otherwise lead to war.

But would the United States Senate agree with him? The American Constitution says that the Senate must ratify, or approve, all treaties made with foreign governments, and early in February the President made a quick trip back to Washington. At a meeting in the White House, he showed the members of the Senate Foreign Relations Committee a rough draft on the plan for a League of Nations, and asked for suggestions. As a result of that meeting, Woodrow Wilson felt reasonably certain that the Senate would ratify the Treaty, of which the League was a part. When he returned to Paris, the suggestions made by the Committee were presented to the Peace Conference and adopted.

Finally, on June 28, 1919, the Treaty of Versailles was signed in an impressive ceremony, and the President left again for home. Word had reached him that opposition to his plan had been growing, led by some of the same Senators who apparently had approved of it a few months earlier. But Woodrow Wilson's conviction that the League was "the first real step forward" in preventing future wars gave him confidence.

"The united power of free nations must put a stop to aggression," he told the Senate on July 10, "and the world must be given peace. Shall we or any other free people hesitate to accept this great duty?"

For the rest of that summer, there were heated discussions in the Senate. The chief opponent of the Treaty was Woodrow Wilson's bitter political foe, a Republican, who also was chairman of the Foreign Relations Committee. But there were other leading Republicans, including ex-President Taft, who were heartily in favor of the League and made speeches urging its adoption.

Some of the Senators honestly believed that it would not be in the best interests of the United States to join. Others wanted reservations or changes. The President's reply was that the changes suggested by the Foreign Relations Committee already had been made. If he were to ask for further changes at this late date, then the representatives who had signed the Treaty on behalf of all the other countries would have to be granted the same privilege.

By the end of August, the arguments in the Senate were still going on. Woodrow Wilson, realizing that the Treaty stood in grave danger of defeat, decided to go on a long speaking tour. He wanted the people of the country to understand the truth, he said. He wanted them to realize that the future peace of the world might depend upon the League of Nations. Then an aroused public opinion might influence the Senate to vote in its favor.

When Mrs. Wilson learned of her husband's plan, she protested. Dr. Grayson, the White House physician, warned him that a long, strenuous trip would seriously endanger his health. He had never been a husky man. The strain of the war years had worn down his strength, and he had been ill during the Peace Conference. But Woodrow Wilson was not thinking of himself. He was thinking of the soldiers whom he, as commander-in-chief, had sent to Europe. They had not turned back when faced with danger in battle, and he could not turn back either.

"What does my health matter?" he asked wearily. "The League of Nations is now at crisis, and if it fails, God knows what will happen to the world."

On September 3, the President's special train pulled out of Washington on a trip that was to take him across the continent. He spoke to huge audiences, and was much heartened by their approval. He shook hands with thousands of well-wishers who came up to speak to him after a meeting or who crowded about the back platform of his train whenever it made a brief stop.

One day two tramps were discovered preparing to stow away for a free ride underneath one of the cars. When they learned whose train it was, they asked one of the Secret Service men if the President would be willing to shake hands with them.

Their request, repeated to President Wilson, was promptly granted. He even offered the two shabby gentlemen a ride—not under the train but in it—but they replied that they would wait for "the regular."

"I know he's got everything and we've got nothing," one of the tramps told the Secret Service man, "but we would not change places with him. With the heavy load he is carrying, we will do nothing to add to it."

Perhaps the tramps had noticed the tired lines in Woodrow Wilson's face. Although he had severe and frequent headaches, he refused to rest. Public opinion, he felt, was turning in his favor. His speeches had caught the imagination of the public, and the crowds grew larger and more enthusiastic as his train sped westward. They listened thoughtfully when he spoke of the danger of another war.

"I do not hesitate to say," he told one audience, "that the war we have been through, though it was shot through with terror of every kind, is not to be compared with the war we would have to face next time."

By September 25, the presidential party had traveled all the way to the Pacific coast and a third of the way back across the continent. That afternoon the President spoke in Pueblo, Colorado. The liberation and salvation of the world, he said, might depend upon the decision of the United States to join the League of Nations. Never had he been more eloquent. Never had his audience been more deeply moved.

That was the last major speech Woodrow Wilson ever made. A few hours later he was stricken with paralysis, and for the rest of his life he was an invalid. Although the Senate voted not to join the League, he never lost faith in his great dream.

"I would rather fail in a cause that I know someday will triumph," he said, "than to win in a cause that I know someday will fail."

THE TWENTY-EIGHTH PRESIDENT *at a Glance*

Woodrow Wilson

Born: December 28, 1856   *Died: February 3, 1924*

Early life. (Thomas) Woodrow Wilson was born in Staunton, Va., but most of his boyhood was spent in Augusta, Ga., and Columbia, S.C. After graduating from Princeton (1879), he studied law at the University of Virginia and was admitted to the bar in 1882. He practiced law in Atlanta, Ga., for a year and in 1883 entered Johns Hopkins University as a graduate student, receiving his Ph.D. degree in 1886.

As an educator. Woodrow Wilson taught history and political economy at Bryn Mawr College (1885–1888) and at Wesleyan University (1888–1890). He was professor of political economy and jurisprudence (the science of law) at Princeton (1890–1902) and president of Princeton (1902–1910).

Political career. Wilson was almost 54 when he was elected Governor of New Jersey, his first political office. As governor (1911–1913), he obtained passage of a law regulating public utilities and a workmen's compensation law. These and other reform measures made him nationally known, and the Democrats nominated him as President (1912).

As President (1913–1917; 1917–1921). Among the important measures Wilson persuaded Congress to pass during his first term were a law reducing tariff rates; a Federal Reserve Act, which reorganized the country's banking system; an antitrust law stronger than the old Sherman Act; and a law establishing an eight-hour day for railroad workers. In 1916 Wilson was elected for a second term, largely because he had been able to keep the country out of World War I, which had broken out in Europe two years earlier. When German submarine attacks on American ships made neutrality no longer possible, Wilson asked Congress to declare war on Germany (April 2, 1917). On January 8, 1918, the President proposed Fourteen Points as the basis for a just and lasting peace. The Fourteenth Point called for "an association of nations." In October, 1918, Germany asked for a peace treaty based on the Fourteen Points, and an armistice was signed (November 11, 1918). Establishment of a League of Nations was included in the Peace Treaty that President Wilson helped to write at the Peace Conference (January–June, 1919) held at Versailles, near Paris. When Wilson submitted the signed treaty to the U.S. Senate for ratification, bitter arguments arose concerning the League of Nations. While on a speaking tour to gain public support for the League, the President had a paralytic stroke (September, 1919) and thereafter was an invalid. The Senate finally rejected the Versailles Treaty, and the U.S. never joined the League. In recognition of his efforts in behalf of world peace, Wilson was awarded the Nobel Peace Prize (1919).

The President's family. The President's first wife, Ellen Axson Wilson (1860–1914), died during her husband's first term in the White House. The President later married a widow, Edith Bolling Galt (1872–1961), who accompanied him to the Versailles Peace Conference and who took devoted care of him after he was ill. The President and his first wife had three daughters. Eleanor, the youngest, married William G. McAdoo, Secretary of the Treasury, at the White House (1914).

Other happenings. The British steamship, the "Lusitania," was sunk by a German submarine (1915). More than a hundred Americans were among the 1,198 passengers who perished. After the Mexican bandit, Pancho Villa, raided Columbus, N. Mex., American troops under General John Pershing pursued him into Mexico (1916). Troops were later withdrawn because of Mexican objections to the invasion. The 18th (Prohibition) Amendment to the Constitution was adopted (1919). The adoption of the 19th Amendment (1920) gave women the right to vote. Radio developed swiftly after the opening of the first commercial broadcasting station (WWJ, Detroit, 1920).

The nation's population. According to the 1920 census, the population was about 105,700,000.

Wilson as author. Among the most important of Wilson's writings are *Congressional Government* (1885), *A History of the American People* (1902), and *Constitutional Government in the United States* (1908). *The New Freedom* (1913) containing material from his 1912 campaign speeches, expressed the political beliefs which he put into effect during the first part of his Presidency.

WARREN HARDING *Trusts His Friends*

Warren Harding walked into the office of the Caledonia *Argus,* the village newspaper, and looked around. Over in one corner of the office, the owner of the paper was running a printing press. Warren touched him on the arm.

"Please, sir," he asked, "would you give me a job? Could I come here and work after school?"

The owner stopped the press, and eyed the tall, twelve-year-old boy appraisingly. He was the son of "Doc" Harding, and there was no man in central Ohio who was more respected. The Hardings lived on a farm nearby, and Warren attended school in town.

"If I hire you," the newspaper owner asked, "would you work hard?"

"Oh, yes," the boy promised. "I like to write. I've written essays about Napoleon and Alexander Hamilton, and I make up poems, too."

"Can't say I need any poets to work on my paper," the owner replied drily. "But if you can come in every day after school, I could use you as a printer's devil."

"A printer's devil!" said Warren. "I'd like that, sir. May I start right away?"

"Yes, come in tomorrow."

Warren's first task was to learn to set type. The owner of the *Argus* also showed him how to run the printing press. As sheet after sheet of the white paper rolled off the press, it was filled with words and lines and sentences. It seemed like magic to the boy—magic that a printer could create again and again.

Two years later Warren entered Ohio Central College in the town of Iberia. Here the course offered was much the same as high school courses of a later time. Warren earned most of his expenses by cutting corn for neighboring farmers, painting barns and selling brooms. Yet he found time to make good grades and to edit the college newspaper. The work was so interesting that he decided he was going to be a newspaper man and someday have a paper of his own.

He also joined the village band. He started out by playing the cornet and ended by learning several of the instruments.

"I've just heard," he said at band practice one day, "that there's to be a state-wide tournament up at Findlay, with prizes for the best bands. Why don't we enter the contest?"

"We haven't any money to pay our railroad fare," someone objected.

That stopped Warren, but only for a moment. "We might ask some of the merchants in town to put up the money," he suggested. "The town would feel mighty proud of us if we came back with a prize."

He sounded so confident that the other boys agreed that it wouldn't hurt to try. The merchants agreed to pay their expenses, and the day of the contest found the members of the Iberia Band gathered in the Findlay concert hall. When their turn came to play, they marched upon the platform and did their best. And then they took their places in the audience again, to listen to the rival bands.

Several of the bands played so well that the Iberia boys felt discouraged. Most of them were convinced that they could not win, and one by one they slipped out of the concert hall. Only three of the members were left—one clarinet player, one bass drummer and Warren, grasping his cornet. He stirred restlessly in his chair when one of the judges stepped upon the platform.

"Ladies and gentlemen," said the judge, "after I have announced the winners in the tournament, the bands that I name will form in line outside. Each band may play one selection as it marches through the streets."

Warren glanced anxiously at his companions. What if the Iberia band did win? he wondered. How much music would one bass drum, one clarinet, and one cornet be able to make?

The clarinet player grinned. "Why worry about it?" he whispered. "We haven't a chance anyway."

But Warren wanted to win, and he listened carefully as the judge continued. "The first prize," he said, "goes to the —— Band."

A burst of applause greeted his announcement, but Warren's heart sank. The judge had named another band.

"The second prize goes to the band from ——"

The town the judge named was not Iberia. There was only one prize left.

"The third prize——"

The judge paused. Warren sat forward on the edge of his chair. "The third prize goes to the Iberia Band."

Warren and his two companions took their places in the procession. "We're going to have to play good and loud," he said.

He raised his cornet to his lips. The notes came out, pure and clear. The clarinet joined in with its high treble, and the bass drum rumbled a brave accompaniment as the three-man band marched down the street. The next day they returned to Iberia in triumph.

A year after Warren finished college, he moved with his parents to the larger town of Marion. Here he applied for a job as a reporter on the Marion *Mirror*.

The editor looked him over. "I'll hire you at a dollar a week. If you make good, I'll raise your pay to two dollars."

Warren nodded eagerly. At nineteen, he had started toward his goal—to be a newspaper man.

He liked his new job, but he had one worry. The *Mirror* was a Democratic paper, supporting Grover Cleveland in the presidential campaign of 1884. Warren wanted James A. Blaine, the Republican nominee, to win. He joined a Blaine Club, whose members wore gray plug hats as a symbol of their party.

One day Warren grew so excited at a meeting that he wore his campaign hat when he went back to the office. His employer looked at it and grew red with rage.

"Get out of here, you Republican," he shouted. "You're fired."

Warren put on his gray plug hat—the hat that had caused all the trouble—and walked out of the door. Was all his hard work on the Caledonia *Argus,* then on the college paper, and now on the Marion *Mirror* to be wasted? There was another newspaper in town, the *Star,* but it would do no good to apply there for a job. Business had not been good, and the owner was trying to sell. Suddenly Warren had an idea, and he went to see Jack Warwick, a printer that he knew.

"Listen, Jack," said Warren, "the *Star* can be bought cheap. Why don't we buy it and run our own newspaper?"

"Wouldn't it cost several hundred dollars?"

"Yes, but we can borrow the money. I had some good experience editing the college newspaper, and now I've been a reporter on the *Mirror*. Both of us know about printing, and between us we can do all the work ourselves."

When Dr. Harding heard of the plan he thought it over carefully. "All right, Warren," he said. "If you and Jack can borrow the money from the bank, I'll go on your note."

The two partners started for the bank, where they obtained a loan of several hundred dollars. This was not much capital on which to run a newspaper, but it was enough to buy the Marion *Star*, with a little left over. Warren had ambitious plans for increasing the circulation and for selling more advertising space. But business trickled in slowly. Even though the partners did all of the work, their money was getting low.

"I know what we need," said Warren. "A telephone."

"A telephone?" Jack exclaimed. "Do you know what those new-fangled contraptions cost?"

"But you and I have so much to do, we can't be everywhere at once. We could save a lot of time, phoning new advertisers, and people who want to subscribe would find it easier to reach us."

"No," said Jack stubbornly. "A phone would be an extravagance. We're never going to make a go of this paper anyway. We might as well give up."

Warren was far from being willing to give up. He borrowed some more money and bought out his partner's interest. Jack was relieved, and Warren was in high spirits. The *Star* was all his now. He made up his mind that, in time, he was going to make it one of the best newspapers in Ohio.

Becoming a successful newspaperman took time, as Warren Harding soon found out. Gradually business improved, and though his funds were still low, he had to hire helpers. He was probably the most considerate boss in town.

"I never heard him talk cross or speak rough to any man," said one employee. "He had another way of getting what he wanted—kindness was his way. Why, Mr. Harding would often see to it that his employees all got their money on Saturday night, and then go home himself without a cent left."

Such measures were no longer necessary after a few years. Warren worked hard, and the *Star* became one of the most successful newspapers in the state. He used his paper to promote various public improvements—paved streets, electric lights, and new parks. No man in Marion was better known, or better liked. He was generous and he was kind.

A man so popular could hardly escape going into politics. Warren G. Harding was elected a state senator, then lieutenant governor. In 1915 he went to Washington to take his seat in the United States Senate. He would have been content to be a senator or a newspaper publisher for the rest of his life, had not his friend, Harry Daugherty, an Ohio lawyer, decided to boom him for the Presidency.

At the Republican convention held in Chicago, in June, 1920, the names of seventeen different candidates were presented. After several days of voting, it became apparent that not one of them could count on enough votes to win the nomination.

Meanwhile Harry Daugherty had laid his plans carefully. The weather was hot, and the weary delegates were anxious to go home. At just the right moment Senator Harding's name was presented as a candidate, and he was nominated on the tenth ballot. Everything had worked out the way Mr. Daugherty had wanted.

During the election campaign that summer Mr. Harding promised a "return to normalcy," if he was elected. He meant that everyone could go back to the old safe, comfortable ways of living they had known before the war. This was exactly what the majority of American voters wanted to hear. They were tired of war, and Warren G. Harding was elected by a landslide.

Certainly, the year 1921 was not an easy time to take office, but President Harding leaned heavily on the advice of his cabinet. The cabinet included such able men as Charles Evans Hughes, a former Associate Justice of the Supreme Court, as Secretary of State; Andrew Mellon, a well known banker, as Secretary of the Treasury; and Herbert Hoover as Secretary of Commerce. He was much admired for his work in feeding millions of hungry people in war-torn Europe. These were men the President knew that he could trust.

But, unfortunately, he also trusted some men who were unworthy. He appointed to high office a number of old friends who later were to take a cruel advantage of his friendship.

It was said that Warren G. Harding—tall and handsome, with a shock of graying hair—really looked like a President. He sincerely wanted to be a good one. But after a few months many of the people who had voted for him were disappointed. They felt that he was making no real effort to solve the problems of the day.

"He simply closed his eyes to disagreeable facts," said one journalist who heard him speak. "It was pathetic; you were sorry for the man, sorrier still for the country."

The journalist would have felt even sorrier for the President, had he known how some of his friends were betraying him. His Secretary of the Interior had accepted a bribe of $100,000. This sum was paid to him after he had leased government oil reserves at Teapot Dome, Wyoming, and Elk's Hill, California, to private oil companies. There were other dishonest deals by government officials of which the President knew nothing at the time.

When he began to suspect that something was wrong no one knows, but he seemed deeply troubled when he started for Alaska in June, 1923. Herbert Hoover, the Secretary of Commerce, was a member of the Presidential party as the ship *Henderson* nosed its way through the Inland Passage between the mainland of Alaska and the many small islands that fringe the coast.

One afternoon, as the President stood at the railing with some of the other passengers, he seemed lost in thought. Was he really seeing the rugged coastline? Was he aware of the gaunt beauty of dark forests set against steep mountain sides? Or was he remembering some of the events of the past two years?

He had some accomplishments to his credit, he reflected. Certainly he was proud of a recent meeting he had held with leaders of the iron and steel industries. In the past laborers in steel mills had been working twelve hours, sometimes fourteen hours, a day. The President had persuaded several leaders to limit the working day for their employees to eight hours.

That, thought Warren Harding, was his greatest triumph. But his satisfaction over that victory could not make him forget the feeling of despair that almost overwhelmed him. He had not had a moment free from worry since he had begun to suspect what some of his friends had done.

The next day, the President asked Herbert Hoover to come to his cabin. "Mr. Secretary," he said, "if you knew of a great scandal in our administration, would you, for the good of the country, expose it publicly? Or would you bury it?"

"I would publish it," Secretary Hoover replied. "You would at least get credit for integrity on your side."

The secretary asked a few questions. The President mentioned fraud in some of the government departments but did not explain more fully. His face was wan, like that of a man stricken by a great grief. He did not mention the matter again.

During the remainder of the journey, Warren Harding made an effort to appear cheerful. He was the first President to visit Alaska, the vast, beautiful possession which one day was to become the forty-ninth state. In every town where he and his party stopped, streets and houses were decorated with flags. Indian bands played patriotic airs. Receptions and parades were held in the President's honor, and native girls dressed in white strewed flowers in his path. In the warmth of the people's welcome, he seemed more like his old genial self.

In speech after speech the President assured his audiences that the Federal Government was deeply interested in their welfare. He had come several thousand miles, by land and by sea, so that he might learn more about their problems. He called his trip "a journey of understanding."

"Understanding—that is what the world and the nation most need," he said.

A few years later, after Herbert Hoover had become President, he visited Marion, Ohio. He was there to dedicate the tomb of Warren G. Harding, who had died soon after he left Alaska. After his death, some of the men he had appointed to important positions had been brought to trial for defrauding the government. But their acts, Mr. Hoover stated, had never touched the former President.

The new President glanced up at the magnificent monument which had been erected in memory of the town's best loved citizen.

"Warren Harding," said Herbert Hoover, "had a dim realization that he had been betrayed by a few of the men whom he had trusted, by men he had believed were his devoted friends. It was later proved in the courts of the land that these men had betrayed not alone the friendship and trust of their staunch and loyal friend but they had betrayed their country.

"That was the tragedy of the life of Warren Harding."

THE TWENTY-NINTH PRESIDENT *at a Glance*

Warren Gamaliel Harding

Born: November 2, 1865   *Died: August 2, 1923*

Early life and career. Warren Harding was born in Corsica (now Blooming Grove), Ohio. His family soon moved to Caledonia, Ohio, where Warren spent his boyhood. He attended Ohio Central College in Iberia (1879–1882). At the age of 19 (1884) he bought a small newspaper, the Marion, Ohio, *Star,* which he gradually built into one of the most important papers in the state. He served as a state senator (1900–1904), as lieutenant governor of Ohio (1904–1906), and as U.S. Senator (1915–1921). In 1920 he was nominated by the Republicans for President and was elected.

As President (1921–1923). Although President Harding opposed U.S. membership in the League of Nations, he urged American cooperation in the League's Permanent Court of International Justice. He also invited several leading nations to send delegates to a Disarmament Conference in Washington to discuss ways of stopping the world armament race (1921–1922).

The President's wife. Florence Kling Harding (1860–1924) had worked with her husband on the Marion *Star* and had helped make it a successful newspaper. The Hardings had no children.

Other happenings. When Harding was President, the Tomb of the Unknown Soldier of World War I was dedicated at Arlington National Cemetery, Va. (November 11, 1921), and the Lincoln Memorial was dedicated in Washington (May 30, 1922). Some of the men that Harding had appointed to high office betrayed his trust by taking bribes and making corrupt deals. The President was taken ill while returning from a trip to Alaska in the summer of 1923 and died in San Francisco.

"Silent Cal" COOLIDGE

"Father, may I have a cent to buy a stick of candy?" asked Calvin. John Coolidge laid down his newspaper and walked over to the fireplace. On the mantel there was a jar in which he kept spare coins. He took off the lid, then replaced it.

"I'm sorry, Cal," he said, looking down at his redheaded son. "I can't let you have that cent after all."

Cal did not reply. He only closed his thin lips a little tighter.

"You see, it's this way," his father explained kindly. "We are about to elect a new President. If General Hancock wins, times may be very bad for the next few years. Of course, if General Garfield becomes President, it will be different."

"All right, Father. I'll go now and drive the cows home."

As Calvin started up the long slope toward the pasture, he kicked at a stone, but he gave no other sign that he was disappointed. He understood why he could not have a penny to buy candy. His father was a Republican and believed that a Democratic victory that fall might bring hard times to the country. If his father thought so, it must be true, Cal decided.

He stopped and took a long, deep, contented breath. Vermont was never more beautiful than in the autumn. The village of Plymouth where he lived lay at the head of a valley enclosed by hills now blazing with color. A white church spire pierced the sky. From where he stood he could see several white houses like his own home, each enclosed by a prim white picket fence. Looking toward the east, he could see the higher mountains raising their green peaks like a pro-

255

tecting wall to shut out the world. Calvin was whistling as he drove the cows home from pasture.

After the boy had fed and watered the stock, he drew a pail of water from the well and started for the house. Outside the kitchen door he paused. He could hear voices; his mother was entertaining company. Calvin always dreaded to meet visitors. For several minutes he stood quite still, but he knew that he could not stay outdoors all evening. He set down his pail, ran his hand over his pale red hair and straightened his jacket. Then he opened the door and went inside.

Nothing alarming happened. The visitors looked up and greeted him pleasantly. But Cal was afraid that the next visitors would be just as hard to face.

A few weeks later Cal found his father in the parlor, reading his paper by the light of a kerosene lamp on the center table. "Well, son, General Garfield has been elected. I guess the country will be safe for another four years."

A smile softened the stern corners of John Coolidge's mouth as he walked over to the mantel. He took the lid from the coin jar. "Here you are, son." And he held out a one-cent piece.

"Thank you, Father." Not by a flicker of an eyelash did Cal show how pleased he was, but John Coolidge knew.

Farming in Vermont meant a continuous round of work. In the winter there was wood to be laid in every afternoon after Cal came from school. Even before the snow was off the ground, the maple-sugar season began. Cal helped to tap the trees and carried big buckets of sap into the sugar-house where it was boiled down into sirup and sugar. After the spring planting was done, it was time to shear the sheep. There were many other chores to keep a boy busy, and Cal even learned to hitch the big pair of oxen to the plow. By the time he was twelve he did much of the plowing alone.

Of course, life was not all work. Cal found time to go fishing in the meadow brook. The circus was an annual event in a town nearby, and sometimes he and his father arose at three in the morning so as to get there early. Almost as much fun was the county fair held every fall.

Cal's mother died when he was twelve, and after that he and his father seemed even closer. Because his father was interested in politics, Cal was, too. Many years before, while serving on the governor's staff, John Coolidge had been given the honorary title of "Colonel," and people still called him Colonel Coolidge.

Ever since he was a young man, he had spent part of his time holding public office. He was a notary public, and he was also a constable and a deputy sheriff. Sometimes he had to arrest persons charged with a crime and bring them for trial before the local justice of the peace. Cal often attended court while a trial was being held, and gradually he came to understand why laws were needed.

He also looked forward to the town meeting in the stone schoolhouse, where the citizens of Plymouth met once a year to decide many questions about their town government. Cal was talking about it one day when he was visiting his grandmother on the adjoining farm.

"When your father was a boy, he liked to go to the town meetings, too," his grandmother replied. "Do you know what he did when he was your age?"

"No, Grandma, what did Father do?"

Mrs. Coolidge smiled. "Why, he used to take apples and popcorn over to meeting to sell."

"Then that is what *I* want to do," said Cal decidedly.

When the villagers gathered in the schoolhouse for the next meeting, Cal was there, walking up and down the aisle with apples and popcorn balls for sale.

When Calvin was thirteen, Colonel Coolidge decided to send him to Black River Academy in the town of Ludlow, twelve miles away. The morning they left, the temperature was thirty below zero. Cal's breath on the frosty air looked like a curl of smoke when he climbed into the seat of the long sled beside his father. In the back were his two small suitcases beside the fatted calf which the colonel was taking to market. When the team reached the brow of the hill, the boy turned for a last look at the white house set in a cluster of farm buildings. Although the sky was still dark, the snow outlined every building, every bush and twig.

And then the sun came out, making a shining path of the road. Cal looked straight ahead. He was starting on his first great adventure.

In Ludlow, Cal lived with a private family and attended classes in the red-brick academy building. He studied hard, and on Saturdays he earned extra money in a village shop where toys and baby carriages were made. The other pupils thought he was something of a dandy because he was always so careful of his clothes; yet even sedate, solemn young Calvin Coolidge sometimes got into mischief with his schoolmates. One morning, when the janitor arrived at the academy to make a fire in the furnace, he heard a strange noise: *"E-aw! E-aw! E-aw!"*

The sound came from above, and the janitor raced up the stairs two steps at a time. Throwing open the door of one of the classrooms, he stopped short.

"A donkey!" he exclaimed. "Now what boys could have done this, I wonder."

The principal also wondered, but when the pupils assembled for chapel they all looked equally innocent. The principal's glance took in the entire room. That studious boy, the one with the freckles and red hair—was he smiling? The next instant, Calvin Coolidge was looking solemn again, but the principal had his suspicions.

Of all his subjects, Cal liked history best, and toward the end of his first term, he read the Constitution for the first time. Later, seated by the window in his room, he read the Preamble again:

> *We the people of the United States in order to form a more perfect union . . . and secure the blessings of liberty to ourselves and our posterity do ordain and establish this Constitution for the United States of America.*

Laying the book down, he looked out toward the mountains. The dull brown tones of winter were gone, and the peaks were a pale, faint green against the sky. The mountains were always changing, as the seasons came and went, as the sun rose and set. Yet they were unchanging, too. "Here we are," they seemed to say. "Here we always shall be."

The United States Constitution was like that, he thought. The history teacher had said that it could be changed by adding new amendments. Yet it could always be counted on to safeguard the liberties of the American people. In that way it was like the mountains—always the same. Throughout his life Calvin Coolidge was to find the Constitution more interesting each time he read it.

"Things always seemed to come right for Calvin," Colonel Coolidge once remarked. The son was graduated with honors from Amherst College in Northampton, Massachusetts, in June, 1895, and a few days later he was asked to call at the office of two Northampton lawyers. They had been present at the Commencement exercises, where Calvin had delivered one of the class orations. The lawyers had been so impressed by his ability that they offered him a chance to work in their office while he studied law.

This was the beginning of what Calvin's friends called "Coolidge luck." Two years later he passed his law examination and opened a law office of his own. At the age of twenty-seven he was elected to the city council. During the next seventeen years he held a number of public offices and had the remarkable record of never once being defeated at the polls.

In some ways the years had changed him very little. At forty-four he was elected lieutenant governor of Massachusetts, but he was still quiet and shy. "Silent Cal," his friends called him. He believed in working, not talking, and unlike many politicians he seemed to shun the limelight. Callers at his Northampton home where he lived with his wife and two young sons were amused by the sentiment that hung above the fireplace:

> *A wise old owl lived in an oak;*
> *The more he saw the less he spoke.*
> *The less he spoke the more he heard;*
> *Why can't we be like that old bird?*

Although this motto caused a few chuckles, the lieutenant governor's habit of silence only seemed to increase the confidence of the voters. When he did speak, he said what he felt needed to be said in a few crisp words that stuck in men's memories. Soon these sayings were being repeated throughout the state, and Calvin Coolidge was so well liked that, in November, 1918, he was elected governor. One day a newspaper reporter asked him why he talked so little.

"I've usually been able to make enough noise, to get what I want," was the reply.

What Calvin Coolidge wanted was what he thought was for the good of the people. When three-fourths of the members of the Boston police force deserted their posts and went on strike, the governor was indignant. Boston, the capital, was a city with a population of several hundred thousand. Without an adequate police force it was at the mercy of hoodlums and other criminals. Store windows were smashed and stores broken into. Citizens were held up and robbed, and the governor called out the state militia to restore order.

"There is no right to strike against the public safety by anybody, anywhere, any time," he said.

By the next day those fifteen words were being quoted in newspapers throughout the nation. The nation was impressed, and Calvin Coolidge became a national figure overnight. He was much admired for the way he had handled the police strike. The following June, when the Republican convention nominated Warren G. Harding for the Presidency, the nomination for Vice President went to the taciturn governor from Massachusetts.

His election followed a few months later, and the Coolidges moved to Washington, where the new Vice President was still known as "silent Cal." He attended many receptions and dinner parties but was as sparing of words as ever. One evening he was seated next to a very talkative woman.

"Oh, Mr. Coolidge," she chattered, "you are so silent, but you must talk to me. I made a bet today that I could get more than two words out of you."

The Vice President gave her a thin smile. "You lose," he said.

At least once a year he and Mrs. Coolidge returned to his father's farm for a visit. Colonel Coolidge, at seventy-eight, still farmed his rocky acres, and Calvin enjoyed helping him just as he had as a boy. On August 2, 1923, the Vice President pitched hay all day. Here among the hills that he had always loved, he felt content. It always rested him to come back to the farm. But that night he was tired, pleasantly tired. It was not yet nine o'clock when he climbed the narrow stairs and went to bed.

In his sleep he may have been dimly aware of a pounding on the front door. He was awakened by the sound of his father's voice.

"Cal, Cal," Colonel Coolidge called. "You'd better get up."

The old man's voice trembled, and his son hurried to open the bedroom door. "What is the matter, Father?"

"It's a telegram. President Harding has just died. You, son, are the President."

For one dazed moment Calvin Coolidge did not move. He had known that Warren Harding was ill in San Francisco, but the doctors had reported he was getting better. The colonel held out a second telegram. It was from the Attorney General, asking that the Vice President take the oath of office as soon as possible. It was then past midnight. But the country must not be without a President.

"Father, are you still a notary?"

"Yes, Cal."

"Then I want you to give me the oath of office."

As always, Calvin Coolidge dressed carefully. By the time he and his wife were ready to go downstairs, his secretary had driven over from the hotel in a nearby town where he was staying. Several newspaper reporters who had been staying in Ludlow had also heard the news, and they drove over the narrow mountain roads at breakneck speed. Calvin Coolidge dictated a telegram of sympathy to Mrs.

Harding and a statement for the reporters to send to their news-papers. A book was found containing the Constitution. The oath which a President must take was copied on a sheet of paper and handed to the colonel. By this time it was past two o'clock in the morning, and several friends had assembled in the parlor.

It was an old-fashioned parlor, with a low ceiling. In the center of the room was a table covered with a red tablecloth. A kerosene lamp cast a dim light over the faded wall paper, a large wood stove, and a few chairs. Colonel Coolidge adjusted his spectacles and looked down at the sheet of paper in his hand.

Calvin Coolidge laid his left hand on the family Bible, which lay open on the table. With right hand raised he repeated, phrase by phrase, the oath of office which his father read aloud.

"I do solemnly swear," said Calvin Coolidge in a low voice, "that I will faithfully execute the office of President of the United States, and will to the best of my ability, preserve, protect, and defend the Constitution of the United States. So help me God."

By seven o'clock the next morning the new President was ready to leave for Washington. Early though it was, more than two hundred people from Plymouth and neighboring villages had gathered to say good-bye to him. That same day millions of men and women he had never seen were reading in their newspapers about his inauguration. For the first time in history a father had administered the oath that made his son the President of the United States, and the simplicity of the scene in the parlor of the Coolidge farmhouse only made it seem more dramatic.

The first part of the Coolidge administration was filled with drama. Soon after his inauguration stories began appearing in the news-papers about the dishonesty, or suspected dishonesty, of some of the government officials under the late President Harding. The public was shocked, as was Calvin Coolidge himself. An investigation was started by the Senate, and in time the suspected officials were brought to trial. Several of them were convicted of defrauding the govern-ment and sent to prison. Several other public officials were forced out of office. The private companies which had leased government oil lands were ordered to pay for the petroleum they had taken, and the property was restored to the government.

From the beginning, even when the scandals were first exposed, the majority of American voters were convinced that Calvin Coolidge himself was scrupulously honest. In 1924 he was elected President in his own right, and during his second term there was much talk about "Coolidge prosperity." Many people were making more money than ever before, and they were spending it recklessly. They invested their savings in wild schemes which they hoped would make them rich overnight. Even prudent businessmen made investments which later proved to be unwise.

President Coolidge himself was a very thrifty man. He doubtless disapproved of the wild spending but did nothing to check it. He may have felt there was nothing he could do. A few business leaders, who warned that in the past a boom had always been followed by a depression, were seldom listened to.

There was a general feeling that the so-called "Coolidge prosperity" would last forever, and each year seemed to add to the President's popularity. "Coolidge stories" continued to be told—not only jokes about his dry wit but anecdotes which illustrated his concise way of summing up old truths.

One popular story concerned a heated discussion at the White House about a new book about George Washington. It was called a "debunking" book. One of the President's callers insisted that the author, instead of trying to present the truth, had merely been trying to be sensational.

"The so-called facts have been twisted and distorted," said the visitor. "The book is not true, and it is unfair to George Washington. What is your opinion, Mr. President?"

Calvin Coolidge did not answer at once. Perhaps the thought went through his mind that a really great man cannot be hurt by idle criticism. Slowly he walked over to a window that looked out on the south garden. In the distance he could see the tall white marble shaft that grateful citizens had erected to the Father of His Country.

"Well, I see his monument is still there," said Calvin Coolidge.

THE THIRTIETH PRESIDENT *at a Glance*

John Calvin Coolidge

Born: July 4, 1872   *Died: January 5, 1933*

Early life. Calvin Coolidge was born on a farm in Plymouth, Vt. His father was a farmer and a storekeeper. After his graduation from Amherst College (1895), Calvin studied law in Northampton, Mass., and was admitted to the bar in 1897. He served as city councilman, Northampton (1899), city solicitor (1900–1901), clerk of the courts (1904), member of the Massachusetts house of representatives (1907–1908), mayor of Northampton (1910–1911), and member of the state senate (1912–1915). He was lieutenant governor of Massachusetts (1916–1918) and then governor (1919–1920). His firm handling of the Boston police strike (1919) as governor brought him into national prominence. At the Republic Convention in 1920 Warren G. Harding was nominated for President and Coolidge for Vice President. The Republicans won the election. When Harding died (Aug., 1923), Coolidge became President.

As President (1923–1925; 1925–1929). Because of Coolidge's insistence on strict economy in government, the national debt was greatly reduced, and income taxes were lowered. Except for the farm areas, the country as a whole enjoyed great prosperity. A bill limiting immigration was passed by Congress and signed by the President (1924). Although Coolidge opposed U.S. membership in the League of Nations, he supported American participation in the Kellogg Pact, which outlawed war in international disputes (1928). Meanwhile Coolidge had been elected President in his own right by a large majority in 1924. In 1928 many Republicans wanted him to run again. It was then that he made his famous remark, "I do not choose to run for President in 1928."

The President's family. The First Lady, Grace Goodhue Coolidge (1879–1957), was greatly admired for her charm and graciousness. The Coolidges had two sons: John (born 1906) and Calvin (1908–1924). The entire nation was saddened by young Calvin's death during his father's Presidency.

Other happenings. When Coolidge was President, Charles A. Lindbergh made the first nonstop flight from New York to Paris in his monoplane, the *Spirit of St. Louis.* The flight took 33 hours, 29 minutes, 30 seconds (May 20–21, 1927). After the release of *The Jazz Singer,* a part-talking picture (October, 1927), silent movies were gradually replaced by "talkies."

HERBERT HOOVER *Sees the World*

It wasn't much fun being the youngest, Bert Hoover decided. He was sitting on the bottom step of the narrow stairway leading to the attic, while upstairs his big brother, Tad, and his cousin, George, were reading *Robinson Crusoe*. Bertie was acting as lookout, and his orders were to whistle a tune if he heard anyone coming. After a while he could not stand the suspense any longer. He wanted to know more about that far-off desert island where Robinson Crusoe had been shipwrecked. He left his place and tiptoed up the stairs.

"What's happening now?" he asked in a loud whisper.

"You get back to your place," said Tad, giving him a push toward the stairs. "You go down there and *sit,* so you can warn us if you hear anyone coming. You know what will happen if we get caught."

The Hoovers were Quakers, and in those days Quakers did not approve of reading stories just for fun. Of course, Bert did not want his brother to get caught, but it was hard not to know what was happening to Robinson Crusoe.

And then his round face brightened, as he remembered his secret treasure. This was a collection of stones which he had picked up along the railroad embankment. Reaching into his pocket, Bert brought out his favorite stone—a pebble marked with pale pink streaks. He moistened it with his tongue and rubbed it on his sleeve to make it shine. Then he looked at it again. He wished that he could find more stones just like it to add to his collection. Maybe someday he would.

Herbert grew from a chubby little boy to a tall, spindling one of nine, who helped his busy mother with the work. He and Tad chopped wood and brought in water from the well. They swept the two-room cottage, washed the dishes, and helped look after their little sister, May. Their father was dead, and their mother took in sewing. She also was a minister of the Society of Friends in the little town of West Branch, Iowa, where they lived. She often preached at the meeting house, and Quakers from miles around came to hear her. One cold February Sabbath, she came home shivering with a chill and took to her bed.

A week later Mrs. Hoover was dead, and the relatives met to decide what should be done about the children. May, the youngest, went to live with her Grandmother Minthorn, and Uncle Davis Hoover offered to take Tad. Another uncle, Allan Hoover, put his arm around Bert's shoulder. Like most Quakers, he used the words "thee" and "thou" instead of "you."

"Thee shall come and live with me," he said.

With a heavy heart Bert climbed into his uncle's wagon for the ride to a farm several miles from West Branch. He felt as if he had lost not only his mother but a brother and sister too. But when he arrived at his new home, Aunt Millie, Uncle Allan's wife, smiled at him tenderly. She said that he was her boy now, and he did not feel quite so lonely.

As the weeks passed, Bert and his cousin, Walter, who was about the same age, became good friends. They went to the same district school. They did their chores together—weeding the garden, currying the horses, milking the cows and looking after the new little calves born that spring. There was one heifer they liked so much that they tried to make a pet of it.

One day the following summer the boys were carrying buckets of cold water to the men working in the hay field, when they paused to look at Mr. Hoover's new mowing machine. Bert watched, fascinated, as the wheels turned and moved the shining blade through the coarse grass.

"See how that blade slices into the timothy," he said admiringly. "I have an idea, Walter. I'll show you, after while."

Not another word would he say until the buckets of cold water had been passed around among the men. Then Bert, with Walter following, raced toward the junk pile back of the barn. Here among odd bits of dismantled machinery were rusty bolts and screws, bits of tin, scraps of iron, and several rusty wheels. At last Bert found what he was looking for. He held up a crosscut saw.

"This is exactly what we need," he told his cousin. "Some of the teeth are missing, but that won't matter. Doesn't it look like the blade of a mowing machine?"

"Yes, but——"

"What do you say that we make a mowing machine of our own?"

"Sure, let's try it," Walter agreed.

The boys set to work. Soon they had a mowing machine that ran on wheels and turned the saw blade with a slow, uncertain movement. The young inventors were much pleased by their success, and even Uncle Allan was impressed. Encouraged by his praise, they decided to make another improvement and furnish motive power for their machine.

"Let's hitch our pet heifer to it," Bert suggested.

But what seemed like a good idea to the boys did not please the calf. She bolted across the vegetable garden, dragging the machine at the end of the traces. Bert pulled at the lines with all his strength, but the frightened calf was not going to be stopped by any ten-year-old boy. The mowing machine cut a wide swath across the garden, leaving a trail of beets and carrots behind it. Just ahead loomed a tree. The runaway calf swerved around the tree just in time. But the mowing machine was hurled against the trunk and fell apart in a dozen rusty pieces.

Walter looked at the mass of wreckage. "All our work for nothing," he said ruefully.

"We can invent something else," Bert replied.

The next invention was a sorghum mill made out of an old clothes wringer. Bert had other ideas, too, but before he could carry out any of them a letter came from his Uncle John. Dr. John Minthorn, his mother's brother, was the physician in Newberg, a Quaker settlement in Oregon, and he was starting an academy. His only son had recently died, and he and his wife, Laura, wanted Bert to come west and live with them. Allan Hoover read the letter aloud. He glanced at Aunt Millie, who seemed to be having a hard time to keep the tears back. Then he turned to his nephew.

"It will be for thy own good to go to Oregon," he said. "Thee can get a better education in John Minthorn's academy than in the district school near here. But we shall miss thee, Herbert—thy Aunt Millie and I. Yes, and Walter, too."

Herbert felt his throat go tight. The thought of getting used to another new home was rather frightening. At the same time he looked forward to taking a long journey more than halfway across the continent.

A friend of Uncle Allan's, who was moving west with his family, agreed to look after Bert. The boy took along a bundle of bedding, for each car of the emigrant train on which he traveled was furnished with only a few bare bunks. At one end of the car, there was a kitchen stove where the travelers cooked their meals. The locomotive poured forth clouds of black smoke, covering the passengers with soot as the cars bumped and jolted over the rough roads.

Herbert Hoover did not mind a few inconveniences. He sat with his face close to the window as the train left behind the flat prairies he had always known and began the steep climb into the Rockies. These were the first mountains he had ever seen.

When the train finally reached Portland, Oregon, he was met by his uncle, and the last lap of the journey was made by steamboat down the Willamette River. Dr. Minthorn was kind but so dignified that Bert could not think of anything to say. Not until they reached Newberg and he met his Aunt Laura did he get over his shyness. She and her three daughters were in the back yard, stirring something in a wash boiler over an outdoor fire.

"These are thy cousins, Herbert," she said kindly, "and they are making pear butter for the winter. Thee may stir if thee wishes, and thee may eat all the pears thee wants to."

Herbert did not wait to be asked a second time. After several days on the train, with mostly beans and bacon to eat, he thought he had never tasted anything so delicious as those pears. Then Aunt Laura gave him a long-handled spoon and he began to stir the bubbling mixture in the big wash boiler. He believed that he was going to like Oregon.

He liked it more and more as the weeks passed. He liked the deep, dark forests, the streams where he went fishing, the golden wheat fields, and the orchards where the tree branches hung heavy with fruit. Bert lived in Newberg for several years, helping with the chores and attending his uncle's academy. Later, when Dr. Minthorn moved to Salem, Oregon, to take charge of a land development company, Bert went along as office boy. The work was interesting, and he never tired of listening to his uncle's customers.

Some of these men wanted to buy farms, and reminded Bert of the farmers back in Iowa. There were other customers who were more interested in what they could discover under the rich Oregon soil. Sometimes they showed Bert specimens of iron and copper ore which they had found, and there was much excited talk about the mines they hoped to develop.

Herbert had been in Salem about a year when Robert Brown, a mining engineer from the East, dropped into the office. The tall, sixteen-year-old office boy was writing a letter on the typewriter. But he left his desk and came closer to listen when Mr. Brown began to talk of his experiences.

A mining engineer, Mr. Brown said, spent much of his time outdoors. He had many problems to solve—exciting, challenging problems. Suddenly the engineer was aware that Herbert was regarding him with an expression almost like awe.

"Why don't you go in for engineering, son?" asked Robert Brown.

"I'd like to," Bert answered. "Only——"

"You'd be smart to go to college first," the engineer went on. "Senator Leland Stanford is opening a new university down in California next year, and Dr. John Branner will be at the head of the mining and geology department. He is a great scientist and a great teacher. You couldn't study under a better man."

Bert flushed, and Robert Brown guessed the reason. "If you should decide to go to Stanford," he said, "I am sure that a bright boy like you could earn his way."

After Mr. Brown left, Bert went back to his typewriter, but he scarcely saw the keys. Instead, he was seeing himself as a mining engineer, visiting far places and searching for valuable minerals. During the next few months he thought of little else.

Herbert Hoover knew what he wanted to do with his life. But first he must go to Stanford, where he could study under Dr. Branner.

When the new Stanford University was formally opened in Palo Alto, California, in the fall of 1871, Herbert Hoover was barely seventeen. He had very little money, but he was able to obtain a position in the university office at five dollars a week. He added to this income by delivering newspapers and laundry on the campus. During the summer vacations, he earned sixty dollars a month helping to make geological surveys for the government. These sums enabled him to pay all of his expenses, but he organized his work so well that he found time to take part in many college activities.

He also did well in his studies, especially in his geology courses. Dr. Branner, his professor, encouraged him to go ahead with a mining career, and as soon as Herbert graduated in 1895, he set out for Nevada City. This was a gold mining center where, he felt confident, he could obtain a good position as an engineer. Instead, the only job he could find was that of a laborer at two dollars a day. For several months he worked a night shift for ten hours at a stretch, seven nights a week, pushing a car in the lower levels of a mine. Finally he saved enough money to pay his railroad fare to San Francisco.

Here he applied for work with Louis Janin, one of the best known mining engineers on the Pacific coast. Unfortunately, the only position Mr. Janin could offer him at the moment was that of a temporary clerk in the office. The pay was small, but Herbert decided to accept, on the chance that something more interesting would turn up later. One day his employer handed him a sheaf of papers.

"I need a technical report on one of my mines," Mr. Janin said. "Here are some figures and other information that may help you. Anyway, see what you can do with it."

Perhaps Herbert realized that this was his big opportunity. He worked all day and all night on the report. Mr. Janin read it in amazement.

"Where did you get so much practical information?" he asked.

"Working underground in a mine," Herbert replied.

"Your time was certainly not wasted," Mr. Janin went on. "This report is good—very good indeed. I believe I can now find an opening for you in one of my Colorado mines."

Herbert liked his new job much better, but after a few months he was called back to the San Francisco office. Mr. Janin was holding a cable in his hand.

"I have had a request from a British mining firm," he said, "to recommend an engineer to go out to their gold mines in Australia. The British seem to think very highly of the mining methods we use here in California."

Then abruptly he added, "How old are you, Herbert?"

"Twenty-three, sir."

"That is rather young, but you have been doing excellent work, and I have confidence in you. In fact, I had hoped to keep you with me for a long time, but I don't want to stand in your way. This job in Australia offers you a great opportunity, with a starting salary of six hundred dollars a month."

"You mean you are recommending me?" asked Herbert. He found it almost impossible to believe that anything like this was really happening to him.

"I am indeed," said Mr. Janin. "The job is yours, if you want it."

Herbert took a deep breath. "Of course I want it, and thank you, Mr. Janin."

Australia was the first of many countries that Herbert Hoover was to visit in his work as a mining engineer. Early in 1899 he returned to California to marry his college sweetheart, Lou Henry, and during the next fifteen years she accompanied her husband to many distant places, wherever his work called him. His rise was rapid. In a short time he had his own business as a consulting engineer, with offices in San Francisco, New York, London and cities in Russia, Australia and China. Not only was he an excellent engineer, but he showed remarkable talent as an organizer. Heads of mining enterprises that were not showing a profit frequently sought his advice, and he became known as "a doctor of sick companies." For his services he received huge fees, and he made profitable investments in some of the enterprises that interested him. As a result he was a rich man by the time he was forty. That was in 1914, the year that World War I broke out.

The Hoovers happened to be in London that summer, when American tourists began pouring into the city. Thousands of Americans who had been spending their vacations abroad now wanted to go home. One difficulty was that most of the British ships that had carried passengers across the Atlantic were now needed to transport British soldiers and supplies. To make matters worse, many of the tourists had no money left by the time they reached London; nor could they cash checks, because all of the banks were closed. Hour after hour, day after day, anxious men and women, and sometimes whole families, crowded into the American embassy to ask for help. The ambassador in desperation called on Herbert Hoover to try to bring some order out of the confusion.

He responded in his usual quiet, efficient way. Special arrangements were made for ships to take stranded Americans home. The officers of a bank in London agreed to cash American checks, after Mr. Hoover personally guaranteed the bank against loss. He raised five thousand dollars in cash of his own money to provide a loan fund for those in need. Meanwhile he had set up headquarters in the ballroom of a large hotel.

Here he and several volunteer helpers, each seated behind a small table, interviewed hundreds of Americans. Most of them were frightened; some were close to panic. One morning Herbert Hoover was astonished to find a dozen Indians in buckskins and war bonnets lined up before him. With them was a blond, blue-eyed boy about thirteen.

"I am Black Feather," said the leader of the group. He and the other Indians, he explained, were members of a Wild West Show. They had been playing in Austria when the war came, and they had just enough money to travel as far as Hamburg, Germany.

"That's where we found this kid, wandering around the steamship docks all by himself," Black Feather went on. "He was plenty scared, and we've been looking after him."

Herbert Hoover, who had two young sons of his own, looked at the boy in quick sympathy. "How did you happen to be in Hamburg alone?" he asked. "Are you an American?"

"Yes, sir," said the boy, "but my grandparents live in Poland. I was on my way to visit them. But when my boat got to Hamburg, some men told me I couldn't go any farther. They said the Polish border was closed. I didn't know what that meant, and I didn't know what to do."

"Well, you are going to be all right now," said Mr. Hoover reassuringly, and turned back to Black Feather. "I can arrange steerage passage for all of you to New York. I'll pay for your tickets out of our loan fund."

"Thank you, but there's something else." Black Feather seemed to hesitate.

"Yes, what is it?" Mr. Hoover asked.

"It's as I told you," said Black Feather. "By the time we reached Hamburg, our money was gone, and the boy gave us all he had. Do you suppose you could give him his money now? I own two hundred acres out in Montana, and I'll pay you back when I get home."

This request was promptly granted, and that evening Mr. Hoover told the story to a rich American woman who had engaged a first-class passage for the voyage across the Atlantic. "The boy can go home with me as my guest," she said.

This invitation was extended to the boy when he returned with the Indians the next day for their steamship tickets. "Please thank the lady," he replied, "but I don't want to leave my friend, Black Feather. I'd rather go in the steerage with him."

Difficult though it was to find transportation for so many people in war time, by the middle of September the last of the stranded Americans were on their way home. Mr. Hoover himself was almost ready to sail when he received another call from the American ambassador.

This time his help was needed for an even harder task. German armies had invaded Belgium, a small industrial nation that usually imported most of its food. Since that was no longer possible with an enemy army occupying the country, ten million people would starve unless a way was found to feed them. The American ambassador, as the representative of the richest neutral country in the world, had been appealed to for aid.

"Mr. Hoover," he said, "I can think of no one who is better fitted to go to the relief of Belgium. Will you do it?"

That night Herbert Hoover paced the floor, trying to decide. This Belgian assignment would probably last for the duration of the war, and he would have to give up all of his business connections at once. His plan had been to work a few more years, until he had accumulated a big enough fortune to provide a lifetime income for his family. And then he wanted to devote the rest of his life to public service.

And now the chance to be of service had come, only much sooner than he had counted on. Millions of people were faced with starvation. With his great talent for organization, he knew that he could help them. The next morning when he came down to breakfast, he turned to a friend who was visiting him.

"What does a fortune matter anyway?" Mr. Hoover said. "I'm going to do it."

On his first visit to Belgium, when he saw the gaunt ruins of the fine old churches and the many homes that had been destroyed, he knew that he had made the right decision. He had the feeling that he was in prison. Instead of children at play he saw German soldiers patrolling the streets. "The depressed, unsmiling faces of the Belgians," he said later, "matched the mood of the dreary winter landscape."

For the next three years the Commission for the Relief of Belgium, which Herbert Hoover organized, kept millions of Belgians alive. Feeding such a large number cost twelve million dollars a month. Part of this sum came from private gifts and part of it from huge loans voted by the American Congress. Mr. Hoover, as the director, refused any salary and paid all of his own expenses. Volunteers, mostly young men and women who came from America to help him, received only expense money.

And then in April, 1917, the United States entered the war against Germany on the side of the Allies, and all Americans had to leave Belgium. The volunteers turned over the work of distributing the food among the people to relief workers from two nations that were still neutral—Spain and Holland. However, even after he went back to the United States, Mr. Hoover continued as the director of Belgian Relief and saw to it that the money was raised to carry on the work.

Shortly after his return to his own country, in the spring of 1917, Herbert Hoover was appointed Food Administrator. In this new position his task was to see that the United States raised enough extra food to feed the Allies and the American soldiers at the front. Although he had no authority to ration food, he appealed to the patriotism of his fellow Americans. More than fourteen million families signed a pledge to waste no food and to use substitutes for wheat and sugar and fats that were especially needed abroad.

The war ended in victory for the Allies, and soon after the Armistice of Novemeber 11, 1918, Herbert Hoover was back in Europe. Four years of fighting had taken a sad toll, with many homes and towns destroyed. Mr. Hoover was particularly distressed by the plight of the children. Many had been left orphans and had no place to go. They wandered through streets and along country roads, ragged and hungry. In Paris and in many other places, child feeding stations were set up. Boys and girls were gathered together in orphanages where they were given nourishing meals.

Of all the countries in Europe, none had suffered more from the war than Poland. Hundreds of thousands of Poles had died of starvation by the time a team of American relief workers arrived early in 1919. From then on, monthly shipments of food saved many lives, and there were special soup kitchens for the children.

Excitement ran high when it was learned, the following August, that Mr. Hoover himself was coming to Warsaw, the capital of Poland. Trainloads of boys and girls, about fifty thousand of them, arrived from surrounding towns and paraded past a grandstand where he and his party waited. This parade went on several hours, but no one seemed tired, least of all the children. They waved paper banners, combining American and Polish colors. They shouted and cheered. The words were Polish, but the meaning was clear: "Mr. Hoover! Mr. Hoover! Long live Mr. Hoover!"

And then suddenly the line of march was broken. A rabbit had scurried through the grass, and some of the children gave chase. One boy captured it and carried it to the grandstand. He bowed and solemnly presented the rabbit to Mr. Hoover. Just as solemnly Mr. Hoover accepted it. He understood that this boy and all of the other children in the parade were trying to say "Thank you."

"In all history, Mr. Hoover," said a general who stood beside him, "there has never been a review of honor which I would prefer for myself to that which has been given you today."

In his own country, as well as abroad, Herbert Hoover was honored as a great humanitarian. After his return to the United States, he served as Secretary of Commerce, and in 1928 he was elected President. Like many of his countrymen, he believed that the prosperity the nation had known under President Coolidge would last forever. Business seemed to be booming.

The new President entered the White House with high hopes. "We in America today," he said, "are nearer the final triumph over poverty than ever before in the history of the land."

Unfortunately the new President had been in office only seven months when the stock market crash of October, 1929, threw the country into a panic. The crash was the result of the wild spending and speculation of the preceding years when so many people had hoped to become rich almost overnight. Now suddenly the prices of the shares of stock in the great industrial firms of the country began to go down, and the people who had invested in them lost a great deal of money.

But worse was to come. The stock market crash was followed by the most severe depression in the nation's history. Banks closed and hundreds of thousands of bank customers lost their savings. Many factories and stores had to shut down. By 1932 there were twelve million men and women out of work. They and their families were suffering from the poverty that Mr. Hoover had believed was soon to be abolished.

In the beginning he felt confident that the depression would soon be over. Toward the end of his term, with conditions steadily growing worse, he suggested to Congress a number of measures which he hoped would help. These measures, however, were not enough to bring the hard times to an end, and for that reason many people blamed the President. He was nominated for a second term, but during the summer of 1932 when he set out on a speaking tour, he was sometimes heckled by his audiences. He was met at railroad stations by crowds of dissatisfied voters carrying signs. One sign read:

"In Hoover we trusted; now we are busted."

This was a distressing experience for a man who, a few years earlier, had been acclaimed throughout the world. That November the rival candidate, Franklin D. Roosevelt, was elected President. Herbert Hoover had been defeated by a landslide.

"Only tough old John Quincy Adams," said a leading news magazine, "had gone out of the Presidency so thoroughly unpopular."

The resemblance did not end with Mr. Hoover's defeat. Like John Quincy Adams, Herbert Hoover was to find other ways to serve his country. For twelve years he was busy with writing and speaking and helping various philanthropic causes. Then came World War II, and many countries were threatened with famine. After the war, another President, Harry S. Truman, invited Mr. Hoover to call at the White House.

"Mr. President," said Harry Truman, addressing Herbert Hoover by his old title, "during and after the First World War you saved many Europeans from dying of hunger. Now there is danger of widespread famine, not only in Europe but in Asia. We must do everything we can to help these starving people, both for their own sake and for the sake of building a permanent peace."

Mr. Hoover nodded. "Famine is always the sad aftermath of war," he said, "and the countries that can produce food must help."

Both men agreed that most of the help would have to come from the United States, in Mr. Hoover's words "the last great reservoir from which starvation could be halted." Would he be willing, Mr. Truman asked, to act as chairman of a Famine Emergency Committee and to make a survey of the conditions in the famine areas of the world?

Although Herbert Hoover was then past seventy, he welcomed this new opportunity to be of service. In April, 1946, he started on a tour of twenty-two countries and traveled more than thirty-five thousand miles. Much of the journey was made in unpressurized army planes, and sometimes the pilot had to climb to great heights to avoid storms. The frequent changes in air pressure permanently injured Mr. Hoover's hearing, but the people he saw nearly every day were in such desperate straits that he had no time to think about himself.

When he returned to the United States, his report to the President included a month-by-month list of the food products each country would need during the months ahead. Although he had found conditions in the famine areas even worse than had been expected, he had concrete suggestions as to how the needs could be met.

Once more Mr. Hoover had been able to help millions of his fellow men.

In 1961, at the age of eighty-seven, Herbert Hoover was hard at work on a four-volume history which he planned to call *An American Epic*. These four books tell the inspiring story of how the United States has aided other countries.

"Never before has a nation undertaken such burdens . . ." he said in his introduction, "that human life and even civilization might be preserved."

THE THIRTY-FIRST PRESIDENT *at a Glance*

Herbert Clark Hoover

Born: August 10, 1874

Early life. Herbert Hoover was born in West Branch, Iowa. Orphaned by the time he was 9, he was brought up by relatives in Iowa and Oregon. He specialized in mining engineering at Stanford University, graduating in 1895. At the age of 23 (1897) he went to Australia as a mining engineer. Later his work took him to China, Russia, and many other parts of the world (1899–1914). In London, when World War I broke out (1914), he directed the work of getting stranded American tourists back to the U.S. He was head of the Relief of Belgium (1915–1919) and U.S. Food Administrator (1917–1919). After the war he organized projects for distributing food to devastated areas of Europe (1919–1921).

Political career. As Secretary of Commerce (1921–1928) Hoover extended American foreign trade, encouraged commercial aviation, established regulations for the new radio industry, and negotiated an agreement among seven Western states for construction of a great dam on the Colorado River. This dam, the highest in the U.S., was completed in 1936 and is now known as the Hoover Dam. Hoover ran for President on the Republican ticket (1928).

As President (1929–1933). The stock market crash (1929) that occurred during Hoover's first year in office was followed by America's worst business depression. The President believed conditions would soon right themselves and that the government should not interfere. Later, as the depression deepened, he recommended the establishment of a program for constructing roads, public buildings, and waterways, which would provide work for some of the many unemployed. He also supported the creation of the Reconstruction Finance Corporation (1932), a government agency that made loans to help business and industry. The situation was too desperate to be remedied by these and other measures suggested by the President, and he was defeated for re-election (1932).

The President's family. Lou Henry Hoover (1875–1944) had met her future husband when they were both Stanford students. After their marriage she accompanied him on his travels, and together they translated from the Latin an important old book on mining.

The older of two Hoover sons, Herbert, Jr. (born 1903) was Undersecretary of State (1953–1956) during the Eisenhower administration.

Other happenings. While Hoover was President, Congress officially adopted "The Star-Spangled Banner" as the national anthem (1931). Amelia Earhart Putnam (1898–1937) became the first woman to make a solo flight across the Atlantic Ocean (1932). The 20th Amendment to the Constitution was proclaimed (January 23, 1933). This amendment designated January 20 as the day on which the term of a new President should begin. (Previously, Presidents had been inaugurated on March 4.)

The nation's population. According to the 1930 census, the population was almost 123,000,000.

As Ex-President. After World War II, at President Truman's request, Mr. Hoover visited famine areas throughout the world and worked out plans for supplying their populations with food (1946–1947). President Truman later appointed him chairman of a commission (1947–1949) established to recommend ways for simplifying the organization of the executive branch of the government. Hoover also served as head of a similar commission (1953–1955) under President Eisenhower.

The Hoover Library. The Hoover Institute and Library on War, Revolution and Peace at Stanford University contains millions of original documents—pamphlets, maps, and foreign newspapers—collected throughout the years from all over the world by Mr. Hoover, members of his staff, and friends in many nations.

FRANKLIN ROOSEVELT *Finds a Way*

So this was the White House! As the carriage drew up before the North Portico, Franklin looked up at the tall white pillars.

A few minutes later he was being introduced to his father's friend President Cleveland. He was a big man with a shaggy mustache, and looked very tired. His broad shoulders drooped.

"I have a strange wish for you, Franklin," Grover Cleveland said, patting the little boy's shoulder. "I hope you will never be President of the United States."

Franklin seemed puzzled. Was it so hard to be President? he wondered. With quick sympathy, he smiled up into the kind blue eyes.

After this visit to the White House Franklin returned to the family farm in Dutchess County, New York. Here, near the village of Hyde Park, he lived with his parents in a big, comfortable house overlooking the Hudson River. From his bedroom window he could see for miles up and down the broad, beautiful stream, and sometimes his father told him stories of Henry Hudson, the explorer, who had discovered the river nearly three hundred years before. Perhaps even more exciting were the stories his mother, Sara Delano Roosevelt, had to tell of her seafaring ancestors. Her grandfather Captain Delano had owned a fleet of sailing vessels, and Sara, as a little girl, had sailed to China and other far-off ports. The river and the sea! Franklin loved them both.

Young though he was, he had already crossed the Atlantic Ocean with his parents, and during the next few years they took him on several other trips abroad. He enjoyed the long voyages, and when he came home he played games about the sea. Once he built a crow's-nest in the top of the tall hemlock tree. Archie and Edmund Rogers, who lived on the big estate next door, helped him. From this high point the boys peered up and down the river, pretending to be on the lookout for pirate ships.

Another time the three friends built a raft near the boathouse. They cut down several beech trees, notched the logs, and bound them together. Franklin looked at the raft admiringly.

"Isn't she a beauty?" he said. "Come on, let's go fishing."

Archie and Edmund were following him on board, when—crash! —the raft sank beneath the surface of the water. Franklin came up dripping but laughing. He realized their mistake: beechwood was too heavy a wood to stay afloat under the combined weight of fishing tackle, picnic lunch and three sturdy boys.

Much as Franklin Roosevelt loved the water, he also loved the land. He liked to make the rounds of the five-hundred-acre farm on which he lived. With his father he visited the stables and the fields. He learned about the livestock and observed the plants on the farm —how they sprouted, flowered, and seeded. On hikes through the forest, he learned the names of many trees, and by the time he was eleven he knew the name of nearly every bird in the neighborhood.

The year Franklin was eleven, he started to make a collection of birds, always being careful not to shoot more than one bird of each species. He was very patient, sometimes waiting under a bush for hours until he succeeded in bringing down the bird he wanted. But stuffing and mounting his specimens proved harder than he had expected. The task made him rather ill, but when his parents suggested that this part of the work be given to someone else, he stubbornly shook his head.

"Not until after I do a few of them myself," he said.

The work did not grow any easier as he went on, but he finally proved to himself that he could do it. Then, and not before, would he allow the rest of the specimens to be sent to a professional taxidermist to be mounted. At the end of two years he had more than three hundred varieties, the most complete collection of the birds of Dutchess County ever made.

Birds were by no means Franklin's only hobby. He also started a stamp collection. After dinner he would lie on a rug before the fireplace, sorting and pasting stamps in his album while his mother read aloud. His favorite stories were about history and the sea, but he was interested in all kinds of subjects. One evening when his mother went upstairs to his room to say good night to him, she found him sitting up in bed with a dictionary on his knees.

"Why, Franklin," she exclaimed, "what on earth are you doing with the dictionary up here?"

"Reading it," he said in a matter-of-fact voice. "There are lots of words I don't understand; so I thought I would find out what they meant. I am almost halfway through."

Mrs. Roosevelt was not too surprised. Franklin was curious about almost everything and he liked to study. Nearly every day he rode Debby, his pony, down the winding path to the estate next door where he and Archie and Edmund had lessons under the same teacher. For a while Franklin had his own governess, Mademoiselle Sandoz, who taught him French. After her return to the French part of Switzerland, he wrote her a letter.

I would very much like to know who is President of Switzer-land. Is there a representative of each canton? I have to go out now. Hoping you will reply to all my questions, I am

Your faithful
Tlevesoor

There was a mischievous look in Franklin's blue eyes; he could make a joke even out of signing his name. Another letter, written to his parents, once when they were away from home, was signed "Tlevesoor D. Nilknarf."

His mother smiled. "I never saw a boy," she said, "who seemed to enjoy himself so constantly."

What Franklin enjoyed most were his visits to Campobello. On that Canadian island, not far from the Maine coast, the family had a summer cottage. The family sailboat, the *Half Moon*, had been named after the ship in which Henry Hudson had explored the Hudson. Franklin learned to sail when he was ten and soon became very good at handling a boat. He was always careful, and his mother knew she need not worry, even when he stayed out for hours at a time. There was nothing he liked better than exploring the bays and inlets off the rocky coast of Maine.

"Father," he said one evening, "when the time comes for college, I'd like to go to Annapolis. I want to go into the Navy."

Mr. Roosevelt looked at his son thoughtfully. The United States Naval Academy in Annapolis, Maryland, would offer excellent training for a young man who wanted to be a naval officer. But when Franklin grew up, Mr. Roosevelt explained, he would probably have to look after the family property. He would need a different kind of training, and it would be better for him to go to Harvard.

"All right, Pops," said Franklin cheerfully. He was not the kind of boy to worry about what could not be helped. Besides, he could always read stories about the sea and biographies of naval heroes; he had a large collection of such books already. He could build ship models. And he could sail his own boat.

At fourteen Franklin entered the famous boys' school at Groton, Massachusetts, to prepare for Harvard. At Groton he was kept busy making good grades, singing in the glee club, and taking part in debates. He liked athletics, and some of his letters home fairly bristled with enthusiasm.

"I am hoarse, deaf, and ready to stand on my cocoanut," he wrote in describing a Groton football victory. "OUR team played a wonderful game."

Another letter told about the visit of his fifth cousin, Theodore Roosevelt, the Assistant Secretary of the Navy. Before going to Washington to take this position, he had been head of the Police Board in New York City. "After supper tonight," Franklin wrote, "Cousin Theodore gave us a splendid talk on his adventures when he was on the Police Board. He kept the whole room in an uproar for over an hour, by telling us killing stories about policemen and their duties in New York."

Less than a year after Theodore Roosevelt's visit to Groton, the Spanish-American War began. He resigned from the Navy Department, and the newspapers were filled with stories of a regiment he was helping to organize. Franklin, who was sixteen years old at the time, also wanted to have a part in the fighting, but he was afraid his parents would consider him too young. Certainly the headmaster at the school would not approve.

One Wednesday Franklin and his roommate, Lathrop Brown, looked up to see a fat, lazy horse trundling a cart toward the school grounds. In the cart was the pieman who came twice a week to sell pies and cookies. With a whoop of delight the boys raced to meet him, fingering the coins in their pockets.

"Well, well," said the pieman, "have you heard the news?"

"What news?" asked Franklin.

"The Navy is enlisting men to go to Cuba."

The Navy! Franklin's eyes brightened. He had never forgotten his desire to go to sea. He stole a glance at Lathrop. Lathrop looked back at him. They were thinking the same thing. Both of them were tall and looked much older than sixteen.

"Where," Franklin asked the pieman, "can a fellow go to enlist?"

"Why, up in Boston, on the Long Wharf."

"Are you coming back to the school this Saturday?"

The pieman nodded, and the boys exchanged another understanding glance.

Franklin lowered his voice. "Would you let us ride in your cart to the first station where we can catch a train for Boston?"

The pieman hesitated, but the boys persuaded him to agree. Franklin had not been a star member of the debating team for nothing.

Carefully he and Lathrop laid their plans. With the help of the pieman they could get to the nearest railroad station five miles away. They had enough pocket money to take them from there to Boston. There were no classes on Saturday, and they probably would not be missed at school until Sunday. By that time they hoped to be regular Navy men on board a transport far out on the high seas.

"Everything ready?" Franklin asked his roommate on Friday night. His eyes burned and there was a parched feeling in his throat, but he tried to shake it off.

Lathrop nodded. He seemed to find it hard to talk.

Franklin slept fitfully. That burning sensation spread up into his face, down his back, and into his arms down to the very finger tips. His head ached. On Saturday morning he awoke with the knowledge that this was the morning he was to run away. And to his surprise he found that he did not care whether he ever ran away or not.

"I feel sick," said Lathrop.

Franklin looked at the reddened cheeks of the other boy. Then he glanced at his own flushed face in the mirror and went back to bed. A life in the Navy seemed much less to be desired than it had the night before.

Later that morning the doctor came to see the boys. "Scarlet fever," he said shortly.

Again, Franklin's wish to go into the Navy had been denied him. And again he took his disappointment good-naturedly.

As the years went by, Franklin Roosevelt continued to sail his own boats just for the fun of it. For the most part they were happy years, filled with quick successes. He attended Harvard, where he was managing editor of the *Crimson,* and everything seemed to come easily to him. Handsome and charming, he made many friends. While still in college, he fell in love with Eleanor Roosevelt, the niece of "Cousin Theodore." By then Theodore Roosevelt was President of the United States, and when the young couple were married, he came up to New York City to give the bride away.

After his marriage, Franklin went to law school and then found a position with a law firm. But he was more interested in politics, and when some of his Hyde Park neighbors suggested that he be a candidate for the state senate, he accepted the challenge.

It was a real challenge. The Hyde Park Roosevelts were Democrats, and they were living in a community where most people were Republicans. It had been a long time since a Democrat had been elected from Dutchess County. But Franklin roared through the countryside in a bright red automobile, determined to call on every farmer in his district. No one had ever campaigned in an automobile before, for motor cars were still something of a novelty in 1910. Many people who otherwise might not have paid much attention began to take notice. The candidate was likeable and friendly. He had a quick, easy smile. That fall he was elected.

As a member of the New York state legislature, Franklin—like his Cousin Theodore thirty years earlier—was soon making news. Just as Theodore Roosevelt had once opposed Republican "bosses," Franklin Roosevelt took a firm stand against the "machine" politicians among the Democrats. He supported liberal laws, and in 1912 he worked for the election of Woodrow Wilson as President.

One day Franklin went to call on the Presidential candidate, who was much impressed by the young state senator. After Woodrow Wilson's election, there was some talk that Franklin was to be offered an important position in the Federal Government. One day, shortly after his thirty-first birthday, he received a telegram from Josephus Daniels, the new Secretary of the Navy, asking him to come to Washington. When he was seated across from the Secretary's desk, Mr. Daniels came to the point at once.

"I have been authorized by the President," he said, "to offer you the post as Assistant Secretary of the Navy. Would you accept?"

Would he accept? Franklin Roosevelt thought of the books and pamphlets about the Navy that he had been collecting ever since he was a boy. He had never stopped reading and learning about it. He flashed his warmest smile. "Mr. Secretary," he said, "all my life I have loved ships. I have been a student of the Navy. The post you offer me is the one above all others I would love to hold."

The seven years that Franklin Delano Roosevelt was Assistant Secretary of the Navy were a grave and stirring time. World War I broke out, and the United States was drawn in on the side of the

Allies. Franklin wanted to resign and join the fighting forces, but the President sternly forbade it.

"Tell that young man," Woodrow Wilson said to Josephus Daniels, Franklin's boss, "that his only and best war service is to stay where he is."

Never before had the young man labored such long hours. He was impatient of red tape—of regulations and rules that stood in the way of getting things done. After the Armistice he was sent to France on Navy business, and returned home on the same ship with President Wilson. The two men had several conversations about the League of Nations, which the President hoped that the United States would join. Only through such an international organization, Woodrow Wilson declared fervently, could future wars be prevented.

Franklin Roosevelt never forgot those conversations. He remembered them in the summer of 1920 when the Democratic convention nominated him for the Vice Presidency. He was thinking about them the day he stood on his front porch at Hyde Park and accepted the nomination. By then President Wilson was seriously ill. The question of the League was still being argued throughout the country.

"Some people," young Mr. Roosevelt told the large audience gathered on the lawn, "are saying, 'We are tired of progress; we want to go back to where we were before.' They are wrong. This is not the wish of America. We can never go back."

No, America must go forward, he insisted. The nation must be prepared to live in a new kind of world. During the next two months he made several hundred speeches. In nearly every speech he told why he thought the United States should become a member of the League of Nations.

But the majority of the American people were not yet ready to take such a giant step. They preferred what Warren G. Harding, the Republican candidate for President, called "a return to normalcy." In November he was elected. Calvin Coolidge became Vice President, and Franklin Delano Roosevelt returned to private life.

Franklin's friends were convinced, however, that he would soon be back in politics. That was what he wanted, too, but not for a while. In New York City he found an excellent position which gave him more time to spend with his family. By 1921 he and Eleanor had been married for sixteen years, and had five children—"the chicks," their father called them. In August he joined them at Campobello, where they had been spending the summer.

The whole family had been looking forward to his vacation, Franklin most of all. On the afternoon of August 10 they all went for a long sail. On the way back they spied a forest fire and made for the shore. Putting out the fire proved to be hot, grimy work, and after they reached home the boys and their father went for a swim. The water was icy, and Franklin was shivering when he came indoors and sat down in his wet bathing suit to look over his mail.

"I think I'll go to bed," he said finally. "I seem to have a cold."

But he had something much more serious than a cold. For several days he was in terrible pain. He could not move, but the two doctors who were called in were not sure what was wrong. There were no nurses on the island, and Eleanor nursed her husband night and day. She became increasingly worried and finally phoned a well-known specialist in Newport, Rhode Island.

When the specialist arrived at Campobello, he told Eleanor that her husband had poliomyelitis. He must be moved to a New York hospital as soon as possible, but his recovery was uncertain. Even if Franklin Roosevelt lived, he might never be able to walk again.

Early in September, four men carried the patient downstairs on a stretcher. As the children gathered around him, they could only stare out of wide, frightened eyes. It did not seem possible that their father—their strong, handsome father—could be so helpless. But he looked up at them with his gayest smile.

"Good-bye, chicks," he said, "I'll be seeing you."

After several weeks in the hospital Franklin Roosevelt was well enough to be moved to his home in New York City. He was no longer in pain, and he could sit up in bed, but his legs were helpless. His mother, fearing that he would always be an invalid, wanted him to come up to Hyde Park to live. Certainly, he could never go back into politics, she said.

There were three people who did not agree. One was his wife. The second was Louis Howe, who had been a newspaper correspondent when young Roosevelt was a state senator, and the two men had been friends ever since. Louis had decided long before that Franklin had in him the makings of a President. It could still happen, he insisted, but people must not be allowed to forget the name of Franklin Roosevelt. Louis then began to write letters to leading Democrats throughout the nation. At his suggestion Eleanor joined several Democratic organizations in New York. Although she was a rather shy young woman at that time, she learned to make speeches, and she brought interesting people home to talk with her husband.

A third person who refused to give in to fear was Franklin himself. "Polio is a child's disease," he exclaimed impatiently. "Don't tell me a grown man can't beat it."

To his friends he seemed gay and lighthearted, and he seldom spoke of his illness. But the struggle to regain his health was bitter and constant. For several weeks he had to wear heavy, painful casts on his legs. He was given treatments of hot packs and massage. He tried exercises to restore his useless muscles, and he kept on trying, hour after hour, day after day. The first time he was able to wiggle his foot he considered it a great triumph.

During the long months when he was trying to get well, he had plenty of time to read and to think. The genial young man brought up in luxury had always known there were many people less fortunate than himself. He had realized there was suffering in the world. Now he understood how it really felt to suffer.

Little by little, he began to get better. Much of the credit for his improvement, he told his doctors, should go to his wife—to her patient nursing and understanding. "Without her," he said, "I never could have done it."

The following spring his legs were fitted with heavy steel braces, and he learned to swing himself along on crutches. On June 26, 1924, at the Democratic convention in New York City, he made his first political speech since his illness.

Because he could not climb stairs, a ramp had been built leading to the speaker's platform in Madison Square Garden. When the time came for him to speak, his oldest son, Jimmy, tall and strong at sixteen, helped his father out of a wheel chair and handed him a pair of crutches. The audience, watching the tall man's difficult progress up the ramp, began to cheer. The cheers seemed to shake the very rafters of the building when at last he reached the speaker's stand at the front of the platform.

The purpose of his speech that evening was to nominate his friend Al Smith for the Presidency. He called Al "the Happy Warrior of the political battlefield." The same words might have been used to describe Franklin Roosevelt, in the opinion of those who knew him best. During the slow months of his recovery, he had never admitted that he might not be able to walk unaided. A few weeks after the convention he learned about a young man with polio who had regained partial use of his legs after swimming in the waters at Warm Springs, Georgia. Franklin Roosevelt decided to try the same treatment.

Warm Springs had once been a summer resort, but a first glimpse of the rundown hotel was disappointing. The swimming pool, however, fed by an underground spring, was pleasantly warm. Many victims of polio who are unable to walk find it easer to use their muscles under water. The water in the pool at Warm Springs—so some of the townspeople said, although doctors did not always agree—had a special quality. Perhaps it was because the water was filled with mineral salts. Whatever the reason, the patient improved more in six weeks than he had in three years. In the pool he could walk and stand erect.

So enthusiastic was Franklin about Warm Springs that he returned again and again. Other people who had suffered from the same disease learned of his improvement and began coming. He was eager to help them, as he had been helped, and in 1927 he organized the Warm Springs Foundation. New buildings were constructed, and a special fund was set up for polio patients who could not afford to pay for medical care. All of this was made possible by contributions from interested people throughout the nation. Much of the money was furnished by Franklin Roosevelt himself, sometimes at great personal sacrifice, for he was not then a rich man in his own right.

He did much more than furnish money. He helped the patients by showing them how to take exercises under water. He encouraged them by his own courageous example. He was especially interested in the children, many of whom called him "Uncle Rosy." From the time the Foundation was started, he made it a practice to eat Thanksgiving dinner with the patients. Some of them were able to walk on crutches; others had to be carried on stretchers into the dining hall, or came in wheel chairs. Most of them were cheerful, and the boys and girls shouted words of encouragement when "Uncle Rosy" stood erect to carve the turkey.

In spite of the sadness all around him, Franklin always enjoyed his visits to Warm Springs. It was a satisfaction to know how many of the patients were being helped. Certainly, he had reason to feel encouraged about his own improvement. Although he still had to wear the uncomfortable steel braces, he could walk, after a fashion, without crutches. In his left hand he held a cane. He linked his right arm through the arm of a strong man walking on his right. In this way he could propel himself forward for a few steps. In time, he believed, he would regain full use of his legs if he continued to exercise in the warm pool and avoided the cold northern winters.

Yet he missed public life. In 1928, when he was urged to be a candidate for governor of New York state, he finally agreed to accept the nomination. There was some talk among his political opponents that he was not well enough to undertake the duties of a governor. Franklin Roosevelt was determined to prove them wrong, and few candidates ever put on a more strenuous campaign. He spoke several times a day, and he kept it up week after week. His audiences saw a man whose shoulders had broadened through constant exercise. His cheeks had a healthy glow. He flashed his listeners a smile, and when he began to speak they forgot he was a cripple.

Certainly his family never thought of him as an invalid. He was nearly always gay; he could nearly always laugh. One evening he told them about an amusing experience that had happened in the afternoon. It had been very hot riding along the dusty roads, between the towns where he was making speeches. Several times he had dozed off, only to be aroused by one of his companions.

"Mr. Roosevelt," he was told, "someone is waving at you."

Almost automatically, the candidate would wave and smile—and then go to sleep again.

Suddenly he came to with a start, awakened by a noise. Still half asleep, he started to wave. He started to smile. But no one shouted a greeting. Instead he heard a loud "Moo!" A cow was placidly gazing at him from the other side of a fence.

It was his ability to relish a joke, even on himself, that helped to make the Democratic candidate so popular. Another reason was the friendly interest he showed in the voters. He promised them liberal reforms, and that fall he was elected governor. Two years later he was re-elected by a very large majority.

By the time his second term began, the nation was suffering from the worst depression in its history. In New York, as in other states, thousands of men and women were out of work. Thousands of families were going hungry. Governor Roosevelt felt it was the duty of the government to aid people who were in distress through no fault of their own, and New York was the first state to use funds from the state treasury to help citizens in need. A system of public works also was started to provide jobs for men and women who were unemployed.

The success of these measures, as well as a number of other laws passed while Franklin Roosevelt was governor, made him better known throughout the nation. In the summer of 1932 the Democratic convention meeting in Chicago nominated Governor Roosevelt for the Presidency, and he flew to Chicago to accept the nomination in person.

"I pledge you, I pledge myself," he told the large, enthusiastic audience, "to a new deal for the American people."

The words "New Deal" became a slogan during the weeks that

followed. What the American people wanted most, the Democratic candidate said, was work and "a reasonable measure of security." He proposed to give them both. After his election in November, many Democratic bands blared out the old, familiar tune, "Happy Days Are Here Again."

But the weeks that followed were anything but happy for many discouraged Americans. More than twelve million of them were out of work. Banks had failed. Men and women had lost their life savings. Thousands had lost their homes or could not pay the rent. Would their new leader be able to find a way out of the depression? many people wondered. On Inauguration Day, March 4, 1933, although the streets of Washington were decorated with flags and bunting, an air of gloom hung above the city. There was gloom throughout the nation.

Franklin Roosevelt looked very solemn, almost stern, as he took his place on the inaugural stand before the east front of the Capitol. Looking down at the crowd of one hundred thousand spectators, he could see fear on many of the faces. But the man who had refused to be conquered by polio refused to be frightened now.

"This is the time to speak the truth, frankly and boldly," he said in his inaugural address. "Nor need we shrink from honestly facing conditions in our country today. This great nation will endure as it has endured, will revive and prosper . . . The only thing we have to fear is fear itself."

In his inaugural address, Franklin Delano Roosevelt promised "action—and action now," and he proceeded to get it during the breathtaking weeks that followed. With the help of his advisers, the President suggested law after law to fight the depression. These laws, which were promptly passed by Congress, were his way of giving the American people the New Deal he had promised them.

The ones to be helped first were those in immediate need. They were given relief in the form of surplus foods or small sums of money until they could start working again. Plans were made for public works, such as new roads, bridges and public buildings, to give jobs to men and women who were unemployed.

Still other laws provided for reforms which, it was hoped, would prevent depressions in the future. Such New Deal measures as social security and the insurance of bank deposits proved to be very popular. Other measures were less successful and had to be dropped.

Franklin Roosevelt, realizing that the nation was faced with new conditions, was willing to experiment.

"It is common sense to take a method and try it," he once said. "If it fails, admit it frankly. But above all, try something."

In a series of "Fireside Chats" on the radio, the President spoke to his fellow Americans, not as an orator, but as a neighbor who had dropped into their living rooms for a visit. F.D.R., as he was often called, took his listeners into his confidence as to what he was trying to do. They felt that he wanted to help them, and they responded to the friendly warmth in his voice. Not everyone did, of course. He made enemies as well as friends, especially among some of the rich business leaders whose profits were being cut down by New Deal laws. Mrs. Roosevelt, Sr., proud though she was of her son, was puzzled by the remarks of some of her friends and neighbors.

"Franklin," she asked him one day, "why is everyone opposed to so much of your program?"

He smiled up at her reassuringly. "I think I know some of the people you have been talking with," he replied. "Their only worry is that they might find themselves having to get along with two automobiles instead of three. They don't give a hoot for the man who not only can't afford a car but is unable to feed and clothe his family. These are the people that I am concerned with."

F.D.R. realized that not everyone who opposed his policies did so for selfish reasons. Many Americans were honestly worried by the high cost of the New Deal. The President was just as firmly convinced that American citizens suffering from the depression must be helped until such time as they could take care of themselves. They must be helped, even if the government did have to go into debt. He soon found, however, that not all the problems of the depression could be solved in a few months, or even in a few years. They had not all been solved by 1936 when he ran for re-election.

But several million men and women who had been out of work in 1936 now had jobs. Many stores, dairies and other businesses, once closed, were open again. The majority of the voters looked forward to the future with more confidence than they had felt in many months, and Franklin Roosevelt was elected to a second term.

Under a Constitutional amendment, adopted four years earlier, his second inauguration was held on January 20, 1937, instead of on March 4, as in previous years. In his inaugural address, President Roosevelt spoke of what had been accomplished. He also reminded his audience of what remained to be done.

"I see one-third of the nation ill-housed, ill-clad, ill-nourished," he said. "It is not in despair that I paint you this picture. I paint it for you in hope—because the nation, seeing and understanding the injustice of it, proposes to paint it out."

What gave the President his greatest feeling of satisfaction, perhaps, was that the reforms of the past few years had been brought about without sacrificing the liberty of the people. This had not been true in parts of Europe. Several countries which had suffered great hardship after World War I were now ruled by dictators. "The people," President Roosevelt said, "were so desperate, they chose to sacrifice liberty in the hope of getting something to eat."

In Germany, the dictator was Adolph Hitler, head of the Nazi party. It was the "mission of the German people," Hitler boasted, to be masters of the world. In September, 1939, his armies raced across Poland in tanks and armored cars, while Nazi airplanes dropped bombs from above. The country was conquered in three weeks.

The invasion of Poland marked the beginning of World War II. Great Britain and France, having agreed to defend Poland, declared war on Germany. A few months later the Nazis conquered Norway, Denmark, and Holland in quick succession. France surrendered in June, 1940, and Great Britain was left to fight alone.

Nor was Hitler the only dictator who dreamed of world conquest. Mussolini, the Fascist dictator of Italy, had attacked Ethiopia. On the other side of the world, Japanese military leaders had gained control of their government. They had conquered large areas of China, and were planning further invasions. In September, 1940, Japan joined Germany and Italy in a military alliance known as the Axis, and secret plans were laid to attack the United States, both on the Pacific and Atlantic coasts. England must be defeated first, but Hitler felt confident that England could not hold out much longer.

Although the American people did not know about these plans until later, they watched the swift march of events with grave misgivings. "When peace is broken anywhere," warned F.D.R., "it is broken everywhere."

The appeals which he sent to the dictators to halt their aggressions were ignored. By 1940 the danger was so grave that America might be drawn into the war that he accepted his party's nomination for a third term. In November he was re-elected. It was the only time in the nation's history that a President was to serve for more than eight years.

This victory at the polls assured Franklin Roosevelt that he had the support of most of his countrymen. They agreed when he said that the "greatest hope" of staying out of the war was to help Great Britain. In his annual message to Congress in January, 1941, he asked for authority to send desperately-needed war supplies to those countries that were fighting the aggressor nations. In this same speech he spoke of the ideals which would have to form the basis of any lasting peace after the war was won.

"We look forward to a world founded upon four essential freedoms," he said.

The freedoms he listed were freedom of speech, freedom of worship, freedom from want and freedom from fear. The American people were greatly stirred by this speech and, a few weeks later, Congress passed the Lend-Lease Act. This law made it possible for the President to lend or rent ships, planes and other supplies to countries at war with the Axis. It was felt that these countries, in defending themselves, were aiding in the defense of the United States.

In the meantime America had started to train a larger army. It was building up its navy and air force. Although many people continued to hope that the nation would not be drawn into actual fighting, this hope grew dimmer as the weeks passed. By October the military leaders in Japan seemed bent on conquering all of eastern Asia and the islands of the Pacific, including islands that belonged to the United States. Warnings to halt their aggressions from the American Secretary of State went unheeded. President Roosevelt sent a personal letter to the emperor, but there is some doubt that he ever saw it. The military leaders then firmly in control of the Japanese government may not have allowed the letter to reach him.

This was the situation when F.D.R. went to Warm Springs in late November. The cluster of attractive white buildings set down among the trees of a Georgia forest looked very different from the shabby resort he had first visited in 1924. It always seemed to rest him to go to Warm Springs, and the patients drew courage from his buoyant spirit.

Especially did they look forward to Thanksgiving, but this year the President seemed more serious than usual when he gave his customary talk after dinner. He spoke of the blessings of liberty, which Americans still enjoyed at a time when most inhabitants of the world were living under dictators.

"I think we can offer up a little prayer," he said, "that these people will be able to hold a Thanksgiving more like our own Thanksgiving, next year. That is something of a dream, perhaps."

It was indeed a dream. On December 7, a few days after Franklin Roosevelt had returned to Washington, he picked up his telephone to be informed that Japanese airplanes had bombed the American naval base at Pearl Harbor in Hawaii. The attack had come without warning, at the very moment when two Japanese diplomats were waiting in the office of the American Secretary of State, supposedly to discuss terms of peace. As a result of the attack, more than three thousand people in Hawaii had been killed or injured. A large part of the American fleet was destroyed, as well as one hundred and seventy-seven American planes which had been grounded at the time.

These losses placed the United States in great danger. The President's face was grim the following day when he addressed a joint session of Congress. Because of the treacherous attack on Pearl Harbor, he said that December 7, 1941, was a day that would "live in infamy." He asked for a declaration of war against Japan. Three days later Germany and Italy, Japan's allies, declared war on the United States.

The next three and a half years were filled with the bitterness and pain and the heartbreak that are always a part of warfare. American sailors and Marines fought in the Pacific. American and British soldiers, with help from others who had once lived in the conquered countries, fought in Africa. In eastern Europe Russia had been invaded by the Nazis, and the Russians were desperately defending their homeland. How long they could hold out, or how long the British could hold out, no one knew. There were times when the American forces seemed perilously close to defeat. But if F.D.R. ever felt discouraged, no one ever knew it. A way must be found for the Allies to win, and he was confident that they would win. In the darkest days his spirits seemed high.

His courage seemed to communicate itself to America's fighting men. General Eisenhower once spoke of the confidence and strength he had drawn from Franklin Roosevelt's "indomitable spirit." There were many other people who were not so generous. F.D.R.—like other popular Presidents who had been both loved and hated in their own time—was accustomed to criticism. He was accustomed to attacks that were unfair, but as a rule he ignored false stories. In the summer of 1944, however, he learned of one rumor that was so exaggerated it was funny.

This rumor concerned a friend and constant companion—a pert, shaggy, black Scottie named Fala. Some days Fala received almost as much publicity in the newspapers as his master, and he accompanied the President on several trips. In the summer of 1944, he was on board the vessel which carried the Presidential party to Hawaii and then returned to the west coast by way of the Aleutian Islands. This was all that was needed to start a rumor that the small black Scottie had been left behind on the Aleutians by mistake, and a Navy destroyer had been sent back to pick him up.

And this time Franklin Roosevelt's sense of humor came to the rescue. In a speech which he made a short time later, he referred to falsehoods told by political enemies, not only about himself, but also about his wife and family. And now the attacks, he went on solemnly, included his little dog Fala.

"Unlike the members of my family," he said, trying to keep a straight face but not quite succeeding, "Fala resents this. When he learned that I had left him behind on an Aleutian Island and had sent a destroyer back to find him—at a cost to the taxpayer of two or three or twenty million dollars—his Scotch soul was furious. He has not been the same dog since."

The audience burst out laughing. People listening to their radios at home chuckled over the story about Fala. By ridicule the President had shown how foolish the rumor was. This speech was made during his fourth campaign for the Presidency, and Mrs. Roosevelt believed it helped him to win.

The day after his fourth inauguration, Franklin Roosevelt left on another long journey of nearly seven thousand miles. In the town of Yalta in Soviet Russia he met with Prime Minister Churchill of Great Britain and Premier Stalin of the Soviet Union. By February, 1945, victory in Europe seemed near. "The Big Three," as the three leaders were called, had many important questions to decide. How should a defeated Germany be governed? What should be done about the nations liberated from the Nazis? Poland and the countries in eastern Europe, which had been invaded by Nazi soldiers earlier in the war, had now been reconquered by Soviet troops. Premier Stalin was already in control. He agreed, however, that free elections were to be held in Poland. The Polish people were to be allowed to live under a government of their own choice.

Still other agreements reached at Yalta concerned the wartime alliance known as the United Nations. It was made up of countries fighting the Axis, but President Roosevelt hoped that after the war it could be turned into a permanent organization to keep peace in the world. To him, the great triumph at Yalta was the decision to hold a conference at San Francisco in April. To this conference forty-six nations were invited to send delegates. Together they would work out plans for a permanent UN.

When F.D.R. returned home, he looked ill and tired. No man had ever served as President for so long a time. No President had ever seen history made so fast and so furiously. And history was still being made, not all of it to his liking. He was worried and angry when several weeks passed by and Premier Stalin had not made a start on keeping some of the promises made at Yalta.

But the San Francisco Conference was soon to meet. The thought of that Conference, on which he had insisted and which he hoped would do away with war, brought Franklin Roosevelt more satisfaction than any other accomplishment during his crowded, busy years. He was to welcome the delegates on April 25. When he went to Warm Springs earlier in the month for a brief rest, he was thinking of the speech that he would make.

First, however, he must write another address which he was to deliver over the radio on Thomas Jefferson's birthday. As he dictated it to his secretary, he spoke of the new and awesome responsibility that faced the American people. They and all other peoples must learn to "live together and work together, in the same world, at peace," he said, if civilization was to survive.

When the speech was brought back to him, neatly typed, he read it over carefully. He picked up a pen and added a few words in handwriting. His last sentence read:

"Let us move forward with a strong and active faith."

THE THIRTY-SECOND PRESIDENT *at a Glance*

Franklin Delano Roosevelt

Born: January 30, 1882   *Died: April 12, 1945*

Early life and career. Franklin D. Roosevelt was born on a farm near Hyde Park, N.Y. Until he was 14, he was educated by private tutors. He then attended Groton School (1896–1900), Harvard University (where he graduated in 1904), and Columbia University Law School (1904–1907). He and a distant cousin, Eleanor Roosevelt, the niece of Theodore Roosevelt, then President of the U.S., were married in 1906. After practicing law in New York City (1907–1910), Franklin served as senator in the New York State legislature (1911–

1913) and as Assistant Secretary of the Navy (1913–1920). In 1920 he was nominated as Vice President on the Democratic ticket but was defeated.

Polio and politics. In 1921 a severe attack of polio threatened to bring an end to Franklin Roosevelt's political career, but after a few years of treatment and exercise he regained a limited use of his legs. Because of the help he received from swimming in the pool at Warm Springs, Ga., he started a nonprofit treatment center there for other polio victims. To the Warm Springs Foundation, organized in 1927, he contributed two-thirds of his own fortune. As time passed, thousands of other Americans contributed through "March of Dimes" and other fund-raising campaigns. Meanwhile, in 1928, Roosevelt was elected governor of New York State and served two terms (1929–1933). He was nominated on the Democratic ticket for President in 1932, when the nation was going through the worst depression in American history. During the campaign, F.D.R., as he was called, promised the voters "a new deal," and was elected.

As President (1933–1937; 1937–1941; 1941–1945; January 20–April 12, 1945). With the help of his advisers, F.D.R. suggested a number of new laws, which were passed by Congress. Most of these New Deal laws were administered by special agencies, including the FERA (Federal Emergency Relief Administration, proposed by the President in 1933), which gave huge sums to the states to help Americans in need; the PWA (Public Works Administration, started in 1933), which constructed such public works as bridges, dams and government buildings, gave employment to thousands and helped to restore purchasing power; and the CCC (Civilian Conservation Corps, founded in 1933), which put a quarter of a million jobless young men to work reforesting public lands and caring for the nation's other natural resources. A number of reform laws also were passed, in the hope of preventing depressions in the future. Later the U.S. Supreme Court declared several New Deal laws unconstitutional, and they had to be dropped.

New Deal measures. Among the successful New Deal measures which have been retained are the following: TVA (Tennessee Valley Authority, founded in 1933), which built a series of dams in the Tennessee River, thus helping to control floods, furnishing cheap water power and light to a large, underdeveloped area in the South, and bringing prosperity to several million people in parts of six states; FDIC (Federal Deposit Insurance Corp., founded in 1934), which insured bank depositors against loss up to $10,000 in any one bank; the SEC (Securities and Exchange Commission, founded in 1934), which protected investors by requiring stock exchanges and persons selling stocks and bonds to tell the truth about the securities they offered for sale; the FCC (Federal Communications Commission, first established in 1934), which now regulates wire, radio and TV communications; and the Social Security acts of 1935 and 1939, which provided for monthly payments to retired workers over 65 (based on their average earnings before that age) and also for special benefits for unemployed persons, for widows and dependent children, and for many others in need. Although the New Deal was not liked by most business leaders, among the Americans who benefited were owners of small business firms, the majority of farmers, and laboring men.

Only four-term President. In 1936 F.D.R. was re-elected. Because of the grave world situation, he was elected to a third term in 1940, and to a fourth term in 1944. He was the only President in American history to serve more than 8 years.

F.D.R. in peace and war. In his first inaugural address (March 4, 1933), the President said the U.S. wanted to be a "good neighbor" to other nations. His "good neighbor policy" resulted in a much friendlier feeling between the U.S. and Latin American countries. After World War II began in Europe (1939), Roosevelt believed that the U.S. would have a better chance of staying out of the conflict if the Americans gave all help "short of war" to the nations fighting the Nazi and Fascist aggressors. At his suggestion Congress passed the Lend-Lease Bill (March 11, 1941) which gave him authority to lend or lease war supplies wherever he felt they were most needed. During a secret meeting (August 14, 1941) with Prime Minister Winston Churchill of Great Britain, on a battleship in the Atlantic, the two leaders issued a joint statement. In this "Atlantic Charter" they expressed the hope that after the war a peace could be established which would "afford to all nations the means of dwelling in safety within their own boundaries." After the U.S. entered the war (December 7, 1941), the President made a number of trips outside the country, to confer with other Allied leaders. He helped to plan the strategy for winning the war, but he believed it just as important to "win the peace" that would follow. With Winston Churchill, he worked out tentative plans for the United Nations. This name was first used (January 2, 1942), to designate a wartime alliance, but it was Roosevelt's hope that someday it would be transformed into an organization to settle international disputes by peaceful means. Suggestions for a United Nations Charter were made at the Dumbarton Oaks Conference when UN representatives met in Washington, D.C. (September–October, 1944). At the Yalta Conference in Russia (February 4–11, 1945), Roosevelt, Churchill and Premier Stalin of the

Soviet Union agreed to invite delegates from 46 nations to meet in San Francisco for the purpose of turning UN into a permanent organization. Among other questions discussed at Yalta was what should be done about Germany, after that country had been defeated, as well as several countries in eastern Europe, once conquered by the Nazis but recently reconquered by Soviet troops. Roosevelt, although not altogether satisfied with the results of the Yalta Conference, had no way of knowing that Stalin was not to keep a number of his promises. When F.D.R. returned to the U.S., he was looking forward to welcoming UN delegates to the San Francisco Conference, which was scheduled to begin April 25, 1945. Thirteen days earlier he died suddenly in the cottage he had built at Warm Springs, Ga.

Other happenings. When Roosevelt was President, the Century of Progress International Exposition was held in Chicago (1933–1934). The 21st Amendment to the Constitution was adopted (1933); this Amendment repealed the 18th, or Prohibition, Amendment. In the 1930's severe droughts and sandstorms turned parts of several states in the Great Plains area into a vast "Dust Bowl," ruining many thousands of farms. Admiral Richard E. Byrd headed his second exploring and scientific expedition (1933–1935) and a third expedition (1939–1940) to the Antarctic. The labor leader, John L. Lewis, organized the CIO (Congress of Industrial Organizations, 1935). Nylon, a synthetic material derived from water, air, and coal, was introduced (1938) after ten years of research. The Golden Gate International Exposition was held in San Francisco and the New York World's Fair was held on Long Island (1939–1940). The first self-sustained nuclear chain reaction leading to the development of the atom bomb was produced at the University of Chicago (1942).

The nation's population. The population was about 131,700,000 (census of 1940).

The President's family. The First Lady, Eleanor Roosevelt (born 1884), was deeply interested in New Deal relief measures. She traveled extensively, reporting to the President on conditions found in different parts of the country. She lectured, appeared frequently on radio and television, contributed to magazines, and wrote a newspaper column. Her books include *This Is My Story, This I Remember,* and *On My Own.* After her husband's death, Mrs. Roosevelt served as a U.S. representative to the UN General Assembly (1945–1952). In 1946 she was made chairman of the Commission on Human Rights. The Roosevelts had five children, two of whom became Congressmen: Franklin, Jr. and James.

HARRY TRUMAN'S *Job*

"Put down that newspaper, Harry," Dr. Thompson said. "I know it's fun trying out your new glasses. But I want you to listen to me carefully, and remember what I say."

Eight-year-old Harry Truman looked up from the newspaper. Even behind his thick-lensed glasses, a sparkle of excitement could be seen in his hazel eyes.

"I can read as easy as anything!" he said in amazement. He turned to his mother, who was sitting beside the oculist's big desk. "Why, Mama, I can read everything in the paper, even the things in little letters!"

"That's fine, Harry!" Mrs. Truman smiled at her son's enthusiasm. She had taught Harry to read when he was five. The boy had been quick to learn his letters and soon had been able to read almost anything—if the words were printed in very large type. But recently he had been wanting to read the newspaper, and that was another matter.

"He couldn't make out anything in the paper except the headlines," Mrs. Truman told the doctor. "That's when his father and I figured he probably needed spectacles."

"He certainly did need them," Dr. Thompson agreed, "and not just for reading. He should wear them all the time. He's not going to be able to play in games or——"

"Not play in any games?" asked Harry in dismay.

"No ball games," the oculist went on earnestly, "or any kind of games where your spectacles might be broken. Your eyes could be badly injured by pieces of glass, and you must not take any chances. That's what I want you to remember, Harry."

"All right, I'll try," said Harry mournfully.

"You'd better do more than try," the doctor grumbled. Then he could not help smiling at the solemn boy, whose round face looked more owlish than ever in the thick-lensed glasses.

"The next time you're here in Kansas City," he added kindly, "stop by and tell me how you like seeing the world as it really is. You're in for some surprises."

The Trumans lived not far from Kansas City, in the small town of Independence, Missouri, where Harry's father was a buyer and seller of livestock. At the Truman place there was a big yard where Harry and his younger brother, Vivian, and a still younger sister, Mary Jane, liked to play. The yard was also a favorite gathering place for the children in the neighborhood. When Harry and his mother reached home after their visit to the oculist, they saw several boys and girls standing in a group near one of the barns. Harry ran over to them, eager to show off his new glasses.

But Harry's friends scarcely noticed him at all. Their eyes were on the two goats harnessed to a little wagon. Vivian was sitting in the driver's seat. He had just pulled the team to a stop, and he looked worried. Every boy and girl there seemed to be trying to talk louder than the others. They always liked to drive the goat team, and each wanted the next turn in the wagon. How could six-year-old Vivian decide? Then he saw that his brother was back home, and the decision was easy.

"Harry's next," said Vivian firmly.

Harry quickly took his brother's place in the wagon. On another day he might have lined up his friends, according to age or height, and then placed himself among them to take his turn in order. But on this day, the day of the new glasses, he was in a hurry to see what his home really looked like.

The Trumans owned several acres of land, and Harry rode from one end of them to the other, eagerly inspecting everything. The house, the barns, the trees stood out sharply against the sky. On the fruit trees he now saw apples, instead of the blobs of red that he had seen before. Up ahead, a rabbit ran across the path—why, he knew it was a rabbit! Yesterday it would have been nothing but a moving shape.

Harry could hardly believe what he was seeing. He pulled the goats to a stop and took off his glasses. Everything became fuzzy and dim. He put the glasses back on, and all was sharp and clear again.

"These spectacles sure are wonderful," Harry said to himself. "They're mighty, mighty wonderful."

Wonderful as the new glasses were, Harry soon discovered that the oculist was right. There were many games in which he could not take part, and reading became his greatest interest. His mother gave him a set of books called *Heroes of History*, which he read and reread many times during the next few years. He also read twice through the big family Bible. Then he started in on the books in the public library, and by the time he was thirteen he had read every book there, even the encyclopedia.

Most of all he liked books that told the story of the United States and its leaders. But he also enjoyed reading about ancient Greece and Rome and about England, France and Germany, and other European nations. In high school, history was his favorite subject. Often after school he would go to the library to read more about some fact he had learned that day in class. "I guess one can learn a lot about the world today from reading about the past," he reflected.

Of course, Harry could not spend all of his time reading. He had chores to do at home. Every day the cows must be milked and the horses curried. Great stacks of wood must be carried into the kitchen for the stove. Once each week Harry and Mary Jane went by trolley to Kansas City for their music lessons. Music lessons meant practicing, and Harry often rose at five in the morning and practiced on the piano before starting his chores.

Until Harry had been fitted with glasses, his poor eyesight had kept him from going to school. He had not even entered first grade until he was eight and a half years old, but once started, he made rapid progress. By the time he was seventeen, he was ready to graduate from high school.

On graduation night in June of 1901, one of Harry's classmates had a question for Miss Tillie Brown, the English teacher. "Which of us is most likely to become President of the United States?" he asked her.

Miss Brown thought for a moment. It hardly seemed likely that any of the seventy-two new graduates would ever be President. But she tried to make a guess. "There is one boy—" she began.

She seemed to hesitate. The boy she had in mind wasn't the most brilliant pupil in the class. But he was a hard worker. He was honest and straightforward. He was able to think things through. Whenever he had a job to do, he gave it everything that was in him.

"*If* any one of you ever became President," Miss Brown said finally, "it would be Harry Truman."

If Harry heard Miss Brown's remark, he probably did not take it seriously. He had not yet decided what career he wanted; but he knew that he did want to get some more education. Because of financial losses, his father would not be able to send him to college. Earlier that year, however, a Congressman from the Trumans' district had obtained for Harry an appointment to the United States Military Academy. But Harry must still pass various examinations before he would actually be admitted to the West Point academy.

Never had Harry wanted anything so much as to go to West Point. Through his study of history he had become interested in military matters, and he wanted to learn more about them. Even more important, at West Point he could continue his education in other subjects. He studied hard all summer, and that fall he took the tests. He waited anxiously to hear the results.

And then he learned that he was not to be admitted. Harry was smart enough; he had done well in all the written tests. But he had not passed the physical examination. His eyes were not good enough for the military academy.

Disappointed though Harry was about not going to West Point, he wasted no time feeling sorry for himself. He soon went to work as a timekeeper on a railroad construction job. Later he worked in Kansas City, first in a newspaper mailroom and then in a bank. In 1906, when he was twenty-two, he gave up his job as a bank clerk in order to help his father run a six-hundred-acre farm in Grandview, Missouri.

The Grandview farm belonged to Harry's grandmother. Harry had spent many happy times there when he was a little boy. Now, as a young man, he settled down to the usual life of a Missouri farmer. He plowed the rich earth, and, as his mother said later, "learned to plow the straightest row in the county." He planted corn and wheat and oats. He milked the cows, fed the hogs and helped with the harvesting, threshing and baling of hay.

In spite of the hard life and the never-ending work, Harry liked being a farmer, and he expected always to be one. But in 1917 the United States entered the First World War, and Harry, after eleven years at Grandview, left the farm to serve in the Army. He was a lieutenant by the time he arrived in France, and later he was promoted to captain. Captain Truman was a firm commander, but a just one, who won the loyalty and devotion of his men. They fought together, and they fought bravely, during some of the bitterest battles of the war. When he sailed for home several months after the Armistice, Harry—like many another returning soldier—had the satisfaction of knowing that his had been a job well done. But he was looking forward to being a civilian again.

Most of all he looked forward to seeing Bess Wallace, his childhood sweetheart. They were married a few weeks later and settled down in Independence to live. His brother was running the family farm at Grandview, and Harry decided he would rather go into business. With a wartime friend, he opened a men's clothing store in Kansas City. Independence was close enough so that he could easily go back and forth to work every day. The future looked bright. He was popular in Kansas City. He liked the work at the store, and business was good.

At least, business was good for a while. Then, in 1921, there was a depression, and customers were scarce. Harry had invested all of his savings in the clothing store, and when it was forced to close, he found that he had lost every cent. Not only that—he had gone into debt. It was quite a large debt, but grimly he made up his mind that he was going to pay back every cent he owed.

Also he had to find a way to earn a living. Some time before his business failed, a man influential in local politics had come to see him. This politician had heard a great deal about Harry Truman. His family was well thought of in Jackson County. His war record was good, and he was popular with veterans. He would be a "vote-getter," the politician said, and offered to back him if he wanted to run for county judge.

Harry finally decided to accept this offer. After the store closed he became a candidate for judge in the eastern part of the county, and his victory at the polls marked his entrance into politics. Several years later he was elected judge for the entire county. County judges in Missouri—unlike judges in most states—do not conduct trials in courts of law. Instead they are in charge of county roads and buildings and charitable institutions. Harry spent millions of dollars of the county's money in the construction of new roads and public buildings. He spent the money as carefully as if it had been his own, and was greatly respected for both his honesty and efficiency. In 1934, twelve years after his start in Missouri politics, he was elected to the United States Senate.

At first he made no great stir in Washington. A modest man, neatly dressed, his eyes somewhat magnified behind his thick-lensed spectacles, the new Senator from Missouri did more listening than talking. He had a new job to learn. He read speeches and reports by his fellow Senators. He found out everything they stood for, what they believed in. Gradually he began to make friends among them. And, after his re-election in 1940, he had his big chance to prove himself.

By then World War II had broken out in Europe. Members of Congress, fearful that the United States might become involved, voted to spend huge sums for defense. There were rumors of waste and extravagance in munition factories, at navy bases, and in army camps. Senator Truman decided to visit some of the camps and defense plants to see for himself, and he found that the rumors were true.

The same thing had happened during World War I, he reflected, but the waste had not been fully realized until after the war was over. In a speech which he made to the Senate in 1941, he suggested that this time waste should be stopped before it had a chance to gain headway.

"The thing to do is to dig this stuff up now and correct it," he said.

Realizing the wisdom of the suggestion, the Senate appointed him chairman of a committee to investigate defense production. After the United States entered the war in December, 1941, the work of the Truman Committee became increasingly important. During the next few years the committee saved the government billions of dollars, and its hardworking chairman became known as the able "watchdog" of the war production program. In the summer of 1944, the Democratic convention nominated him for Vice President. President Franklin D. Roosevelt was a candidate for a fourth term, and in November both men were elected.

As Vice President, it was Mr. Truman's duty to preside over meetings of the Senate. Often, in the late afternoon, after the Senate adjourned for the day, he would stop in at the office of Sam Rayburn, the Speaker of the House of Representatives, to talk over Congressional matters. On April 12, 1945, when he entered the office, the Speaker had a message for him.

"Harry," Sam Rayburn said, "Steve Early has been trying to reach you by phone. He wants you to call right back."

Mr. Early was President Roosevelt's press secretary, and Harry Truman picked up the phone at once. The press secretary's voice sounded strained, but all he said was, "Please come right over to the White House."

The Vice President was puzzled by the sudden summons. Two weeks earlier Franklin Roosevelt, weary from his wartime responsibilities, had left for Warm Springs, Georgia. He must have returned earlier than expected, Mr. Truman decided, as his car sped toward the White House. When he walked through the wide front entrance, he was ushered into the elevator and taken into a room on the second floor.

But it was not Mr. Roosevelt who was waiting to see him. It was Mrs. Roosevelt. She stepped forward and placed her hand on his shoulder.

"Harry," she said, "the President is dead."

For a moment Mr. Truman could not speak.

Then he said, "Is there anything I can do for you?"

"Is there anything *we* can do for *you?*" Mrs. Roosevelt replied gently.

There were many things that must be done immediately; the country must not be left without a President any longer than necessary. The members of the Cabinet were summoned. Mr. Truman went to the President's office, where he phoned the Chief Justice, requesting him to come to the White House to administer the Presidential oath. He also called his wife and daughter, and asked them to join him.

A short time later members of the Cabinet, leaders of Congress, and Mr. Truman's wife and daughter gathered in the Cabinet Room. There Harry Truman, standing erect and firm, took the oath that made him President of the United States. After the brief ceremony he held a meeting of the Cabinet. The Cabinet members had just taken their places around the huge conference table when the press secretary entered the room.

"Mr. President," he said, "the reporters want to know if there will be any change about the San Francisco Conference. Will it take place as planned?"

The press secretary was referring to a conference scheduled to meet two weeks later for the purpose of establishing the United Nations as a permanent organization. The new President had to make his first decision, but he did not hesitate.

"Tell the reporters," he replied, "that the conference will take place as President Roosevelt had directed. It is of supreme importance that plans be made now that will help keep the future peace of the world."

President Truman turned back to the members of the Cabinet. He wanted all of them to stay on in the positions they had held under Franklin Roosevelt, he told them. "But since I am the one who is now President," he added, "I will take full responsibility for my own decisions."

The Trumans would, of course, live in the White House after Mrs. Roosevelt had had time to move. But that night Harry Truman returned to the five-room apartment where he and his family had lived for several years. Little had he dreamed, when he left it that morning, that before the day was over he would be the head of the most powerful nation in the world.

The thought of his new responsibilities seemed almost overwhelming when he awoke the next morning. The country was still engaged in fighting the greatest war in history. Harry Truman had been Vice President for less than three months. During that time he had not been briefed on many of Franklin Roosevelt's plans for winning the war and building the peace that would follow. There must be a million men, he thought sadly, who were better qualified to be President than he was. But he was the one who had the job, and he was determined to give it the best that was in him.

That morning on his way to his new office in the White House, he turned to a friend riding beside him in the car. "There have been few men in history," he said, "the equal of the man whose shoes I am stepping into. I pray God I can measure up to the task."

Harry Truman was not the only person who was wondering about his qualifications for the difficult tasks that lay ahead. For twelve years the country had known no other President than Franklin Roosevelt. His wartime leadership during the past four years had made him possibly the best known man in the world. But not many people, even in the United States, knew much about Harry Truman. What was he like? What kind of President would he make?

Many of the newspapers called him the "average man," and perhaps in many ways he was. But he certainly knew more about history than the average man, for he had never stopped studying the subject that had interested him so much as a boy. As a result he had a vast knowledge of American history and government. Fortunately, for there was no chance to get used to the new job gradually, he also had the courage and the ability to make decisions. He had to decide many grave matters, almost from the moment he took office. For the commander-in-chief of the armed forces there was much to learn about America's war plans and foreign policy, and he had long talks with leading government and military officials. In the secret Map Room of the White House, he studied the locations of the battle

lines. And he read endless numbers of reports from the State Department.

On May 8, Harry Truman's sixty-first birthday, he had gratifying
news to announce to the country: Germany had surrendered. But the
war with Japan was not over. In order to bring the war in the Pacific
to an end, elaborate preparations were being made to invade the
Japanese home islands. The invasion was scheduled to take place in
the fall. A force of two million men would be needed, unless . . .

Thinking of those two million men, the President's eyes grew
thoughtful behind his thick-lensed spectacles. Shortly after becoming President, he had been amazed to learn about a super-secret
project. For several years some of the world's leading scientists working for the American government had been experimenting with a
new kind of bomb—an atomic bomb. But the bomb was not yet
ready to be tested. Would it actually work? As yet no one really knew.

In the meantime, there were many postwar problems to be settled
in Europe. In July President Truman went to Potsdam, Germany, to
confer with Prime Minister Churchill of Great Britain and Premier
Stalin of the Soviet Union. These two nations had been allies of the
United States during the war, and the leaders must decide what was
to be done about the future of a defeated Germany. In Potsdam the
President was quartered in a beautiful house in a wooded area near
a lake. But he had little time to enjoy his peaceful surroundings.
The morning after his arrival he received a message of utmost importance from his Secretary of War: the first test of an atomic bomb
had just been made in New Mexico, and the test had been successful.

The United States now had the most powerful weapon of destruction the world had ever known. Should it be used against Japan? The
question called for a momentous decision—and only the President
could make it.

A number of high-level government and military officials had accompanied Mr. Truman to Europe, and he summoned them to a
meeting.

"How long will it take to invade and defeat Japan if the bomb is
not used?" he asked them. "How many Americans and Japanese will
lose their lives before the islands can be conquered?"

"Without the bomb, it will take at least a year," General George
Marshall told him. "The Japanese would defend their home islands
desperately. A quarter of a million Americans and probably millions
of Japanese would be killed before Japan surrendered."

What should be done? If the bomb was dropped, the invasion probably would not be necessary. Terrible as the new weapon was, to use

it would mean less loss of life than another year of bitter warfare, he concluded.

President Truman made his decision. The bomb was to be used as soon as possible.

On August 6, when the President was returning to the United States following the Potsdam Conference, he received the news on shipboard. An atomic bomb had been dropped on a city in Japan. In spite of the terrible destruction, no offer of surrender came from the Japanese, and three days later a second bomb was dropped. On August 14, 1945, Japan surrendered. At last World War II was over.

But though the bitter fighting had ended and the guns were silent, President Truman soon realized that peace—real peace—had not come. During the war Soviet troops had conquered several countries in eastern Europe which had previously been conquered by Germany. But these countries were still not free. Communist governments were set up in Poland and in several other nations once controlled by Nazi dictators. These same nations were now Russian satellites, ruled by dictators backed by the Soviet Union.

It was the belief, frequently stated, of members of the Communist party in Russia and elsewhere, that their form of government should be extended throughout the world. By 1947, Soviet leaders were putting pressure on Greece and Turkey in an effort to extend Communist control to those nations. Members of the Communist party in France and Italy and other countries of western Europe were encouraged by the Soviets to stir up trouble for their own governments.

The newly-formed United Nations could do little to ease the tensions caused by Russian ambitions. The Soviet Union was one of the five members of the UN Security Council that had the right to veto any decisions made by other Council members. And the Russians used the veto time and again.

President Truman was deeply disturbed to see that Russia was setting out on a program of expansion all too similar to the German and Japanese programs of expansion that had led to World War II. Communism must be "contained," he insisted; that is, it must not be allowed to spread. Free peoples that needed help to keep their independence must be given that help. For this reason the President urged that money and military advisers be sent to Greece and Turkey.

"The free peoples of the world," he said in a speech before Congress in March, 1947, "look to us for support in maintaining their freedoms. If we falter in our leadership, we may endanger the peace of the world—and we shall certainly endanger the welfare of our own nation."

At the end of the speech, the members of Congress rose and applauded. Later they voted to aid Greece and Turkey, and as a result both countries were able to maintain their independence. The President's recommendations for helping free nations to resist Communism became known as the Truman Doctrine, and marked the beginning of a new foreign policy for the United States.

Later that same year, still another foreign-aid program was announced by General George Marshall, the President's new Secretary of State. Under the Marshall Plan, the United States sent money, machinery and technical experts to European nations to help them rebuild their war-shattered cities and industries. The plan was offered to all European nations that were willing to work together for the recovery of Europe.

The Soviet Union refused to take part in the plan or to allow the satellite countries in eastern Europe to do so. But sixteen other European nations cooperated in the program, and as poverty and despair gave way to prosperity and hope, Communist propaganda lost much of its influence in western Europe.

The President's foreign policy was approved by most of the members of both political parties, but his domestic policies were not so popular. His Republican opponents had a majority in Congress and were able to defeat much of the program which the Democratic President wished to carry out at home.

Their success in Congress led many Republicans to believe that their party was sure to win the next Presidential election. "It's time for a change," became their slogan, and most of the newspapers in the country agreed that Harry Truman did not have a chance. Public opinion polls strongly indicated that most of the American people would vote Republican in the coming election.

At the Democratic convention in July, Mr. Truman received his party's nomination for President. But there were some Democrats, as well as many Republicans, who had not approved of all of his policies. Thirty-five delegates from the Southern states, in protest against the President's civil rights program, walked out of the convention. They organized the "Dixiecrat" party, which then nominated another Presidential candidate. The Democratic party was split still further when a number of extremely liberal members joined a new Progressive party, which also had its own candidate for President.

Neither the Dixiecrats nor the Progressives could hope to win, but many people would vote for them who might otherwise vote for Harry Truman. He could not possibly be elected, the political experts said. There was going to be a landslide victory for the Republican candidate, Thomas Dewey.

Even the President's most loyal friends were discouraged. It really seemed a waste of effort for him to campaign. He was beaten before he started—that's what almost everyone seemed to think. But "almost everyone" did not include Harry Truman. It never occurred to him not to make the fight, and two months before election, he started on a whirlwind campaign.

He traveled by train from one end of the country to the other, speaking in big cities and small ones, and at whistle stops. Sometimes he addressed large audiences in stadiums and armories. More often, he spoke from the rear platform of his train to groups of people gathered at railway stations.

The President seldom made a prepared speech. Instead, he spoke "off the cuff" and in plain terms expressed what was in his heart and in his mind. He no longer seemed the quiet, unassuming man from Missouri that many people had once thought him. His speeches were fighting speeches. He tore into the Congress that had opposed the laws he had suggested for reforms at home. He reminded farmers and factory workers of the many gains they had made in the past fifteen years. If they did not want to lose those gains, he told them bluntly, they'd better get out on election day and vote for him and his party.

As the campaign continued, the crowds became larger and more enthusiastic. "Pour it on, Harry," they would yell, as he lashed out at his opponents.

But did the people really like him? Were they really listening to what he had to say? Or did they think of his colorful speeches simply as entertainment and enjoy them as they might a good show?

Most important, would they vote for him? Would the people who had heard him speak in Detroit, Des Moines, and Denver; in San Francisco and Los Angeles; in Duluth and Miami; in Provo, Utah, and Sparks, Nevada; and in dozens of other towns, large and small— would these people vote for him on November 2?

The public opinion polls indicated that they would not; at least not enough of them would. The political experts and the newspapers agreed. But no matter what anyone else thought, Harry Truman himself expected to win.

On election day he voted in his home town of Independence, Missouri. Then, accompanied only by two secret service men, he slipped away to a quiet hotel in a town nearby to await the results. The President had no intention of sitting up all night listening to the radio, however. After eating a sandwich and drinking a glass of milk, he went to bed.

Early in the evening, a few scattered returns showed that Mr. Truman was ahead. "That means nothing," some of the radio commentators said. "The tide will soon turn."

But the tide did not turn. At four o'clock in the morning, the President was awakened by a knock on his door.

"I think you will be interested," one of the secret service men told him, "in listening to the broadcast."

The President turned on the radio. A commentator was saying, "Truman is now two million votes ahead."

"Well," the President remarked dryly, "it looks very much as if we may be in the White House for four more years. Maybe I'd better get up."

To him the news came as no surprise. But other people throughout the nation listened to their radios that morning with dazed expressions on their faces. Harry Truman, the underdog, had won! What had happened? they asked themselves.

"I just don't know what happened," was the only explanation the head of a prominent poll-taking organization could give.

But there was an explanation after all. There had been a last-minute swing to Harry Truman, a swing missed by the pollsters and the newspapers. The President's energetic one-man campaign and his fighting heart and words had won him the admiration of millions of his countrymen. The result had been one of the greatest political upsets in American history.

Two days after the election the triumphant President returned to Washington and a tremendous welcome. The streets were gaily decorated with flags and bunting. Crowds stood eight deep on the sidewalks to cheer him as his car drove from the railroad station to the White House. "I'm just wild about Harry," they sang, to the music of the bands along the way.

Harry Truman was smiling broadly as he waved to the crowds. He was pleased that he had been elected President in his own right. But what gave him even greater satisfaction was the knowledge that he would now have the chance to carry out, at home and abroad, the policies he believed were in the best interests of the American people.

By the time Harry Truman was inaugurated as President in his own right, in January, 1949, what was called "the cold war" was alarming many people both in the United States and in the other free nations of the West. It was with the hope of avoiding "a shooting war" that NATO was formed. This North Atlantic Treaty Organization was an alliance of the United States, Canada, and ten nations of western Europe. Each nation agreed that in the case of attack on any one of them, the others would assist in its defense. With the free nations standing together, it was believed that the Communists would not dare to start a shooting war in Europe.

On the other side of the world, however, Communist ambitions were soon to lead to bitter warfare. The country of Korea, on a peninsula in southeast Asia, had belonged to Japan before World War II. For several years after Japan's defeat, Soviet troops had occupied the northern half of the peninsula of Korea. During the same period American forces had occupied the southern half. Late in 1947, the UN General Assembly arranged for a commission to hold free elections in both occupation zones. The Soviets refused to cooperate and set up a Communist government in North Korea. But in South Korea, the elections were held and a free republic was proclaimed in August, 1948.

By 1950 the occupation forces of both the United States and the Soviet Union had withdrawn from the divided country. Then suddenly, in June of that year, a North Korean army equipped with Russian tanks and planes invaded South Korea in an attempt to bring all of the peninsula under Communist control.

President Truman was spending a few days in his home town of Independence, Missouri, when news of the North Korean aggression was phoned to him from Washington. He knew that he must return to the capital at once, and he sent word to have the Presidential plane, the *Independence,* made ready for the trip.

As the DC-6 droned its way high above the wheatfields and cornfields of the Middle West toward Washington, President Truman considered what would happen if this new and unexpected Communist aggression in Korea was not stopped. What other small nation would be next? Unless the free nations were willing to help South Korea, the next small nation to be attacked might decide it was useless to try to resist the powerful Communist armies.

The President's thoughts went back nearly twenty years. Had Hitler and Mussolini been stopped in time, World War II might have been avoided. Now unless the Communist dictators were checked, might not their aggressions lead to a third world war?

Soon after his plane landed, the President went into conference with his top advisers. While the conference was going on, the Security Council of the United Nations also was meeting to consider the Korean question. There was no Russian delegate present, for the Russians, angry over another matter, were boycotting the Security Council. The other members, however, passed a resolution accusing the North Koreans of aggression and ordering them to withdraw their troops from South Korea.

But what if the North Koreans ignored this order? What was to be done then? In Europe the Russian Communists had used threats and propaganda—they had even stirred up riots and revolutions— but they had not resorted to full-scale, open warfare. The American foreign-aid programs and Russian fear of NATO had prevented them from attaining their full goal in Europe. The situation in Korea was very different, where a powerful Communist army had launched an armed invasion on a free nation.

The UN resolution condemning the North Koreans was passed on June 25, 1950. Would the United States, as leader of the free world, take action to uphold the authority of the United Nations? President Truman knew that people throughout the world were waiting for the answer. When word came the next day that the South Koreans could not hold out much longer, the President ordered American air and navy forces to go at once to their aid. On June 27 the UN Security Council met again, and called on all UN members to assist South Korea. President Truman then ordered American ground troops to Korea to help the South Koreans fight the Communist aggressors.

Leaders throughout the free world were greatly reassured by President Truman's swift and decisive action, and soon they, too, were sending soldiers to Korea. South Koreans and Americans formed the greater part of the fighting forces, but Britain, the Netherlands, Canada, France, Turkey and a number of other democratic countries also had troops in Korea. In July the United Nations asked the United States to appoint an over-all commander, and General Douglas MacArthur was chosen to head the UN forces.

For the first time in history an army made up of soldiers from many nations was fighting under one banner—the blue and white flag of the United Nations—to oppose aggression.

By late October, the UN troops had pushed the aggressors out of South Korea and were driving deep into North Korean territory. But in November two hundred thousand so-called "volunteers"—Communists from the mainland of China—had arrived to help the North Koreans. UN forces were now greatly outnumbered. The fighting was still going on in December, 1952, when President Truman's term in office was drawing to an end.

One night just before Christmas, the President stood before a brilliantly lighted tree on the White House lawn as he delivered his Christmas greeting to the nation. In his message he spoke of Korea. With conditions as they were in the world, he was convinced that the action of the United Nations had been the best way, the only way, to halt further aggression.

"The struggle there has been long and bitter," he said. "But it has a hopeful meaning because it is the common struggle of many free nations which have joined together to seek a just and lasting peace . . . We seek only a universal peace where all nations shall be free and all peoples shall enjoy their inalienable human rights."

When he had finished his message, President Truman walked back to the White House. He seemed lost in thought, as he stood in the doorway and looked again at the giant Christmas tree. In another month his job as President would be over, and he would be back in Independence, Missouri.

He had no intention of taking it easy, however. He had decided to devote the rest of his life to teaching the coming generation about the American form of government. He would lecture in schools and colleges, and he would write books. In every way he could, he would draw upon his knowledge and experience to help young people learn what had made their country great and what they must do to keep it that way.

As the President turned from the Christmas tree and went indoors, he was thinking of the future with interest and enthusiasm. Peace for the world and a fair deal for every American had been his goals as President. They were the goals he would always strive for.

THE THIRTY-THIRD PRESIDENT *at a Glance*

Harry S. Truman

Born: May 8, 1884

Early life. Harry S. Truman was born in the small town of Lamar, Mo. The initial "S" in his name was given him because his family could not decide whether his middle name should be "Shippe" for one grandfather or "Solomon" for the other grandfather. Harry moved with his family to a farm at Grandview, Mo., when he was 3 and to Independence, Mo., when he was 6. After his graduation from high school at 17 he was a timekeeper on a railway construction job (1901–1902). He worked in Kansas City, Mo., in the mailroom of a newspaper (1902) and as a bank clerk (1903–1906). In 1905 he joined the Missouri National Guard. For 11 years he helped run the family farm at Grandview (1906–1917). During World War I he served (1917–1918) as 1st lieutenant, as captain, and then as major in the Field Artillery. After the war he was a partner in a men's clothing store in Kansas City (1919–1922).

Political career. Truman served as judge of the Jackson, Mo., County Court (1922–1924; 1926–1934) and as U.S. Senator (1935–1945). In 1944 he was nominated for Vice President by the Democrats and was elected. He succeeded to the Presidency when President Franklin D. Roosevelt died (April 12, 1945).

As President (1945–1949; 1949–1953). World War II was drawing to a close when Truman became President. Germany surrendered May 7, 1945; Japan on August 14, 1945. After the war, it soon became clear that Communist Russia was setting out on a program of expansion. Truman believed this Russian policy was a threat to world peace and that the U.S. must help other free nations to resist Communist pressures. The Greek-Turkish Aid Program, proposed by the President (1947) and the European Recovery Program, outlined by his Secretary of State, George Marshall (1947), both helped to check Communist expansion. When Russia blockaded all land routes to West Berlin (1948), American and British planes airlifted food and coal into the city until Russia called off the blockade in 1949. After the President's election (1948) to a second term, some of his domestic measures were passed by Congress, including a law for slum clearance and low-cost housing and a law raising the minimum wage. In foreign affairs, Congress supported a new foreign-aid plan, proposed as "Point Four" in the President's inaugural address (1949). Under the Point Four Program, American technical assistance was given to underdeveloped countries to help them raise their standards of living. In 1949, NATO, or the North Atlantic Treaty Organization, was formed by the U.S., Canada, and 10 European nations. When NATO asked Truman to select a supreme commander for its defense forces in Europe, the President named General Dwight D. Eisenhower (1950). When an army from Communist North Korea invaded the free republic of South Korea (June, 1950), the United Nations called on all UN members to help drive back the aggressors. President Truman immediately ordered American troops to Korea. The Korean conflict was still going on when he finished his second term (January, 1953).

The President's family. The First Lady, Bess Wallace Truman (born 1885), had gone to grade and high school in Independence, Mo., with her future husband. They were married in 1919. The Trumans' only child, Margaret (born 1924), became a concert singer and television actress. She married Clifton Daniel, a New York City journalist (1956).

Other happenings. When Truman was President, the United Nations charter was signed (June, 1945). The Philippines became an independent republic (1946). After a long civil war, Chinese Communists gained complete control of mainland China, and their opponents, the Chinese Nationalists, fled to the offshore island of Formosa (1949). The U.S. did not give official recognition to the Chinese Communists. The 22nd Amendment to the U.S. Constitution, limiting future Presidents to two terms in office, was adopted (1951). Puerto Rico became a U.S. commonwealth (1952). The U.S. exploded the first hydrogen bomb (1952).

Truman as Ex-President. After leaving the Presidency, Truman lectured on history and government in many colleges throughout the country. He also wrote his *Memoirs,* an account of his years as President (2 volumes; published 1955, 1956). In 1961, at the request of President Kennedy, he accepted the chairmanship of the United States Freedom from Hunger Foundation. The letters and documents of Truman's Presidency are preserved for the public at the Harry S. Truman Library in Independence, Mo.

Plans were announced (1962) to erect a statue in Athens, Greece, in commemoration of the Truman Doctrine, which by sending aid to Greece after World War II had saved the country from being taken over by Communists.

DWIGHT EISENHOWER, *Hero*

I'm here, Dwight. They said you wanted to see me." Edgar Eisenhower stood beside the bed looking down at the flushed face of his younger brother.

A few days earlier Dwight had fallen and skinned his knee. With six boys in the family, a skinned knee was nothing unusual, and the fourteen-year-old boy had not even mentioned the injury. But then an infection had set in, his leg began to ache, and he realized he must tell his parents what had happened.

When they saw that his leg was swollen and that dark streaks of purple were spreading from his knee, they sent for the doctor. He was now in the hall talking with Mr. and Mrs. Eisenhower. Dwight, tossing feverishly on his bed, had asked for his brother.

Edgar was not quite two years older than Dwight. Though both boys had quick tempers and often settled their frequent arguments with their fists, they were devoted to each other.

"I'm here, Dwight," Edgar repeated. "Did you want to see me?"

"Listen, Ed," Dwight said. The boy's lips were parched and his voice was weak, but his words were clear and emphatic. "Don't let them do it!"

"Do what?" asked Edgar. "What do you mean, Dwight?"

A flash of anger lit up Dwight's fever-dulled eyes. "The doctor says they'll have to cut off my leg!"

In those days there were no wonder drugs to fight infections. When blood poisoning in an arm or leg threatened to spread to other parts of the body, amputation was usually the only means of saving the patient's life.

"Don't let them do it!" Dwight demanded again. "Promise me you won't. No matter what happens! I'd rather die than lose my leg. Promise me, Ed!"

Cut off Dwight's leg! Edgar could think of nothing more terrible. He knew how he himself would feel, how any boy in their home town of Abilene, Kansas, would feel about an amputation.

By the time the Eisenhower boys were growing up, the cattle drives were over, and Abilene—the old railroad shipping point at the end of the Chisholm Trail—had become a quiet, pleasant town of some five thousand people. But stories of the cowboys and of the deeds of the famous town marshall, Wild Bill Hickok, were still told there. The boys who heard such stories grew up feeling they must be physically strong in order to make their way in life. Yes, Edgar knew exactly how his brother would feel about losing a leg.

Edgar pulled a chair to the side of Dwight's bed and sat down firmly. "I won't let it happen," he said. "Word of honor."

As the hours passed, Dwight's fever rose higher and higher. He became delirious with pain. Edgar allowed the doctor to examine Dwight and give him medicine, but that was all he would let him do. Again and again the doctor appealed to the boys' parents. "Make Edgar leave that room. Let me operate if you want Dwight to live."

Mr. and Mrs. Eisenhower also realized what the loss of a leg would mean to Dwight. Besides, they were a little afraid of surgery. There had been very little illness in their home. Good food and rest and prayer could cure most ills, they believed. And yet the doctor should know, they told each other anxiously. In this crisis they simply did not know what to do.

But Dwight had made a decision, and Edgar had made a promise. For two long days and nights, the older boy stayed beside his brother's bed. On the third day when the doctor entered the room, he gave Edgar an angry look. Then he took Dwight's temperature and carefully examined the infected leg.

Slowly the doctor turned to the parents who were standing, white-faced, in the doorway.

"I can't understand it," he said, and there was awe in his voice. "The leg is much less swollen, and the fever has gone down. Your son is going to be all right."

From then on, Dwight made steady progress. Within a few weeks he was going to school again and was doing his share of the family chores.

There were many chores to be done. Mr. Eisenhower was a mechanical engineer at the Belle Springs Creamery in Abilene. His salary was not large, but fortunately most of the family's food could be raised at home. There were hollyhocks growing in the front yard of the white frame house, but most of the three-acre lot was given over to a vegetable garden, fruit trees and a corn field. There were a cow and a horse in the big barn, and the family also kept chickens.

It was up to the boys to take care of the animals—to milk the cow, curry the horse and feed the chickens. They also helped in the garden. When the farm produced more than the family needed, the boys would load a small wooden wagon with peas, beans, corn and tomatoes and sell the vegetables to people without gardens. When Arthur, the oldest son, went to Kansas City to take a job in a bank, his chores were divided among the five younger brothers. Even the two smallest ones, Earl and Milton, had chores to do.

The boys also helped in the house, and Ike liked to cook. One day he made a pie, but it turned out to be pretty tough. Dwight suspected that was because he and his brothers had played ball with the dough before he rolled it out. It had been great fun to play catch with a ball of dough. Maybe it had been a little hard on the pie.

The next Sunday the family had apple pie for dinner. "It's delicious," said Mrs. Eisenhower approvingly. "Much better than your first pie. What did you do this time that was different?"

Dwight grinned. "I guess it's what I didn't do," he said.

Dwight and Edgar were graduated from high school in the same class, in 1909. Edgar decided to study law. He would work in Abilene during the summer and then go to the University of Michigan.

Dwight wasn't sure what he wanted to do. At the time of the Spanish-American War, when he was eight years old, he had thought that he would like to be a soldier when he grew up, but he had never mentioned this idea at home. His parents were pacifists; opposition to war was part of their religion. Dwight knew that they would not approve of any military ambitions, but the idea of military service had remained in the back of his mind.

There had been times when Dwight had daydreamed of being a famous baseball player, preferably with the Pittsburgh Pirates. But he had to be honest with himself. He was a competent player but not a remarkable one. Anyway, he didn't really want to make baseball his career. He wished he knew what kind of a career he did want. Perhaps he'd better go on to college and then decide.

In order to earn money, Dwight took a job in the creamery

where his father worked. Within a year he was made night engineer, which meant that he had to be at the creamery from six at night until six in the morning. Often there wasn't much work to do, and he was glad when "Swede" Hazlett, a high school friend, stopped in to see him.

Swede's Congressman had recommended him for an appointment to the Naval Academy at Annapolis, providing that he passed the required examinations. Swede was studying hard, and hoped to enter the next year. Many times that summer he talked to Dwight about the wonders of the Naval Academy.

"Say, Ike," he said one night, "why don't you try for Annapolis, too? The government pays all expenses, you know."

Dwight soon caught some of his friend's enthusiasm. Through Senator Bristow, he was given the chance to take a competitive examination, along with the other young men who had applied for recommendations. The Senator would decide, on the basis of the examinations, which of the applicants to recommend for the appointment. This was also true of the applicants for West Point.

Although Dwight really preferred the Naval Academy, in his letter to the Senator he asked for either West Point or Annapolis. Perhaps if one academy turned him down he would be accepted by the other.

After taking the competitive examinations, Dwight was gratified to learn that he had made the highest grade among the applicants for Annapolis. Then came a bitter disappointment. He had just passed his twentieth birthday, and at that time it was a rule of the Naval Academy that no cadet over twenty could be accepted.

But he was not too old to enter the military academy. Later he passed the West Point examination with a very high grade. He was so pleased that he almost forgot that Annapolis had been his first choice.

Since Dwight's parents were pacifists, they could not share in his enthusiasm. When his mother heard the news, she was so unhappy that she hurried to her room to cry where no one could see her. It was a great disappointment that her son should be going to West Point, where young men were trained to be officers in the United States Army. But a boy had a right to choose his life work, she believed. Dwight had chosen to be a soldier, and she would not ask him to change his mind. . . .

Ike, as Dwight soon was known to his classmates, studied hard. No West Point cadet would be able to pass the required technical courses without plenty of study. But the young man from Kansas was no grind. His chief interest at the Academy was athletics, just as it had been in high school. In his first year he played on the plebe football team, and the next year he made the Army football squad as a halfback. His running and tackling in the early games of the season soon had the sports writers predicting that he would have a great football career.

"Watch Eisenhower," they said. "He's got the makings of a great back."

In November, Army played the Carlisle Indian School. The members of the Carlisle team were known for their strength and skill, and their captain was the world-famous athlete Jim Thorpe. Thorpe, a Sac and Fox Indian, was expert on the baseball mound and in track and field events; but his specialty was football, and the newspapers that fall were calling him one of the three or four greatest halfbacks football had ever produced. The members of the Army team had been looking forward to the chance to play Carlisle, and they fought hard during every minute of the game. But they could do little to stop the rush of Jim Thorpe and his Indians, and the game wound up with the score Carlisle 27—Army 6. Ike emerged from the game battered and bruised, but he had the satisfaction of knowing that he had played a good game. With one of his tackles he had downed the great Jim Thorpe.

A week later the Army played Tufts. This time the Army won. But during the game Ike wrenched his knee so badly that a substitute had to be sent in to replace him.

"You'll be out of football for the rest of the season," the doctor said as he taped up Ike's knee. "But it's not too bad an injury. Just don't do anything for a while that might make it worse."

The doctor's verdict ruled out Ike's chance to play in the final and most important game of the season: the Army-Navy conflict. Ike was badly disappointed, but a football player has to expect injuries. By the next fall, his doctor assured him, his knee would be in good shape again and he would be ready for another football season.

Before long the knee had improved so much that the doctor said he might resume his riding lessons. The young cadet was cautioned, however, to be careful in mounting and dismounting. After Ike arrived at the cadet riding hall, the riding master looked at him scornfully. He had noticed how awkwardly and slowly the young man had mounted his horse.

"What's the matter? Are you afraid of a horse? That was disgraceful. Dismount and mount again immediately."

Ike was too furious and too proud to explain about his knee. His eyes were blazing and his mouth was grim as he swung himself off his saddle. He stayed through the entire lesson, mounting and dismounting many times on orders from the riding master.

And that was the end of Ike's football career. For weeks his knee was in a cast, and though he later coached a plebe football squad, his own playing days were over. But he had already taken part in enough games to win his "A," and the name Eisenhower can be seen today on a bronze plaque in the West Point gymnasium, along with the names of the other "A" winning athletes in the class of 1915.

The knee injury that ended Ike's football career came close to ending his Army career also. During his last two years at West Point, although his knee improved, it did not heal perfectly. As graduation day approached, the West Point doctors wondered whether it would be better not to let him have an Army commission.

"Eisenhower may always have a trick knee," one of the doctors said. "It might give way some time when he is on active service."

Except for his knee, Ike was husky and strong, and the doctors reported that he met all other physical fitness tests. It was decided that he should get his commission after all.

"We saw in Eisenhower," one of his West Point instructors said many years later, "a not uncommon type—a man who would thoroughly enjoy his Army life, giving both to duty and recreation their fair values. We did not see in him a man who would throw himself into his job so completely that nothing else would matter."

Ike himself had no expectation of rising to the top of his profession. A few members of his class might eventually become generals, he realized. His friend and football teammate, Omar Bradley, for example, would probably make it. As for himself, Ike hoped that someday, maybe, he would be a colonel.

Stationed in Texas, Ike met and married pretty Mamie Doud, a girl from Denver. Promoted to first lieutenant, he became a captain shortly after the United States entered the First World War in April, 1917. Eager to go overseas, he was sent instead to one training camp after another in the United States. Tanks were something new in warfare. At Camp Colt near Gettysburg, Pennsylvania, Ike taught the six thousand men under his command how to use the new vehicle in battle. After the war he was promoted to major.

As one of his first assignments during the post-war years he was sent to the Panama Canal to serve as executive officer under General

Fox Conner. General Conner was not only a brilliant officer but a serious student of history, and he was convinced that nothing had been really settled by the recent war.

"There's bound to be another world war in twenty or thirty years," he told his young assistant. "We'll be in that war, and, as before, we'll be allied with other countries. Moreover, if the allies are going to win that war, their leaders will have to learn to work together under a unified command."

For ten years after Major Eisenhower left Panama, he had a variety of assignments and attended several advanced military schools. Although he did well and learned a great deal, his work and study were routine, and he was much pleased in 1935 when he was sent to the Philippine Islands. Here he was senior military assistant to General Douglas MacArthur. It was Ike's job to help the general establish a military organization for the islands, which were scheduled to become completely independent of the United States in a few years.

While serving in the Philippines, Ike became a lieutenant colonel. His friendliness and tact made him popular with the Filipino people, but in the fall of 1939, he felt that he must leave. War had just broken out in Europe, and Ike was convinced that Fox Conner's predictions were now coming true. There was going to be another global war, and the United States would become involved. If his country must start preparing for that war, Ike wanted to be on hand to help with the preparations. After his return home, however, he found that very few people shared his concern.

It was only after Hitler's armies had conquered Denmark and Norway, and swept through Holland and Belgium the following spring, and after France itself had fallen to the Nazis, that most Americans became worried. Gradually at first, and then with increasing swiftness, the country began to prepare for whatever the future might bring.

In the fall of 1941 large-scale war games were held in Louisiana between the Third Army and the Second Army. The Third Army "won," and Eisenhower, recently appointed Colonel and serving under General Kruger, was highly praised by the military "high brass" for the important part he had played in the maneuvers.

He was also made a brigadier, or one-star, general, but outside of the Army he was still practically unknown. The reporters could not even get his name right. At the end of the Louisiana maneuvers his picture appeared in a newspaper in a group photograph. The names of the other officers in the picture were given correctly, but Ike was identified as "Lt. Col. D. D. Ersenbeing."

"At least they got the initials right," Ike remarked later.

Ike had worked extremely hard while on the maneuvers, and he continued to work for long hours every day. Very carefully he sifted the information that had been gained from the war games, and wrote long reports. On Sunday, December 7, 1941, feeling weary and worn out, he decided to take a nap after lunch. He had just fallen into a deep sleep when there was a knock on his door.

"Well, what is it?" the general demanded. "Come in, come in."

One of his aides entered the room. "Sir," he said, "the news has just come. Pearl Harbor is being attacked by Japanese planes!"

The United States was now at war. By December 12, five days after the attack on America's great naval base in Hawaii, General Eisenhower was on his way to Washington, D.C. His orders to report to the War Department had come from General George Marshall, the Chief of Staff of the Army. Ike had been hoping for a troop command, but it looked as if he would be sitting out World War II at a desk in the War Department.

For six months Ike did sit at a desk, working from early morning until late at night on plans for defensive strategy in the Pacific and for future offense actions in Europe. Then one day in June General Marshall said to him, "Eisenhower, you are going to command the European Theater."

In nonmilitary language, this meant that General Eisenhower was to command all the United States forces which would be taking part in the war in Europe against the Axis powers. Ike was astonished to receive what would eventually be an immense command.

But General Marshall knew that Ike was both tactful and persuasive. He was self-confident and optimistic—the kind of leader who would inspire confidence in his associates.

A short time later General Eisenhower left for London. England was to be the base of operations for an invasion of northwestern Europe, which was under German control. But to cross the English Channel and conquer Hitler's Europe would be a mighty undertaking. Months would pass before the necessary troops and supplies could be sent to Britain from America.

After careful consideration, it was decided to try to conquer North Africa while waiting for the massive build-up of supplies and men needed for the cross-channel invasion.

Both American and British forces were to take part in the African expedition, and General Eisenhower was named Allied Commander-in-Chief. On the night of November 7, 1942, great Allied fleets arrived in the harbors of Casablanca, Oran and Algiers, three ports in North Africa. The next morning American and British troops poured ashore. Bitter warfare had been going on in this important region between British and German troops, but after several more months of hard fighting Tunis and other towns fell to the Allies. The Germans were finally driven out of Africa. The Allied armies then invaded Sicily, where the Axis was defeated in six weeks.

Meanwhile, on the Italian mainland, the people had grown weary of war and of the harsh rule of their dictator, Benito Mussolini. He was ousted from his office and imprisoned, although later he escaped. A new Italian government surrendered unconditionally, just as the Allies were about to invade the country.

But there were many German forces in Italy, and they had no intention of surrendering. After a hard-fought battle, the Allies finally gained a beachhead south of Naples. The city was soon captured. But from then on the Allies, in their northward march up through Italy, met stubborn German resistance all the way.

Meanwhile, preparations had been going on in England for the great Allied invasion across the English Channel. By the fall of 1943, it had been decided that this invasion, known by the code name of "Overlord," was to take place the following spring. The expedition, made up of American, British, and Canadian troops, as well as a number of other units formed by men who had escaped from their Nazi-conquered lands, was to serve under one over-all command. Inasmuch as the United States would be supplying the largest share of the manpower and equipment, Winston Churchill, the British Prime Minister, had suggested that an American should be named as the Supreme Commander, and President Roosevelt selected Ike.

No soldier in history had ever been given a more difficult assignment than Dwight D. Eisenhower. Hitler had had four years to turn western Europe into a great fortress. But a successful Allied invasion would shorten the war and put an end forever, it was believed, to the Nazi tyranny. That being the case, Ike told his old West Point friend, Omar Bradley, the invasion would succeed—because it had to. On Ike's recommendation, General Bradley, who had held one of the top commands in Africa, was now placed in charge of the American ground forces preparing to invade the continent. He was one of several thousand officers, one of many times that many soldiers from a number of different nations, serving under General Eisenhower. The success of the undertaking depended on their willingness to work together.

"I am almost fanatic in my belief," Ike once said, "that only as we pull together, each of us in the job given him, are we going to defend and sustain the priceless things for which we are fighting."

By March, 1944, when Ike set up his headquarters in a trailer near the English Channel, most of England looked like an armed camp. Airports had been built. Ports were jammed with ships. In many of the villages there were more American soldiers than Englishmen. There was a feeling of tenseness in the air. The troops realized there was to be an invasion soon, but few knew where and when it would take place. The decision to try to invade Normandy on the northwest coast of France was still a carefully-guarded secret.

In making final plans General Eisenhower and his staff officers were helped immeasurably by members of the French resistance movement. At great risk to themselves the "underground" sent short-wave messages—in code, of course—giving the Allied commanders important information concerning the enemy. At one of the meetings where the Supreme Commander and his staff were making final plans, Winston Churchill was present.

"Generals," he said, "I have every confidence in you. The destiny of the world is in your hands."

The date for the invasion—"D-Day," the officers called it—had been tentatively set for June 5, 1944. On that night there would be a late-rising moon which would make it easier for paratroopers and other airborne troops to be dropped behind the lines. The tide would be right for the landing of the thousands of soldiers who would cross the channel on ships. And then because of weather— the worst weather on the channel in twenty years—D-Day had to be postponed.

On the night of the fourth, General Eisenhower and his staff officers met with three meteorologists, or weather experts, from the British Royal Air Force. What were the weather prospects for June 6? Would the skies clear by then? the general asked. The meteorologists replied that the forecast was for better flying weather the night of the fifth, and the following morning. During that period the planes could take to the air; but by noon the next day the skies would be overcast again. There would probably be a very rough sea, making it more difficult for the seaborne troops to reach the Normandy beaches.

The general's face was white and drawn. Whatever he decided, he would be taking a grave risk. Bad weather might cause the expedition to fail, even after months of careful planning; but if he postponed D-Day again, it would be several weeks before there would be the right combination of moonlight and tides for the invasion of the Normandy coast. With thousands of soldiers feeling tense after weeks of waiting, and curious as to what was going to happen next, the secret could not be kept much longer. And secrecy was necessary for the success of the plan.

"I don't like it," said General Eisenhower slowly, "but what else can we do? I am going to give the order to go ahead."

The night of the fifth, the general stood in the doorway of his trailer looking up at the dark sky. The first planes were taking off for France to drop the parachute fighters behind the lines. The task of the parachute troops would be to capture the crossroads and open the way for the main body of the invaders. By dawn of June 6— D-Day—hundreds of ships would have crossed the channel. How many of the men disembarking from those ships in the face of enemy gunfire would reach the shore? How many would never come back? There were tears in the general's eyes as he turned back into his trailer.

After that there was nothing to do but wait. Nor was the general the only one who waited. With the invasion launched, there was no longer any reason to keep it a secret. Londoners heard the news as they were going to work the next morning. The American people read it in their newspapers, a few hours later. In Philadelphia the Liberty Bell began to toll as it had on another historic day in July, 1776.

Seated in his trailer, General Eisenhower sat hunched over his radio hour after hour. At last came the news that he had been waiting for. Details were still lacking, but the Allied Troops had established a beachhead on the Normandy coast. He immediately broadcast a message, beamed to the captive countries across the channel.

"People of western Europe," he said, "a landing was made this morning on the coast of France. This landing is part of the concerted United Nations plan for the liberation of Europe. . . . Although the initial assault may not have been made in your country, the hour of your liberation is approaching. . . . Great battles lie ahead. I call upon all who love freedom to stand with us. Keep your faith . . . together we will achieve victory."

After the general established his headquarters in France, the Allied soldiers continued to win victories. Town after town—in France, in Belgium, in Holland, and in Luxembourg—was liberated by the Allied troops.

The Allied victories did not come easily. In December the Germans made a desperate counterattack, and many Allied lives were lost in the Battle of the Bulge. After ten days the Allies began driving the Germans back toward the borders of their own country.

Then the situation became hopeless for the once-powerful Nazis. Russian troops were battering Germany on the eastern front. General Eisenhower's troops entered from the west. Hoping to shorten the war, he issued a proclamation. He reminded the Germans that further resistance was hopeless and would only add to their misery. But many of them also lived in the grip of fear—fear of the Nazi secret police—and they continued to fight.

Soon afterward General Ike visited his first concentration camp. Although he had heard about the brutality in such camps, he was deeply shocked when he saw the evidence of it with his own eyes. Fortunately, such horrors had now ceased. The man chiefly responsible, Adolf Hitler, committed suicide when he realized that his mad schemes to dominate the world were doomed to failure.

Eight days later Field Marshall Alfred Jodl of the German Army appeared at the Allied headquarters in Reims, France. Here he signed the terms of an unconditional surrender. Ike's Chief of Staff, General Bedell Smith, signed for the United States, and then conducted the German officer before the Supreme Commander. The American general's eyes were like cold blue steel when he glanced up from his desk.

"Do you understand the provisions of the document you have just signed?"

"*Ja,*" the field marshall replied.

"Then," said the general coldly, "you will officially and personally be held responsible if the terms of this surrender are violated . . . That is all."

It wasn't all, so far as the liberated countries were concerned. Western Europe was free after years of slavery. The people rejoiced, and the man they desired to honor above all others was General Ike.

When Dwight D. Eisenhower returned to the United States in June, 1945, a few weeks after Germany's surrender, he received a hero's welcome. In New York City more than four million people lined the jampacked streets to cheer the man who had led the Allies to victory in Europe.

"Ike! Ike!" the people shouted. In the days that followed, the cry was repeated by other welcoming crowds—in the nation's capital, in Abilene, Kansas, where the general had lived as a boy, and in a number of other towns and cities. Although he seemed to be enjoying himself hugely, he looked forward to retiring. During twenty-nine years of marriage he and Mamie had lived in temporary quarters in many places, but they had never had a permanent home of their own. Now at last, they thought, they would be able to buy a house and settle down.

But the general soon found that his country, which he had served for thirty years as an Army officer, still needed him. In November, when George C. Marshall resigned as Army Chief of Staff, Dwight D. Eisenhower was appointed to succeed him. In 1948 General Eisenhower retired from active duty in the Army and became president of Columbia University, but he soon went back into military duty at the request of President Truman.

Because of Russian ambitions to expand the Communist system, Europe was threatened with another war, and it was in the hope of stopping further aggression that the North Atlantic Treaty Organization (NATO) was formed. Dwight Eisenhower was asked to become Supreme Commander, and in December, 1950, he flew to Paris, to take command of the NATO forces.

Even with the country's favorite hero thousands of miles away in France, the general's popularity seemed to be increasing month by month. For several years there had been a great deal of talk of having him for President. When the suggestion was first made to him, Ike had brushed it aside.

"Why can't a simple soldier be left alone to carry out his orders?" he had asked.

But "We like Ike" soon became a campaign cry that swept the country. Finally, early in 1952 "Ike" gave in to the popular clamor, resigned his NATO command, and returned to the United States to campaign for the Presidency on the Republican ticket. From the moment he gave his consent to run, his nomination was practically a certainty, and so great was his popularity that his election followed almost as a matter of course.

From the time Ike took office, he let it be known that he would do everything in his power to work for world peace, and he resolved to show the Soviet Union that the United States sincerely wished to end the cold war.

As the months passed, however, the two great powers in the world, the Soviet Union and the United States, became more fearful and distrustful of each other. Each nation was developing new and terrible weapons. President Eisenhower feared that if they ever went to war they might destroy themselves and a large part of the world besides.

Some drastic action must be taken, he decided, when in July, 1955, he flew to Geneva, Switzerland. Here he was to take part in a "summit" conference with the leaders of several other governments, the British, French and Soviet, and their aides and assistants. When he stepped off his plane he was warmly welcomed by Swiss government officials.

"I came to Europe once before," he told them, "with an army, a navy, an air force, with a single purpose: to destroy Naziism . . . This time I come armed with something far more powerful: the good will of America—the great hopes of America—the aspirations of America for peace."

In his opening speech before the conference, President Eisenhower suggested that the United States and the Soviet Union give each other a complete blueprint of their military establishments. Representatives from the two countries were to be allowed to inspect one another's military preparations from the air, taking photographs of military installations. By this simple "open skies" plan, the President urged, the two leading powers in the world could provide against the possibility of surprise attack.

"It is not always necessary," he said, "that we should think alike and believe alike before we work together. The essential thing is that none should attempt by force or trickery to make his beliefs prevail." What *was* necessary, he added, was that new forces should be put in motion to set the nations "truly on the path to peace."

Most of the people who heard that speech were deeply impressed by the sincerity of the President's "open skies" proposals. After the conference closed, the foreign ministers of the four countries represented continued to meet. The meetings, however, ended in a deadlock. The Russians refused to allow representatives from other countries to visit their military bases and other military establishments. The Americans and their Western Allies refused to accept Russian promises unless the Russians would guarantee, by opening their country to inspection, that their promises were being kept. There had been too many broken promises in the past.

During the next few years relations between the two great powers blew hot and cold. By 1959, the tensions had relaxed enough so that Premier Khrushchev accepted the President's invitation to visit the United States. The two leaders agreed that peaceful means must be found to settle the problems that divided them, and plans were made for another summit conference in Paris the following June.

Unfortunately, just before the conference began, an American U-2 reconnaissance plane was brought down over Soviet territory. Such flights had been undertaken after the Soviet refusal to accept the President's "open skies" proposals at the Geneva conference. The flights were considered necessary by American authorities; the pictures obtained might prove vital for defense if the United States should be attacked. But Premier Khrushchev bitterly denounced the President, and the conference was abandoned.

Meanwhile in 1956 Dwight D. Eisenhower had been elected to a second term. His personal popularity remained high, not only in his own country but in other countries, too. Throughout his eight years in office, this President, who had gained his first fame as a soldier, continued to have one overriding ambition. He wanted to bring permanent peace to the world. One way he tried to do this was by personal diplomacy. In the course of a number of good-will trips to twenty-six different nations, he traveled more than 100,000 miles. To people in Canada, in Latin America, in Europe, in Africa, in the Philippine Islands and on the mainland of Asia he carried a message of friendship from the people of the United States.

The people in almost every town and city that the President visited gave him an enthusiastic welcome. In Formosa, familiar signs were displayed: WE LIKE IKE. In Ankara a young Turk also had a sign which he held up for the President to see. It had been crudely lettered in crayon, and the English was garbled, but it expressed what many people in many lands were thinking: IKE LIKE WE. In Buenos Aires, the capital of Argentina, great crowds warmed to the friendly smile of the simple, unpretentious man who had been one of the great heroes of World War II.

"Hereafter," said one New York newspaper, commenting on the President's good-will trip to South America, "in the memories of many thousands of Latin Americans, Uncle Sam will look like President Eisenhower, a man who did not pretend good will but honestly felt it."

In spite of many disappointments, Dwight D. Eisenhower continued to work for world peace, and after eight years as President he found comfort in the knowledge that war had been avoided. He and his wife were looking forward to living in the farmhouse which they had purchased and remodeled near Gettysburg, Pennsylvania. But he was still chiefly concerned about what was going to happen in the years ahead. In a radio and TV address three days before he left office, he reminded the American people that they had a good right to be proud of their accomplishments throughout their long adventure in free government.

"Understandably proud . . . yet we realize," he said, "that America's leadership and prestige depend, not merely upon our unmatched material progress, riches and military strength, but on how we use our power in the interests of world peace and human betterment."

THE THIRTY-FOURTH PRESIDENT *at a Glance*

Dwight David Eisenhower

Born: Oct. 14, 1890

Early life. Dwight D. Eisenhower was born in Denison, Texas. When he was a few months old, his family returned to Kansas where they had lived previously. Dwight was the third of seven sons, one of whom died in infancy. Ike, as Dwight soon became known, grew up in Abilene, Kansas, where his father worked as a mechanical engineer in a creamery. After graduating from high school (1909), Ike also worked in the creamery for a while. In 1911 he entered West Point and was graduated in 1915.

Military career. After receiving his commission, Dwight was assigned to the 19th Infantry at Fort Sam Houston, Texas. He was promoted to first lieutenant in 1916. He advanced through grades to General of the Army (5 stars) in December, 1944, having served in the Panama Canal Zone, France, in the Philippines (1935–1939) and (after World War II broke out) in Africa and Europe.

In World War II. After the Japanese attack on Pearl Harbor, Eisenhower was summoned to Washington to serve in the War Plans Division of the War Department. In February, 1942, he became head of this division. When the War Plans Division was replaced by the Operations Division a short time later, he became its first head. In June, 1942, Eisenhower was assigned to the European area as commanding general of all American troops in Europe. He was commander of the Allied forces for the invasion of North Africa (November, 1942). In the summer and fall of 1943 he directed the invasions of Sicily and Italy. He was appointed Supreme Commander of the Allied forces in western Europe (December, 1943) and commanded the D-Day invasion of Normandy (June 6, 1944). On May 7, 1945, he received Germany's surrender at Reims. He commanded the U.S. occupation troops in Europe until November, 1945, when he returned to the U.S. to become Chief of Staff of the Army. He served as president of Columbia University (1948–1952), and then was called back to active duty in the Army to command the NATO forces in Europe. He held this post until May, 1952, when he resigned to campaign for the Presidency on the Republican ticket.

As President (1953–1957; 1957–1961). Eisenhower, unlike earlier Presidents, set up a "staff system" (very much like that he had used as a general), making each Cabinet member and other important executives in the government responsible for the work in particular areas. He was a moderate in his domestic policies but retained most of the reforms brought about by his two Democratic predecessors. In his "Atoms for Peace" address to the UN (1953) he urged that nations with atomic materials and information cooperate to use atomic energy for peaceful purposes. At the "Big Four" summit conference in Geneva (1955) the President made his "open skies" proposal for disarmament, suggesting that the U.S. and the Soviet Union open their military establishments for mutual aerial inspection. After prolonged negotiations, the Russians refused.

The President suffered a heart attack (1955), and in 1956 he underwent surgery. He recovered from both illnesses and was elected to a second term (1956). The following year (1957), in an address before Congress, the President warned that the U.S. would intervene if the Communists tried to extend their conquests further in the Middle East. The Eisenhower Doctrine, as it was called, was applied in Jordan (1957) and in Lebanon (1958) where revolts seemed to be Communist-inspired. In an effort to reduce tensions between the U.S. and the Soviet Union, the President invited Nikita Khrushchev, premier of the Soviet Union, to visit the U.S. (1959). Plans were made to hold another summit conference in Paris. As the conference was about to begin (May, 1960), an American U-2 reconnaissance plane was brought down over Soviet territory and Premier Khrushchev broke up the conference. As President, Eisenhower made several good will tours to distant lands. On his final tour (1960) before leaving office, his proposed visit to Japan had to be canceled because of student riots against military alliances. In the countries he visited, however, he was received with honor and enthusiasm.

The President's family. Mamie Doud Eisenhower (born 1896) was a popular First Lady. One son, Dwight David, died at an early age. The other, John Sheldon Doud (born 1923) attended West Point and served in the Korean War.

Other happenings. A few months after Eisenhower became President, a truce was signed (July, 1953) which ended the fighting in Korea. The U.S. Department of Health, Education and Welfare was established (1953) by Congress. The U.S. Supreme Court ruled

(1954) that racial segregation in public schools was unconstitutional. SEATO (Southeast Asia Treaty Organization) was formed in 1954 by the U.S. and seven other nations (Australia, France, Great Britain, New Zealand, the Philippine Islands, Pakistan and Thailand) to resist threats from Communist China and prevent conquest by Communism in the Far East. Early in 1955 Congress passed a resolution authorizing the use of U.S. armed forces to protect the Chinese Nationalists on the island of Formosa, in case they were attacked by Chinese Communists from the mainland. Two large labor organizations, the American Federation of Labor and the Congress of Industrial Organizations, with a combined membership of 15,000,000, merged under the name AFL-CIO (1955). A vaccine to give protection against polio, developed by Dr. Jonas E. Salk, was pronounced a success (1955) after extensive experiments. A Civil Rights Act passed by Congress (1957) established a Civil Rights Commission to investigate any cases where Americans may have been denied voting rights and equal protection of the laws because of color, race, religion or national origin. An economic recession (1957–1958) resulted in more than 5 million unemployed. Recovery from the recession began soon afterward. The St. Lawrence Seaway was opened (1959). Toward the close of the Eisenhower administration, the U.S. broke off diplomatic relations with Cuba after the Castro regime became closely allied with the U.S.S.R. (January 3, 1961).

Population and growth. Two new states, Alaska and Hawaii, were added (1959) to the Union, bringing the total number to fifty. According to the 1960 census, the U.S. population was over 179,300,000.

Eisenhower as author and ex-President. Eisenhower's book *Crusade in Europe* (1948) told of his experiences in World War II. After leaving the White House, the former President and his wife retired to a farm which they had purchased near Gettysburg, Pa. The home in Abilene, Kan., where the Eisenhower brothers had grown up, has been preserved, and a museum has been built close by to house the Eisenhower trophies and medals.

JOHN KENNEDY said, *"Let Us Begin"*

LYNDON JOHNSON said, *"Let Us Continue"*

When Jack and Joe Kennedy were children, Jack wanted to be a writer. Joe was the one who wanted to be President. He was smart and he was handsome. Whatever he did, he did well. As the eldest of nine children, he considered it his privilege and his duty, especially when his father was away from home, to boss the younger members of the family. When they went sailing or swimming at their summer home in Hyannis Port, Massachusetts, on Cape Cod, it was Joe who looked after the smaller ones and he expected them to obey without question.

None of them seemed to mind very much except Jack. He was only two years younger than Joe and did not like to be bossed. The two boys often got into fights, and Joe, who was bigger and stronger, always won. Jack had been sick a great deal and was rather frail. But he never lacked courage. He never gave up. Whether the brothers were wrestling or playing touch football or taking part in a sailing race, each had the same grim determination to win.

It was the same way when they went to Harvard. Joe was an upper-classman when Jack entered as a freshman in the fall of 1936. Again, the younger brother was living in the shadow of the older one. Joe was hero of the varsity football team. Jack, a tall, skinny six-footer, tried out for the freshman team. He and a friend were practicing a forward pass one day, as Joe watched.

"You'd better forget about football," Joe advised. "You don't weigh enough, and you're going to get yourself banged up."

Jack flushed with anger, but later he had to admit that Joe was right. Jack did get himself "banged up." During practice one day, his back hurt badly. A disc had been ruptured in the lower part of his spine, and he was in great pain. Even after he felt better, he knew he would never make the varsity. But he could still swim, and he became a member of the Harvard swimming team.

During the next two years Jack seemed more interested in sports than in his studies, but then something happened that changed his point of view. Joseph Kennedy, Sr., had been appointed ambassador to Great Britain, and Jack and Joe spent their summer vacation at the American Embassy in London. Grave and exciting events were taking place in 1938. Hitler, dictator of Germany, was making more and more demands of the neighboring countries, and it was feared that he might plunge Europe into war. When Jack returned to college for his junior year, he did much better in his classes. He was majoring in government and taking courses in history, and he could see a definite connection between his studies and what was happening in the world.

"Kennedy is surprisingly able," one of his professors said, "when he gets down to work."

Though Jack found his classes interesting, he decided he could learn more by viewing history close up, and he received permission to spend the second half of his junior year abroad. In several months of travel he visited France, Poland and Russia, among other countries. He talked with all kinds of people and saw for himself the tensions building up in Europe. He was not surprised when—shortly after his return to Harvard in September, 1939—World War II broke out.

During his senior year Jack wrote a thesis about England's lack of preparation. In spite of the Nazi menace, he said, most Englishmen had refused to face the fact that they might become involved in war again. Jack's professors thought so highly of his thesis, and he did such good work in his classes, that he was graduated with honors the following June. From London came a cable from his father.

"Two things I always knew about you," the cable read. "One that you are smart. Two that you are a swell guy. Love, Dad."

⛉

The summer of 1940 was one the Kennedys would always remember. The parents and their nine children—everyone from Joe, now twenty-five and a student at Harvard Law School, down to eight-year-old Teddy—came back to Hyannis Port for a reunion. They sailed, went swimming, and played football on the lawn. Those glorious weeks in the big, comfortable cottage overlooking the waters of Cape Cod were the last time they would all be together.

Much had happened before another summer rolled around. Jack had rewritten his thesis and expanded it into a book called *Why England Slept*. It soon became a best seller, an unusual honor for a book by a young man one year out of college. Joe, believing the United States would become involved in the war, had joined the Navy as an aviation cadet. Jack tried to join but was turned down. He tried the Army and was turned down again. Doctors said that his back, which he had hurt playing football, could not stand the strain of combat.

Jack refused to give up. After five months of exercises to strengthen his back muscles he was finally able to pass the Navy fitness test. Late in 1942 he was assigned to a motor torpedo boat squadron, made up of small patrol torpedo boats—an ideal assignment for a young man who had been handling small boats since he was a child.

And those PT boats, as they were called, were really something to handle. Made of plywood, they offered little protection to their crews in battle. But a PT boat was fast. It could dodge through heavy gunfire from a warship, and fire its own torpedoes at close range. Then it could escape, if the crew was lucky. "Fire—dash—pray!" was a popular saying among the sailors who rode the small, dangerous craft.

After weeks of intensive training, Jack shipped out of San Francisco for the Solomon Islands in the South Pacific. In April, 1943, he was given command of his own boat, the PT-109. On the night of August 1, he was on patrol duty with a crew of ten enlisted men and two ensigns.

As Jack stood at the wheel he must have thought of Joe, thousands of miles away in England. As a Navy lieutenant and pilot, Joe had flown a number of successful missions against the enemy in Europe. Well, Jack was also in the Navy—a lieutenant junior grade. He had a part in the vast combination air-sea-ground counterattack against the enemy in the Pacific.

On that night the PT-109 was one of a squadron of PT boats patrolling the stretch of water known as Blackett Strait. The engines were muffled as the boats passed close to the shores of islands still held by the Japanese, and the crews kept a sharp lookout for enemy destroyers. On Lieutenant Kennedy's boat, Ensign George Ross stood at the bow peering through a pair of binoculars.

Suddenly Ross turned and pointed toward a vague shape in the darkness. It was a Japanese destroyer. As Jack spun the wheel to prepare for an attack, there was a sound of splintering wood. The larger boat had rammed the smaller boat, and the force of the impact threw

Jack violently to the deck. He looked up to see the destroyer slicing through the PT-109, splitting it in half. With a blinding flash, the gasoline ignited and part of the boat caught fire.

"So this is how it feels to be killed," thought Jack.

But he was not killed. He was hardly aware of being hurt. After the destroyer had dashed off into the darkness, everything was quiet except for the low hissing sound of burning gasoline. The gasoline had spread over the surface of the water, making it appear that the water was on fire. The part of the boat where the fire had broken out had sunk. The part to which Jack clung was half submerged.

The two ensigns and four crewmen also were clinging to the hull. What had happened to the others? Jack called, and was answered by several feeble shouts a hundred yards away. He and the two ensigns swam to the rescue.

The life jackets the crewmen were wearing had kept them afloat, but the men had been stunned by the force of the ramming. Several were almost unconscious from inhaling the gasoline fumes. The engineman, Patrick McMahon, aged thirty-seven and called "Pop" by the younger men, had been badly burned. When Jack reached him, Pop protested.

"Go on, skipper," he said. "I've had it."

Jack paid no attention. Fighting a strong current, he towed Pop back to what was left of the PT-109, and then went to help other members of the crew. Finally, ten of his men were accounted for. Two were missing. They had gone down when the boat was rammed.

For the rest of the night the survivors tried to keep their balance on the slanting deck. The boat was slowly sinking, and daylight brought the danger of capture. The shipwrecked crew was in enemy territory, in plain view of several islands. There might be a Japanese base on one of the larger islands. Others seemed to be mere dots on the water, but beyond them was a green oval of land with tall trees. It looked big enough to shelter eleven men but too small—Lieutenant Kennedy hoped—to interest the Japanese. Anyway, the risk must be taken. His men could not stay where they were.

Two of the crew could not swim, but a plank was found to serve as a float. With four men on each side, and a ninth man at the end, they could hold on to the plank with one hand and paddle with the other. All of them could kick. Lieutenant Kennedy took charge of Patrick McMahon. After easing the badly burned man into the water, he grabbed a strap from Pop's life jacket. Holding the strap between his teeth, he towed the injured man through the water toward the island three and a half miles away.

It was a painful swim for both of them. Pop's body felt as if it were on fire, and for Jack every stroke was torture. His fall on the deck had aggravated his old back injury, and the pain was getting worse. None of his companions knew how badly he had been hurt, Pop least of all.

"Is it much farther, Mr. Kennedy?" he asked.

"Not much farther," Lieutenant Kennedy replied.

With the strap clenched between his teeth, he could not keep his lips closed tight, and the salt water he had to swallow made him ill. Occasionally he stopped to rest, and it took nearly four hours to reach the island. Jack lay on the beach, too tired to move, his feet still in the water.

But he and Pop did not dare to lie for long on the exposed beach; they would make easy targets for an enemy plane. After a few minutes they dragged themselves to the safety of some bushes. From there Jack saw his other shipmates swimming with their plank. He stood up and waved. A few minutes later they were all together again—eleven weary men who had been without food or fresh water for fifteen hours. As they crouched under the bushes, no one spoke. There was only the sound of their loud breathing.

Then came the hum of an approaching motor. Peering from their hide-out, they saw that it was a Japanese boat. Had they been seen? Were they to be captured after all?

But the motor boat did not stop. The sound of its engine grew fainter in the distance.

Jack's back was throbbing, but at least his men were safe—for a while. He had brought them through their first ordeal. He had brought Pop McMahon through.

Even Joe could not have done better.

However, the enemy was too close to risk a long stay on the island, and after a brief rest Jack started out on another long swim. With him he took a ship's lantern wrapped securely in a kapok life jacket and fastened to his belt. Perhaps he would be able to signal an American boat patrolling the waters in the darkness. The following night Ensign Ross tried the same plan. Neither he nor Jack had any success. Both returned to their companions exhausted and numb with cold.

By the third day the situation was desperate. All of the men were ill, and they had to have food. The few coconuts found on the island were soon gone. The castaways swam to another island where they could see coconut palms growing. Again Jack towed Pop McMahon. Pop's condition was pitiful, but he never complained.

Nor did the young lieutenant, though by now he was in constant pain. In the distance he could see Rendova Peak, rising high above the American PT base. It was less than forty miles away, but the men had almost given up hope of being rescued.

Then, the next afternoon, they were found by two natives. The natives, whose names were Biuku and Erono, could speak very little English, but they seemed friendly. Jack husked a coconut, and with his knife scratched a message on the smooth part of the shell. "Eleven alive," he wrote. "Natives know position. Kennedy."

He handed over the shell and pointed in the direction of the American base. "Rendova, Rendova," he said.

The natives nodded and climbed into their dugout canoe. They pushed out into the water, but Jack wondered if they had really understood. . . .

As it turned out, his message did finally reach Rendova, and a PT boat came to the rescue of the castaways. Ill and half starved, they arrived back at the base seven days after the ramming of their boat. They were warmly welcomed. The other PT crews in their squadron, after seeing the 109 catch fire, had not believed it possible anyone could survive in that flaming sea.

Later, Lieutenant John Kennedy was awarded the Navy and Marine Corps medals for his "courage, endurance and excellent leadership" which "contributed to the saving of several lives." Saying nothing about his injured back, he volunteered for another tour of duty, but the pain steadily grew worse. He also had malaria, and was finally sent back to the United States. In the spring of 1944, he entered the Chelsea Naval Hospital, not far from the family summer home at Hyannis Port. One day his Harvard roommate, Torbert Macdonald, came to see him. In the doorway, Torbert stopped short in surprise.

Jack had had a spinal operation and lay on his bed, strapped to a board. His skin was of a yellowish tinge because of the anti-malaria drug he had taken, and he had lost thirty-five pounds. He raised a bony wrist and waved.

"How are you, Jack?" asked Torby, trying to sound cheerful.

"I feel great," said Jack.

"Great?" asked Torby.

Jack managed a grin. "Well, great, considering the shape I'm in."

By August he was much better, and soon he would be going home. Joe, too, was expected home on a furlough. All the Kennedys looked forward to the reunion.

Then came the tragic telegram: Joe's plane had been destroyed in the air while he was flying a dangerous mission over an enemy rocket base. Brilliant, handsome Joseph Kennedy, Jr., the star of the family —the young man who had intended to go into politics and who had confidently expected to be President—was dead.

While still in the hospital, Jack began to compile a book, *As We Remember Joe*, made up of reminiscences of family and friends. There may have been moments in his boyhood when he had resented Joe's domination, but he had been intensely proud of his talented older brother. Now he was grateful, as well. He realized that his determination to be as good as Joe had prodded him into doing better work at school. Yes, and in the war, too, perhaps.

Jack knew his father wanted him to take Joe's place, and the whole family seemed to expect him to go into politics. A political career would have been a natural for his friendly, outgoing older brother; but Jack, more quiet and reserved, often felt shy with strangers. Though deeply interested in government, he had never thought seriously of running for public office. He was more interested in writing, and he decided to try journalism first.

After he was given a medical discharge from the Navy, Jack found a position as a newspaper reporter. In April, 1945, he was sent to California to cover the San Francisco Conference of the United Nations. In July he went to Germany to report on the Potsdam Conference. He was fortunate to have such interesting assignments, but he was not completely satisfied.

"Instead of doing things," he told a friend, "I am writing about other people who do things. The job is too passive. I want to go into politics."

It had been Joe's plan to run for Congress, and Jack hoped to start his political career in the same way. In 1946 he and nine other would-be Congressmen entered the Democratic primary for the 11th Congressional District in Massachusetts. Jack decided that the way to win was to work harder than his rivals, and he visited voters in their homes, stores, and offices. It was not easy, but he even stopped strangers on the street and asked them to vote for him.

One worry Jack Kennedy did not have: he had plenty of money to conduct his campaign. However, he discovered that the family wealth might be a disadvantage. One day, several of the candidates had been asked to speak at a political picnic, and Jack soon noticed a certain sameness in the introductions.

"We shall now hear from a great American," the chairman would say, and pause impressively. "He's a man who came up the hard way."

Each time, this statement was heartily applauded, but when young Mr. Kennedy's turn came to be introduced, the chairman seemed at a loss. Jack had begun to feel uncomfortable, but he met the problem head on.

"I'm the one," he said dryly, "who didn't come up the hard way."

The audience roared with laughter.

During the final days of the campaign, Jack never relaxed his efforts, and the work brought results. He won the Democratic nomination and then the election. At the age of twenty-nine, he went to Washington to take his seat in Congress.

John F. Kennedy served in the House of Representatives for six years, and in 1952 he was a candidate for the United States Senate. Nearly every weekend he flew from Washington to Massachusetts. He drove his car all over the state, meeting people and making speeches. Again his hard work paid off, and he was elected.

The following year Senator Kennedy was married to a beautiful and brilliant girl, Jacqueline Bouvier. He seemed to have everything a man could want—a lovely wife, many loyal friends, wealth, and a successful career; but when he was thirty-six, pain from his old back injury began to trouble him again. He tried to ignore it, but by 1954 he was forced to walk on crutches. His only hope of relief was another delicate operation. He was warned that he might not survive surgery, but he decided to take the chance.

During the next five months Senator Kennedy had two operations. Jacqueline was with him constantly. Twice, his parents were summoned hastily to his bedside. It did not seem that he could possibly live, but he did.

"He fought his way out of it," his father said later. "Jack's always been a fighter."

After the Senator began to get better, he was taken on a stretcher to the airport and flown to his parents' winter home in Palm Beach, Florida. He had orders to rest for several more months, but he could not bear the thought of doing nothing. He was planning another book, a book about courage. He had seen plenty of raw courage in the Pacific, but since his election to the Senate he had become interested in a different kind of courage. He wanted to write about some of the Senate leaders—Daniel Webster and Sam Houston among others—who had risked their careers to do what they thought was for the public good.

Jack set to work. The Library of Congress sent him cartons of books, but under the circumstances he needed additional help. His friend and assistant Ted Sorenson did research in Washington, collecting interesting incidents and checking facts. Several historians had suggestions. But he did the writing himself. When *Profiles in Courage* was published early in 1956, it became an immediate hit, and Jack was a best-selling author again by the time he returned to the Senate in May.

Soon he was back in the old swing, attending Senate sessions and committee meetings and making speeches. "I married a whirlwind," Jacqueline once said.

The "whirlwind" was gathering force as the time for the 1956 Democratic convention drew near. Jack's friends wanted to boost his nomination for the Vice Presidency. When Jack left for Chicago in August, he hoped to be his party's nominee for Vice President of the United States.

It was a close race between him and Senator Estes Kefauver. During the voting Jack sat before a TV set in his hotel room, and when he saw that his rival was going to win, he rushed to the convention hall. Here he made a brief and gracious speech.

"Let's make the vote unanimous for Senator Kefauver," he said.

A cheer went up from the delegates—not only for the winner, but also for the good sportmanship of the loser. Many television viewers were seeing Jack Kennedy for the first time, and they liked what they saw—a calm, polished young man who could smile in defeat.

"Don't worry," a friend assured him. "You are going to be a shoo-in for the Vice Presidential nomination in 1960."

"I'm not running for Vice President any more," said Jack quietly. "I'm now running for President."

Almost at once, Jack Kennedy began making plans to be a candidate for President. His bid for the Vice Presidency had made him better known, and a few months later, *Profiles in Courage* was awarded the Pulitzer Prize as the best biographical work of the year. Thousands who read it were much impressed. They also were impressed by Senator Kennedy's speeches, but many people felt that he was too young to be elected President.

With his usual persistence, he set out to prove them wrong. In 1960 he put on a vigorous campaign to win the nomination and then the election. Though only forty-three, his quiet self-confidence assured many voters who saw him on television that he could provide the strong leadership the country needed. It was a close election that November, but Jack Kennedy was the winner.

The afternoon before Inauguration, ten weeks later, Washington was struck by a blinding snowstorm. Snow blanketed the city, and three thousand men worked all night to clear the streets in time for the inaugural ceremonies. By noon on January 20, 1961, a mammoth crowd had gathered before the east front of the Capitol. The crowd shivered in the cold wind that whipped across the plaza, but listened with rapt attention as the new President gave his inaugural address. Whether or not they had voted for John F. Kennedy, they knew they were listening to a great speech.

It was a speech not only to the American people but to the people of the world. He pledged friendship to American allies. To the peoples living in huts and villages of half the globe, who were struggling to break the bonds of poverty, he promised that Americans would try to help them help themselves. Of those nations that would make themselves enemies of the United States, he made a request "that both sides begin anew the quest for peace." All that needed to be done, he pointed out, could not be accomplished in a few days, or perhaps even in the lifetime of those listening to his voice.

"But let us begin," he said.

The three years and ten months that followed were filled with both triumphs and disappointments. Some of the laws President Kennedy recommended won Congressional approval. But other laws he considered necessary for the welfare of the country failed to pass.

In his dealings with foreign nations he also had reason to be both encouraged and deeply concerned. A Peace Corps was formed, made up of trained volunteers to work in underdeveloped countries where the government had asked for their services. Within a year these volunteers were teaching, improving health and sanitation, working on farms and helping with many other important tasks. The Corps was a great success, but at the same time there were a number of crises in foreign affairs.

A special threat to American security was Cuba, ninety miles off the coast of Florida. This island was ruled by Fidel Castro, a Communist dictator under Soviet influence. In 1962 Russian technicians were sent to Cuba, and aerial photographs taken from American planes showed a massive buildup of Russian military equipment. Jet bombers were being assembled capable of carrying nuclear weapons. The pictures also showed missile bases under construction, with some medium-range missiles trained in the direction of United States cities.

The President, faced with the greatest crisis in his career, acted promptly. To make sure that neither missiles nor bombers would ever be used against any part of the Americas, he ordered a naval blockade of Cuba. At the risk of nuclear war, he demanded that the Soviet Union withdraw its missiles and dismantle its bases on the island so close to American shores.

Nikita Khrushchev, premier of the Soviet Union, realized for the first time, perhaps, the mettle of the young American President. He knew that John Kennedy was not bluffing, and the United States was assured the offensive weapons would be sent back to Russia. The threat of a nuclear war had been averted.

"Kennedy," Premier Khrushchev once said, "is a man you can disagree with and still respect."

The President's greatest hope at all times was to keep the peace—"the kind of peace," he said, "that enables men and nations to grow and to hope and to build a better life for their children."

For five years, American leaders had urged that both the United States and the Soviet Union stop testing nuclear weapons in the atmosphere. Finally, in the summer of 1963, the Soviet leaders agreed to a test-ban treaty, providing for a partial ban on nuclear testing. President Kennedy knew this marked only one step toward permanent peace, but many consider it his greatest achievement.

"Let history record," he said, "that we, in this land, at this time, took the first step."

The test-ban treaty increased John F. Kennedy's popularity. "J.F.K.," as he was often called, obviously enjoyed being President, but he was deeply in earnest about the grave responsibilities of his office. On his frequent television appearances, his quick thinking, his wit, his good looks and his confidence and cheerful nature combined to make him a national favorite. Most writers, artists and musicians liked him because of his special interest in them. Scholars considered him brilliant.

"He noticed everything, responded to everything, forgot nothing. He lived his life so intensely that in retrospect it almost seems he must have known it would be short and that he had no time to waste," said one well-known historian, Arthur Schlesinger, Jr., who had worked closely with the President.

Like most human beings, J.F.K. liked to be liked. He was anxious to be re-elected in 1964, but he had the courage to take unpopular stands. His stand on equal rights for all citizens brought him much bitter criticism. Nearly a hundred years had passed since Negroes had been granted citizenship by the Fourteenth Amendment to the Constitution, yet thousands still were denied many privileges white citizens take for granted. Though J.F.K. realized his action would lose him more votes than he would gain, in June, 1963, he asked

Congress to pass a civil rights bill that would give Negroes their full rights as Americans.

The opposition in parts of the South was especially strong. In November, 1963, the President and Mrs. Kennedy visited Texas. Although the state was supposed to be hostile, nearly everywhere they went they were acclaimed by cheering crowds. In Dallas, where J.F.K. was to speak on November 22, five thousand people were waiting at the airport to welcome him.

After shaking a few hands, the President and First Lady took their places in the back seat of an open car for the drive into the city. In the jump seats in front of them sat Governor and Mrs. John Connally of Texas. In the second car of the motorcade rode the Secret Service men. Next came the car in which Vice President and Mrs. Lyndon B. Johnson were riding.

No one noticed the barrel of a rifle protruding from a sixth-story window of a building on the motorcade route. No one saw the man with the twisted mind who held the rifle.

Mrs. Kennedy had never looked lovelier than she did that day in a raspberry-colored suit, with a bunch of red roses that had been presented to her on her arrival. The President was smiling. There were waves of applause from the crowds lined up eight and ten deep along the sidewalks. They cheered themselves hoarse. It was a tremendous ovation.

Mrs. Connally turned to speak to the occupants of the back seat. "Mr. President," she said, "you can't say that Dallas doesn't love you today."

Those were the last words John F. Kennedy ever heard. A shot, a second shot, and then a third, crackled through the air. The Governor was wounded, and the President slumped forward.

"Oh, no, no!" his wife cried out.

In an instant, as the terrified crowd watched, a Secret Service man climbed into the car. It sped toward a hospital, bearing the unconscious President, his head cradled in Jacqueline's arms. Her suit was spattered with his blood, but she did not seem to notice. Outside the emergency operating room where doctors were trying to save her husband's life, she waited. With her were Vice President and Mrs. Johnson and several of John Kennedy's close friends and advisers who had accompanied him on the trip.

Then the announcement came. John F. Kennedy who had faced death twice before—in the Pacific and in a naval hospital—was dead.

Ninety-eight minutes later, on the plane that was to carry the dead President back to Washington, Lyndon Johnson, the new President, took the oath of office. The woman judge who administered the oath could not keep her voice from trembling, but Jacqueline Kennedy stood beside him, calm and composed. There were marks of suffering on her face, but even her husband could not have shown greater courage. While the plane was en route to Washington, she began to plan the impressive funeral services that would follow.

Jacqueline Kennedy's grief was too deep for tears, but throughout the world there were many who wept. In the United States, in Britain, in Japan and in other far-off places, the people shared a common sorrow. Leaders from ninety-two nations—an emperor, a king, a queen, princes, premiers, and generals—attended the funeral. Tens of thousands of mourners lined the streets of Washington. Millions watched on television.

The burial was in Arlington National Cemetery, across the river from Washington. The widow had asked that a light burn forever at John Kennedy's grave, and at the end of the burial service she lighted the eternal flame. She wanted people always to remember the young man with the compassionate heart who had died before his work was done.

During the next few weeks Mrs. Kennedy received nearly eight hundred thousand letters, and she appeared on television to thank all those who had tried to comfort her. She would never forget the warmth of the tributes paid to her late husband.

"All his bright light gone from the world!" she said. "All of you who have written to me know how much we all loved him"—her voice caught, but she did not pause—"and that he returned that love in full measure."

Lyndon Johnson, the new President, was thinking of that "bright light gone from the world," of which Mrs. Kennedy had spoken, when he addressed Congress a few days after the tragedy. He said that no memorial or eulogy could honor the late President more eloquently than the early passage of some of the bills for which John Kennedy had struggled. President Johnson was thinking, too, of the Inauguration Day nearly three years before.

"On the twentieth of January in 1961," he reminded his hushed and solemn listeners, "John F. Kennedy told his countrymen that our national work would not be finished in the first thousand days, nor even in the life of this Administration, nor even, perhaps, in the lifetime of this planet.

" 'But,' he said, 'let us begin.'

"Today, in this moment of new resolve," President Johnson went on, "I would say to all my fellow Americans, *let us continue.* This is our challenge—not to hesitate, not to pause, not to turn about and linger over this evil moment, but to continue on our course, so that we may fulfill the destiny that history has for us."

THE THIRTY-FIFTH PRESIDENT *at a Glance*

John Fitzgerald Kennedy

Born: May 29, 1917   *Died: November 22, 1963*

Boyhood and youth: John F. Kennedy, son of Joseph P. Kennedy, well-known financier and U.S. ambassador to Great Britain (1937–1940), was second in a family of nine children. He was born in Brookline, a suburb of Boston. He attended Choate, a well-known preparatory school in Connecticut, and was graduated from Harvard with honors in political science (1940).

War and politics. Jack Kennedy served in the U.S. Navy (1941–1945). As a lieutenant (j.g.) he was sent to the Solomons, where the PT boat he commanded was sunk (August, 1943) by a Japanese destroyer. For heroic conduct in saving his crew, Jack was awarded the Navy and Marine Corps medals. He underwent spinal surgery (1944) in Chelsea (Mass.) Naval Hospital. After a medical discharge from the Navy, he became a reporter for International News Service (1945). He served in the U.S. House of Representatives (1947–1953) and later in the U.S. Senate (1953–1961). During his Senate career he had two critical spinal operations (1954–1955). In August, 1956, he attended the Democratic convention and narrowly missed being nominated for the Vice Presidency. In 1960 he was elected President—the first Roman Catholic to hold that office.

As President (1961–1963). During Kennedy's first year in office, Congress approved almost half of his legislative requests, including a housing bill, new federal financing for highways, and an increased minimum wage for labor. The President also set up a U.S. Peace Corps to work in underdeveloped countries, and proposed an Alliance for Progress to improve conditions in Latin America, with the cooperation of the U.S., over a ten-year period. Later, the Alliance was approved by all Latin American countries except Cuba. In June, 1961, he met Khrushchev, premier of the Soviet Union, in an attempt to ease tensions between East and West. J.F.K. took a firm stand toward Communists seeking to extend their power in Laos and other parts of southeast Asia. He pledged continued aid to the pro-Western South Vietnam government in defending their country against Communist guerrillas. He reaffirmed the U.S. policy of refusing admittance of Communist China to the United Nations. Difficulties with Congress increased during the latter part of the Kennedy administration. A number of bills which he considered important for the welfare of the country, including medical care for the aged under Social Security and federal aid to education, failed to pass. One of the President's triumphs was the Trade Expansion Act, which Congress passed in 1962. This act gave the President new powers to regulate tariffs so that the U.S. might compete more effectively with the six-nation Common Market in Europe.

The chief domestic problem of the Kennedy administration was that of civil rights. A mass demonstration of over 300,000 Negroes and white sympathizers was held at the Lincoln Memorial in Washington (August, 1963) to arouse public support of the Negroes' demand for full civil rights. A civil rights bill and a tax reduction bill were among those under consideration by Congress when the President was assassinated (November 22, 1963).

Other happenings. During the early part of the Kennedy administration, the 32d Amendment to the Constitution gave residents of the capital the right to vote for President. "Freedom riders," groups of Negro students who were often joined by white youths, protested segregation by riding segregated buses. In September the Interstate Commerce Commission ruled that, after November 1, 1961, passengers on interstate buses were to be seated "without regard to race. . . ." Many events in other parts of the world during 1961 affected the U.S. The UN voted to use force to bring civil war to an end in the Congo. In April, Cuban exiles, said to have been trained by U.S. agents, invaded their homeland, hoping to overthrow the Cuban dictator, Fidel Castro, but the invasion failed. In August, Communist East Germany, backed by the Soviet Union, built a concrete wall along a 25-mile border between East and West Berlin, to prevent refugees from escaping Communist rule. In September, the Soviet Union began testing nuclear weapons again, although in 1958 it had agreed, as had the U.S. and Britain, to suspend testing. On October 30, despite UN protests, the Soviet Union set off a bomb more powerful than any earlier nuclear blast. Great advances in space travel were made during 1961: In April, the Soviet Union launched the first man into outer space. Later, U.S. astronauts Alan B. Shepard and Virgil E. Grissom rocketed more than 100 miles into space. John H. Glenn, Jr., who orbited the earth three times (February, 1962), was the first American to make an orbital space flight. That same year, Astronaut Walter M. Schirra, Jr., orbited the earth six times. In 1963, Leroy Gordon Cooper orbited the earth 22 times.

Kennedy as author. Kennedy's first book, *Why England Slept* (1940), expanded from a thesis he wrote in college, became a best seller. *Profiles in Courage,* written while he was convalescing from spinal surgery, was awarded the Pulitzer Prize as the best biography of 1956. A third book, growing out of his desire to avoid war, was called *The Strategy of Peace* (1960).

The President's family. Jacqueline Bouvier Kennedy (born 1929) was the youngest First Lady since Mrs. Grover Cleveland. Beautiful and talented, she was primarily responsible for the redecoration of the White House begun in 1961. The Kennedys had two children, Caroline (born 1957), and John, Jr., called "John John" by his father (born 1960). A third child, Patrick Bouvier (born August, 1963), lived less than two days.

THE THIRTY-SIXTH PRESIDENT *at a Glance*

Lyndon Baines Johnson

Born: August 27, 1908

Early life. Lyndon B. Johnson, the son and grandson of members of the Texas legislature, was born on a farm near Stonewall, Texas. Finishing high school at 15, he worked at a variety of jobs, then attended Southwest State Teachers College. After his graduation (1930) he taught in Houston public schools (1930–1932).

Political and war experience. President Franklin Roosevelt appointed Johnson Texas state administrator of the National Youth Administration (1935). In 1937 he entered the U.S. House of Representatives. During World War II he served in the Pacific (1941–1942) and was decorated with the Silver Star. After his war service he returned to the House of Representatives. He was elected to the U.S. Senate (1948) and became majority leader (1952). As Vice President (1961–1963) he was one of President Kennedy's most trusted advisers and "trouble shooters." After Kennedy's death, he was sworn in as President (November 22, 1963) and was greatly admired for the efficient manner in which he took over his new and difficult duties.

The President's family. Claudia ("Lady Bird") Taylor Johnson (born 1912) was the daughter of a successful Texas rancher and businessman. After her marriage (1934) she became owner of a radio-television station in Austin, Texas. The Johnsons have two daughters. Lynda Bird was 19 when her father became President, and Luci Baines was 16.

ABOUT THE AUTHORS

FRANCES CAVANAH finds it hard to decide which she has enjoyed more—writing or editing for young people. After graduating from De-Pauw University in her native Indiana, she joined the staff of the old *Child Life* magazine, where readers' letters gave her invaluable insight into the thinking of the youthful subscribers. Later she was director and editor of *Real People,* a series of biographies widely used in schools. Now living in Washington, D.C., Miss Cavanah does much of her research at the Library of Congress. In recreating other periods of history, she seeks primarily firsthand sources, which, together with her ability to tell a story well, accounts for the sense of immediacy that has made her books so popular. She is the author of *Two Loves for Jenny Lind; We Came to America; They Lived in the White House,* about the younger members of the Presidential households; and *Friends to Man: The Wonderful World of Animals,* an anthology of stories about some famous and unusual pets.

ELIZABETH L. CRANDALL is a graduate of Vassar and a former textbook editor. Her further experience in research and writing for textbooks and encyclopedias has made her a valuable collaborator in the job of re-creating for this book the contemporary background of each President's administration. A resident of Santa Fe, N.M., Mrs. Crandall lives in a Spanish pueblo-type house on a hill with a view of the Sangre de Cristo mountains on one side by day, and below, on the other side, the jewel-like lights of the city by night.

Date Due

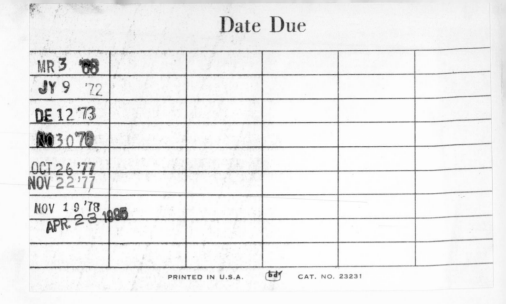

MR 3 '68				
JY 9 '72				
DE 12 '73				
NO 30 '76				
OCT 26 '77				
NOV 22 '77				
NOV 19 '78 APR 23 1985				

PRINTED IN U.S.A.   CAT. NO. 23231

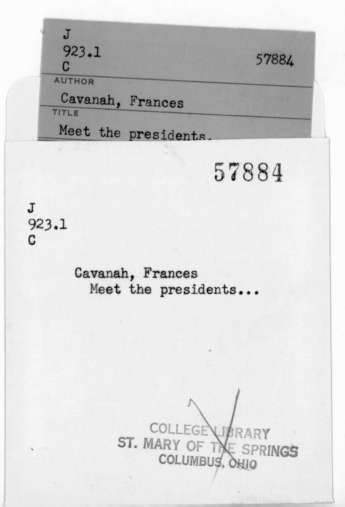